The Efficient Epworthian

Being

"Epworth League Methods"

REVISED   ENLARGED   REWRITTEN

By

DAN B. BRUMMITT
Editor of The Epworth Herald

PUBLISHERS
Eugene, Oregon

Wipf and Stock Publishers
199 W 8th Ave, Suite 3
Eugene, OR 97401

The Efficient Epworthian
Being the "Epworth League Methods"
By Brummitt, Dan B.
ISBN 13: 978-1-59752-811-5
ISBN: 1-59752-811-0
Publication date 7/5/2006
Previously published by The Methodist Book Concern, 1922

CONTENTS

CHAPTER		PAGE
I.	IN THE BEGINNING,	7
II.	THE ORGANIC LAW,	24
III.	HOW TO ORGANIZE A CHAPTER,	38
IV.	OVERSEEING THE CHAPTER'S WORK,	47
V.	WORKING EFFICIENCY IN THE LEADERS,	64
VI.	THE WEEKLY DEVOTIONAL MEETING,	89
VII.	THE MORNING WATCH, PERSONAL EVANGELISM, AND BIBLE STUDY,	132
VIII.	THE LEAGUE'S WORLD INTERESTS,	165
IX.	SOCIAL SERVICE,	208
X.	CULTURE AND RECREATION,	262
XI.	MAKING THE RECORD AND FINANCING THE WORK,	320
XII.	THE LEAGUE'S RED LETTER DAYS,	341
XIII.	CEREMONIAL OCCASIONS,	375
XIV.	THE EPWORTH LEAGUE PLEDGE,	385
XV.	SUPERVISION, INSPIRATION, AND INSTRUCTION,	393

Introduction.

THIS volume is "Epworth League Methods" revised, rewritten, enlarged, brought down to date.

Much old material has been left out, and much more new material has been added. The League moves, and any writer who hopes to deal adequately with its activities must be able to see that yesterday's methods are not all usable to-day, though yesterday's principles have not changed.

The purpose of the book is not to offer exhaustive discussion of the League's many-sided life. It is meant to be, mainly, suggestive and provocative of independent work. It leaves much to the initiative of the resourceful young people of the Epworth League. Also it is a guide to the sources of ten times as much practical aid as is given within its limited compass.

The groups of brief paragraphs scattered through the book will be found of much use in stimulating the inventive and aggressive faculties of League officers and leaders. These paragraphs will serve that purpose again and again, without being of much immediate use for particular problems.

The present volume is the third revision of the original "Epworth League Methods." Since 1906 thousands of members of the League have found it useful, and every year it finds new friends. This is largely due to the fact that "The Efficient Epworthian" is in no sense the work of one writer. It owes a debt which cannot even be stated, to hundreds of successful workers in this field. Some have provided the suggestion for a single paragraph; others are indirectly responsible for entire sections of the book. Of course, I assume responsibility for all matters of arrangement, wording and emphasis.

If names were called for, the time would fail me to tell of Jacob E. Price, B. E. Helman, Joseph F. Berry, P. Ross Parrish, Peter Jacobs, Edwin M. Randall, Wilbur

INTRODUCTION.

F. Sheridan, Francis E. Clark, Amos R. Wells, Annie E. Smiley, S. G. Ayres, Jesse L. Hurlbut, Grace Scribner, George F. Sutherland, Ralph E. Diffendorfer, Ralph S. Cushman, S. Earl Taylor, Charles E. Guthrie, Thomas Kane, George F. Durgin, Francis H. Case, and many others.

The best acknowledgment I can make for all the material on which I have so freely drawn is to put this book just as freely at the service of all those who are at work in the hopefulest enterprise in the world,—the great adventure of young life, as it follows Jesus Christ.

Dan B. Brummitt.

CHAPTER I.
IN THE BEGINNING.

THE CHURCH AND YOUTH.

THE Epworth League is the young people's society of the Methodist Episcopal Church. Under its banners practically all the young people of the Church are enrolled.

No other Church has succeeded in organizing its young life so extensively, and, at the same time, so intensively, as has the Methodist Episcopal Church by means of the Epworth League.

But it must not be supposed that this Epworth League movement was the initial effort of Methodism to promote the social, intellectual, and spiritual culture of her young people. During all the years of her eventful history individual Churches have maintained societies for the special benefit of their younger members.

In the years immediately preceding the birth of the Epworth League these organizations had multiplied until, in the larger Churches, they had become quite common. Many of the distinguishing features of these local organizations were retained in the more general organizations, and, in turn, have been inherited by the Epworth League.

The first movement to provide a uniform organization dates back to the year 1872. Some time previous to that date there had been organized by the Rev. Dr. T. B. Neely, in the Fifty-first Street Methodist Episcopal Church, Philadelphia, a Church Lyceum, the chief object of which was to encourage a systematic reading of approved books. Several similar lyceums were formed in neighboring Churches, and soon it was thought best, for purposes of mutual cooperation, to unite these in a city union.

At a meeting of the Board of Managers of this central body, held March 3, 1872, it was resolved to memorialize the General Conference, then soon to assemble at Brooklyn,

THE EFFICIENT EPWORTHIAN.

N. Y., asking formal recognition of the Lyceum. The memorial was referred to a committee, which made a favorable report, but, owing to the great pressure of business at the close of the General Conference session, the recommendations of the committee were not acted upon. At the succeeding General Conference, that of 1876, the request for official recognition was renewed. The Conference adopted *verbatim* the paragraph sent up in 1872.

The Lyceum was received with much favor in different parts of the Church. It did good work in stimulating the intellectual life of the young and in promoting a taste for the pure and upbuilding in literature. The organization was destined, however, to give place to the Oxford League, a society which retained the idea of intellectual culture, but provided also for special activity in the realm of social and spiritual life.

THE FIVE ORIGINAL SOCIETIES.

The Epworth League is the resultant of the amalgamation of five other societies—the Young People's Methodist Alliance, the Oxford League, the Young People's Christian League, the Methodist Young People's Union, and the Young People's Methodist Episcopal Alliance.

Of these the oldest was the Young People's Methodist Alliance. It came into existence August 25, 1883. Its birthplace was a woody grove on the old and historic Desplaines Camp-ground, not far from the city of Chicago. It emphasized the highest spiritual existence, mutual helpfulness, daily Bible study, the avoidance of doubtful pleasures, and ardent loyalty to all that is embodied in the word "Methodism."

The prime mover in the organization and development of the Oxford League was Dr. John H. Vincent. The General Conference of 1876 made provision for the Lyceum, but it was found that the purpose of this organization did not meet the needs of the young people. Dr. Vincent, keenly alive to the real requirements of the multitudes of young Methodists, sought to supply the vital thing which the Lyceum lacked. He proposed to organize a young people's society that should provide symmetrical spiritual and

IN THE BEGINNING.

intellectual culture. This society was called "The Oxford League," after the famous English university in which the "Holy Club," to which the Wesleys belonged, was founded. The new organization was received with favor by many pastors and leading laymen, and was given hearty and significant indorsement at the centennial anniversary of the "Christmas Conference," which was held in Baltimore, December 9-17, 1884.

The late Rev. Dr. J. H. Twombly was the originator of the Young People's Christian League. Years before, in his early pastorate, he organized the young people for service. One of his dreams had been the gathering of a great Methodist international meeting of young people. The hour of the fulfillment of his dream was not far off when the Young People's Christian League was started with broader plans than any society then existing in the Church. The Young People's Methodist Alliance at that time had only one class of members, and the Oxford League required a uniform constitution, and neither of these societies was able to group together the already existing societies which were in many of our Churches. The Young People's Christian League aimed to unify the interests of these older societies, Lyceums, Guilds, Bands, etc., with their local histories and associations, by making them auxiliary to a central body without requiring any change of name of constitution or method of work, wherever these were acceptable to their local Church.

The Methodist Young People's Union had its headquarters in Michigan. The organization was the outcome of a meeting of certain alert Detroit Conference pastors. For some time they had been impressed that the time had come for the formation of a society for the social and religious culture of their young people—a society better fitted for this high purpose than any of those already in existence. The matter was first broached in November, 1887, and a Conference organization was formed, known as the "Young People's Society of Detroit Conference." A comprehensive constitution was adopted. Many of its best features were ultimately wrought into the plan of the Epworth League.

THE EFFICIENT EPWORTHIAN.

The fifth of the "original societies" was but an infant when the consolidation took place. The organizers doubtless hoped that they had found the solution of the problem that was vexing the leaders of the younger hosts of Methodism. One who was high in the councils of this new organization said that the North Ohio Conference Methodist Episcopal Alliance was the outgrowth of a desire for the consolidation of all Methodist Episcopal societies of young people into one great connectional society.

The Birth of the Epworth League.

There are certain localities of historic interest to which Methodists instinctively turn with gratitude and pride. Epworth, the home of the Wesley family, is one of them. City Road Chapel, in London, is another. Old John Street Church, in New York City, is still another. Others are old St. George's Church, in Philadelphia, and Lovely Lane Chapel, in Baltimore.

Future historians of Methodism will need to place Cleveland, Ohio, in their list of favored names, for in that city the Epworth League was born. The event occurred on May 15, 1889, in the Central Methodist Episcopal Church. The old building in which the historic meeting was held has been removed, and a handsome modern structure, known as Epworth Memorial Church, a very hive of activity and efficiency, has taken its place.

As indicated in the foregoing paragraphs, negotiations had been carried on for some time between representatives of the five general young people's societies of the Church looking toward a possible union. That some steps ought to be taken to centralize and harmonize the work was freely admitted. But just what method would most easily and successfully bring about the desired consummation was a question not easily answered.

Finally the leaders of the Young People's Methodist Alliance proposed a conference. This plan met with favor. In due time an invitation was extended by the Rev. B. F. Dimmick, the pastor of Central Church, Cleveland, to representatives of the various societies to meet in that

IN THE BEGINNING.

church. The invitation was accepted. On the morning of Tuesday, May 14th, the leaders met face to face.

The work of the Cleveland Conference was not accomplished without serious and thorough discussion. The representatives of the various organizations had come together on purpose to unite on a plan of organization. But each one was naturally inclined to favor the distinctive features of his own society. Several plans were proposed as a basis of union, and at the beginning of the conference these plans differed so widely that some despaired of reaching an adjustment.

The Oxford League stood for all-round culture, and took as its model the Holy Club of Wesley's Oxford days. The Young People's Methodist Alliance was intensely spiritual in its purposes and aims. The Young People's Christian League was more a federation than a compact organization, seeking to affiliate all classes of young people's societies through a central body. The Methodist Young People's Union had large aims for spiritual, literary, and social work. The North Ohio Conference Methodist Episcopal Alliance had scarcely been at work long enough to develop any peculiarities of plan or organization when the historic meeting at Cleveland was called.

Two days were spent in the discussion of various proposals looking to a union of all existing societies. At one point in the proceedings the representatives of one of the organizations felt impelled to withdraw from the conference. Later they returned, and the work of finding a basis of union issued, toward midnight of the second day, in the unanimous decision to organize THE EPWORTH LEAGUE, and to make it the successor and sole heir of all the societies represented at the conference.

The years that have intervened since that memorable Cleveland Conference have been years of stirring history. A new Epworth League host has come to the front since then. Some of the workers of that day have passed on to the other life. Many are leaders of thought and action in the Church. But no other service they can render will so greatly make the Church their debtor as the work they did

THE EFFICIENT EPWORTHIAN.

so faithfully and so unselfishly when they called into being the Epworth League.

THE LEAGUE'S GROWTH FROM WITHIN.

The history of the Epworth League is a record of development from within. The major activities which now occupy its attention have been begun, for the most part, in a small way by individual chapters and by local groups of chapters. The Central Office has wisely assumed the functions of a clearing house, choosing rather to suggest, co-ordinate, and counsel than to originate plans and hand them down ready made.

The Win-My-Chum movement has become an annual observance in thousands of chapters,—a time when the young people face and accept responsibility for the definite enlistment of their friends in the beginnings of Christian experience and service. In many churches it serves as a preparation for the wider evangelistic program of the winter under the direction of the pastor.

The growth of the Institutes has been one of the wonders of contemporary Methodism. Between the days of six Institutes a year, and the days of more than a hundred summer Institutes, and almost as many winter Institutes, there is an interval of about fifteen years. And the Institute method of training is as yet in the early stages of an inevitable revolution toward forms of usefulness as yet but dimly perceived.

The General Conference of 1920 made the Epworth League one of the benevolent societies of the church, and gave its governing Board representation in the Council of Boards of Benevolence, on a parity with the other Boards. The finances of the Board of the Epworth League are supervised and approved by the Council.

The League's income differs from that of other Boards in that while it is fixed by the Council, it is provided in various ways by the young people themselves, and not by the gifts of the churches.

THE LEAGUE TESTED BY TIME.

A third of a century has passed since the Cleveland meeting. Many people have asked and are asking whether the outcome of these years has proven that the founders of the

IN THE BEGINNING.

Epworth League were as wise as they have been proclaimed by enthusiastic Epworthians.

The ordinary facts of to-day's life in the Church are sufficient answer. There is no disposition to claim that the Epworth League has accomplished everything which its founders dreamed might be done. But its shortcomings are the flaws in a record whose value can not be estimated.

The League has stood for three great ideas in Christian life and service—democracy, initiative, and fellowship. In organization and operation it is beautifully democratic, and there is constant exchange of position by every member,—to-day, leader; to-morrow, follower; and not long in any one department of the organization.

The League manages its own affairs, not for offensive self-assertion, but for training in responsibility and capacity. Its whole work is determined by it, not for it, and this has been one great element in the value of the League's training. Its activities have been "our" business, and so have been regarded with a loyalty and affection not otherwise attainable.

And the League's fellowship, maintained by conventions, institutes, rallies, and, in large measure, by *The Epworth Herald*, has had very much to do with keeping up the *esprit de corps*, the enthusiasm, and the unity of the great multitude, which, in widely separated places and under infinitely varied conditions, is one "League,—offensive and defensive," in the service of Jesus Christ.

The League must be judged not by how much more it might have done, but by how much less would have been done without it. The great majority of Methodists have come into the Church since the League was organized, and have always known it as a part of the Church. Its work has been taken for granted. But there can be no doubt of the value of its service to the Church and the community.

The Epworth League has sustained a weekly prayer-meeting, which, by its democratic atmosphere and its simple directness, has been a distinct addition to the Church's social means of grace. This meeting has been a training-school in devotion, in Christian confession, in fellowship, and in leadership.

THE EFFICIENT EPWORTHIAN.

It has discovered great fields of practical service which, before its advent, were almost wholly unoccupied by the young people. The Social Service (formerly known as Mercy and Help) work in the Methodist Episcopal Church, the similar work in the Methodist Episcopal Church, South, and the corresponding work in Canadian Methodism, have done much to make pointless the criticism that Methodists were too busy getting happy to pay much attention to the needs of those about them.

The remarkable Deaconess Movement, which has grown side by side with the Epworth League, has been very largely helped by the League. Scarcely a League convention is held but the deaconess is there to invite and direct the practical philanthropy of the young people, and to enlist young women for deaconess service. Hospital, orphanage, and training-school have been benefited by this co-operation in many ways, for the gifts of money and supplies have been crowned by the gift of self. Nearly every wearer of the white ties is a gift of the Epworth League to the Church.

He would inquire unwisely who left the League out of his studies of the present missionary revival. The "parish abroad" idea derives its chief support from large or small organizations of the League. In a single State the Epworth League has assumed the entire support of a score of missionaries in the foreign field. This plan, which provides the personal element so much needed in the support of mission work, would have been, at the outset, almost a negligible quantity but for the Epworth League.

Apart from this form of missionary activity, the League has furnished a direct and easy channel for the diffusion of missionary intelligence. Mission study classes, missionary institutes, the emphasis on missions in conventions and rallies are only the outward signs of a great missionary concern in the League. And the supply of missionary recruits in the past two decades has come mainly from the ranks of the Epworth League, in which missionary interest has fired missionary zeal, which has fused the purposes of many a life into the white heat of personal dedication to the missionary enterprise.

IN THE BEGINNING.

The Conferences of Methodism are very largely the business meetings of a great and complex institution. They are necessarily cumbered with much serving. The Epworth League, with its minimum of machinery, has had opportunity to provide in its conventions general gatherings for the cultivation of the spirit of fellowship, for the emphasis on the connectional idea, and for the conduct of exceedngly profitable "Conversations on the work of God."

The Epworth League, through its consistent and continually increasing emphasis on personal dealing with the unconverted, has helped to provide a fruitful means of evangelism. And in the stated revival efforts of the local Churches there is a mass of unassailable testimony which accords the League high place as a loyal and effective agency, affording aid of the utmost value to the pastor and the officiary in the work of reaching the unsaved.

There is more giving, more generous giving, and more systematic giving among the young people because of the work and influence of the Epworth League. There is more private prayer, more religious meditation, more devotional reading of the Word of God in Methodism than there could have been without the efforts of the League.

In brief, every activity of the Church, every outgoing of Christly service, every element in the upbuilding of strong and symmetrical Christian character, every interest of the Kingdom of God, has been blessed and profited through the providential use and spread of the Epworth League throughout the Methodist world.

The Wheel That Became a Cross.

The changes in the Epworth Cross, made in 1913, marked one more step in the evolution of a device that is now at least thirty years old.

In organizing the League, at the memorable Cleveland meeting, the founders united in a new plan of organization. The scheme, when printed in chart form, became the forerunner of the famous "Epworth Wheel," which later gave place to the "Epworth Cross," the present graphic form of showing the varieties of League work.

THE EFFICIENT EPWORTHIAN.

It is interesting now to see what the young people of the late nineteenth century were trying to do. We have small reason to say of our own League time that it is so much more wonderful than the days of old; we are the heirs of great thinking and large purpose in the former generation.

The descriptions of the six departments, in the Cleveland plan, were arranged in a hexagon, around a circle marked "President." As now, there were four Vice-Presidents, a Secretary, and a Treasurer.

The department of Christian work was under the First Vice-President. It had these subdivisions: (1) The Conducting of a Weekly Prayer-meeting, (2) Missionary Work, (3) The Spiritual Welfare of Members, (4) Carrying on Christian Work Among the Young, and (5) Sunday School Interests.

The second department was that of literary work, including: (1) Lectures and Literary Entertainments, (2) Lyceum Reading Circles, Papers, Magazines, Library, and all Educational Work; (3) C. L. S. C. Reading, (4) Oxford League Readings, and (5) Home Culture Circles.

"Social Work" was the name of the third department. Its divisions were: (1) All Sociables and Social Entertainments, (2) Systematic Visitation, (3) Reception and Introduction of Members, (4) Look-up Legion Work, (5) Social Purity, and (6) Temperance.

The department of entertainment was the Fourth Vice-President's care. It provided for: (1) Music for all Meetings, and Selection of a Chorister; (2) Excursions and Picnics, (3) Amusements for all Meetings, (4) Flower Mission Work, (5) Badges and Signals, and (6) Children's Day Exercises.

The only points needing special attention in the Secretary's department are that this officer was expected to gather historical and other statistics, and that he was to keep a record of the Chapter's literary work.

Looking through these divisions of the work of one group of Oxford Leagues, it is easy to see why so much of the idea has been preserved until now, and also why some things have been dropped.

IN THE BEGINNING.

Missions has grown from being one-fifth of a department until it is a department by itself. The work among children has come to such proportions as were not dreamed of in the Cleveland "wheel." Literary work, though changed in form, has not lost in earnestness or interest, and has gained in directness

Children's Day exercises are no longer conducted by the League, nor does the League provide for Chautauqua Circle work or Home Culture Circles.

Now we are thinking a little more than formerly about serving and helping the community. We have an entirely new notion about what Christian stewardship means. We talk about personal evangelism, and do more of it. We think of amusements and entertainments as something we owe to the whole neighborhood.

These new movements are germinal in the old. The League could not live and grow without producing new applications of old principles.

But—and this is the significant thing for us of to-day— the Wheel long ago became a Cross! In 1903 that happened.

And there's a difference. A wheel carries the burden; a cross is itself to be carried. A wheel runs with the minimum of effort; it costs something to take up a cross. A wheel is good for the beaten path; a cross must be borne wherever One goes before who has said, "Follow Me."

In a word, we know now, perhaps a little better than was known twenty-five years ago, that the Christian work of young people is as serious, as urgent, as imperative, as any other form of Christian work. It is not mere drill work nor wooden gun parade. It is, for the moment, the business of life.

They felt something of that in the other days when the League was seeking to be born. But the time of its full realizing came later. And when that time arrived, that which had been a Wheel became a Cross.

"If any man will come after Me, let him take up his Cross daily and follow Me."

THE EFFICIENT EPWORTHIAN.

The Vindication of the League's Church Relationship.

In the beginning the Epworth League was organized as a Methodist young people's society.

At the outset it met with more than a little adverse criticism from people who felt, in all sincerity, that the proper thing to do was to merge it into an organization which might include the young people of all Churches.

The Epworth League was thought to be too narrow a society, too exclusive. It was urged to be broad and inclusive; to make itself a part of a great interdenominational demonstration of the unity of the Churches.

At that time there existed a great, all-inclusive organization for work among the children and young people, in which Methodists worked side by side with other Christians of all names. That was the International Sunday School Association. It provided the Uniform Lessons, and was completely organized, with auxiliary associations reaching down through provincial, State, county, and township associations, clear to the little Sunday school at the forks of Elk Creek.

That organization is here yet.

But not as it was; and the difference is an endorsement of the wisdom which, at the outset, held the Epworth League to the denominational form of organization and control.

In February, 1913, two groups of leaders came together at Dayton, Ohio. One group represented the long-established, far-reaching International Association. The other represented the official leaders of denominational Sunday school work in North America.

But the meeting was of the highest interest to all workers in denominational societies of every sort.

It forecasted the taking over by all the denominations, sooner or later, of the control of their Sunday school work. They are no longer willing to leave it largely to an interdenominational association, *although they are more than ever willing to work together in the Sunday school movement.*

IN THE BEGINNING.

The thought of the Sunday school executives who are chosen by the Churches, and responsible to them, was expressed with great clearness in the report of the secretary, Dr. H. H. Meyer.

Because two paragraphs of that report state the exact principles on which the Epworth League was founded, they are reprinted here. We have taken the liberty of substituting for the words "Sunday School," wherever they occur, the words which are printed in italics:

Every denomination at all equipped and organized for *Young People's* work is awake and disposed to regard its responsibility seriously, and to strengthen its own agencies at every point, from the local society to the denominational supervising board or committee. This does not mean an unwillingness on the part of any denomination to enter heartily into fellowship with interdenominational *Young People's* leaders, either in the local or in the general field. It does mean, however, that the seriousness of the task with which every denomination is confronted, and responsibility for the fulfillment of which rests upon the denominational *Young People's* leaders, will make it quite impossible for the denominations permanently to co-operate with each other in interdenominational *Young People's* work through the channels offered by an outside, independent organization, in the inner councils of which the responsible denominational *Young People's* executives, as such, have no voice.

The principle for which the council stands, and stands as a unit, is that of denominational autonomy in matters of *Young People's* administration and instruction. The corollary of this principle is that the denominations, as such, can not conduct their co-operative educational and extension propaganda except through channels over which they have immediate control. There will always be a broad field of usefulness open to independent organizations, but ultimately, though perhaps gradually, every important department of work, on both the educational and administrative sides, must be taken over by some organization officially

THE EFFICIENT EPWORTHIAN.

constituted by and for the co-operating denominations themselves.

Now, these words do not speak the thought of narrow-minded partisans. There is no fencing-out, no disfellow-shiping of the other man. There could not be in this day of enlarged and enlarging comity among the Churches.

For example, the Federal Council of Churches is a pretty broad affair. So is the Home Missions Council. And the missionary secretaries of the various Churches are doing an amount of united, co-operative work that would have staggered the imagination of the most aggressive Church a few years ago. These secretaries can not possibly be denominational hardshells.

But they are all seeking to get their own Churches as compactly organized, as denominationally self-conscious as possible, *for the very reason that the Churches must work together more efficiently!*

To do the large tasks which are the present business of the Protestant Churches, every Church must first be, in every department, efficiently organized and operated within itself.

Then it can bring to bear in Sunday school work, in Social Service, in the Missionary enterprise, in Young People's work, a force which, by its very concreteness and compactness, can be used in co-operation with the like forces which its denominational neighbors have developed.

For, as Secretary Meyer says, in another part of the report which is quoted above:

> Let us not deceive ourselves with regard to the present trend of the development of every department of Church work in the larger field. This is obviously and most definitely in the direction of direct co-operative denominational control of interdenominational activities.

This subject is not referred to here to revive a forgotten controversy, which has no present-day interest save as history.

This, rather, is the thing the League should consider: If the League was so wisely directed in the days of its

IN THE BEGINNING.

beginnings, that, after twenty-four years, the leaders of the Churches began to apply the same principles to other departments of religious activity—what have we of the League to do but to justify our birthright, by working with all our might to make ourselves fit for Methodism's share in the co-operative work of the Churches?

The Church must shape and control the League, because only so can it make the League its efficient vocational school. Inside that control the League must develop individual initiative, personal responsibility, ability for spontaneous service, which marks the work of a good vocational school.

And, in the measure that the League reaches this ideal, it will echo Matthew Simpson's declaration: "We live to make our own Church a power in the land, and to love every other Church that exalts our Christ."

More than that, it will be able, as a part of the Church, and with the other Churches, to give a twentieth-century fulfillment to John Wesley's eighteenth-century longing: "I desire a League, offensive and defensive, with every soldier of Jesus Christ."

Why the League Works As It Does.

A man asked one day, "What's the reason for the League, anyway?"

Readers of "Nicholas Nickleby" will remember the Squeers system of education; first the boy spelled the word, "w-i-n-d-e-r, window," and then he went out and washed the thing which the word denoted.

Mr. Squeers was an ignorant and conscienceless villain; but he was not entirely astray in his principles of pedagogy. The new education says, "We learn to do by doing."

The Epworth League does much teaching, exhorting, appealing. It seeks to deal largely with the inner life of its members. It is cultural, inspirational, didactic.

But its great word is *action!* It is trying to wash the "winder."

The Sunday school may do more teaching. The preaching service may be more appealing and inspiring. But the League is not satisfied unless its members are getting education and inspiration out of their round of service.

THE EFFICIENT EPWORTHIAN.

Not much does it matter that the service is crude, even blundering at times. Both spelling and washing the "winder" may leave much to be desired. What the League seeks, and what the Church needs, is a body of young people able to harness their principles to their Christian opportunities.

Mission study is expected to produce—and does produce—missionary giving, even to the giving of self.

Social service is to be something bigger than a new convention-institute talking point. It means charity, helpfulness, intelligent acquaintance with the common needs of the neighborhood, and a readiness to help in meeting them.

The "love thy neighbor" teaching is in the League's course of study, but it is also being worked out in the varied activities of the recreation and culture department, as well as in social service.

And the spiritual work is real work. It is often shallow, often cheap, often based on a shaky theology. But it is done. The Sunday night spectacle of thousands of religious meetings, in which young men and women talk about the great spiritual themes, and direct one another's thought to religious certainties and their meaning for life—that is a sight the angels rejoice over, in spite of all the too true complaints that the devotional meeting is not anything near what it should be.

The League desires to link Christian profession to broad, all-inclusive Christian living. It seeks to provide expressional deeds to make young people's religion a thing of worth in every-day actual living.

And its members are encouraged to do all this on their own initiative and in their own way. That's the reason for the League.

THOUGHTS IN THE EVOLUTION OF LEAGUE LIFE.

No Epworth League Chapter can live on last year's banners.

What people want the Epworth League to have is not perfection, but vision.

The Chapter that never made a mistake has disbanded for fear of spoiling its record.

IN THE BEGINNING.

"The Epworth League a failure in our Church? Why, it hasn't really been tried yet."

When you would answer anger with anger, remember that Beelzebub does not cast out devils.

If you have your doubts about the League, get busy at some of its work. Your doubts will die of neglect.

If no Epworth League Chapter had ever suffered from its own folly, there would be fewer wise Chapters than there are.

Certainly the Epworth League can be trusted. But it needs as much training in moral distinctions as the rest of the Church.

It would stiffen many a weak backbone to remember that the Epworth League is one of the plans of God, and that God's plans always mean something.

The one thing the League ought not to endure is the refusal of any Church or any people in the Church to take it seriously. Better have enemies than belittlers.

The Epworth League is not a Church cut down to fit young folks. It is a part of the Church, and fits young folks just as the whole Church does, which was made for them.

Graduate Epworthians are running the Methodism of to-day. Without looking at the records, we could name ten great leaders who were started, inspirited, and trained in the Epworth League.

Whatever good or bad is in the Epworth League, it is the only Epworth League there is. We may make the best of it or the worst of it. But to ignore it or to wipe it out would be equally foolish.

Don't believe anybody who tells you that young folks are not ready to make sacrifices for the sake of others. There was an heroic age. But also there is now an heroic age. Every age is heroic, because in every age the world's young people are ready for high adventure and noble self-forgetfulness.

CHAPTER II.
THE ORGANIC LAW.

THE scheme of League organization is in harmony with the connectional theory of Methodism. The parent body is the Epworth League of the Methodist Episcopal Church, with its supervising Board. Then comes the District League, and, as the unit of organization, the Chapter in the local church. There are other organizations, such as the Conference League, the State League, and General Conference District League, fully sanctioned by the law of the Church, but these are not essential to the connectional scheme.

The Epworth League exists by the authority of the General Conference, and is entirely under the control and direction of that body. The General Secretary, who is the executive officer of the League, and the Editor of *The Epworth Herald* are both elected by the General Conference, and all the legislation concerning the League either originates in the General Conference or is delegated by it to the Board of the Epworth League.

The Board of the Epworth League consists of a Bishop, the General Secretary, the Editor of *The Epworth Herald*, one member from each of the fifteen General Conference Districts, and five at large. Three of these five must be laymen. The District representatives and members at large are nominated by the Board of Bishops and elected by the General Conference. The Board holds an annual meeting, and its Executive Committee, of five members, meets every two months at the Central Office in Chicago.

The chapter in the Discipline which relates to the Epworth League provides a Constitution for the government of the entire organization, framed by the General Conference. This is called, for convenience, the General Constitution. It can be altered or amended only by the General Conference.

GENERAL CONSTITUTION.

ARTICLE I. *Name.* The title of this organization shall be, "The Epworth League of the Methodist Episcopal Church."

THE ORGANIC LAW.

Article II. *Object.* The object of the League shall be to promote intelligence and vital piety in the young members and friends of the Church, to aid them in the attainment of purity of heart and constant growth in grace, and to train them in works of mercy and help.

Article III. *Organization.* With a view of carrying out the objects of the League, the Chapters and such other young people's societies as may be approved by the Quarterly Conferences shall be organized into District Superintendents' District Leagues, and may also be formed into General Conference District Leagues. The District Superintendent shall be *ex officio* a member of the District Cabinet. Other groupings may be arranged for the advantage of the work, such as Annual Conference Leagues, State Leagues, and City Leagues, and whenever such organization shall be made, it shall become thereby a regular Disciplinary organization within the provisions of this section.

The Chapter shall be under the control of the Quarterly Conference and pastor. Any Young People's Society may become an affiliated Chapter of the Epworth League, provided that it adopt the aims of the League, that its President and other officers and its general plans of work are approved by the pastor and Official Board of Quarterly Conference, and that it is enrolled at the Central Office.

§ 4. Article IV. *Government.* The management of the Board of the Epworth League shall be vested in a Board which shall consist of a Bishop, General Secretary, the Editor of *The Epworth Herald,* and one member from each General Conference District, and five members at large, three of whom shall be laymen; the District representatives and members at large to be nominated by the Board of Bishops and elected by the General Conference.

The Bishop shall be President of the Epworth League and of the Board of the Epworth League. The Secretaries of the Junior League, of the German work and of the colored work, shall be advisory members of the Board. In case of a vacancy in the office of General Secretary during the quadrennium, the same shall be filled by the Board of the Epworth League. Any vacancy occurring in the

THE EFFICIENT EPWORTHIAN.

District membership of the Board of the Epworth League by a District member's removal from the District from which he was elected, or by any cause whatsoever, shall be filled by said Board from the Conference to which said member belonged. The Board of the Epworth League shall meet at least four times during each quadrennium.

§ 5. ARTICLE V. *Officers.* The Officers of the League shall be a President, a Vice-President, a General Secretary, a Recording Secretary, and a Treasurer. The President shall be chosen as hereinbefore provided. The Vice-President and Recording Secretary shall be chosen by the Board of the Epworth League from its own body. The General Secretary shall be elected by the General Conference, and shall be the executive officer of the League. He shall have charge of the correspondence, shall keep the records of the League, and may speak or provide speakers for Annual Conference anniversaries, and perform such other duties as the Board of the Epworth League may direct. The Editor of *The Epworth Herald* shall be elected by the General Conference, and shall perform such duties as relate to the editorial departments of Epworth League publications. The Treasurer shall be elected by the Board of the Epworth League. These Officers shall be elected quadrennially, and shall hold office until their successors are chosen. Vacancies in any of the above-mentioned positions, except the Presidency and the Editorship of *The Epworth Herald,* shall be filled by the Board of the Epworth League.

§ 6. ARTICLE VI. The Board of the Epworth League may elect, upon nomination by the General Secretary, such field or departmental secretaries as may be deemed necessary.

§ 7. ARTICLE VII. *Finances.* The salary of the Editor of *The Epworth Herald* shall be fixed by the Book Committee and paid by the Book Concern. The salaries of the General Secretary and of other Secretaries and the administrative expenses, such as may be authorized by the Board of the Epworth League, shall be paid from contributions from the local chapters and Churches and the profits on Epworth League publications and supplies and other resources.

THE ORGANIC LAW.

ARTICLE IX. *Central Office.* The Central Office of the Epworth League shall be in Chicago, Illinois.

ARTICLE X. *Local Constitution.* The Constitution for local Chapters shall be determined by the Board of Control; provided, however, that no enactment shall be made which shall in any manner conflict with this General Constitution.

ARTICLE XI. *By-Laws.* The Board of Control shall have power to enact such By-Laws for its own government as will not conflict with this Constitution.

ARTICLE XII. *Amendments.* This Constitution shall be altered or amended only by the General Conference.

LOCAL CONSTITUTION.

The Local Constitution, which applies to and governs the individual Chapters, is framed by the Board of Control.

The Local Constitution may be changed by the Board of Control, but only so far as the changes may be in harmony with the General Constitution. It can not be changed by local Chapters, and is not subject to adoption by them. Whatever modifications are made in it from time to time by the Board of Control become immediately operative in every Chapter, and the work should be adjusted to these changes promptly. The Local Constitution, as it now stands, is as follows, as revised by the Board of Control in 1918:

ARTICLE I. *Name.*—This organization shall be known as the Epworth League of the .... Methodist Episcopal Church of ...., and shall be subordinate to the Quarterly Conference of said Church. It shall be a Chapter of the Epworth League of the Methodist Episcopal Church.

ARTICLE II. *Object.*—The object of the League is to promote intelligent and vital piety in the young members and friends of the Church; to aid them in the attainment of purity of heart and in constant growth in grace, and to train them in works of mercy and help.

ARTICLE III. *Membership.*—1. Membership shall be constituted by election of the Chapter, on nomination of the Cabinet; and, as far as practicable, membership shall be

THE EFFICIENT EPWORTHIAN.

confined to persons between the ages of sixteen and thirty-five.

2. The pastor shall be *ex-officio* a member of the Chapter and the Cabinet.*

(Footnote to Article III, Section 2.)
*Whenever a Chapter so decides, there shall be two classes of members, active and associate. Active members shall, in addition to election as provided in Section 1, subscribe to the following pledge:

"I will earnestly seek for myself, and do all that I can to help others attain the highest New Testament standard of experience and life. I will refrain from taking such diversions as can not be used in the name of the Lord Jesus. I will, so far as possible, attend the devotional meetings of the Chapter and the worship of the Church, and will take some active part in them."

In such cases, active members only shall be eligible to election as officers of the Chapter. Associate members shall be entitled to all other privileges of membership excepting the right to vote in the election of officers or to hold office.

ARTICLE IV. *Departments.*—The work of the League shall be carried on through four departments, as follows: 1. Department of Spiritual Work. 2. Department of World Evangelism. 3. Department of Social Service. 4. Department of Recreation and Culture.

The distribution of work under each department shall be as follows:

1. *Department of Spiritual Work.*—This department shall arrange for the regular devotional meetings of the Chapter. It shall look after the spiritual welfare of the members, inviting those who are interested to join the classes of the Church. To it shall be committed the work, wherever possible, of organizing and training a personal workers' class. It shall, at least once each year, present the subject of the Morning Watch Enrollment, endeavoring to enlist all the members and friends of the League and Church in the movement. It shall endeavor to interest the

THE ORGANIC LAW.

young people in systematic daily Bible study, and shall have supervision of the Bible Study Classes. To this end is is recommended that a Committee on Bible Study be appointed. It shall encourage enlistments for life service, and assist in equipping those so enlisted. It shall instruct the membership of the Chapter in the doctrines, polity, history, and present activities of the Methodist Episcopal Church, and the other denominations of the Church universal. It may plan special revival meetings, and neighborhood outdoor and cottage services, and other meetings of like purpose. It may also conduct devotional meetings for special classes of persons, as sailors, railroad men, etc. It shall promote and assist in the conduct of Junior Leagues, wherever practicable, and may also conduct prayer-meetings for children where there is no Chapter of the Junior League. To it shall be committed all the evangelistic and devotional activities of the Chapter. Where the work of the League is so divided that the work of the different departments is interwoven, the Department of Spiritual Work shall arrange for the devotional services in sociables, lectures, and all meetings of similar character.

2. *Department of World Evangelism.*—This department shall endeavor to interest the young people in the missionary and other benevolent interests of the Church. It shall enlist the members in the systematic study of Christian missions, and in the formation of mission study classes. It shall have charge of the circulation of Missionary literature. It shall cultivate the habit of prayer for world evangelism. At least once each year, it shall present to the Chapter the claims of Christian Stewardship and shall encourage the members in the study and practice of Christian Stewardship.

3. *Department of Social Service.*—This department shall arrange for the systematic visitation of the members of the Chapter, the sick of the neighborhood, the aged, and the newcomers to the community. It shall promote the study of social service among the members, and, wherever practicable, conduct a social survey of the community. It shall interest the League in the charities of the place, and plan to give aid when needed. It shall promote a commu-

nity consciousness of the necessity for prohibition, temperance, moral reform, and the enforcement of law enacted in behalf of the same. It shall have charge of social purity work, tract distribution, Christian citizenship, and kindred activities. All kinds of charitable work, when undertaken by the Chapter—such as visiting hospitals, nursing, distributing flowers, starting industrial schools, conducting employment bureaus, coffee houses, day nurseries, etc.—shall be under its care.

4. *Department of Recreation and Culture.*—It shall be the aim of this department to give stimulus and direction to general Christian culture, to do what it can to quicken the intellectual and social life of its members and of the community. It may open, wherever practicable, libraries, reading rooms, art rooms, night schools, and the like. It shall arrange for lectures and literary gatherings, when members of the Chapter and others shall present essays, papers, talks, debates, etc. It shall endeavor to extend the circulation of *The Epworth Herald,* and of the other publications of the Church. It shall be on the lookout for new members, and be ready to receive them and introduce them at all meetings of the Chapter. It shall have charge of the social part of all gatherings. The music of the Chapter (except that of the devotional meetings) and its entertainments shall be under its care. It may provide flowers for the pulpit, ushers when needed, and attend to procuring badges, emblems, banners, decorations, etc., and be the custodian of all such effects belonging to the Chapter. Athletic events, indoors and out-of-doors, and all such recreations as picnics, excursions, and other outings shall be under its care.

ARTICLE V. *Officers.*—1. The officers shall be a President, First Vice-President, Second Vice-President, Third Vice-President, Fourth Vice-President, Secretary, Treasurer, and Junior League Superintendent.

2. The President, who shall be a member of the Methodist Episcopal Church, shall be elected by ballot on a majority vote. The other officers, who shall be members of the Methodist Episcopal or some other evangelical Church, shall be elected in the same manner, except the

THE ORGANIC LAW.

Junior League Superintendent, who shall be appointed by the pastor.

3. After approval of the President by the Quarterly Conference, the names of the officers, with their addresses, shall be promptly forwarded to the Central Office of the Epworth League.

4. The President shall perform the duties usually assigned to his office. The Vice-Presidents, in the order named (beginning with the First Vice-President), shall represent and have charge respectively of the Departments of Spiritual Work, World Evangelism, Social Service, and Recreation and Culture. The officers, together with the Pastor, shall constitute the Cabinet of the Chapter.

5. The Secretary shall keep a complete record of the membership, of all the meetings, and of all courses of reading and study pursued by the Chapter. It is desirable that he send reports of its meetings to local papers; also that he keep copies of all programs, newspaper and other notices of Chapter affairs, and all memorabilia relating to its doings. He may carry on correspondence with absent members and other Chapters, and read the replies at the meetings of the Chapter, as the Chapter may order. He shall conduct all correspondence with the Central and District Offices, and be the custodian of all the records of the Chapter. Through him members in good standing shall be recommended to other Chapters. The Secretary may choose one or more assistants to aid him in his work.

6. The Treasurer shall present to the Chapter plans for meeting the financial needs of the Chapter. He shall collect all dues and receive all moneys, disbursing the same as the Chapter may direct. He shall make regular remittances to the Central Office of the Epworth League, Chicago, Illinois, of such amounts as the Board of the Epworth League shall request for the general expenses of the Epworth League.*

*The Board of the Epworth League, in November, 1921, adopted the Twenty-four-Hour-Day plan (which calls for payment of two cents per week by Senior members and one cent per week by Junior members) as the official method of discharging the obligations of the local chapter to the world-wide work of the League. A minimum enrollment of 25% of each chapter's membership was designated to supersede the former Central Office dues of ten cents per year per member. The minimum expectation of 25% is general and applies to all Leagues, except chapters in certain Areas, Conferences and Districts, where a larger percentage has been accepted for special programs."

THE EFFICIENT EPWORTHIAN.

7. The Superintendent of the Junior League shall have charge of all work in the Junior League. For specific directions as to methods of work, see the local Constitution for the Junior League.

8. For the purpose of enlisting all in the work and rendering it more effective, the Cabinet shall assign each member of the Chapter to at least one department of work. Each Vice-President shall name to the Chapter a committee of from three to five members for the management of his department, the officer being *ex-officio* chairman. If for any cause all the offices of a Chapter shall be vacated, a special meeting may be called by the pastor to fill the vacancies.

9. It shall be the duty of the Cabinet to organize a Junior League, under the control of a Superintendent, to be appointed by the pastor.

ARTICLE VI. *Meetings.*—The Chapter shall hold a devotional meeting on .... evening of each week, under the direction of the Committee on Spiritual Work. Other meetings shall be held as the Cabinet may arrange for them.

ARTICLE VII. In case of immorality, unchristian conduct, or neglect of duty, the Chapter, at any regularly called meeting, may, by a majority vote of the members present and voting, exclude the offender upon the recommendation of two-thirds of the Cabinet. The accused shall have the right to be heard by the Cabinet before any decisive action is taken.

ARTICLE VIII. *By-Laws and Amendments.*—The Chapter may adopt such by-laws, consistent with the Constitution, as may be needed. Amendments to said by-laws must be submitted in writing to the Cabinet, and, when approved by it, may be adopted by a two-thirds vote of those present at any regular meeting; provided, however, that all by-laws must be in harmony with the League pledge.

The following paragraphs from the Discipline define certain duties of the President, the District Superintendent, and the pastor.

THE ORGANIC LAW.

THE PRESIDENT.

The President of an Epworth League Chapter must be a member of the Methodist Episcopal Church, and shall be elected by the Chapter and confirmed by the Quarterly Conference, of which body he shall then become a member if approved by it for membership therein. It shall be his duty to present to the Quarterly Conference a report of his Chapter, together with such information as the Conference may require and he may be able to give.

DIRECTORS OF SOCIAL AND RECREATIONAL LIFE.

Whenever a chapter of the Epworth League is organized and maintained, the fourth Vice-President of the same, when confirmed and approved by the Quarterly Conference, may be designated as Director of Social and Recreational Life.

DISTRICT SUPERINTENDENTS AND PASTORS.

It shall be the duty of the District Superintendents, when holding a District or Quarterly Conference, to inquire into the condition of Epworth League Chapters and such other Young People's Societies as may be under the control of the Quarterly and District Conferences, and to ascertain whether they are conducting their affairs in harmony with the purpose and Discipline of the Methodist Episcopal Church.

It shall be the duty of Pastors to organize and maintain, if practicable, Chapters of the Epworth League.

It shall be the duty of the Pastor to cause each Church under his charge to observe Epworth League Anniversary Day on the second Sunday in May, or a Sunday as near thereto as possible. Whenever convenient, the Anniversary shall be observed at the regular preaching hour.

It shall be the duty of the Pastor to appoint Superintendents of Junior Leagues when needed, who shall continue in office until a successor is appointed.

It shall be the duty of the Pastor to cause to be transmitted to the Central Office a complete list of the Epworth League officers of his Charge immediately after each election.

THE EFFICIENT EPWORTHIAN.

By-Laws.

The by-laws, which relate to the minor details of the Chapter's business, may be changed by the local Chapter at its pleasure, with the single condition that all changes shall be in harmony with the Epworth League Constitution. A set of by-laws, given below, is offered by way of suggestion:

Article 1. The Chapter shall hold a devotional meeting weekly on .... evening, to be led by the members, under the direction of the Department of Spiritual Work.

Article 2. The Chapter shall hold a business meeting on the .... evening of each month. (Insert in the blank, "First Monday," "Second Monday," or whatever evening may be chosen.)

Article 3. At each business meeting, all the departments shall present reports of their work through their respective chairmen.

Article 4. The following shall be the Order of Exercises at the business meeting: (a) Devotional service, to consist of singing, the reading of Scripture, and prayer by a member, or the Lord's Prayer by all in concert. (b) Minutes of the last meeting, and their approval. (c) Reports from the departments of work. (d) Reports from special committees. (e) Unfinished business. (f) Propositions for membership. (g) New business. (h) Adjournment.

Article 5. At any business meeting, ... members shall constitute a quorum for the transaction of business.

Article 6. The annual meeting for the election of officers shall be held on the .... evening in the month of May.

Article 7. At the annual meeting, each officer shall present a written report of the work in the department under his charge during the year.

Article 8. After the election of officers, the Secretary shall report in writing to the Official Board of Quarterly Conference of the Church the name of the President-elect for their approval; and shall also report the names and addresses of the newly-elected officers to the Central Office

THE ORGANIC LAW.

of the Epworth League; and, as soon as practicable, shall communicate the action of the Official Board upon the President to the Chapter. The President shall attend, as a member, each session of the Quarterly Conference.

ARTICLE 9. A remittance shall be made, on or before May 1st, to the Central Office of the Epworth League, 740 Rush Street, Chicago, Ill., of such an amount as the Board of Control shall request for the general administrative expenses of the Epworth League.

When the Twenty-four-Hour-Day plan (which has been officially recommended by the Board of the Epworth League) is adopted as a method of financing the Chapter, remittances should be made to the Central Office at the beginning of each quarter.*

ARTICLE 10. Amendments to these by-laws must be submitted in writing to the Cabinet, and when recommended by the Cabinet, may be adopted by a two-thirds vote of those present at any regular meeting, provided, that all are in harmony with the Discipline of the Church and the Constitution of the Epworth League.

ARTICLE 11. Any of these By-Laws, except Article 5, may be suspended at any meeting, for that meeting only, by a two-thirds vote of those present.

ARTICLE 12. The following is the Form for the Report of the Local League to the Quarterly Conference:

```
            Report of Epworth League, Chapter......
   ....................Methodist Episcopal Church.  ....................Charge.
   ................District.       ................Conference.   For..........Quarter.
   Number of Active Members...........    Number of meetings held...............
   Number of Associate Members........    Religious ............................
   Number of Honorary Members.........    Social or Literary....................
   Total ...............................  Business .............................
            Number at last report..........   Increase or decrease...........
Study Classes and Enrollment.
   ..............................................................................
   ..............................................................................
   ..............................................................................
Notable items concerning the work.
   ..............................................................................
   ..............................................................................
   ..............................................................................
```

---

*The Board of the Epworth League, October, 1918, fixed the amount at a sum equal to ten cents a member for each Senior Chapter, and five cents a member for each Junior Chapter, plus enough to raise any fractional part of a dollar to a full dollar. (This provision is really obsolete, having been made altogether insufficient by the enlarged program of the Centenary. It is unnecessary when the Chapter has adopted the Twenty-four-Hour-Day plan.)

THE EFFICIENT EPWORTHIAN.

The following person has been elected to serve as President for the period of ....,
subject to your approval:

....

The following officers have also been elected for the term of ....:
  1st Vice-President, 3d Vice-President, Secretary,
  2d Vice-President, 4th Vice-President, Treasurer.

OTHER DETAILS OF ORGANIZATION.

Pledge.—The Epworth League has a pledge, the adoption of which is optional with the Chapters. That is, each Chapter may decide for itself whether the pledge shall be made a condition of membership. No Chapter has any authority to change the pledge in any way. The pledge reads as follows:

I will earnestly seek for myself, and do all that I can to help others attain, the highest New Testament standard of experience and life.

I will refrain from taking such diversions as can not be used in the name of the Lord Jesus.

I will, so far as possible, attend the devotional meetings of the Chapter and the worship of the Church, and will take some active part in them.

The adoption of the pledge automatically determines that the Chapters adopting it shall have two classes of membership, active and associate. The active members are those who have taken the pledge. It is expected that where the pledge is adopted all members of the Chapter who are also members of the Church shall take it. Associate membership is not provided, except as a stepping-stone to active membership, and all members of the Methodist Episcopal Church are practically pledged to do all that the formal pledge of the Epworth League requires.

Colors.—The Epworth League colors are red and white. The most usual form is a white ribbon with a scarlet thread running through its center.

Badge.—The badge of the Epworth League is a Maltese cross. In the center is a smaller cross. This cross is encircled by a series of small circles, each one of which bears a letter of the motto, "Look up, lift up." On the arms of the cross are the initials of the Epworth League. These badges are made in a variety of sizes and materials.

Watchwords.—Two significant sentences have been incorporated into the activities of the Epworth League from the beginning. The first is from John Wesley:

THE ORGANIC LAW.

"I desire to form a League offensive and defensive with every soldier of Jesus Christ."

The second is a declaration made by Bishop Matthew Simpson:

"We live to make our own Church a power in the land, while we live to love every other Church that exalts our Christ."

Elections.—For the sake of uniformity, the Central Office of the Epworth League suggests that all Chapters hold their election in April or early in May, so that the new officers may be installed on Anniversary Day, which is the Sunday nearest the fifteenth of May.

GENERAL OFFICERS.

For the four years ending with June, 1924, the general officers of the Epworth League are as follows:

President—Bishop Adna W. Leonard, San Francisco.
General Secretary—Rev. Charles E. Guthrie, Chicago.
Editor of *The Epworth Herald*—Rev. Dan B. Brummitt, Chicago.

The Board of the Epworth League for the quadrennium ending June, 1924, is composed of the following ministers and laymen:

District Representatives: I. Rev. A. E. Morris, Bangor, Me. II. J. E. Fisher, New York. III. Rev. W. E. Brown, Syracuse, N. Y. IV. Rev. J. W. Engle, Clarksburg, W. Va. V. Rev. W. E. Hammaker, Youngstown, O. (Vice-President). VI. Rev. J. S. Hill, Morristown, Tenn. VII. Rev. C. S. Stanley, New Orleans, La. VIII. Rev. H. A. Gordon, Independence, Kan. IX. Rev. H. E. Hutchinson, Spencer, Iowa. X. Rev. J. T. Jones, Rock Island, Ill. XI. Rev. W. W. Martin, Fort Wayne, Ind. XII. Rev. J. W. Taylor, Minneapolis, Minn. XIII. Rev. J. L. Panzlau, La Crosse, Wis. XIV. Rev. E. N. Edgerton, Grand Junction, Colo. XV. Rev. J. C. Harrison, Bellingham, Wash.

At large: Laymen, Carl F. Price, New York (Recording Secretary); E. H. Forkel, Chicago (Treasurer); M. C. Tifft, Minneapolis, Minn. Ministers: Rev. Carl M. Warner, Sacramento, Calif.; Rev. D. L. Marsh, Pittsburgh, Pa.

CHAPTER III.

HOW TO ORGANIZE A CHAPTER.

The Preliminaries.

The organization of an Epworth League Chapter is not now as common an event as in the first years of the League's existence. Chapters have been organized in the great majority of our Churches. But there is need in many places for a reorganization.

And here and there are a few Churches which have not yet organized their young people. There is, in most places, no good reason for delaying longer. The League is by now a fairly permanent institution. Its value has been abundantly demonstrated. It works.

The method of organization is simple enough. The smallest and weakest charge on the remotest circuit, as well as the resourceful and more numerous membership of the great city Church, can start a Chapter and keep it going.

Usually the pastor will take the first step. The need of it may occur to him before it occurs to any one else. Perhaps he will be confident that an organization can be effected when other people will be less sanguine.

But if the pastor does not take the initiative, and the conviction has come to a group of young people that it is time to organize, or reorganize, an Epworth League Chapter, the pastor should by all means be consulted before definite or organized action is taken.

Then get information. Take no leaps in the dark. The Central Office of the Epworth League exists to serve as a clearing-house of Epworth League information. All its resources are at the service of those who need them.

Send to that office for the necessary literature. Most of it is free, although there is some for which a small fee must be charged. It is abundantly worth it.

HOW TO ORGANIZE A CHAPTER.

The pastor should by all means be enlisted in the new movement. He will "talk it up," both in the pulpit and out of it. He is to be recognized officially and personally as the leader of the work. He will be from the outset the Chapter's cordial and resourceful friend.

Appoint an evening for considering "to organize or not to organize," when the business in hand will be certain to have complete right of way. Advertise widely and persistently. Make a personal canvass of the young people who should be present. Provide some simple social feature, which will help to dissipate any feeling of strangeness and put everybody on an equality.

Before the day of the meeting those who are most interested in it must take themselves to prayer. The Epworth League is committed to implicit faith in prayer. If a new Chapter can not be begun in the prayerful spirit, and with definite dependence on God, better not begin it at all.

At this preliminary meeting, after the devotional exercises, some one will explain the purpose of the gathering. Often one of the officers of the District League will be glad to come and talk of the spirit, purpose, and plan of the organization. By the time this speech is over the question will be, "Shall we organize a Chapter of the Epworth League?" It is presumed, of course, that all will answer "Yes." But do not limit discussion. Hold it to the question, but let everybody be free to say his say.

With the other literature received from the Central Office will be a copy of the Epworth League Constitution. This should be pasted on a large sheet of paper, and after the vote to organize has been taken, all who will may sign the document. Distribute additional copies of the Constitution so that those who have joined may study the details of the organization at their leisure.

The question of by-laws should be left to a committee, instructed to report at the next meeting, presenting such a set of by-laws as are given on page 33. Another committee should be appointed to make nominations for the Chapter's first officers. Then the meeting may be adjourned for a week.

At the adjourned meeting let the reports of the Committee on By-Laws and on Nominations be heard, discussed, and adopted. Then the Chapter is ready for definite and aggressive work.

Membership.

There is no legal age limit in the Epworth League. The Constitution says that "as far as practicable the membership shall be confined to persons between the ages of sixteen and thirty-five." Under ordinary circumstances, therefore, when a Junior League exists, the Epworth League will not receive members who are under sixteen years of age.

The maximum age limit should be considered in the light of two facts. First, that the Epworth League is a young people's society; second, that youth is usually, but not always, a question of years.

At the second meeting of the Chapter the question of the pledge should be considered. Should it be adopted or not? Here is a short and simple answer to that question. Adopt the pledge wherever it is possible. But it can not be made an essential everywhere. Some Chapters for a time may be better without it. If the pledge *is* adopted, do not make it easy for professing Christians to become associate members. Associate membership was not provided for actual Christians. It can have no meaning for them.

Keep the associate membership list constantly changing by the taking in of new associates, and by steady promotions. That is to say, win over associate members to Christ and His Church, and so make active members out of them.

The Nominating Committee.

The Nominating Committee, which was chosen at the preliminary meeting, should invite the pastor to meet with it. Let the Chapter members trust the committee to select the best available material to fill the offices. Random nominations for officers in open meeting are seldom wise. And it is almost never wise to have two tickets in the field at an election. The committee will do its best work if it is free to choose those members who, in its opinion, will make the

HOW TO ORGANIZE A CHAPTER.

best available officers. Then, unless there are very weighty reasons against it, accept the committee's report at its face value and elect the nominees.

The Nominating Committee should, of course, take plenty of time. Perfect frankness should be the rule. Consider all the possible material for officers. Discuss the whole subject with freedom, and yet with Christian courtesy. Weigh well the qualifications and needs of every suggested nominee. The committee is in charge of a confidential business. It is taken for granted that whatever is said about individuals in the committee meetings is not to be repeated outside, any more than the things that transpire in a Bishop's Cabinet at an Annual Conference are to be retailed outside of the Cabinet room.

OFFICIAL RECOGNITION.

At the first Quarterly Conference after the election of officers, the name of the President should be submitted to the Quarterly Conference for its approval and for election to membership in that body. That makes him the official link between the League and the Church.

The names of all the officers should be sent as soon as possible after the election to the Central Office of the Epworth League, Chicago, and a charter secured from the same office. The charters are of three kinds: a card charter, which is free; a large charter in blue and gold, which is furnished for 50 cents; and a still larger and more elaborate document, beautifully engraved and engrossed, the price of which is $1.50. This last charter is in all respects the best. Wherever possible, it is the one which should be secured. Then frame it and hang it in a conspicuous place in the League room.

THE UNVEILING OF THE CHARTER.

After a Chapter has been organized and recognized by the Central Office, at the first public meeting of the Chapter make a place on the program for the unveiling of the charter.

The charter is the certificate of a great fellowship. The young people of the Methodist Episcopal Church are

THE EFFICIENT EPWORTHIAN.

banded for the winning of the young people to Jesus Christ, and training them for service. The new Chapter has come into that union of effort to be a part of it and to make its work more effective. The charter is the visible sign of that, and of much more. It grants rights and privileges, stands for certain truths and beliefs, and certifies to enrollment and recognition.

Let the charter be decorated with the Epworth League colors, so arranged that they will conceal it until the moment of unveiling. The pastor, or some other speaker, should make an inspiring and convincing address. Then, at the proper moment, a slight pull at the cords which hold the draperies will draw them back and reveal the charter.

Organizing the Departments.

The plan of the Epworth League is now nearly ideal. It is intended to provide for every form of social, moral, and religious activity among the young people of the Methodist Episcopal Church.

In the first department the spiritual life is cultivated. Emphasis is placed upon private and public prayer, on witness-bearing, on the study of the Bible for personal spiritual growth, on the study of Christian experience and personal evangelism, and on the actual evangelization of the young people of the community.

In the second department there is opportunity to take up and study the work of the Kingdom of God in its greater aspects, looking out upon the world-wide field and facing the varied avenues through which the progress of the Kingdom of God is to be secured.

In the third department the emphasis is upon service and sacrifice, the union of those who love in behalf of those who suffer. This work is remedial and also preventive. It believes in lighthouses as well as lifeboats.

In the fourth department the intellectual and social natures are provided for. Means of proper and satisfying recreation are discovered and used.

All these phases of Epworth League work are essential to a well-rounded Christian character. And, in some form

HOW TO ORGANIZE A CHAPTER.

or other, the work of every department can be carried on, wherever it is possible to organize a Chapter at all.

The plan of the Epworth League provides for every member. "To every man his work." There can be a definite place for every individual, with duties easily understood, and with real service and personal growth involved

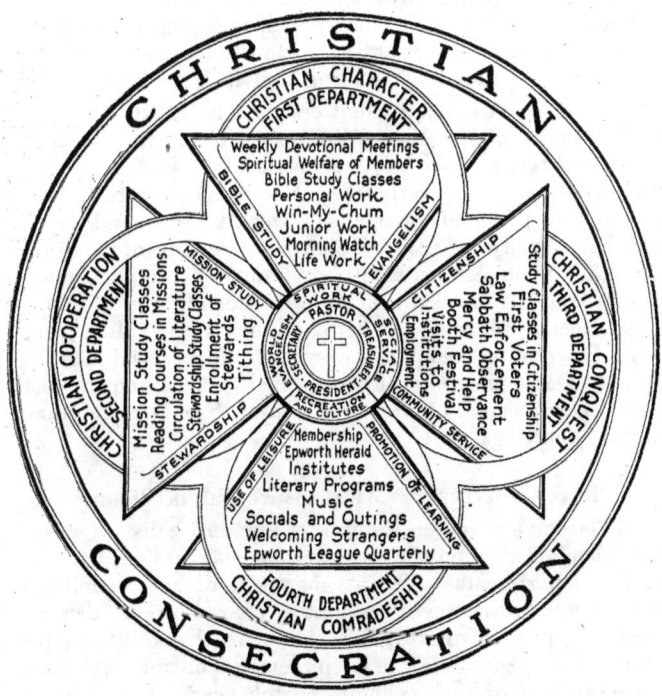

in every duty. The League works on the theory that we are all members one of another. What one does for another in the first department, for example, may be returned to him in service of equal value by the fourth department.

Organize all the departments. In some places local conditions will put stronger emphasis on one or the other

THE EFFICIENT EPWORTHIAN.

of the four, or on one phase or another of the different departments, but no Chapter can do its full work without attempting at least something in each department.

The Constitution provides for departmental committees of three to five, appointed by the several Vice-Presidents. But the whole membership should be assigned to the various departments as personal fitness and the needs of the work may suggest. It will be well if each department can have a large committee, so that the various subdivisions of department work may each be provided with workers.

Let the department committees be subdivided according to the scheme of the Epworth Cross. That will give four sub-committees to each department, as follows: First Department—spiritual welfare of the members, study and practice of personal evangelism, weekly devotional meeting, Bible study. Second Department—study of missions and other benevolences, monthly missionary meetings, study of Christian stewardship, definite missionary work. Third Department—Mercy and help, studies in social service, good citizenship, temperance reform, and social purity. Fourth Department—athletics, social entertainments and music, new members and *The Epworth Herald* circulation, literary meetings.

The Assigning of Members to Their Work.

This belongs to the Cabinet. The entire list of members should be gone over and each member assigned to one of the departments. The arrangement of sub-committees may be left to the Vice-President in charge of each department. It is not best to make an entire change of assignments every year. Plan to keep members on for two years, changing half of each committee each year. Then a good working minority, at least, of members who have had some experience in a department will be retained as a nucleus around which to gather the department forces.

When persons are elected to membership in the Chapter they should be assigned at once to department work. Even a brief delay at the beginning of membership may make it difficult later to secure the member's active co-operation.

HOW TO ORGANIZE A CHAPTER.

Meetings.

Much of the work of an Epworth League Chapter is done by and in meetings. There is room for a large variety of gatherings, and each of them may be made indispensable in the work of the Chapter.

The central assembly, of course, is the weekly devotional meeting. It should be held every week, without interruption, except when circumstances absolutely prevent its assembling. That means a meeting every week when the church doors can be open for anything at all.

This meeting is the heart of the League. It is the place of power. It is the general gathering place. More members are present than at any other time. But there is not room here to do more than hint at the possibilities of this devotional meeting. For a complete discussion of its work and methods, see "The Practice of Devotion," in this series.

The business meeting is of large importance. Shall it be held monthly, semi-monthly, or bi-monthly? All things considered, most Chapters will find the once-a-month business meeting the most satisfactory, especially if some social feature is combined with it. For a fuller discussion of the business meeting, see page 22.

There will be frequent department meetings. These, being small as to attendance, will do a large amount of distinctly constructive work. They should be in charge of the various Vice-Presidents. All departments should hold meetings often enough so that the department committees will have an understanding of their work and a sense of the responsibility which belongs to it.

Some departmental committee meetings must be held at certain periods, because of the needs of the work. The first department's committee on devotional meetings will meet twice a year, to assign leaders for the weekly meetings. This is important work, and ought not to be left to the judgment or inclination of a single individual. This same committee may arrange to hold a preliminary prayer-meeting just before the weekly devotional meeting, inviting the more earnest members to unite in a few minutes of prayer for the success of the larger gathering. This is done in many places with great benefit.

THE EFFICIENT EPWORTHIAN.

The study class committees in the Bible, in missions, in social service, and in other subjects, will each hold an important meeting well in advance of the respective rally days. They will plan for class work and prepare for the proper observation of these study rally days. After the classes are organized, the class activities will furnish a good opportunity for occasional meetings of the several committees. Their members may join in the work of the class, and tarry awhile at the close to discuss the situation and to consider means of enlarging and improving the work committed to them.

These smaller meetings may seem to be spending a good deal of time over trifles. But they are not trifles at all. In these smaller gatherings one single interest dominates. There is unity of purpose, direct location of responsibility, opportunity for the survey of the field work, and time to consider. The smaller number makes for informality and freedom, and there can be entire frankness and fullness of discussion.

CHAPTER IV.

OVERSEEING THE CHAPTER'S WORK.

THE OFFICERS.

The President.—The President of an Epworth League Chapter needs four things: spirituality, sense, tact, and grit.

The first goes without saying. The President of an organization with such high spiritual purposes as those of an Epworth League Chapter would be utterly helpless and lost if he were not a spiritually-minded Christian. He certainly would be finding requirements and problems entirely beyond his power to meet. Much of his work would be entirely meaningless to a mere nominal Christian, and the responsibility which belongs to the President would be a load upon him so great that he would either resign at once, as he should, or keep up the hopeless attempt to *be* what he has not yet *become*.

The word "sense" is so large and inclusive that if all it involves can be found in one Chapter President, that Chapter will possess a jewel. It means that he must understand folks and understand his work. He will need to be able to see the difference between visionary schemes and plans for real work.

And "tact"—who shall define that word? But the idea for which it stands is perfectly understood. The Epworth League President is dealing with many people, possessing many peculiarities. He must be, in Paul's sense and with Paul's motive, all things to all men. He must know how to reduce friction, to smooth over the difficulties which occur in all associated effort. Without offensive self-assertion he must make himself a necessary friend of the pastor and of the Sunday school superintendent, and especially of the Cabinet and membership of the Chapter. He must be firm and yet gentle, vigorous and yet tender, exacting and yet

THE EFFICIENT EPWORTHIAN.

considerate, businesslike and yet forbearing; hoping all things, believing all things, enduring all things.

"Grit" is a modern Americanism for an energetic courage that will not be denied. There are many opportunities in religious work for discouragement and for letting things alone. These opportunities are temptations, and the President who yields has not only missed his mark as President, but he has wasted the powers and possibilities of the entire membership.

The League is represented in the Quarterly Conference through its President. He should not consider his membership as a mere form; he is expected to be the voice of the League in the council of the local church.

The President of the Epworth League should be entirely satisfactory to the pastor. These two must work together so closely that it would be unwise to select a President with whom the pastor could not hold the most cordial and intimate friendship.

I KNOW A LEAGUE PRESIDENT.

He's a true Methodist.

He reads *The Herald* every week.

He never forgets the real business of the League.

He knows a few things about parliamentary law.

He helps the Sunday school superintendent in many ways.

He knows how to step in and take anybody's place in an emergency.

He is a systematic and sympathetic friend of the Junior League Superintendent.

He does most of his work, and his most effective work, away from the public eye.

He's good at getting other people to work, preferring that to doing the work himself.

He attends all the department meetings so far as he can, but he does not dominate them.

He is in the confidence of each department officer, knowing the problems, difficulties, and resources of them all.

He does n't let things die on his hands. When any work ought to be discontinued, he insists on its being done decisively.

OVERSEEING THE CHAPTER'S WORK.

He has a good temper, large patience, a sunny outlook on life, a perfect faith in the Epworth League, and a deep and vital Christian experience.

He has no ambition to break any records for continuity of presidential service, and is always on the lookout for possible successors who can be trained for the work.

He has a program for his administration, and has it planned so that the things the Cabinet will attempt can all be done by concerted and intelligent effort.

He carries an Epworth League notebook with pages for plans, dates of coming events, outlines of workable methods, hints, suggestions, class lists, book lists, and miscellaneous. "Miscellaneous" takes most of the room.

Isn't he worth knowing?

First Vice-President.—The First Vice-President is intrusted with a place of superlative responsibility. Four great tasks are committed to him: the direction of the weekly devotional meeting, the organization of the Chapter for Bible study, and the provision of systematic study in Christian experience and the promotion of personal evangelism. He must be both spiritual and intelligent. He must believe in the spiritual value of the devotional meeting. He must expect it to produce both direct and deferred results. He should make it largely evangelistic and wisely constructive to win the unconverted, and to help the young converts in the early days of their Christian life.

This officer ought not to be afraid of the sound of his own voice in public. If he has been so hitherto, he must get over it by speaking, though not at length, whenever he finds opportunity. He must be a lover of his Bible, and if the holding of this office drives him to a closer, more continuous, and more devotional study of the Book, his term will be as great a blessing to him as it will be to the Chapter.

The First Vice-President should hold himself ready, on short notice, to lead any devotional meeting in case the leader assigned fails to do his part.

In planning the work of Bible study, the First Vice-President will need a large stock of tact and persuasiveness and intelligence. People must be convinced of the

THE EFFICIENT EPWORTHIAN.

value of Bible study. They have a sentimental belief in it, but actually they ignore it.

The First Vice-President is called to leadership in spiritual things. He needs to be an inspiring Christian in his ideals and conduct, attracting the members to the highest standard of personal life, not only by his example, but by simple and loving speech. He is in a peculiar sense the successor and heir of the old-time class leader, who dealt with his members directly concerning their progress in grace. He will organize and supervise, wherever it is possible, classes for the study of Christian experience, as more fully set forth in another chapter.

And the work of personal evangelism, now happily bulking so large in the activities of Epworthians, is largely dependent on the zeal and discretion of the First Vice-President. He it is who must direct the efforts of the Chapter's growing group of personal workers. To do all this he must have the spirit of an evangelist, eagerly enthusiastic in the work of leading young people to Jesus Christ.

Second Vice-President.—The Second Vice-President is in charge of "World Evangelism," that department of Epworth League work which was created in May, 1903. World evangelism is a cardinal principle in the League, but not every member is as yet ready for all that it means. So the Second Vice-President must be a sort of pioneer. He must believe in missions, home and foreign; in every form of gospel spreading; in stewardship as the rule of life for Christians; in intelligence about all the Church's great enterprises, and he must see that the Chapter's members get every chance to believe in these things also.

Third Vice-President.—It is not too much to say that the old Department of Mercy and Help did more than any other one thing to develop the spirit of Christian kindliness and practical benevolences which to-day exists in so large measure among the young people of the Church.

The work of this department, under its new name and with its larger functions, is popular, and the people are glad to support it. But it is toilsome work, and the Third Vice-President will need large devotion and constant consecra-

OVERSEEING THE CHAPTER'S WORK.

tion. He should be a sympathetic lover of men and women and of children. The work of systematic visitation, when wisely done, may be of the very highest value to the Church. Care for the poor and sick is a fruitful and yet laborious task. The great and widening field of social service, with its need for careful study, as well as strong conviction, includes an endless variety of interests and opportunities for successful activity.

Of course, the Third Vice-President will be inspired by the knowledge that everything done in this department is meant to bring people into the Kingdom of God, and to discover some citizens of the Kingdom who had been counted as on the outside. All the ministries of comfort and love and service which spring up in this department have their explanation and source in the love wherewith Christ hath loved us, and to forget this is to rob the work of most of its power. Social service must exalt, not the department, nor the Chapter, but the Christ, and carried on in this spirit may be made a marvelous evangelizing agency.

Fourth Vice-President.—The legislation of June, 1913, simplified, without making any lighter, the work of the Fourth Vice-President. The incumbent of this office requires now more than ever to seek both culture and resourcefulness. Whatever literary work the Chapter may do will be done under the direction of this department, and the recreational and social life in the Church and Chapter will very largely depend upon it.

In many Chapters a most important work of this department will be the securing of new members. That demands a thoroughly human interest in the people whom it is sought to reach. They must be sought mainly for their own sake. To seek members just to lengthen the Chapter roll is to defeat the very purposes for which the League is organized. The Chapter exists for its members, not the members for the Chapter.

Here there is danger that we shall forget the need of definite religious purpose. The Chapter is a perfect dynamo of life and power, because it is made up of people whose life-forces are at their highest and fullest strength. But the joy of living, to which this department particularly ministers, must not be the mere exuberance of youthful spirits; it can be made a mighty means of winning the young and light-hearted to a Savior who, instead of robbing them of their gladness, will give it a new, an abiding, and a more gracious meaning.

The Cabinet.

The Cabinet of an Epworth League Chapter is a peculiarly distinctive feature of the organization. It is the heart of the Chapter. It is more than an Executive Committee, for every activity of the Chapter, in every department, is represented here.

The Cabinet is the body which sifts, discusses, and puts into shape for consideration all the varied items of business which later will require action by the entire Chapter. That makes the Cabinet a time-saving organization. It unifies the work of the Chapter. It co-ordinates the operations of the various departments, strengthening the weak places by applying to them the overplus of strength which is developed elsewhere. It considers them in a business meeting. It is not hampered by any rules of debate, or any other restriction, except the ordinary rules of courteous conversation.

The Cabinet is a clearing-house for the entire Chapter. All the Chapter's resources are centered here. The officers can see the defects of the work sooner than any one else, and may perhaps repair them without making them public at all.

The Cabinet may be of exceeding value to the pastor. If he can consider this central body as his general staff, he can keep his fingers on the keys of Epworth League power. The members of the Cabinet will know what is being thought and said and done among the younger members of his Church with a definiteness which few of the older members can possess concerning each other.

Through the Cabinet the pastor may very often set in motion plans and purposes which are urgently needed, but which it may be difficult or unwise for him to attempt directly.

OVERSEEING THE CHAPTER'S WORK.

The Cabinet is composed of all the Constitutional officers of the Chapters, including the Junior Superintendent. This does not include such officers as chorister, organist, auditor, etc. The pastor, of course, is *ex-officio* a member.

The Cabinet must plan for a regular and fully-attended meeting, preferably once a month. This ought to be insisted upon, and attendance at the meeting should be expected of each officer as a part of his ordinary duty. Hold these meetings, if possible, at a fixed place, and preferably in the home of one of the members. Let the Secretary's notification be regular and definite, so that no member can possibly have any excuse for forgetting the recurrence of the stated session.

The Cabinet meeting is not a particularly formal affair, and its business may be transacted without undue attention to the necessity of parliamentary discussion. There will be the utmost frankness and freedom of expression, of course, and many of the things that are said in the discussion will properly be considered as privileged communications, not to be talked about outside the Cabinet group.

The informality of the Cabinet meeting, however, should not be made an excuse for puttering or frittering away the time. There is a way by which important matters may be attended to promptly without sacrificing the freedom of a friendly, face-to-face consultation.

The great business of the Cabinet, in the beginning of its work, should be to see that every member of the Chapter has a chance and a place. It should distribute the work well, with reference not only to the needs of the work, but also to the needs of the individual members. It will seek to develop each of them in all the things that go to make up a well-rounded Epworthian.

This assignment of the members to departments should be made at the first meeting of the Cabinet after its election. No member should be omitted from the scheme of assignment, except for entirely sufficient reason. Do not consider that it is necessary to have exactly so many members in each department. Be flexible. Some departments will need more members than others, and some members

THE EFFICIENT EPWORTHIAN.

ought to be especially interested in one department rather than another.

At every Cabinet meeting each department should be represented. If the chairman can not be present, he should send some member of his committee who is familiar with the department work.

It will be well to hear all the reports from the departments before taking up the recommendations which the various members will make. After all reports have been heard, recommendations can be considered, not only on their own merits, but in relation to each other, and intelligent and harmonious action can be taken.

The Secretary will keep a sufficient record of the Cabinet proceedings so that he can make a clear and concise report to the business meeting of the Chapter. This record of the proceedings should be read at the close of the Cabinet meeting, especially if the Cabinet meets a few days before the regular monthly business meeting of the Chapter, as in most cases it will.

At the business meeting of the Chapter the Secretary will present the proceedings of the Cabinet, so far as they involve recommendations to the Chapter for action. In most matters the Cabinet can not act on its own initiative. It can study the interests of the Chapter carefully, discuss proposed plans, while they are yet only plans and not definite policies, and so can relieve the business meeting of any necessity for discussing unprofitable things, or for discussing things in an unprofitable way. It can keep the balance between departments, and prevent disorder and clash of interests. But it can not decide matters which belong to the whole Chapter. For instance, it can not elect members, but must nominate them. It can not nominate persons for election to League offices. It can propose a budget, but the Chapter must adopt it. It can not spent money, except by a vote of the Chapter.

In every way the usefulness of the Cabinet is entirely sufficient to justify all effort to keep it in perfect working order.

OVERSEEING THE CHAPTER'S WORK.

The following is a suggestive order of business for the Cabinet meeting:
1. Devotional moments.
2. Roll call.
3. The record of the last meeting, read for information.
4. Reports from the officers of all work done during the month.
5. Recommendations from the several officers, of plans and methods, for consideration.
6. Nomination of candidates for membership.
7. Assignment of members to departments. Transfers between departments.
8. Are there any members who need special attention?
9. What should be the important feature of the next business meeting?
10. Miscellaneous business.
11. Reading of the record of the meeting.
12. Adjournment.

The Cabinet may help greatly in the work of the Church by arranging a conference with the Sunday School Board. At this conference these questions would naturally arise: How can the Sunday school and the Chapter be of mutual service? Are there any points at which the work of the two bodies seems to conflict? If so, what can be done to remedy the difficulty?

If difficulty is found in getting the department committees together, the following plan will often be of value. Set apart one night in the month as committee night, when all the committees shall meet at the church, each committee going to its own part of the room. The committees may take an hour for the consideration of their work, after which will come an informal social time, shared in by all the committee members present.

In dealing with the question of membership the Cabinet will need much wisdom and Christian charity. All applications for membership are first submitted to the Cabinet. Now, the Chapter is not a club, from which all uncongenial persons may properly be excluded. It is rather a company

THE EFFICIENT EPWORTHIAN.

of people seeking to be of the largest possible service to one another and to the world outside. Personal considerations must not be allowed to control in the admission of members. The Cabinet, which decides whether an applicant shall be recommended or not, possesses thus a power of exclusion which should be rarely exercised. The Chapter, for its own sake and for the sake of the work, should secure as many new members as possible. It may not be easy to see how a proposed member may be of value to the Chapter, or the Chapter to him, if he should be elected. But it is not difficult to see that there will be no value given or received on either side if the candidate is excluded.

It is better to err on the side of admitting to membership doubtful candidates, provided that the Chapter has sufficient vitality and grace to make sure that the new members will not lower the standard of the Chapter's life. Standing in Christ's stead, the Epworth League member is come to seek and to save that which was lost, and the Christ-method of accomplishing that holy work is the method of personal association. The "doubtful" candidate may be just the one who has most need of the Chapter's help and influence, and who will most completely justify any sacrifice of inclination and taste which his admission may make necessary.

It will be found helpful at times if the Cabinet will call the roll of the entire membership, giving opportunity for suggestion and information concerning each member. The main question should be, "What can we do for this member that we are not now doing?" and "What more can that member be induced to do for the Chapter and the Church?" In raising these questions, the special interests represented by the various members of the Cabinet will be enlisted. In one case the Third Vice-President may have just the answer that is needed; in another the Secretary may furnish the suggestion; in another, the chairman of the Social Service Department.

When it becomes necessary to exclude any member from the Chapter, the Cabinet has the delicate duty of recommending such action. The accused member has the right to appear, not before the Chapter, but before the Cabinet, and to be heard there in his own behalf. If, after such

OVERSEEING THE CHAPTER'S WORK.

hearing, it is considered by any that exclusion is the safe and Christian thing, two-thirds vote of the Cabinet is required to recommend that action to the Chapter. Unless there are extraordinary reasons for some other action, the recommendation of the Cabinet should be adopted by the Chapter.

At the beginning of a new term of office the wise Cabinet adopts a policy or program which it will attempt to carry out during the twelve months to come. The advantage of focusing effort and interest on a definite program is evident enough. An incidental gain of this plan is that every department may be given proper attention. Thus the Chapter will grow symmetrically, and avoid the criticism that its interest is all absorbed by one favorite project.

THE BUSINESS MEETING.

For intelligent understanding of the Chapter's work and the proper conduct of its business, a periodical business meeting is necessary. A monthly meeting is preferable to one held more frequently, and in an active Chapter it is not likely that a meeting at longer intervals would be sufficient for the needs of the work. Of course, no Epworth League Chapter will hold a business meeting on Sunday. Indeed, it is not wise to let any secular item of business intrude into the devotional meeting, unless under stress of unusual circumstances.

The question of a quorum will be settled early in the life of a Chapter. The fact that the business meeting is held at a stated time, and that full announcement is made of the meeting as it draws near, gives sufficient publicity so that all members who desire may arrange to attend. A large quorum requirement usually serves no better purpose than to cripple the business of the Chapter, and to alienate the interest of those who may come once or twice only to find that they have their journey for their pains. Better do business with a handful than wait for a crowd.

Wherever it can be done, and there are few places where it can not, the monthly business meeting should be specially considered by the Fourth Vice-President. Through the co-operation of that officer, simple but attractive social features may be prepared, so that at the close of the business session it will be possible to devote thirty minutes or an hour to informal sociability, or to a prepared program of games, etc.

There are advantages in holding the business meeting at a private house, if the Chapter is not too large. But unless it can be made perfectly convenient for friends of the Chapter to open their homes for this purpose without serious disarrangement, the meetings should be held in the church. Do not trespass on good nature. Then you will be the more welcome on those rare occasions when you really need to ask for the opening of a private home for your meeting.

Although, as has been suggested, the social feature may be made a part of the business meeting, do not depend upon that to attract the attendance. Young people, like other people, are attracted by "doings" in which they are interested. If there is real business, business that counts, and business that really appeals to the members of the Chapter, then the business itself will be attractive enough. Most Chapters can find in the course of a month sufficient real business to justify all the interest and enthusiasm of the majority of its membership.

The business meeting is not a mob. On the other hand, it is not a great deliberative body. The happy medium between these two extremes is secured when the Chapter, in its business meetings, is subject to simple but definite rules of order. A knowledge and use of parliamentary law, such as is given in Bishop Neely's "Parliamentarian," will make the meeting not only more resultful, but will shorten the time of the session. No business meeting can be a permanent success if it is a chatter-meeting. On the other hand, it is a real affliction when some members of the Chapter are possessed of the idea that Robert's "Rules of Order," or Cushing's "Manual" is more important than the actual transaction of actual business.

The various officers of the Chapter will make monthly reports. The reports will cover what was done and planned during the preceding month, and perhaps what is proposed for the month to come. The members need to discuss these

OVERSEEING THE CHAPTER'S WORK.

reports. Of course, the discussion is for conference and for results, and not for empty criticism. The less of the faultfinding spirit or of the spirit of carping objection, the better for the Chapter.

The reports of the officers and committees should be written. This can not be too strongly insisted upon. A written report will be prepared with at least a little care to its contents. A verbal report may be anything or nothing, with the chances in favor of its being as near nothing as the conscience of the officer concerned will allow. A written report abides. It is there next month. Last year's record is valuable for comparison, for encouragement, or, it may be, for warning. The Secretary can not be too careful about the filing and preserving of these reports. It may seem a matter of small importance, but in a large measure the work of the Chapter will be indicated and influenced by the sort of reports its officers get into the habit of making.

It will be a great help to the business meeting if each succeeding month a fresh center of interest can be found. Some department of the Chapter's work can be given right of way, so that the entire Chapter may focus its thought and interest on that one particular point.

The business meeting receives recommendations for membership from the Cabinet, and elects candidates to membership. The electing must be done in business meeting, but for the sake of the Chapter and for the sake of the new members, they ought to be received in some formal and public way. This may be done, very briefly, but with sufficient impressiveness, at the first regular devotional meeting following the business session.

Quite frequently it will be found helpful to have a paper or discussion of Epworth League work in a broader and more general way than is possible when discussing the specific problems of the Chapter. Arrange a quiz; invite a district officer; have a debate on some question of League policy. These things will broaden the Chapter's interest in the League as a connectional institution.

Invite the pastor to the business meeting. Do not encourage him to think that the young people prefer his room

THE EFFICIENT EPWORTHIAN.

to his company. In most places it is not true, and for the pastor's sake as well as for the best interest of the Chapter, it ought never to be true. He needs the Chapter, and is needed by it. He will get and give much.

There are two dangers which lie in the path of an Epworth League business meeting. One, that it will degenerate into a perfunctory performance, without life or vigor or interest. If that happens, the attendance will decrease, the work of the Chapter will languish, and the securing of new recruits will fail, because nobody will care to ask them and they will not care to come.

The other danger is that the interest in the various plans and enterprises of the Chapter will be so intense that feelings may be overstrained and a spirit of unfriendly rivalry, or even jealousy, may creep in.

Both of these hindrances may be avoided by remembering that the business meeting is intrusted with interests that are of the greatest importance. The members are set to organize and combine their resources for spiritual and permanent results. For this reason the business meeting calls for the same prayerful spirit and the same sense of God's presence as does the devotional meeting. With this atmosphere prevailing, interest will be deeper and more real, personal differences will disappear in a common loyalty to Jesus Christ, brotherly love and Christian patience will abound, and the business meeting will become a place of the keenest interest and yet of the most complete friendliness and fellowship.

Once a year, early in May, as recommended by the Board of Control, the business meeting will be found of unusual importance. Complete reports for the year will be presented and considered.

If the Chapter is wise it will give large and definite recognition to all the good work that has been done by the retiring officers. Pass a simple but hearty resolution of thanks.

There may be some deficiencies in the finances of the Chapter. These should be provided for at this annual business meeting by some proper and adequate method.

The officers for the year to come are to be elected at

OVERSEEING THE CHAPTER'S WORK.

this meeting. Of course, they will be carefully selected from the best available material, and they will be elected for business, not for fun, nor from prejudice, nor as a mere mark of honor.

It will probably be possible to present the budget for the coming year's activities at the annual meeting, although in many cases that will be left until the new officers have formulated their plans and can estimate the probable cost of carrying them out.

Every annual meeting ought to mark a distinct advance in every feature of the Chapter's work. The Secretary should read, at some point in the meeting, a complete summary of the condition of the Chapter as it was twelve months before, compared with what it is at the date of this meeting.

A simple program for the business meeting, with allowance for any amount of variation to suit local and occasional needs, is as follows:

1. Devotional exercises.
2. The reading of the minutes of the last meeting.
3. Unfinished business.
4. Officers' reports and their discussion.
5. Recommendations of the Cabinet.
6. Election of members.
7. New business.
8. Special. Papers, discussion, or other general features.
9. Reading of the minutes, for information.
10. Social hour.

Samples of League Oversight.

The letters of League leaders to their young people never were so full of optimism and practical idealism as they are in this present year of grace.

The President of the Montana State League, Roy C. Smith, begins his letter to the local presidents in this vigorous fashion:

> "You and I have had a great honor and a great responsibility given to us—to lead and direct the forces of the Epworth League in this great State of ours

THE EFFICIENT EPWORTHIAN.

during the coming year. What are we, you and I, going to do about it? I am wondering if you are as much impressed as I by our opportunity.

"If you were at the convention, you heard about the great things planned for the new year. If you were not, you have heard about them through other Epworthians, the *Messenger*, the State Cabinet, etc. Surely your League is going to do its share this year, and it depends on you and me whether it does or not. Won't you let me help you?"

Here are seven things the first department of the Illinois State League was working for, as set forth in the letter of the First Vice-President to the Chapters throughout the state:

"First: 'The Devotional Meeting.' The motto being, 'Every member a Christian, every Christian a better Christian.'

"Second: 'Personal Evangelism.' Motto, 'Zeal in spreading the gospel.' Organize a Personal Work Committee, which will meet once a month for fifteen minutes before the devotional meeting. Pray for the unconverted members of your Chapter and others in the community. Use every member sometime, somewhere, and somehow. Work with the pastor, secure his influence, help him in his evangelistic services and any other special work he wishes the committee to do.

"Third: 'Bible-study Classes.' The Church's growing interest in the study of the Bible is largely traceable to the activities of the Epworth League.

"Fourth: 'The Morning Watch.' Motto, 'Watch, pray, talk with the Master daily.' Establish a Morning Watch enrollment class and adopt the pledge.

"Fifth: 'The Daily Prayer Lists.' Closely linked with the fourth branch on Morning Watch is this special systematic personal prayer list.

"Over eight thousand prayer lists have been sent throughout the State in a year. In one district alone over three hundred have been benefited by this prayer list. Many encouraging reports have been received of the success of this plan, and we have been advised

OVERSEEING THE CHAPTER'S WORK.

by many to continue the daily prayer lists for another year. Each Chapter should compile such a list, of causes, institutions, and persons.

"Sixth: 'Open-Air Meetings.' From late spring to early fall many Chapters have found open-air meetings a great means of usefulness.

"Seventh: 'Spiritual Welfare of Members.' Establish a praying band to meet occasionally for prayer. Pray especially for those in your community who occasionally visit your meetings who do not claim Christ as their Savior."

These are just samples, symptoms, straws. Wherever the leaders have caught the spirit of the League's relation to the young life of the Church they are working at definite and wholly worth-while tasks.

As more League leadership rises to this level the Church will have a new reason to be thankful in the new reinforcements the League provides.

Deflating Swollen Committees.

The department assignments should be made or, perhaps, be revised for the beginning of each fall's work. What is the system in your Chapter?

Do you put members on the committees for the same reason that influential people are asked to the platform at a political meeting, to bind them a little closer to the cause by giving them a little cheap recognition, or do you put them on because there is work to do and they can and will do it?

The League is interested in a large membership list, but not to the extent of getting members who must be coaxed and coddled and cajoled into loyalty and service.

Let it be understood, when a member is assigned to one of the departments, that the assignment is a business arrangement, and not a compliment or a bribe.

That may mean smaller department committees and fewer schemes of activity. But what of that? Padded lists and paper programs deceive nobody, except perhaps those who contrive them. And only for a little while, even so.

CHAPTER V.

WORKING EFFICIENCY IN THE LEADERS.

SCIENTIFIC MANAGEMENT IN LEAGUE WORK.

SCIENTIFIC management is a thing of the hour. It is even applied everywhere—on the farm, even, as carefully as in the automobile factory.

But its best use is a personal use. The twenty-two rules for efficiency printed below, which are taken from "Tests of Efficiency," by Harold Holmes, reveal ways of applying to one's self the standards of the efficiency engineer. Try them.

And notice how they would fit when applied to Epworth League work.

We suggest that some alert Epworthian take this list, and, by changing a word here and there, make it appropriate for reading in the League meeting or at the convention.

Let the first be stated thus, for example: "It is within the power of every Epworthian to so develop his League efficiency that he can get complete satisfaction out of his labor." And so on.

Even if your paraphrased list is never used, it will do you good to make it.

Here are the items:

1. It is within the power of every man to so develop his efficiency that he can get a good price for his labor.
2. Disraeli says, "Be ready when your opportunity comes."
3. Think out your problems carefully.
4. Let your ambition supply the enthusiasm.
5. Control and centralize your thoughts to develop thought capacity.

WORKING EFFICIENCY IN THE LEADERS.

6. The way in which your hours of freedom are spent increases or decreases your efficiency.
7. Efficiency is the ratio between results and opportunity.
8. A fifty per cent machine, like a fifty-point man, is always open to question.
9. There are many who think it smart to do as little as they can get by with.
10. Every employer wants honesty, loyalty, sobriety, punctuality, and industry.
11. Initiative is the suggestion of methods of action, better methods than those of yesterday, without being told.
12. Do a thing a little better than it was ever done before.
13. Lessen your limitations and you will increase your efficiency.
14. It is not so much what you do, but how you do it.
15. Put your heart into your work, and then work with all your might.
16. Make good rather than make excuses.
17. Give undivided service or none.
18. "A man passes for what he is worth."—Emerson.
19. The successful man is made, not born.
20. Efficiency is measured in deeds, not in reasons why deeds are not performed.
21. Form the habit of concentration.
22. If you want to hold your job, if you want to be in line for a better position, you must render honest, efficient service.

Making the Community Need Us.

"The public invited," "strangers welcome," and similar phrases are a confession of weakness or laziness or ignorance.

If the public and the strangers never discover that you have something for them except as they get the idea from these phrases, your business will one day receive a call from a gentleman who was not invited, and who will not be welcome when he comes.

An Epworth League Chapter which buys a hundred

THE EFFICIENT EPWORTHIAN.

topic cards on which are printed, "You will find a cordial welcome," and calls that "advertising the meeting," will not be troubled to provide chairs for the multitude.

An old friend said one day, "When I find that a thing is really inevitable, I fix myself to get reconciled to it." We may as well "fix ourselves to get reconciled" to the fact that there is no irresistible demands in the community for the work of the Church and the League. We may tell people, as does the washing machine agent, that they "can't keep house without it," but they do n't believe us, or are content to fuddle along in the old way.

What then? Why, the only thing left is to create a demand for something which people need, but did n't know they wanted!

There was once no demand for automobiles, and the first miner of anthracite coal could n't sell the stuff. "David Harum" was refused by more than one publisher. Chicago's Thomas Orchestra began its career playing to empty benches or "paper" houses.

Of late one maker has produced 300,000 automobiles as his season's output. If "David Harum's" author had lived he could have sold his second book at his own price before writing a line of it. Now we are glad to get hard coal, though we pay a big price for it. Thomas Orchestra tickets for the whole winter season are almost all sold before the first week's concert.

The Epworth League Chapter must create a demand for itself and its product, or it will go down. There are plenty of young people who ought to be in its meetings and its work—plenty of what the piano salesman calls "prospects." But they have to be captured by making them want what the League offers.

How? Ay! there's the rub. There are a thousand ways, and not a single one which can be guaranteed to succeed. Everything depends on personal devotion and faith and sense and resourcefulness. Nobody knows the easy road, for there is n't any.

But any Chapter has gone far on the difficult road to success when it recognizes that it must do something more than open its doors and put up a bulletin board.

WORKING EFFICIENCY IN THE LEADERS.

The first great task of every Epworth League Chapter is to create a demand for its output.

("But," warns our friend, the sales manager of a manufacturing concern, "I know a man who went broke because his advertising was so good that he was swamped with orders which he could n't deliver.")

FINDING THE FACTS IN ANY CHAPTER.

Is your Epworth League Chapter organized for efficient work? Have you an efficient President?

Is your President supported by an efficient Cabinet?

Do the other Vice-Presidents really work at the activities of their several departments? (The First Vice-President usually can show a fair average of effort.)

Is the business of the Chapter as well managed as the business of the successful merchants of your community?

Could you write a report of the Chapter's work for last year without padding or vague generalities, that would justify the year's expense and effort spent on the Chapter?

Is your membership list a relic, a guess, a Chinese puzzle, or actually a list of living, accessible, dependable members?

Have you a budget, with plans for the spending of every dollar you purpose raising, or do you take a collection whenever it becomes necessary to get money for some emergency that might have been foreseen, but was n't?

In a word, can you, or *anybody,* prepare a definite survey of your Chapter so that a new pastor, for instance, might study it with the certainty that he was getting exact and essential information about one of the Church's important agencies?

The thing can be done, of course. But in some Chapters the doing of it would be no light labor.

Until such a survey is possible, nobody can tell what your Chapter can do or should do or might be expected to do in a given situation. And when that knowledge is available, your Chapter will be twice as useful, with the same resources, as it could possibly be under the policy of "muddling through."

THE EFFICIENT EPWORTHIAN.

Make a survey! One form is suggested here, and many modifications will occur to expert readers.

QUESTIONS FOR A SURVEY OF THE CHAPTER.

President:
1. When first elected?
2. Previous League offices held?
3. Other Church offices held?

Cabinet Officers (same questions as to each):
1. When first elected?
2. Previous department service?

First Department:
1. Devotional meeting—time? Average attendance? General character of meeting? Leaders—how appointed, frequency of service, nature of preparation, material available for preparation? Topics used? Special features (music, addresses, etc.), ushers, departmental co-operation with leader?
2. Number of Bible-study classes? Text-books used? Enrollment? Is Bible study a regular form of activity? How many weeks annually?
3. Win-My-Chum Week observed—when and how?
4. Evangelistic work—when and where? Public? Personal? Classes in personal evangelism? Enrollment? Results?
5. Morning Watch enrollment? What attempt to encourage Morning Watch?
6. Co-operation with pastor—when, how?

Second Department:
1. Missionary devotional meetings—how led and what nature?
2. Number of mission-study classes? Text-books used this year? Previous years? Enrollment? Results?
3. Christian Stewardship enrollment? Study class? Special effort?
4. Missionary contributions of Chapter? Amount? Objects?
5. Is department in regular correspondence with the Department of Mission Study and Stewardship of the Central Office at Chicago?

WORKING EFFICIENCY IN THE LEADERS.

Third Department:
  1. Systematic visiting? How? Among what people? Results?
  2. Local relief and benevolence—what forms? To what extent? How financed? Records?
  3. Long-distance work—what institutions and objects? Form of help given? Value in money?
  4. Fresh-air work?
  5. Law Enforcement work—what forms? Results?
  6. Christian citizenship work—what forms? What cooperation with other bodies?
  7. Study class in social service? What text-books? Enrollment?
  8. Distribution of literature? What sort? Where? How much?
  9. Social service work? What forms?

Fourth Department:
  1. Plans for regular recreational activity? How financed?
  2. Recreational gatherings within last six months? Attendance? Results?
  3. What plans for educational work? What study classes other than those in first three departments? Reading clubs? Lecture courses? Literary evenings?
  4. What work in securing new members? How many members gained this year? Membership contests? First results? Final effects?
  5. How is *The Herald* club secured? Number of subscribers? How may list be increased?
  6. Flowers for pulpit? Later disposition?
  7. Decorations—when used? Extent and character?

Secretary:
  1. What records are kept? Reports made? Correspondence with District, Conference, or State officers? Are present officers reported at Central Office? Other correspondence with Central Office?
  2. Method of membership transfer and reception?
  3. Publicity methods? General advertising? Special printed matter? Announcements—when and how made?

THE EFFICIENT EPWORTHIAN.

Treasurer:
  1. Financial method? Results?
  2. Annual budget—how prepared and presented?
  3. Relation of Treasurer to the Twenty-four-Hour-Day Plan of the Central Office?

General:
  1. Business meetings—when and how? How well attended? Combined with socials?
  2. Cabinet meetings—function and frequency?
  3. Is a yearly policy formulated? How? What does it cover? How completely is it followed?
  4. Relation to Junior League?
  5. Relation to Sunday school?
  6. Relation to district and other League organizations?
  7. Is pledge used? Is membership grouping, as active and associate, satisfactory in operation?
  8. Membership: Young men? Young women? Resident? Non-resident? Active? Associate? Church members? Workers in other departments of the Church (Sunday school, missionary societies, Junior League, Official Board)?
  9. Distribution of membership—is each member assigned to a department? How and by whom are assignments made?
  10. What special days are observed through the year (Anniversary Day, *Epworth Herald* Day, League Rally Day, Bible Study, Missionary Study, and Christian Stewardship Rally Days)?
  11. Elections and installations—dates, form of installation?
  12. Affiliation with other bodies—City Union? Federation of Young People's Societies? Group? Subdistrict? District? Conference? State? General Conference District? Method of affiliation? Delegates to conventions? Dues? Contributions?

FINDING THE FACTS IN ANY COMMUNITY.

After the Chapter knows itself, it ought to make some searching studies of its field and the work that ought to be done. A suggestive series of questions is here given,

WORKING EFFICIENCY IN THE LEADERS.

which may be added to, or taken from, to meet local needs. Only, do not be satisfied with guesses or generalities. Get the facts!

THE COMMUNITY.

1. Define the community precisely, stating its bounds.

2. If a city community, decide upon the number of blocks to be taken into consideration.

3. If a country community, how many miles?

4. If a village, consider the community as a whole, the village being the unit of study.

THE CHURCH.

1. What is the value of the present church building?

2. Are there social rooms? Club rooms? Is the building attractive to young people? State number of rooms and their use: Auditorium? Sunday school class rooms? Gymnasium? Chapel? Kitchen?

3. Is the building adapted to the needs of the community? Would a better building mean better service? What improvements would you make if you were rebuilding?

4. How often is the building open? What is the total attendance at its meetings in a week?

5. What proportion of the Church membership has no interest in the Church—except that of worship.

6. Are the men organized? Would they take more interest if they were?

7. Describe some organization that your Church could start for the discussion and promotion of community interests.

8. What methods are used by your Church to minister to the unchurched?

9. Mention needs of the community common to all the Churches where they might profitably work together.

10. What are the vital needs in your community in which no Church is showing an interest?

11. In what reforms or enterprises does the Church lead?

THE EFFICIENT EPWORTHIAN.

YOUNG PEOPLE.

1. How many young people over fourteen years and unmarried are in the community? How many of these are boys? How many are girls?

2. How many young men over fourteen years of age are continuing in school? How many young women? How many are away from home at high school? How many away at college?

3. How many after leaving school are at productive work in the community?

4. How many of the young people are Church members? What proportion attend?

5. What societies for young people has the Church? For boys? For Girls? For young men? For young women? For young men and young women together?

6. How often do these hold religious meetings? Social meetings?

7. How many adults are actively interested in work with young people?

8. Are there adult individuals in the community who could be induced to lead activities for young people?

9. Is there any training in community service?

10. What noticeable needs of young people are not met in the community?

THE COMMUNITY IN GENERAL.

1. What opportunities to earn a living does your community offer to its educated young people?

2. Are there any marked forms of disorder among the young people of the community?

3. What corrupting agencies are at work?

4. Are the homes in the community adequate for the social meetings of the young people? Are there frequent social gatherings in the homes?

5. What organizations minister to the social life of the young people?

6. Does the community offer opportunities to the young people in the way of study classes, lecture courses, etc.? Make a list of them.

WORKING EFFICIENCY IN THE LEADERS.

7. Is there any sentiment in favor of adequate education for young people—a "get an education" movement?

8. Does the Church co-operate with other community agencies for betterment? With Health Department? With Charities? With temperance organizations? With housing commissions?

9. Is there any disposition on the part of the Church to initiate new betterment movements?

10. Does the district offer Summer Conference opportunities?

RECREATION.

1. What are the most popular forms of recreation in the community?

2. Which are commercial? Which are society?

3. What agencies are providing recreation for the people without private profit?

4. Does the community permit Sunday baseball with admission fee? Sunday organized play without charge?

5. Is there a public playground? Ball field? Is the play supervised?

6. Is there a Young Men's Christian Association at work in the locality? A Young Women's Christian Association? What forms of recreation do these provide?

7. Where do men and boys meet regularly without formal appointment?

8. Do the parents in the community give their boys regular time off for play?

9. How many young people take their recreation outside the community?

10. How do the young people spend their Sundays besides going to Church? Is any change needed?

11. What proportion of social gatherings are held in the homes of the community?

12. What games are provided in the homes of the community?

13. Do the Churches hold socials? Suppers? Picnics? Are these free, or to raise money?

14. How generally do the people of the community attend?

THE EFFICIENT EPWORTHIAN.

15. Name the social or literary clubs of the community. Give purpose and function of each.

16. What events bring the whole community together and secure general acquaintance?

17. What public tasks that need doing could be performed by a "bee" or "frolic" with good results?

Making Use of the Facts.

The two lists of questions given in the preceding pages are in some sort an Epworth League Survey. They are not painfully scientific, but they will produce a great mass of information. What is to be done with it?

Front the force to the field! Ask your Chapter what revelations it has seen, and what obligations have come to the surface.

Then work out a policy, a program to include the work of all the departments, so that as much of the discovered need is provided for as possible.

To get these facts and not to use them would be like getting seed corn and throwing it into the sewer.

The Test of the League's Permanence.

Nobody who is working at the Epworth League's real business has time to consider whether the League has or has not outlived its usefulness. But a few bystanders raise the question occasionally; and some of them pause for a reply.

This is a busy time, and a very practical time, in religious circles. The Church people of to-day are not such worshipers of tradition that they need much rebuke on that score. They are familiar with the scrap heap, and not specially reluctant to deposit thereon the outworn tools of other days.

The Epworth League *has* outlived its usefulness if it is not rendering a present-day service. If it is doing its work blunderingly, or with less efficiency than some other institution can do it, its end is near. The Church will replace it with the more effective instrument.

We should be sorry for the Epworth League if we thought the Church had lost faith in it, but we should not

WORKING EFFICIENCY IN THE LEADERS.

be alarmed for the Church. It would find another tool, or make one.

All this is beside the mark, however. The Church has not lost faith in the League, nor has it found that the League's work can be better done by some other agency. The peculiar training the League provides is not offered by any other institution of the Church, and can not be.

Nevertheless, League workers need to remember always that the League is not sacrosanct. It is being tested constantly by the law of the survival of the fittest. It faces the perpetual question, What service does it render?

The only danger which threatens the League is from within, that it shall consider itself immortal. If any Chapter is no more of use to the Church, it may not complain that its kingdom is taken from it and given to another. It does not "own" anything. It has not even a ninety-nine year lease of its room.

But the Chapter which is making full proof of its ministry, which is enlisting and training and educating and thrusting out for larger service those young people whom the Church so sorely needs—why should *it* be anxious?

And the Epworth League has thousands of such Chapters.

Way for the Younger!

Each summer's conventions of the past few years have proved that the Epworth League is renewing itself.

It has promoted to the larger, wider work of the Church a multitude of trained and eager Christians.

Their places have been and are being taken by a host of young folk who were born after the Epworth League began and are now in the full strength of their joyous youth.

In the conventions these new young people are making themselves felt. They are better equipped intellectually than the first generation—they have had a better chance. Their appetite for exact and definite knowledge concerning the work that is before them is prodigious. Their desire to do constructive things, unselfish things, is a delight to all who see it.

But there are not enough of them. The Churches have

THE EFFICIENT EPWORTHIAN.

great numbers of other youth, quite as capable, quite as teachable, quite as promising in every way.

Why should the League not have these also? They need it, it needs them. They are at the heroic age; they need only to see an heroic opportunity.

Not good times, not meaningless "rallies," not effervescent enthusiasm that evaporates over night, but the Christian appeal to the generous-hearted, the offer of a task that is worth while and not too easy; that must be our program for them. And we must find them a place in which they can work.

The time is always ripe for a great ingathering of the big boys and girls, to renew the youth of the League.

Make way for the younger!

Promoting the Graduate Epworthians.

What shall we do about the older leaders in the League?

In one month we have heard of active workers, mostly office-bearers, who are forty, fifty, and even sixty years old.

The situation is described in a personal letter which comes from one of the League's most sympathetic friends. And in this letter there is also the hint of a remedy well worth trying:

"Our local Chapter has had perplexing times.

"Officers who have been in the League for ten, fifteen, or more years, by desperate effort of young folks, were not re-elected.

"The young President came in to see me not long ago. He sees the harm to our young folk in the keeping of the same officers in forever-and-a-day. He sees the harm that comes in elections every six months.

"In his talk he said something like this: 'If we could have officers in *for one year, with the understanding that they are not to be re-elected,* we would get our young people used to business methods; they might make some mistakes, but there could be nothing serious if the pastor and older Christians would advise. In each department we could be educating some one for the next chairman of that department. The President of the Chapter could be made one of the Vice-

WORKING EFFICIENCY IN THE LEADERS.

Presidents, a Vice-President might be left on the committee. But a change of officers creates new interest, draws in new members, and, if the officers of this year are in some way in the Cabinet next year, we get their advice, suggestions, help.' "

The trouble is not personal. It is not ambition seeking to supplant experience. It is in the notion that League membership is a perpetual privilege.

The trouble is partly outside the League. If the local Church will understand that the League's training is for the Church's sake, and will draft the more mature for the larger service of the Church, some good workers will drop the active work of the League, and some new material may be brought in.

The trouble is partly inside the League. If members will understand that they are in the League for the sake of a more definite training in Christian service, and will hold themselves ready to render that service when training years are done, the Church will find places and work for them, and the League will be able to train a new generation of young folks.

The one cure for a belated membership in the League is the general adoption of the school theory of League life. For every real school has two great days: matriculation day, when it enrolls new pupils, and graduation day, when it sends its old pupils out to make use of their schooling.

And, in spite of all the wistful thoughts of Commencement time; in spite of the valedictorian's voicing of the keen regret that the class feels in leaving the haunts of learning and the scenes of schoolday joys, everybody knows that graduation is not humiliation. It is promotion.

The Church has need of our expert Epworthians in the wider fields of toil. The Church has need that its young people of the Junior League and Sunday school should have the training in initiative, responsibility, and resourcefulness which the League provides. If we can consider the League as a school, these two needs will be met.

Now then, let us say it all together: "The League is a school. The school remains, but the scholars win through

THE EFFICIENT EPWORTHIAN.

to promotion, to graduation with honors, to service beyond the school walls. And this is as it should be."

The Advantages of Imperfection.

"I like an imperfect League meeting," said a man who is no longer of League age.

"I like it because it is imperfect. These ideal meetings, in which somebody pumps perfectly good religious sentiments into a lot of cramped minds, leave all but the leader in a state of stuffed repletion.

"Give me a meeting where the young people use indifferent rhetoric, and get their metaphors mixed, and quote inappropriate Scripture, and talk an unreasonable theology, and stammer out their determination to be loyal to Christ.

"The League is a school. Therefore, it has its stupidities, its poor recitations, its blunders, its wild guesses at truth, its sense of the ludicrous, its informalities and inaccuracies and vaguenesses.

"And I like to see a school at work. But if it professed to be a parliament, or wanted Commencement orations every week, or had more teachers than pupils, or expected its pupils to do nothing but listen, I should n't enjoy it."

No Epworth League Chapter needs to become slovenly because of what this observant man says. But is n't he almost half right? After all, what would a flawless Chapter mean, except that several promotions were overdue?

If a League Chapter can help its members to keep alive and vigorous the flame of personal devotion to Jesus Christ, and give them a little understanding and a sense of personal concern as to evangelism and missions and social service and wholesome recreation, it has done all that it is called upon to do. The Church, for its larger needs, should have these workers when their training has gone thus far.

Then you can invite recruits into the League, and may expect them to accept your invitation!

League Growth from Below and Within.

When somebody says that the Epworth League has seen its best days, tell him this: The Epworth League was not

WORKING EFFICIENCY IN THE LEADERS.

invented; it was made, for their own needs, by the young people of the Church, under circumstances that gave the word "providential" real meaning.

They ran it at the beginning, and they run it now. They can make it what they will.

And they will make it always better and more fitted to its work, because the Church's young people of to-day are better, clearer-visioned, more broadminded, more responsive to the Christ-call, more eager to serve, than the young people of twenty-five years ago.

Until the Church loses ground so far that it produces an inferior sort of young people, until the magnetism of Jesus Christ for young life loses its tractive power, the Epworth League will not have come on its second-best days.

Changes? Of course. Yes, indeed. The young people will change the League's plans, often. They *have* changed them.

For instance, the Board of Control is too wise a body of men to think that any modifying of the League scheme is the wisdom of a group of men talking together for two' days in a Church parlor.

In 1913 the young people of the Church were doing social service, and liking it, and wanting to do more.

In 1913 the young people of the Church were getting a bigger, clearer notion of recreation and what it meant.

And so the Board changed the Constitution. But the Board did n't evolve the changes. *It just registered them!*

In a word, this Epworth League is the young people of a great Church working out their life ideas and ideals. They get all sorts of help from pastors and bishops and secretaries, and are glad of it.

But if these young people were not religiously alive and dynamic, not all the bishops and pastors and secretaries together could tell the League how and where to go, or, indeed, get it to go at all.

Few Desertions in War Time.

Desertion is a disease of the barracks, not of the firing line. Army officers say that the sure way to stop desertions would be to go to war.

THE EFFICIENT EPWORTHIAN.

Too great a price, that, merely to waken the *esprit de corps* of the United States army; and yet the officers speak truth. Desertion in the face of the enemy is a rare disease. Men are not afraid to fight, but many of them can not endure the monotonous round of meaningless motion on the parade ground.

The Epworth League knows how this bit of human nature works among the young people. Let some enterprise be set afoot, even though it be so slight a matter as a membership contest, and how the lines straighten up! Everybody works, and everybody is eager, for it is possible to record progress and to realize that something is really being done.

But most membership contests are followed by unhappy reaction. After the "banquet," in which the Reds and Blues have complimented each other more or less heartily, a period of low vitality ensues. Everything slumps. Everybody relaxes. The work drags. And then the desertions begin, sometimes without check until all the gain of the contest has been lost, and more.

If you seek the reason for these desertions you will shortly find a young person who will say, frankly, "I quit because there was nothing doing!"

An Epworth League Chapter, like a bicycle or an aeroplane, to keep up must keep going. It was not meant to be stationary, and it can not be at once stationary and successful.

The young people desire activity, and they need it. They will not stay where stagnation is.

But also they ask for justifiable activity. They must have their drill mixed with deeds. They do not care to play at Christian service, to talk endlessly about it without doing any of it. In a word, if they are never led out of the barracks they will abandon the barracks to the leaders who do not lead.

Not always do Epworthians know what to do, but that is not mortal sin. It is rather the opportunity for a tactful pastor, an alert President, a wise Cabinet. The avenues of League usefulness are so many that there need be no lack of variety or reality in the service. Every Chapter

WORKING EFFICIENCY IN THE LEADERS.

has latent ability enough for the doing of whatever needs to be done in its field.

It is useless to complain about want of interest, or to scold for lack of loyalty. Get your Chapter into real and resultful action, and desertions will cease. More than that, new enlistments will begin.

The Ability to Start Something.

The Epworth League has this distinction among religious organizations for young people: it develops initiative.

What is that?

It is the ability to do things without being pushed, coached, coaxed, or bribed.

It is the power to take a suggestion, turn it inside out, cut off the end of it and splice that to the beginning of it, give the whole thing a new complexion and a new direction, and win through with it to a desired result.

It is the capacity which makes precedents when it can't find any, or repeals them when they are in the way, because it means to start something whether something was ever started just that fashion before or not.

Initiative is more interested in putting forces in motion than in discussing why they do n't move as they did in the old days.

Initiative is not always infallible. Some people are always starting what they can't finish, or they lose interest about the fifth inning and let the other team win the game by the simple method that prosperous bill-posters have found useful.

But there's so great need of initiative that we could afford to have a few starters who soon quit in exchange for a lot of quitters who never start.

And, last of all, initiative puts the man above the method.

Where there is no initiative, there *must* be a method, or nothing can be done, of course. But if you can find a "who," he will promptly take his first letter, put it after his last, and make a "how" out of his own personality. He invents his own methods.

THE EFFICIENT EPWORTHIAN.

Plenty of other organizations have some of the Epworth League's methods and plans. But none of them demands and encourages so much this power of initiative. And no human power is needed in the Church to-day as is this same power to get things done without red tape or a Constitutional amendment.

We are not so sure about the referendum, but we are dead certain that the sort of initiative here described is greatly needed all over this broad and lengthy land.

The Four League Vices.

There is a fifth, which deals with the other four. Without it they would not exist.

The fifth vice is a verbal one, and not a hanging matter at all. But it is hopelessly infelicitous, and has a hint of laziness about it. So it ought to be cured, if it can be.

It is the trick of referring to the department leaders of the League as "the first vice," "the second vice," "the third vice," "the fourth vice."

But the Epworth League has no room for vices, even of the verbal sort.

"Vice-president" takes a little more breath to its saying, and a little more ink to its writing.

Nevertheless, who would want to be thought a "vice," which is unpleasant, when really he is a "vice-president," which is honorable among all men, and may be highly useful,—a quality no vice ever had!

Let us make the vice a virtue, by adding to it a president.

Efficiency Hints for Cabinet and Chapter.

If a Chapter's habits need improving, change its activities.

The Chapter which does n't deliver the goods ought not to expect that it can collect the bills.

A religious hurry is as likely as any other to spoil the job. Give your League work time.

Tell your Epworth League methods to some other worker, and they will at once become worth more to yourself.

WORKING EFFICIENCY IN THE LEADERS.

In the task of reviving your Chapter, do n't try to make over every department at once. Begin with one, and let everybody concentrate for a while on developing that.

A man in a motor-boat was troubled because he could n't make headway, until he remembered that he had n't pulled up his anchor. There are Epworth League Chapters like that.

There are cranks and cranks. Maybe your Chapter needs a crank—a dreamer, an innovator, a breaker of new paths. The power of a crank comes from its being eccentric—off the center.

Mince-pie is more than ingredients, but when you improve the ingredients you improve your chances of getting a better pie. Get the best material for the devotional meeting that you can find.

The little things count in League work. Topic cards neatly printed, a word fitly spoken, a bit of inexpensive thoughtfulness, a show of genuine interest—all these are profitable out of all proportion to their cost.

Epworth League education is like any other; the best part of it comes through trying to do something, and not doing it very well, either. So do n't be too critical of the visible results. The invisible results are the ones that count.

Since there's only one kind of people, "just folks," would n't it be worth while to ask seriously why the Epworth League succeeds among one group of young people and fails less than five miles away?

If the Epworth League could use all the wisdom of all its members since the beginning, what a wise organization it would be! But how much of the joy of learning in the school of hard knocks each League generations would miss!

When all the Chapter's eggs are in one basket, the League's future is in danger, even though the basket be the devotional meeting. The League is a training school in the art of watching more than one basket at once.

A League budget will teach every Cabinet officer the value of money, and keep expenses somewhere within rifle-

THE EFFICIENT EPWORTHIAN.

shot of income. Give it a trial and be convinced, as the soap ads say.

How well do your Vice-Presidents know the actual capacity of their helpers? There's a world of ability not yet discovered in every Chapter.

A farm paper says that a good horse can be spoiled by being worked with a team-mate of a different length of step. Every League Chapter knows that it is true with young folks.

"A lazy man," says a Kansas editor, "will take any kind of a job he can't get." Did you ever hear of an Epworthian who was willing to take any office except that he was asked to fill?

Plan no more for your Chapter next year than you can do; but there's no use in discounting your own ability. You can do more than some people think. Don't let them make your program.

Lunches, suppers, dinners, banquets, are all worth using for the sake of getting people together in the breaking of bread. But they are most successful when the other business grips people until they are too interested to eat.

A contest has its good features, but it stimulates some activities that are not necessary, and appeals to some motives that are not advertised on the program.

If you can run the Chapter better than the President is doing it, you will have the chance some day. But for to-day, stand by and help!

The Cabinet officer who won't train somebody to do his work for fear of losing his own office may save his office, but he has robbed the Chapter.

Do too much for the young folks and they will do nothing for themselves. In the League they learn a little resourcefulness by being given a little rope.

It is not a sin to make the League room cheerful.

The League's work sometimes appears to lack variety, but one Chapter we know of helps to support a missionary in Java, another organizes its Junior boys into a Scout patrol, one makes its devotional meetings broadly educational, another makes extra money by selling kodak pictures, and yet another maintains a fine tennis court. The

WORKING EFFICIENCY IN THE LEADERS.

interesting thing about this variety, too, is that practically all of it is within the reach of any Chapter with the right sort of energy and initiative.

If you have somebody in your Church who doesn't believe in the League, elect somebody else as President.

The Epworth League doesn't appeal to a group of young people, but to all the young people of the Church.

Dimes from dues are better than dollars from doubtful entertainments.

Do not hold a social for money-raising purposes alone, unless it is absolutely necessary. And it is never absolutely necessary.

That experimental Chapter which we are going to enlist one of these days will never begin work on any new plan until it has answered three questions: Is it needed? Should we use it? Is there a better way?

The Chapter that can do three things at a time, and do them well, might make a sorry failure of five.

If there are factions in your Chapter, somebody start something big enough to use the abilities of every member on the roll. Then you may have a merger of factions.

Eliminate jumping-jack activities from your Chapter. Up-and-down motion is lost motion, and self-respecting young folks know it.

The Chapter which can have a successful membership contest doesn't need it.

When a Chapter thinks itself bigger than the Church it is time to magnify the Church.

The Chapter that is glad to give its expert members to the Church for larger tasks will always have plenty of experts left for its own work.

Surplus members ought not to be treated as suckers are in a blackberry patch, as though they were weeds. Give them a place and room to grow.

The best cure for a tired business meeting is a dose of actual business.

The Chapter that does most with its own resources is in best condition to make use of outside help.

The Cabinet meeting is worth all it costs if it does

THE EFFICIENT EPWORTHIAN.

nothing but discover, when it looks over the League's machinery, what repairs are necessary.

Make your members travel. Don't keep them serving in one department all the time. They are entitled to a symmetrical training.

It is amazing what a change comes over a Chapter when it has something definite to do.

It is less important to get all the young folks into the League than it is to get them to want to be in it.

The new Epworthian's value to the League begins when he says "our Chapter" instead of "your Chapter."

There are automatic presses and self-acting sewing machines, but the Epworth League Chapter that runs without watching always run away, and often smashes something.

After an Epworth League Chapter begins to produce a few trained and earnest young Christians, the question of disposing of the output becomes important. For, you see, it must be disposed of. No factory would last long that didn't find a market for its product.

The quickest and most profitable way to use sensible Epworthians who have had some training in leadership is to give them work in the Sunday school or the Junior League.

League weather note: About three months after the Institute, look out for light frosts. They will do no harm unless the Chapter has a northeast exposure to the chilling winds of criticism.

The wise Chapter grows its workers instead of importing them.

If the Chapter's new President has a well-trained imagination, his lack of a good baritone voice may be overlooked.

The best book on Epworth League methods is the New Testament.

Many a Chapter does good work with material that a critical Epworthian would consider hopeless.

Training the young people is a great business. And "doing" is the best training.

Steady work proves that a Chapter has passed the

WORKING EFFICIENCY IN THE LEADERS.

enthusiasm stage. Some Chapters effervesce and then evaporate.

"Was n't that a clever ad?" "Yes, perhaps; but what did it advertise?" Put your League achievements to that test.

Many an Epworthian who seems slow and indifferent merely needs the spur of responsibility. Give him something to do.

When General Apathy becomes the commanding officer of a League Chapter, he invites General Debility to share his command.

"Can't do anything in summer" is a popular remark among the members of the excuse club in a Chapter not far from Chicago, and in another near New York.

When a Cabinet officer thinks that the Chapter can't get along without him, it is time for another election, no matter what the Constitution says.

"There is no difficulty," said a man of experience the other day, "in finding plenty of members in every Church who will talk about work, suggest work, and even start work; but there is a plentiful lack of people who just work and keep on working." The need of every Church to-day is young people in its membership who will "just work and keep on working." Are we helping to fill that need, or do we belong to the talkers, starters, suggesters—and shirkers?

To break the grip of custom: Make it a rule in your Chapter, when anybody says, "That is the way we have always done it," to do it some other way. Custom is good until it becomes binding. Then it impedes the circulation of ideas.

The Chapter that pays no attention to its younger members need not worry about its future. There won't be any.

Anybody can run a successful Chapter. It is making the unsuccessful Chapter successful that takes brains and devotion.

You've just been elected to a place in your Chapter Cabinet? Then know that the new way of spelling "office" is "opportunity."

In any Chapter there are people with aptitudes. Mod-

THE EFFICIENT EPWORTHIAN.

ern efficiency says, "Find the apt man and set him to doing what he can do better than the man who isn't apt in that particular work."

If we could convince some people that there's actually more fun in doing a good piece of League work than in just muddling it through, the tasks of some pastors would be wonderfully lightened.

Five signs of a Chapter's prosperity: Team-work in and between the departments; vitality in the devotional meeting; study-classes that study; a business meeting that does real business; offices held by the younger members, and few re-elections.

If there's any royal road to a larger League membership, it is by the way of finding worth-while things for new members to do.

Study your League roll, not to see how many you may cut off, but to discover how many you can keep on if you try hard enough.

Another hour given to the perfecting of your plans for the new League enterprise may make all the difference between triumph and humiliation.

Many a League Chapter has disbanded for want of the thing that makes the bill-poster prosperous. *His* business is to stick.

CHAPTER VI.

THE WEEKLY DEVOTIONAL MEETING.

The best thing about the Epworth League is its weekly meeting for worship and fellowship. We have become so entirely accustomed to it that its high usefulness is sometimes overlooked just because the meeting is taken for granted. But it is a wonderful thing, when you consider it carefully, that the young people should have maintained this meeting all these years and that, whatever else of League work is abandoned, so long as a Chapter has life at all it maintains the weekly devotional meeting.

The reason for these facts is not far to seek. The young people of Methodism find in this meeting opportunity for supplying four great needs: the need of worship, the need of inspiration, the need of education, and the need of service. In the devotional meeting these elemental demands of young life are in larger or smaller measure satisfied. God becomes sensibly near and gracious, the Christian life becomes a blessedly alluring state, intelligence in the things that accompany salvation is developed, and multiplied avenues of spiritual and practical helpfulness are opened to view.

The League's devotional meeting differs from the old-time prayer-meeting in that it has a theme, about which the leader seeks to group the meeting's prayer, testimony, song, exhortation, and invitation. There are times when the topic holds the meeting in too rigid a grasp, and one longs for the freedom of a "social meeting" which shall be like the old-time love-feast.

But for the most part the topics are of the highest usefulness. They encourage and sometimes compel definite thinking on definite religious themes. They make it difficult for members to satisfy easy consciences by taking part in

THE EFFICIENT EPWORTHIAN.

slipshod or stereotyped ways. They bring before the young people in the course of a year a large variety of subjects, and invite the study and expression of personal Christian experience from almost every conceivable point of view. And one convincing proof of the usefulness of the topical method of conducting the devotional meeting is found in the fact that pastors are largely adopting that method for the regular Church prayer-meeting. Even in the British Wesleyan Methodist Church the class leaders, who have been supposed to be the least yielding in their conservatism, have begun to use topics, sometimes announcing them months ahead.

THE CONDUCT OF THE MEETING.
A TALK WITH THE LEADER.

There are four great divisions of the leader's work. Every time an Epworthian is appointed to lead the devotional meeting he should marshal his forces as indicated by these divisions. For the sake of their memory value, the key-words of the divisions may be given thus: *Preparation, Plan, Progress, Purpose*. And there are three words in each division, as shown in the following outline:

The Leader's Twelve Words

Preparation { Early. Independent. Intelligent. }
Plan { Definite. Co-operative. Alluring. }
Progress { Lead. Guide. Guard. }
Purpose { Inspiration. Concentration. Devotion. }

Three things are to be done in the PREPARATION for the devotional meeting. The leader's fitness for his work will

THE WEEKLY DEVOTIONAL MEETING.

be demonstrated as much by his quality and quantity of his preparation as by any one thing.

The first essential of the leader's preparation is that it shall be *early*. Sunday afternoon at 4.30 is at least two weeks too late. Many a leader has unhappy memories of the Sunday afternoon immediately preceding the meeting for which he was responsible. He had been to Church and had come home to a good dinner. He had perhaps enjoyed a comfortable after-dinner nap. Then at 4.30 he awoke to the appalling consciousness that in two hours he was due at the League room to take charge of the service.

The first thing he thought of, after the immediate heart-sinking had somewhat passed away, was to find *The Epworth Herald* with its notes on the topic, but that particular number was two weeks old, and had disappeared. The next expedient, and usually a successful one, was to call on the pastor and borrow his paper. Many a pastor's file is only half complete because of such borrowings. But, in spite of having the paper, the meeting is so imminent that the panic feeling is in the air. No careful reading of the notes is possible, nor any ordered search for other material in Bible or commentary. It is always easy to identify a meeting whose leadership began, continued, and ended in this mood of panic, due to the late beginning of preparation.

There are two great reasons for early preparation. One is that it gives time for the fullest possible study, and the other that it gives opportunity for one's own daily experience to suggest, as it inevitably will, a large number of illustrative and suggestive ideas which bear on the theme. When once our attention is centered on any subject, it seems that all life, both our own and the world's, begins to make contributions to that subject. But all this is a matter of time.

Then, if the leader is going to ask any people to help, as he will if he is wise, he must give them as much time for preparation as he gives himself.

The leader's preparation should be not only early, but *independent*. It can not be independent without being early, but it may easily be slavish, no matter how early

THE EFFICIENT EPWORTHIAN.

it is begun. There is an abundance of helps for the devotional meeting, but in many cases these helps are grossly misused. They are not meant to be substitutes for the leader's own thinking, nor are they offered as crutches to help his limping feet through the difficult ways of the League hour. They are not meant to be taken as though they were food for the sick and the weak, who must needs have predigested nourishment. Least of all are they to be used as though the leader were merely a phonograph, able to say over and over again, "I have been very busy this week and have not had much time to prepare, but I have found something in *The Epworth Herald* which is so much better than anything I could say that I will read that." This statement is doubly unhappy; besides being a confession of weakness and failure, it is also far from being true. No matter how forceful or brilliant the extract from the paper may be, it is in every case less desirable and less usable for the particular need of the hour than the leader's own remarks, however imperfect these may seem.

The leader's preparation must above all be *intelligent*. This might seem a needless caution, but long experience has shown that many a meeting fails because the leader has not distinctly grasped the topic. And so the meeting flounders, because the leader flounders, in a fog-bank of vagueness and guesswork.

One Sunday night the topic was "Cumberers of the Ground," and the Scripture lesson, the story of the barren fig tree—"Cut it down; why cumbereth it the ground?"

The leader had been twice misled, once by the similarity in sound between words which have no kinship of meaning, and once by that snare of the unwary, the Concordance. He had forgotten that the Concordance, even when used on the proper words, is after all a concordance of words only, and not of ideas.

And so, when a reference slip was handed to one attendant at that meeting, he looked up the Scripture, and then, to save a greater embarrassment, he lost the slip so that it could not be found when the references were called for. He lost it because the meeting, which was already

THE WEEKLY DEVOTIONAL MEETING.

vague enough, would have been entirely disorganized if he had read the extract from Isa. 1:8, for which the slip called; —"as a lodge in a garden of cucumbers." To many people that would have been an accidental bit of accuracy, for they consider that if any vegetable is a cumberer of the ground it is the cucumber. But that had nothing to do with the topic.

Let the leader ask himself in all his preliminary survey of his material: "Do I really know what this topic means? Do I understand its whole significance? Do I see its bearing on to-day's life and to-day's thinking? Can I talk about it without running for refuge to pious platitudes or empty phrases? Can I put the meaning of the theme into clear, simple, definite language of my own?"

Now comes the PLAN of the meeting. It must needs be considered, of course, in connection with the preparation. And it will determine at many points the kind of preparation to be made.

First, then, the plan of the meeting should be *definite*. A leader who expects to accomplish something with his single hour of opportunity must marshal his material and construct an outline program covering the sixty minutes which have been given him.

A program implies a point of departure, a direction of movement, and a point of arrival. It should be a sort of railway schedule, but with this difference, that plenty of opportunities should be allowed for variations and stopovers. If a leader has no program, he will be at the mercy, at some point of the meeting, of people whose intentions are thoroughly good, but whose habit of religious testimony is so fixed that it can not adjust itself to varying themes.

A person of this description arises in nearly every meeting, and, instead of speaking on the topic of the evening, gives a rather familiar and intensely personal bit of experience. It is of a sort that has been heard so often that it starts similar mental movements in other persons. The second speaker will carry the subconscious feeling of the meeting a little further from the appointed subject than the first. The third will continue the process. And in a

THE EFFICIENT EPWORTHIAN.

few moments all attention to the topic has disappeared entirely from the meeting.

With a program clearly defined in the leader's mind, this distraction can not occur. He will always know what he desires to do next. He will be able to swing the testimony back to its original center. He can permit all manner of excursions from the main line of the meeting's thought because he has something to come back to.

Another advantage of the program is that the meeting will have proportion and balance. It will not spend all the time on a single and subordinate phase of the subject. It will not miss connections with the purpose for which the meeting is called, and will not end with the main business of the evening untouched and unreached. The leader who has a program which progresses logically from one point to the next will be spared the humiliation of ending the meeting up in the air, with nothing distinct or final resulting from it, and no complete idea to be carried away by those who have been present.

The second element in the plan is that it shall be *co-operative*. The leader is only the leader. He is not the whole meeting. Moreover, if he does not secure followers, how *is* he the leader? Every meeting should have some six to twenty participants whose work has been planned for them by the leader. In the construction of his program he will provide that certain members shall read the lessons and make brief comment on them, that others shall speak for a minute each on some element of the evening's theme, that others shall present striking illustrations which throw light upon the subject. Still others will refer to parallel Scriptures and their significance, while as a rule at least half a dozen may be assigned simple questions for study and answer. The ways of providing co-operation are innumerable, and the value of it is beyond question. The more people who can be enlisted in the preparation for the meeting, the better the meeting will be, and the better the feeling on the part of all who have shared in it.

This co-operative participation reinforces the necessity for an early start in planning the meeting. It is not only unfair, but almost always unsuccessful, to put off asking

THE WEEKLY DEVOTIONAL MEETING.

people to help until the meeting is under way. A leader who must announce a hymn in order to get time for a rapid journey around the room pleading with members by the way, accomplishes nothing but the advertisement of his own unreadiness.

The third element of the plan is that it must be *alluring*. A very large part of the meeting's value will be in its power to capture the attention of those who have not been formally invited to do anything. The simplest possible method of accomplishing this result, if plenty of co-operation has been arranged for in advance, is to make an appeal through the eye of the audience as well as through its ear. A big sheet of paper or a blackboard, with questions on the topic displayed thereon, will do more to hold the attention of the meeting to the leader and the subject than thirty minutes of eloquence. If these questions are put in the first or second person, and phrased with a certain amount of human feeling, they will go far towards abolishing the dismal pauses and the pointless testimony which spoil so many meetings. It is easy for people to take part in a devotional meeting only when it is made easy for them. The thing does not happen of its own accord. It is won by forehanded and intelligent planning.

The third great word of the meeting is PROGRESS. What about the actual course of the service? What shall mark the passing of the sixty minutes between 6.30 and 7.30?

The words that answer this question are all imperatives. The first is *Lead*. You *are* the leader; do you *be* the leader. Retain control of the meeting from start to finish. This does not mean that you are to talk all the time. It means rather that you are not to talk very much any of the time, but that your words are to furnish the thread on which all the other words of the meeting are strung. If at any moment you surrender control of the meeting, your program is also surrendered, and the meeting is at the mercy of general aimlessness. Never permit yourself to make the inane and untrue announcement, coupled as it is to a vain hope, "The meeting is now in your hands; I trust you will not let the time go to waste."

It is the leader's business to see that nothing that hap

THE EFFICIENT EPWORTHIAN.

pens shall defeat the purpose of the meeting. He must be able to relate to that purpose every apparently unrelated thing which befalls. If it has no application, he must make one for it. Especially at the end of the hour is it vital that the leader shall indeed be the leader. All the profit of the meeting depends on that. It is better to endure a leaderless meeting for the first fifty-five minutes than to suffer a meeting to be leaderless in the last five minutes.

Another function of the leader's position is that he shall *guard* the meeting. He can do much of this through his preliminary arrangements. He can see that no disturbing incidentals are provided for. He can make sure that the special music shall contribute to the total impression rather than weaken it. He will see to it that no zealous departmental officer is permitted to spoil the climax of the impressive meeting by interjecting the announcement of a Poverty Social next Friday night.

The devotional meeting is not a bulletin board. It is not its chief function to furnish an advertising opportunity for other meetings yet to come. It has one theme, one direction, one goal. The leader is under bond to see that these are protected from irrelevant material, meaningless comment, aimless testimony, and pointless sentiment.

The leader is not only to guard the meeting; he is to *guide* the meeting. And the essence of perfect guidance is the absence of all mechanical expedients and all compulsion. No leader who guides will number his references, for instance, and then call for them by number. He will put all the machinery into the background. He will pay as much attention beforehand to the mechanics of the service as the choir leader does in rehearsal to the technique of the anthem, leaving nothing to interfere with the uplift and inspiration of the final rendition. He will arrange that the several speakers shall do their part with little or no announcement. This is simple enough if he will give each one his cue. And that is not deception. It is the elimination of everything that would prevent the meeting from going straight through by its ordained path to its desired haven.

THE WEEKLY DEVOTIONAL MEETING.

We have gone through the work before the meeting and during the meeting. What about the results of the meeting? What is its PURPOSE? Without a definite purpose it is of no large significance.

The first result which every devotional meeting should produce is what may be called, for want of a better word, inspiration. That is to say, at the close of the meeting everybody ought to feel that it has been a really good, wholesome, spiritual hour. There should be a consciousness of exaltation, though sometimes not so marked as at others. We ought to go away from the devotional meeting feeling it has been a place of kindred spirits whose fellowship is all the richer because it has been allied to worship.

But besides inspiration, there must be in the aim of the meeting a certain concentration. Some single result, sincerely desired and truly worth attaining, ought to spring out of this hour of consecration and serious thought. Very often the theme of the meeting will suggest what this definite result should be. A class of one sort or another is to be organized, or an enrollment of Christ Stewards, or Comrades of the Morning Watch, or personal workers. A moment of deep and searching self-dedication may be the meeting's climax, or, what is quite as truly religious, a gift to some significant enterprise of the Church or the Chapter. The possible outcomes of League meetings are multitudinous in their variety, and there is no need that any meeting should fail to produce at least one bit of worth-while fruit.

Last of all, perhaps best of all, the purpose of the devotional meeting should be *devotion*. It is in essence a worship meeting. Its origin and explanation are bound up in the consciousness that the members have come together to utilize the mystery of prayer. They do not use prayer as mere spiritual gymnastics, or merely as a means for securing the things they desire. But they should saturate the whole meeting, in the days of preparation as well as in the hour of presentation, with the spirit of prayer. The devotional element in the devotional meeting ought to be a real communion of the mind and heart of every person present with the mind and heart of God in Jesus Christ our Lord.

THE EFFICIENT EPWORTHIAN.

Some Do n'ts About Planning the Meeting.

Do n't be a slave to any program, not even your own. But have a program, so that you will know where the meeting is going, and why.

Do n't put items into your program just because you can. If they do n't belong to the theme, leave them out.

Do n't arrange your program big end first. Make the last five minutes the most important five minutes of the hour.

Do n't expect people to take part intelligently without giving them a chance to think. Therefore, ask them beforehand.

Do n't leave the selection of songs to the chance of the moment that you need them. Appropriate songs are not chosen that way.

Do n't ignore those who do not often take part. It is some trouble to induce them to help, but there is large profit in it for them and you.

Do n't make a program like everybody's else. Yours can be different without being freakish.

Do n't leave out the leader's ten minutes. No one else can sound so effectively the keynote of the meeting.

Do n't forget that you are planning for a *devotional* meeting, not for a study class or an informal lecture. Put into every element of your program the spirit of worship.

Two "Cans" and Two "Wills."

The one thing which the average devotional meeting needs is not better members nor more members, nor help from outsiders, but a simple, positive conviction, which every Chapter can make a part of its consciousness.

It can be put into two sentences: "We can do it *if* we will." "We can do it *and* we will."

The regular devotional meeting can be made a thousand per cent better than it is in nearly every Chapter by a simple working out of these two sentences. Any Chapter can have variety and freshness and effectiveness in its devotional meetings in spite of the fact that it has had monotony and dullness and failure.

And the very same people who have been in the Chapter up to this moment can make the transformation. They need

THE WEEKLY DEVOTIONAL MEETING.

no new intelligence and no new equipment. All they need is to believe that the thing can be done, and then go ahead and do it.

Such a Chapter will abolish the Clipping Habit, will fill up the long pauses that make everybody uncomfortable, and will accomplish in the devotional meeting and through the devotional meeting the highest results that can be desired.

There is no space here to tell in detail how the transformation may be accomplished; but "We can do it *if* we will," and "We can do it *and* we will" are the two sides of a conviction which will work out its own methods and provide its own material.

All this does not exclude the spiritual meaning and atmosphere of the devotional meeting. Rather, it makes a higher spiritual life possible and points out the door by which any Epworthian may find his way into the secret of spiritual power.

SCRAPPINESS OR LEADERSHIP.

The devotional meeting is at the heart of the Epworth League. Its possibilities are simply unreckoned. It may be made a power in the Church the like of which has not been felt since the days of the class-meeting's prime. Or it may be a medium for the absolute frittering away of every spiritual grace and potency which its attendants possess.

Apart from spiritual deadness, the greatest obstacle to the prosperity and power of the devotional meeting is *scrappiness*. One verse of a hymn, two lines of a poem, a string of more or less related "references," "sentence prayers"—as though prayers could be measured with a two-foot rule—these things are too much with us. Each of them is right and good in its way. But they are so common that they have fixed a type, and the type is wholly undesirable.

The "scrap"-meeting method is easy. Half an hour is time enough to prepare for its leadership, and none but the leader needs to make the slightest preparation. The leader's requisites are enough printed helps, a Concordance, a

THE EFFICIENT EPWORTHIAN.

pair of scissors, and a supply of paper slips. The hymns need not bear on the topic at all. Half a dozen will be sung, and five of them are used at three meetings out of every four. They are not important, for their words long ago ceased to have any meaning. Some of them had precious little to begin with.

The "scrap"-meeting is almost wholly a failure. One of its worst effects is that the meeting may seem to have been a good one. The singing has been lively, the prayers numerous, the reading of references prompt, and the leader has taken up as much time as usual.

There is a better way. It is not so easy. No better way is. It depends almost wholly on the leader. It requires study, secret prayer, and intelligent planning for the meeting. It encourages the use of helps, but only as *helps*. The leader studies his material instead of taking it on faith. He finds the center of the theme and makes the whole meeting bend to that. He selects hymns that fit the theme, and is not discouraged if some of them are unfamiliar. He interprets Scripture by Scripture. In his opening address he indicates what he considers the heart of the theme, which will provide a subject for the testimony service, so that whoever takes part in that exercise must do some independent thinking. He believes in intelligent and vital piety.

This better method has not quite so much "go" in it, judging by surface indications. But it has power in it, and the possibility of growth, and it is a hint at the real object for which the devotional meeting was instituted.

The leader of the devotional meeting has a great opportunity. For the space of half an hour, more or less, he may speak the things that he has had on his heart.

If a minister is under obligation to study his sermon, the obligation of the Epworth League leader is, if possible, more insistent. For the preacher will have another opportunity next Sunday. He may expand to-day's sermon into a series. He has abundant means of modifying what he says, or of deepening its impression, or of controlling its effects.

But in most cases the leader has only one arrow in his

THE WEEKLY DEVOTIONAL MEETING.

quiver. He has a single hour of opportunity. In that hour he must make clear the meaning and the teaching of the topic. He must so present it that it will stimulate thought, because otherwise the testimonies will drag. He must control all the exercises of the hour—singing, prayer, and testimony—so as to produce the effect for which the meeting was designed.

It is a big task. It can not be done well by one who glances at *The Epworth Herald's* devotional page or the "Notes on the Devotional Meeting Topics" half an hour before the meeting. It can not be done well by one whose chief anxiety is to "have it over." It takes love and grace and pains and patience.

But when the task is rightly appreciated, and the privilege of it is fairly estimated, it offers a priceless opportunity to do a great thing in a great way.

A School for Leaders.

Leaders of the devotional meeting are made, not born. They must be recruited, enlisted, trained, drilled. This is the First Vice-President's work. If he will make it his special aim to secure a group of capable and effective leaders among the hitherto untrained members of the Chapter, he can make his term of office a great and lasting benefit to the Chapter.

There is not much opportunity for uniform methods in the training of leaders. The conditions vary so widely that no one method could succeed anywhere. In some Chapters the leaders for a month or a quarter may be gathered for a conference on the general ways and means of leadership. In others, the First Vice-President may need to go over the preparation for each meeting with the several leaders, helping, suggesting, supplementing their material and methods.

A Way to Magnify the Meeting.

The First Vice-President had called his department committee together to talk with the leader of the devotional meeting of four weeks hence. He had already talked with all the committee members privately.

THE EFFICIENT EPWORTHIAN.

"I have made up my mind," said he, "that we are accountable for the devotional meetings. And as before I asked you individually, now I ask you collectively: Are you willing to take up the work of helping each leader in turn? Of course, no one member of the committee will be asked to help *every* week, but most of us will have a chance once in two or three weeks."

For a few moments all the committee seemed to be talking at once. And the composite remark seemed to be, boiled down, "Yes, if we can be given something that we really can do without having to make ourselves prominent in the meeting itself every week."

"That can be done," said the First Vice-President, "by our reminding each leader that we are to help him or her, not to take the meeting into our own hands."

"Now, I have already outlined my suggestion. We are to be entirely at the disposal of the leader in charge of any particular meeting. He is to ask for help; we are to provide it to the full measure of our power."

So the leader assigned for the meeting of the last Sunday in the month took the floor and outlined his plan. There is n't room here to tell about any of it except that which relates to the work assigned to various members of the committee.

One was to find nine members of the Chapter who would tell in their own words the stories referred to under "Shepherds, Hirelings, or Robbers," as the Scripture lesson was our Lord's talk about shepherds, and to show how each character could be classified.

Another agreed to find three members who would give three illustrative ideas "To Light Up the Theme," and comment briefly on them.

A third promised to bring a reader who would repeat "De Massa ob de Sheepfol'."

Number four was assigned the duty of finding five people who would tackle as many "Suggestive Queries" and start discussion on them.

The leader announced that he would read the Scripture lesson and make it the basis of his remarks in presenting the topic.

THE WEEKLY DEVOTIONAL MEETING.

One member of the committee raised a question: "Suppose two of us, or three, should go to the same person and ask him to take part?"

The First Vice-President smiled. "That is quite likely to happen," he said, "but it will do no harm. Let the first finder have right of way. The others will seek other folks, but each will also have impressed the importance of the meeting on the mind of every member who is asked twice."

"Now I shall have time to arrange my program," said the leader, "and the only other thing I want of you is that each one here will be ready to take hold in the testimony service when that 'awful pause' threatens."

"It won't come," said one of the committee. "But if it should show its face for even a moment, there are six of us here who can put it to flight *because we shall have the meeting on our hearts!*"

Testimony in the Meeting.

THE REASONS FOR TESTIMONY.

I ought.—That is the reason of duty. The story of our Lord's work for men is spread by testimony and by no other way. I am in the line of that story's progress. It was told me, and worked its wondrous change in me. I dare not refuse to pass it on. Some one is waiting to hear it from my lips, with my experience illustrating it and giving it new proof. So I am bound by duty to testify.

I must.—That is the reason of self-interest. If I do not tell my experience, I shall lose it. He who would keep the joy of salvation must learn the joy of testimony. If I do not make known my hopes, they will vanish. He who would live with Christ hereafter must know how to speak for Christ here. Faith can not live in an atmosphere of concealment; the hidden disciple is the lost disciple. If Jesus Christ is so precious to me that I fear to lose His gracious influence in my life, there is one way to prevent that loss. I must bear testimony to Him.

I love.—Testimony that is given only from duty or self-interest is not complete. The great motive of all Christian service is not force, but desire. I testify because I love.

THE EFFICIENT EPWORTHIAN.

The love of Christ to me is greater than I know, but it has awakened in me a great love for Him. If I kept silence I should give the lie to my love. For I know that His chief joy is in saving the lost. So testimony becomes a way of giving joy to my Lord, by convincing men that He can save them.

Then, my new life in Christ has aroused a new love for men. They seem so much more worth loving now. And I know how great a calamity threatens them if they do not find Christ. I have been delivered from that danger, but I remember still how real and terrible it is. And I know that I can not testify for Christ without helping somebody to find Him. So I testify for love's sake.

Some Detailed Plans for Special Meetings.

We suggest here a number of plans for meetings on special subjects. As to some, pretty full directions are given. As to others, there is something left to the imagination and ingenuity of the leader. But all have their use if they are followed intelligently.

A Meeting for Prayer.—The wisest way to plan this meeting will be to make it a real prayer-meeting. It should not be permitted to drift into a discussion about prayer, or a series of aimless talks on prayer. Pray!

But a prayer-meeting, more than any other, must have definiteness and directness. There should be a careful survey of the Chapter's needs, and a study of the prayer-life of its members. How many Comrades of the Morning Watch are there in the Chapter? Enlist them.

After the leader's opening talk, let there be four "times of prayer:" "Prayers of confession,"—the personal and collective failures and wrongdoings of the members and the Chapter, humbly and penitently acknowledged, and forgiveness for them sought. "Prayers of supplication,"—the needs which seem greatest brought boldly and believingly to the throne of grace. "Prayers of co-operation,"—the work of the Kingdom in the community elsewhere frankly accepted as a direct personal obligation, and greater loyalty to that work gladly assumed. "Prayers of intercession,"—for all who have need, whether in the home Church, in the

THE WEEKLY DEVOTIONAL MEETING.

home town, on the frontier, or out on the edges of heathenism.

Close the meeting with an invitation to those who for any reason desire to be included in your ministry of intercession and are willing to say, "Pray for us."

Another "Prayer" Meeting.—Use these themes for study and comment: Christ as a Man of prayer. The men of prayer of the Bible. The reasons for prayer. Incitements to prayer. The time for prayer. The place of prayer. Victories of prayer. Christ's teachings on prayer.

SCRIPTURE REFERENCES.

Bible Instances of Secret Prayer: Gen. 32:9-12; 2 Kings 20:2; Neh. 2:4; Dan. 6:10; Matt. 14:23; Matt. 26:36-39; Mark 1:35; Luke 5:16; Acts 9:40; Acts 10:30.

Hindrances to the Prayer Life: Job 35:13; Psa. 66:18; Prov. 1:24-28; Prov. 28:9; Isa. 59:2; John 9:31; James 1:6, 7.

Sustainng the Prayer Life: Psa. 27:8; Rom. 8:26; Eph. 6:18; Phil. 4:6; Col. 4:2; 1 Thess. 5:17, 18; Heb. 4:16.

Blessings of the Prayer Life: Psa. 37:8; Psa. 86:5; Psa. 91:15; Prov. 3:6; Amos 5:4; Luke 21:36; John 15:7; James 1:6; 1 John 5:14.

QUESTIONS FOR TESTIMONY.

What is prayer to you, a duty or a delight?

What is it to "pray without ceasing?"

How large a place should be given to thanksgiving in our daily prayers?

How can we use the Bible as a help to prayer?

What are some of the things that hinder the life of prayer?

BOOKS ON THE LIFE OF PRAYER.

Mr. Mott, in his pamphlet on "Secret Prayer," which is itself well worth careful study, recommends the following books: "Prayer; Its Nature and Scope," by H. Clay Trumbull; "With Christ in the School of Prayer," by Andrew Murray; "Secret Prayer," by Professor H. C. G.

Moule, and "The Still Hour," by Professor Austin Phelps. He also recommends three pamphlets: "Prayer and Missions," by R. E. Speer; "Secret Prayer a Great Reality," by Henry Wright, and "The Practice of the Presence of God," by Brother Lawrence. These pamphlets may be had from the International Committee, 124 East 28th Street, New York City.

The Present Christ.—After the leader has spoken, let him set questions before the members, written on a blackboard, or printed on slips, or in some other effective way. Then invite responses during the time set apart for testimony. Such questions as these may be used:

If Christ came to our town—
  Should I be glad to see Him?
  Where should I wish Him to find me?
  What neglect would He condemn?
  What business would He disapprove?
  With whom would He spend most of His time?
  What claims would He make?
  What changes would I make if I had twenty-four hours' notice of His coming?
  How would He be received?
  What work would He begin to do?

Let the testimonies end fifteen minutes before the time to close the meeting. The pastor or the leader may use half of the remaining time in pressing home this application: "In answering these questions we have revealed our present duty and privilege. It is a vision of opportunity to be Christlike, to show that Christ dwelleth in us. What shall we do with the vision?"

Close the meeting with a simple, tender, searching consecration service.

An Evangelistic Devotional Meeting.—The leader has a great opportunity. Enlist the active help of the entire Department of Spiritual Work, and get ready by prayer, by self-dedication, by personal work, for a revival which shall begin in the League meeting.

Ask the pastor to take his place as general director of this meeting. In many cases it will be possible to com-

THE WEEKLY DEVOTIONAL MEETING.

bine the League service with the evening preaching service, in which the pastor will supplement the League's work by a tender, earnest, urgent presentation of Jesus Christ as a Savior from sin. If that can be done, and the League members will co-operate by giving the Christian invitation in person to those of their friends who are not Christians, this meeting may be the most important and resultful of the whole year.

Beginning New Work.—A Cabinet meeting should be held during the week before this devotional meeting, if possible. If the Cabinet decides to take up some new form of work this year, there can be no better time to announce it than now, and to enlist the co-operation of every member. In case this is done, divide the time of the devotional meeting into three parts: the first, for the discussion of the topic in its larger and more general aspect; the second, for the presentation and explanation of the new plans; and the third, for some brief but earnest and definite moments of solemn dedication to and acceptance of the new work.

The Central Office, 740 Rush Street, Chicago, will furnish explanatory literature on Bible study, the Morning Watch, Christian Stewardship, temperance work, and personal evangelism. The Missionary Education Department will furnish literature on mission study. Parish Abroad Office, 150 Fifth Avenue, New York, will send information concerning that most practical and workable method of helping the missionary work of the Church.

The Christian and Amusements.—Plan this meeting with special care. The topic is one which always interests young people. You may have a few in your Chapter who are radical on the subject. Do not try to suppress them. Give them full opportunity to speak.

But select for special participation only those whose spiritual life is such that their words will carry weight. That does not mean the dull members, or the narrow ones, but those who have the most vigorous personal religion and who do not spoil their influence by inconsistency in matters of amusement.

Let the prayer service be as earnest and tender as pos-

THE EFFICIENT EPWORTHIAN.

sible. It is unusually important that the meeting shall rise at once to a high spiritual level and stay there. Pray for the tempted, for the eager ones to whom all life's offered pleasures seem real and lasting, for those who have gone far on the road of doubtful delights. Pray for higher and clearer ideals. Thank God for the power of pleasure, the gift of laughter, and the zest for joy. Pledge a new allegiance to the Lord Jesus, seeking to have the same mind and to follow in His steps.

Hold up worthy ideals. Self-respecting young people do not need to be kept amused constantly. A program outline is appended:

Song service, ten minutes.

Brief prayers, following suggestions above given.

The Scripture lesson.

The leader speaks: "Recreation as a duty."

Members speak: The test of right recreation; a review of Bishop Vincent's "Better Not;" recreation by a change of work; the high purpose of recreation; the border line in the field of doubtful practices; the joys and pleasures of the Christian life.

Testimony.

The League benediction, or this, "Let all those that put their trust in Thee rejoice."

"Let them ever shout for joy, because Thou defendest them."

"Let them also that love Thy name be joyful in Thee."

Who is My Neighbor and What of Him?—What are *you* doing to strengthen your neighbor's faith in Jesus Christ?

Why can not any one of us be a Christian all by himself?

Can the law of love as illustrated by the Good Samaritan be applied to industry and commerce and politics?

Do Christians treat their neighbors, as a rule, better than non-Christians do?

What has your experience with professing Christians in business taught you about them and about the religion they profess?

THE WEEKLY DEVOTIONAL MEETING.

How would the Christian idea of neighborliness transform your town, your street, your school, your store, your home?

What Methodism Stands For.—Methodism is sometimes Episcopalian in its polity, sometimes Congregational, sometimes Presbyterian.

Some of its people worship in log cabins, some in bamboo huts, some in mud houses, and some in great cathedrals.

Some of its preachers are the choicest products of the great universities, while others are barely able to read the Scriptures they expound.

Some of its members are millionaires, while others are as poor as the poorest.

Its parish extends from the Arctic Circle to Patagonia, and from Hawaii in the West to Japan in the East.

Its message is proclaimed in the oldest languages now spoken, and in the latest tongues which its own missionaries have just reduced to writing.

But amid all this diversity—

Every Methodist preacher proclaims the same great doctrines;

The world-scattered congregations of Methodism sing the same songs of salvation;

Her invitation to the sin-sick and weary is the same the world over;

Her experience of salvation in Jesus Christ has the same value and meaning for rich and poor, for learned and untaught, for Caucasian, Ethiopian, Mongolian, Malay;

Her testimony to the witness of the Spirit is as real on the banks of the Ganges as on the shores of the Hudson;

In a word, her abounding life realizes the apostolic picture of diversities of gifts and diversities of operations and diversities of opportunities, BUT THE SAME SPIRIT!

Bishop Vincent's Methodist Ten Doctrines of Grace.—

I. I believe that all men are sinners.

II. I believe that God the Father loves all men and hates all sin.

III. I believe that Jesus Christ died for all men to make possible their salvation from sin, and to make sure the salvation of all who believe in Him.

THE EFFICIENT EPWORTHIAN.

IV. I believe that the Holy Spirit is given to all men to enlighten and to incline them to repent of their sins and to believe in the Lord Jesus Christ.

V. I believe that all who repent of their sins and believe in the Lord Jesus Christ receive the forgiveness of sin. (This is justification.)

VI. I believe that all who receive the forgiveness of sin are at the same time made new creatures in Christ Jesus. (This is regeneration.)

VII. I believe that all who are made new creatures in Christ Jesus are accepted as the children of God. (This is adoption.)

VIII. I believe that all who are accepted as the children of God may receive the inward assurance of the Holy Spirit to that fact. (This is the witness of the Spirit.)

IX. I believe that all who truly desire and seek it may love God with all their heart and soul, mind and strength, and their neighbors as themselves. (This is entire sanctification.)

X. I believe that all who persevere to the end, and only those, shall be saved in heaven forever. (This is the true final perseverance.)

The Ten Points of Church Economy.—I. All who belong to the Kingdom of Heaven on earth are members of the holy catholic Church.

II. The holy catholic Church has many outward branches or denominations.

III. One branch of the holy catholic Church is the Methodist Episcopal, which was organized in 1784, and is, in doctrine, usages, and spirit, in harmony with the apostolic Church.

IV. There are in the Methodist Episcopal two sacraments: Baptism and the Lord's Supper;

V. Four classes of members and candidates for membership: Sunday school scholars, persons baptized in infancy, probationers, and full members;

VI. Ten classes of officers: Bishops, district superintendents, elders, deacons, local preachers, exhorters, class leaders, stewards, Sunday school superintendents, and trustees;

THE WEEKLY DEVOTIONAL MEETING.

VII. Five principal organizations: The General, Annual, District, and Quarterly Conferences, and the Leaders' and Stewards' Meeting;

VIII. Three peculiarities: The itinerancy, the lovefeast, and the class meeting;

IX. Benevolent societies:

X. The promise made by parents at the baptism of their children is as follows: The child to be baptized "shall read the Holy Scriptures and learn the Lord's Prayer, the Ten Commandments, the Apostles' Creed, the Catechism, and all other things which a Christian ought to know and believe to his soul's health."

Preparing for Our Heavenly Home.—Remember that the chief stress of the meeting must be, not heaven, but preparation for heaven.

Make plain the illustration of citizenship, as the granting of privileges and honors, and the imposing of responsibility, so that all may see with new clearness the idea that getting to heaven is not an accident, but a result of meeting the conditions of the Heavenly Kingdom.

The leader's own address—which should not be omitted—may deal with one or the other of the three subjects briefly discussed on this page: "Our Heavenly Citizenship," "Longing for Heaven," or "The Attractions of Heaven." Assign the other two to competent speakers, who should speak not more than three or four minutes each.

General testimony may be stimulated by the use of questions prominently displayed by the blackboard or other device. Use such questions as these: "Why do you desire to go to heaven?" "How much preparation is necessary for heaven?" "What is the difference between you as you are now—a citizen of the Kingdom of heaven—and as you will be hereafter—a dweller in heaven itself?" "If you knew you had just a year for preparation for heaven, how would you employ that year?"

The list of avaliable hymns is almost endless. There are so many great and noble hymns on this theme that no one ought to waste a moment on the shallow ditties whose words and music combine to cheapen and weaken the whole purpose and meaning of the theme. A few hymns are suggested below. They are all to be found in the Methodist Hymnal. The series ascribed Bernard of Cluny (1058-1061) are especially effective when well read.

The Message of the Flowers.—Make this meeting memorable for two things—beauty and practical helpfulness.

The beauty may be secured by the intelligent and tasteful use of decorations. As this is more than a flower service, you may draw on all the resources of the community for the effective display of "green things a-growing." Flowering and foliage plants, cut flowers, vines, ferns, grasses, grains,—all may be used with good effect.

The usefulness of the service may be made certain by the taking up of some form of flower-mission work as the result of this meeting. Decide before the meeting what your Chapter can do. Present the plan during the devotional meeting, and see that it goes forward afterward.

There are many poems available which are appropriate for recitation by some capable member.

For the singing use such selections as "By Cool Siloam's Shady Rill," "The Lily of the Valley," "The Morning Flowers Display Their Sweets."

Ask some members in advance to be ready to speak on the spiritual lessons that may be learned from the well-known poetical symbolism of the flowers and trees: the palm for victory, the violet for modesty, the lily for purity, pansies for thoughts, forget-me-nots for remembrance, the olive for peace, the oak for strength, the vine for fruitfulness, the cedar for permanence, and so on.

A Christmas Gift to the Christ.—Why must my gift to Christ be entirely voluntary?

Why can not I give part of my life to Christ, retaining the rest for myself?

What is the great motive which makes us desire to give gifts—to our friends, to our own kindred, to Christ?

Why is Christmas the ideal time for deciding that we will be wholly the Lord's?

When and where can I begin to prove that I have given myself to Christ?

If we have given ourselves, does it matter whether we give our money or not?

THE WEEKLY DEVOTIONAL MEETING.

What are the chief hindrances in the way of our making a complete dedication of our lives to Christ?

What can we do to-night and to-morrow that will be a Christmas gift to our Lord?

Christian Education.—If possible, get one or two college folk to take part—people who have been to school and know what they are talking about. Have at hand information about the nearest Church school. Here is an outlined program:

Song service, ten minutes.

The Scripture lesson.

The leader speaks: "Right and wrong education."

A member considers the question, "Who can afford to go to college?"

Another asks, "Why go to college?"

Another member inquires, "What kind of a college?"

Two members consider, "How to secure a Christian education if the way to college is not open."

General testimony on "The reasons why all Christians should be educated Christians."

A "Vision" Meeting.—This may be made a beautiful meeting. If it is conducted like an old-fashioned love-feast some people will be inclined to take part who have long been silent.

The leader will need prayer and quietness before beginning his meeting. Go into the secret place and seek a clearer, brighter vision of the Lord. Let Him become real to the leader's heart and He will be real to the people in the meeting.

Ask the members to "tell their experience." Put the invitation to testimony in the form of questions. "What was your first vision of Christ?" "How did it affect your life?" "Has the vision changed?"

You will hear of Nathanael visions and Matthew visions and John Baptist visions and Zaccheus visions and centurion visions, and Wesley visions, Saul visions, Augustine visions, Luther visions. "God fulfills Himself in many ways."

Perhaps it may be helpful to have a few brief recitals of "How Christ reveals Himself to men," describing some of the experiences indicated in the preceding paragraph.

THE EFFICIENT EPWORTHIAN.

Follow these with the personal question, "How did Christ first show Himself to you?"

As the meeting draws to a close the vision of Christ may have dawned for the first time on some one present. Find that one. Devote the last five minutes to the search. You may help a soul into the light of Christ's love.

A Service of Confession.—This meeting will, of course, be largely a meeting of testimony. Plan to give as much time as may be necessary for this part of the program. Let every exercise emphasize the duty of witnessing for Christ.

If you have reason to believe that there will be some present who are trying to be silent disciples, urge the duty of confession. Insist plainly, though kindly, that it is quite as important as following Christ in life. Show that such following can not be complete and satisfying without an open declaration of purpose and allegiance.

Various sub-topics may be assigned to various members, asking them to take these as themes of three or four-minute talks, of course using their own language and finding other ideas besides those suggested.

The testimonies should be pointed and personal confessions of Christ as Lord and Savior, as Redeemer and Master of life.

At the close of the service let the leader or the pastor urge with great tenderness the claims of Christ on those who as yet have not confessed Him. An altar service may be made of great value toward this end.

A Decision Meeting.—Group all remedies for present-day evils around the gospel.

Ask for reasons why other remedies fail—such remedies as Socialism, co-operative colonies, the Anti-Poverty Society, political reform, philanthropic movements, and education.

Let the testimonies be of the "one thing I know" order.

The range of hymns appropriate to this topic is almost limitless. Here are some: "The Great Physician," "Just as I am," "At even, ere the sun was set," "I heard the voice of Jesus say," "Whiter than snow," "Of Him who did salvation bring," "Come, said Jesus' sacred voice," "There is a fountain filled with blood," "Rock of Ages."

THE WEEKLY DEVOTIONAL MEETING.

For Opening the Meeting.

The Canadian *Epworth Era* suggests several good and helpful ways for opening the devotional meeting:

Open with silent prayer.

Open with an appropriate solo.

Open with a series of sentence prayers.

Open with a blackboard talk on the topic.

Open with a word from your pastor, previously asked to give it.

Open with six comments on the six daily readings of the week.

Open directly with some abrupt and striking word about the subject.

Open with an appropriate recitation, rendered by some younger member.

Open with Bible verses brought by the members as their testimonies.

Open with the Scripture lesson read by two members, who will stand before the Chapter and read alternate verses.

Open with a series of Bible verses bearing on the subject, given out before the meeting to a number of members, who will read in the order in which the slips are numbered.

Open with a Bible-reading on the subject, making sure beforehand that the members bring their Bibles. Give out numbered slips containing references, and have them read in order.

In your opening always seek to touch the highest themes. Remember that novelty is of value only as a stepping-stone to interest. If you can get the interest in an old way, do so.

For Variety in the Meeting.

Sing the hymns from memory.

Ask questions, the answers to which are Scripture sayings. This may be used instead of a Bible-reading.

Put all the thought of the topic into half a dozen plain questions or less. Write these on the blackboard, or on a large sheet of wrapping paper, and let the testimony be in answer to these questions.

Secure telegraphic testimonies from absent members,

THE EFFICIENT EPWORTHIAN.

written on regular telegraph blanks, and limited to twenty words.

Exchange leaders with a neighboring society, possibly of a different denomination.

Get special music, if it is appropriate to the theme.

Find one of the great hymns which will illustrate the topic, and get some one to recite it from memory.

Occasionally hold a meeting which shall be exclusively a *prayer-meeting*.

Call for a brief season of prayer at some moment of unusual feeling.

For a change, limit all speakers to one minute.

Try a question box. This should mean vigorous advertising also.

Change the seating plan, especially if it has been stiff and formal. Arrange the chairs in semi-circular fashion about the speaker.

Call for the reciting in concert of familiar Scripture.

Drop all the familiar phraseology that has ceased to mean much. If a Chapter should not hear for fifty-two Sundays the words, "The time is yours; do not let it go to waste," nobody would be the worse for the deprivation.

Let the leaders for a month arrange a plan which will provide a different method and different material for each Sunday.

Put the song service at the close of the meeting one week, in the middle the next. The third week sing only two or three songs in the entire evening.

Announce that the first ten minutes of the testimony service will be for some special class: the new converts, the oldest members, the members who have joined this year, or others.

Soul-winning is never monotonous. If there is the slightest sign of interest on the part of the unconverted, devote the closing moments to the deepening and making definite of that interest.

Have two leaders: one with some experience in the work, the other a comparatively untried member. This will give variety and at the same time be a good training for the younger members.

THE WEEKLY DEVOTIONAL MEETING.

Instead of voluntary testimonies, call on one to speak, who, after speaking, calls on another, who, after speaking, calls on another, and so on. It puts everybody on the alert.

Let the Scripture lesson be given from memory. Sometimes, if it is a familiar Scripture, use it responsively, both leader and congregation giving it memoriter. Expand this plan so as to include all the songs used during the evening.

When your meeting is distinctly evangelistic, use every effort to get your unsaved friends to attend. Set people to work giving personal invitations. Invite testimony on such themes as "What I was without Christ," "How I found Christ," "What Christ has done for me." Be ready to put the meeting into the hands of the pastor whenever there is any sign of intense spiritual interest which may lead to immediate seeking of salvation.

Closing the Meeting.

The closing moments are the most important. It is possible to spoil utterly a good meeting by the use that is made of the last five minutes. Therefore, while ready to take advantage of unusual circumstances, have a definite plan for the closing moments. Do not let the meeting "fade out" or run out from sheer weakness. The moment that it seems best to close, begin on the special plan provided.

In every case where it is possible give the invitation to accept Jesus Christ as Savior.

The repetition in concert of some appropriate Scripture or hymn of devotion will secure the participation of many who have had no opportunity to take part otherwise, or who for various reasons have remained silent up to this point.

Often the pastor is the person to be asked to take charge of the closing moments. He will sum up the lesson and the testimonies, and give a brief, pointed, loving exhortation based on the topic for the evening.

It is rarely out of place to close with prayer, and the more who can be induced to share in the prayer, the more helpful it will be. Silent prayers, sentence prayers, prayers by three or four members called upon for that purpose, chain prayers (in which each one taking part calls on some one else to follow him), prayers quoted from Scripture or from hymns,—all these will be found of value. But always bear in mind that in prayer, of all things, the spirit and the purpose is all-important, while the form is of small moment.

Whatever the method employed, seek to make the last moments of the meeting the most important. Bring the hour to its climax just before it ends. End at the highest point of conviction and feeling, so that it will be the most natural thing for the congregation to go away with its mind made up to some definite form of action. That is the test of every method by which the gospel is presented. If it reaches the will of the hearers, it is well. If not— if it has merely interested the intellectual faculty, or excited the emotions—it is a failure. Our business is to *persuade*. We must do that, or it matters little what we do.

How to Take Part.

By prayer.

By a word of testimony ending with prayer.

By quoting a verse or, preferably, two or three verses of Scripture.

By giving the reason for your appreciation of the Scripture you quote.

By quotations other than Scriptural, given from memory.

By a few words of comment, relating the quotation to the topic and to your own experience.

By appropriate reading from current literature.

By reciting a hymn or other poem.

By telling of some incident within your observation which illustrated and enforces the theme.

By referring to some such incident as the one last mentioned which you have found in the course of your reading.

By a brief expression of your own thought on the topic of the evening.

By personal testimony for Jesus Christ, with special reference to the theme of the meeting.

And personal testimony is of all ways the best!

THE WEEKLY DEVOTIONAL MEETING.

The Singing in the Meeting.

This is a difficult subject. There is plenty of willingness to sing and, as a rule, plenty of singing. But appropriate and heartfelt singing is not so common.

It seems absurd that one should consider it necessary to say, "Select the hymns in advance," but the advice is sorely needed by thousands of leaders. In the serene consciousness that there are half a dozen songs in the book which everybody can sing without the slightest effort of memory or of the reflective powers, the leader trusts to the inspiration of the moment or falls back on the nerveless "Has any one a song to suggest?" It would seem that the frequent ridiculous situations to which this expedient gives rise would in time cause leaders to avoid it. But it still flourishes, and perpetuates the use of many a commonplace song. This drawing a bow at a venture, and its companion method of "leafing through" the book during an awkward pause in the meeting, are deadly enemies of a successful service of song.

Select the hymns after all other preparation has been made. Take the book your Chapter uses and go through the whole list of possible hymns that will fit the theme.

If you have a reasonably proficient organist, do not hesitate to select a few unfamiliar hymns. One of the reasons often given when inviting all to sing is, "This is such a familiar hymn that everybody can sing it." Sometimes that is precisely the reason why many do not sing that particular hymn. Most people enjoy singing the unfamiliar hymns. They give more attention to the words, and are more likely to be struck by the thoughts embodied in them.

Occasionally sing fewer hymns, and utilize the time thus saved in singing the stanzas usually omitted. We are in some danger of thinking that two stanzas of a hymn constitute all of it that is worth singing.

Get the best hymn-books you can afford. Some Chapters are wisely adopting the Methodist Hymnal. They will be a long time exhausting it. The best books are usually as cheap as the poorest, to begin with, and in the end there is no comparison. Do not buy a one-man book. The fact that you have heard a gospel singer render effectively

THE EFFICIENT EPWORTHIAN.

half a dozen of the songs in his latest book is not an infallible indication that your Chapter should have that book. A one-man book, especially if it is of the sort that the man carries with him for sale, is not likely to be worth much to anybody six months after date. Ask a competent musician, who should, of course, be a Christian, to help your committee in the selection of the new book your Chapter has ordered to be bought. He will not save you much in the actual outlay of money, but he will save you some disappointment born of unconscious and unnecessary blundering.

Why not a choir and an orchestra? Both are within the capacity of thousands of Chapters, and a choir is so easily secured that no Chapter need be without one. It will create some new problems, perhaps, but it will solve some old ones.

Select the closing hymn with special care. If you can find one which summarizes the thought of the topic, or which crystallizes the convictions the topic has created, or which expresses some determination or purpose appropriate to the theme, use that hymn. It may not be familiar. So much the better. First read it in concert. Let its meaning be clearly seen, then sing it with feeling and thoughtfulness. It will be surprisingly effective.

The old-time method of impromptu song is often employed with thrilling effect. To avoid possible confusion, let this work of starting a hymn without announcement be given to one or two persons only, and let it be understood between them and the leader what songs they shall start. Of course, this method is impossible with unfamiliar hymns, but it is one of the most valuable and inspiring ways of using the old hymns. For some reason it often happens that more people will join in such an informal outburst of song than will attempt to sing when number or page is given and a prelude is played.

The organist has much to do with the success of the song service. He may control the time of the singing, and often its expression also. He should sit at the organ throughout the meeting, so that all needless pauses may be avoided. He should not play preludes, except for the

THE WEEKLY DEVOTIONAL MEETING.

rarely-used hymns. Ordinarily the chord is sufficient. Interludes, as everybody knows, long ago went out of fashion. Let us hope they will never return.

Colleges have their songs. Why should not Epworth League Chapters have their songs? The students at Drew Theological Seminary have long been in the habit of considering Faber's hymn, "Faith of our fathers," as the seminary hymn. It is sung on anniversary occasions and whenever the loyalty and devotion of the students have been particularly aroused. Such a custom is specially appropriate to the League Chapter. It would be an additional bond of fellowship, and there are many occasions when the use of the "Chapter hymn" would be both appropriate and beautiful. At group meetings, for example, and at conventions, the roll of Chapters might be answered by each delegation singing its hymn. Do not select one which will soon be outworn or which will become tiresome. As a rule, one of the grand old hymns of the Church is more desirable than the latest copyrighted novelty. Try 408, or 416, or 616, or 382, or 407, or 409. In any case, avoid as you would the plague a song whose words are senseless or whose music suggests the music-hall or the circus.

Ushers.

Few Chapter devotional meetings are so small as to be able to do without ushers. In the large Chapters ushers are indispensable.

They should see that the room is properly warmed and ventilated before the meeting begins.

They should see that the seats are properly arranged, that there are song-books and Bibles within the reach of all.

They will strive courteously to fill the front seats first, so that the late comers will disturb the meeting as little as possible.

Ushers have the best opportunity of securing the names of strangers and turning them over to the chairman of the department or the chairman of the Social Service Department.

THE EFFICIENT EPWORTHIAN.

Open-Air Services.

From late spring to early fall many Chapters will find open-air services a great means of usefulness. Contrary to the usual belief, the summer is a most favorable time for revival and evangelistic work—but not in stuffy churches and badly ventilated halls. The widespread habit, which our climate fosters, of spending as much time as possible in the open air during the warmer months, offers a suggestion to the aggressive Christian which ought not to be ignored.

The people are already out-of-doors. A little music will usually draw a large crowd. The open-air service which follows, if it is wisely planned, will hold the crowd which the music draws.

An open-air meeting must not be conducted after the same fashion as one conducted inside a church building. There must be an entire absence of stiffness. The street is not the place for ritual. The meeting must stand entirely on its own merits. It can have no crutches of churchly surroundings, of the dim religious light and Sabbath-like atmosphere of the sanctuary. Whatever is done must be done promptly, and without any break in the chain of exercises.

The singing must be vigorous, confident, and sufficient in volume to sustain itself without any assistance from the crowd. The crowd may choose to join in, but it is well not to be dependent upon it. The hymns that are sung will be set to practicable tunes, tunes that are attractive, if not familiar. But it is not necessary to copy slavishly the methods of the Salvation Army. Methods are not so important as spirit. With the proper knowledge of the character of a street crowd, an intelligent leader can usually devise his own method.

If the open-air service is to be held in an incorporated town, it will be necessary to seek official permission before taking any positive steps. A good location should be selected beforehand. Do not start out, like Abraham, not knowing whither you go. The best location is one which, while being close to the main stream of travel, is not so near as to be disturbed by the noises of the street.

THE WEEKLY DEVOTIONAL MEETING.

In the conduct of the meeting one or two things should be specially noted. Long prayers are fatal to an open-air service. Indeed, it is sometimes wise to omit prayer altogether. A preliminary meeting with the workers may be held in some quiet room, and prayer for the service may there be offered with large prospect of blessing. But when the meeting is on, the crowd must be held. Anything which breaks the magnetic current between the speaker and his hearers will hurt the meeting. A street crowd, once its attention is distracted, is gone.

The speaking should be direct, forceful, and brief. If a sermon is attempted, its introduction and peroration should both be amputated, and what is left set on fire with earnestness. The closer the workers are to the crowd, the better. A prayer-meeting may drag itself along to some sort of a conclusion with twenty feet of empty benches between the people and the leader, but in an open-air meeting the thing is utterly impossible. Hold the meeting, if practicable, so near to the church or other meeting-place that a brief after-service may be held indoors. To this service all who desire to come will be welcome. There direct personal dealing with individuals about their soul's salvation will be entirely in place, and often fruitful of blessed results.

HOME PRAYER-MEETINGS.

The prayer-meeting in the home has long been a most helpful means of carrying on spiritual work. Community prayer-meetings are famous in the history of revivals. The Epworth League Chapter is admirably adapted by its spirit and organization to conduct just such meetings as these. They may be held at homes distant from the church in order to reach people who are not reached by its regular services. The homes of those who are shut in by any manner of infirmity are usually gladly opened for prayer service.

In times of revival a chain of home prayer-meetings may be established in such a way as to include the entire Church. The Epworth League may co-operate with the pastor so effectively in this work that its continuance for

THE EFFICIENT EPWORTHIAN.

two or three weeks before the opening of special revival services will pave the way for instant victory at the very opening of the more public services.

At every home prayer-meeting a number of active Christians should be present to render help in song and prayer. By dividing the departments of the Chapter into small groups a force may be organized sufficient to hold home prayer-meetings in every section of the parish on the same night.

A Description Undesired.

An Epworthian came to his pastor and said, "Where can I get hold of the paper that they cut up for the meeting?"

And the pastor passed the query over to *The Epworth Herald* office.

If the editor believed that one out of a hundred *Herald* readers thought of the paper in terms like those, he would take to the woods—for a while, at least.

Please, O gentle Epworthians, do n't give anybody else cause to describe your paper in such unhappy words. Do n't cut it up!

The Herald's pages on the devotional meeting are written with exceeding care by the best writers to be found. They keep in mind the needs of the meeting and the ability of the leaders.

But they do n't do anybody's thinking for him. The material they provide is not "ready to serve." Nobody can cut it up and use it wisely.

Rather should the leader "read, mark, learn, and inwardly digest" it, and so make it his own. Then *The Herald's* material will really help him, and he will put the impress of his own mind on the meeting which he leads.

Do n't "cut it up!"

Brief Wisdom for the Devotional Meeting.

The songs a Chapter sings tell what soul the Chapter has.

There 's a lot more harm done by dull meetings in the League than by lively games in the gymnasium. But dull meetings are not compulsory.

THE WEEKLY DEVOTIONAL MEETING.

If you want to waste the time of the devotional meeting, do n't begin until everybody is present.

Do n't spoil your meetings by using a poor song-book.

A long prayer-meeting talk is no sign of a good leader.

What should happen in your Chapter if you omitted to sing one of the old stand-by songs for the next month? One answer: The quality and volume of the singing would be noticeably improved.

One reason some young people stay away from the evening preaching service is that they have heard one sermon already. But the devotional meeting is no place for sermons, lay or ministerial.

The superstitious are never afraid when the meeting begins, on time, with an *appropriate* song. For these are signs of a leader who has made preparation, which is the sign of a good meeting.

The leader who says "Never again," would be heartened if he knew that his work had been a help to somebody. And when "somebody" tells him so—!

What makes devotional meeting "helps" so useless as substitutes for individual thinking is the fact that the chief excellence of the meeting is in the individuality that is put into it.

Berating the absentees is a poor way to make those present feel comfortable.

It is not a crime to introduce variety into the methods of the devotional meeting.

To advertise topics too far ahead is to throw away the advantage of surprise.

The leader who says less than he had intended to is not beyond the reach of forgiveness.

In a missionary devotional meeting, ask how those who do n't believe in missions ought to revise the Lord's Prayer.

The Bible is more modern than yesterday's newspaper. To prove that, give it a chance at to-day's life in your next devotional meeting.

The leader who shuffles the hymn-book's pages in search of something appropriate to sing is announcing the fact that he is not prepared to lead.

THE EFFICIENT EPWORTHIAN.

About once in nineteen times the hour may profitably be devoted to the hearing of a single speaker. But don't let it happen when *you* are the leader.

No meeting can be more devotional than the people who attend it.

It is a poor consecration that doesn't last until the next meeting.

One way of putting variety into the devotional meeting is to put new people into it.

Hint to devotional leaders: When you can't think of anything else to say, be sure to tell the people that they mustn't let the time go to waste.

A railway mail-clerk told me the other day that the train he traveled on had been on time at its destination just three times in five years. Some devotional meetings are worse than that. They haven't been on time at their starting point since first the time was set.

Testimony in meeting is a good thing, but it is not absolutely necessary as long as one's Christianity gives to others the sensation of vitality.

An easy testimony may be nothing but cheap talk.

There are seventeen good ways of conducting a League meeting, but beginning ten minutes late is not one of them.

That experimental Chapter of ours will try to fill some of the devotional meeting pauses with silent, concerted prayer.

The First Vice-President at Manhattan, Kans., calls on the leader of the Sunday night devotional service twenty-four hours ahead of the meeting to make sure that the leader will not fail him. If the leader just *can't* be ready, the First Vice-President will have everything in hand, for the meeting must not be a failure. It is a first-class idea for first-class department heads.

Worn-out song-books are no sign of good singing.

Life is too short to spend any of it on long League speeches.

Sunday school teachers who fail are described by an Iowa teacher: the nearsighted teacher who can not see into the background of the pupils' lives; the teacher with a funnel, who pours the mixture into the pupils until the

THE WEEKLY DEVOTIONAL MEETING.

vessel is empty; the Mephibosheth, lame in the feet, who thinks that all the work is done on Sunday; the surgical teacher, whose remarks cut, or sting, or inject unwholesome virus; the geyser teacher, who works by spurts and fits; the Elisha's servant teacher, who can not see the mountains filled with the chariots of God. The League devotional meeting has had leaders like these—sometimes.

Quality costs. A successful devotional meeting has to be paid for. But a shoddy meeting, like a shoddy coat, costs more in the long run.

One reason for giving the familiar hymns a rest in the devotional meeting is that they will mean more when they are sung next time.

Some pauses in the devotional meeting are profitable; like the intervals between the dots and dashes of the telegraph, they help to produce an intelligible message. But not the long, long pauses! They interrupt the message.

If the Epworthians could have their way, the leaders would not read long paragraphs in the devotional meeting—not even *Epworth Herald* paragraphs.

Take your Bible to the League meeting. Maybe the leader, "as should n't," will forget to bring one—and yours will save the day.

Do n't be afraid of the old truths in the devotional meeting. Sin, repentance, faith, salvation, judgment, eternity—they are all here, just as much as ever. No modern improvements on those elemental facts.

Is there anybody in your Chapter who comes to the League meeting only when there 's nothing else to do? Then do n't scold; that merely makes a bad matter worse. But aim for meetings so attractive that all your members will come to feel every week there 's nothing else to do.

Put Jesus Christ into the devotional meeting—not cantingly, but positively. It attracts more people, especially young people, than any other magnet you can use.

You can get an Epworthian to meeting, but you can not make him speak. Make him *want* to speak!

In choosing leaders, give a little attention to the fitting of leaders to topics.

THE EFFICIENT EPWORTHIAN.

THE SUNDAY NIGHT SERVICE AND THE EPWORTH LEAGUE.

In many places the Sunday night service is one of the most serious problems the pastor and the Church are called upon to face. The Church membership is fairly loyal to the morning service, but does not consider attendance at the evening service a matter of vital importance. The out-of-door attractions in fine weather and the charm of the home circle in winter make the work of sustaining the Sunday night congregation very difficult. Some pastors meet this situation by the use of special expedients, such as illustrated sermons, song services, lecture sermons, sermons in series, and so forth. In some places these expedients are quite successful, but in many others they do not sufficiently meet the problem to be considered adequate answers to it.

A serious element in the whole question of the Sunday night service is the feeling which obtains in many quarters that the Epworth League does not support the service as it should. When the pastor sees the young people passing out of the church after the League meeting while the scanty audience for the evening service is gathering, the sight is not likely to cheer his heart or to intensify the eagerness and enthusiasm of his message. The fact that the young people, in places where the complaint is made, are not disloyal in any larger measure than other members, is not considered. The other members have not come near the church. They are not seen turning their backs on the church at the moment when the evening service is beginning. Consequently their offense is likely to be estimated less seriously than that of the young people.

In view of these and other facts with regard to the evening service, suppose we consider a sustained campaign by the League in behalf of the second public preaching.

The point of contact which justifies such a campaign as this lies in three facts which are known to everybody. First, the Epworth League has already a regular service, which in nearly every case is set for the hour immediately preceding the Sunday night preaching service. This is an established institution, to which the Church everywhere is thoroughly accustomed.

THE WEEKLY DEVOTIONAL MEETING.

Second, the League as an organization is in such relation to the pastor and to the Church that it can help the Sunday night service as no other agency can do it.

Third, the Sunday night service is the best opportunity offered to get at the young people of the community through the young people of the Church.

These three facts all point to the Sunday night service as coming legitimately within the scope of the League's activities and interest. Nobody could complain that devotion to this interest was affecting unfavorably any other work of the League or of the Church.

In order to make this campaign really effective, it ought to be carried on in an aggressive and spectacular, though not sensational, fashion. It should be a positive movement, not concerning itself with the fixing of blame upon anybody for the present conditions, but rather with the developing of a new spirit of courage and aggressiveness and confidence.

THE LOCAL LEAGUE'S PART IN THIS CAMPAIGN.

It must be understood always and everywhere that the local Chapter in its work for the Sunday night service is to act always as the helper of the pastor, and under his direction. The interest which the League seeks to arouse is in a service of the Church, not a service of or for the League. The pastor is in charge of every activity of the local Church. He is the commander-in-chief. The Epworth League will work loyally under him and will follow his living leadership with eagerness and devotion.

This campaign is not an intimation from the Epworth League or from anybody that the Sunday night service is a failure. Least of all is it a suggestion that the pastor is less than competent to do the work committed to his hands. Instead of these things, this campaign means a fuller acceptance by the Epworth League of its share of responsibility for the one meeting which most of all belongs to the young people who are just on the edge of the Church community.

THE EFFICIENT EPWORTHIAN

The Two Sunday Night Meetings.

The Rev. P. Ross Parrish suggests some important considerations when he says: "These are mutually and vitally related interests. No Sunday evening preaching service can be a success without the loyal support of the young people who attend the Epworth League. No one can be a failure where the young people stand by with enthusiasm and constancy. Note some of the reasons why Epworthians should generously support the evening service:

"1. It is most important for many reasons. It can be made a popular, evangelistic, and widely profitable service. It must become either a marked success or a dragging failure.

"2. Many of the older people and children who attend the morning service do not come in the evening. The evening service must be supported largely by young people, youngerly people, and casual attendants.

"3. The relation of the Epworth League meeting in point of time to the preaching service creates both the privilege and duty of supporting it.

"4. For Epworthians to withhold help in sustaining it is in a sense to tear it down and to advertise it a failure. Can you imagine the effect on the other young people, the general public, and the pastor when any considerable number of Epworthians turn away from the church at the close of 'their' meeting? We can not expect the general public to attend and appreciate the services of the Church unless we stand loyally by and set the example.

"5. In fact, the fate and character of this service are largely in the hands of the Epworth League and the young people. What can you do? Many things.

"(1) Pray especially for this service and the pastor.

"(2) Talk it up everywhere.

"(3) Help to create enthusiastic loyalty in the Chapter.

"(4) Begin the devotional meeting on time so as to close five or ten minutes before the hour for evening service. Then you can be in your places sharp on time.

"(5) Never go away after the League meeting except in cases of extreme necessity. Nothing is so damaging to the public service and so discouraging to the pastor as this

THE WEEKLY DEVOTIONAL MEETING.

"(6) Let the members attend in a body and sit directly in front of the pulpit. There is no objection to this. It is a reasonable request. There are many reasons for it. It is the key to the situation. Your example will become contagious. You can help the pastor mightily by sympathy, prayer, song, and manifest interest.

"(7) Appoint a 'Welcoming Committee' of young men to greet the people as they come in and go out.

"(8) Various volunteer committees of one or two persons each might select pews and undertake to keep them full on Sunday night.

"(9) In every possible way prove your loyalty to the Church and to the pastor.

"(10) There is especial need for this whole-hearted devotion during the summer. Let us be on hand when we are most needed.

"(11) The Chapter can stand ready to conduct the service now and then at the request of the pastor, or in case of his sickness or absence."

CHAPTER VII.

THE MORNING WATCH, PERSONAL EVANGELISM, AND BIBLE STUDY.

The Practice of the Presence.

It is particularly fitting that the great campaign for the Morning Watch enrollment should be inaugurated on the first Sunday in the year. This day is the beginning of the Week of Prayer, many Churches are in the midst of special revival efforts, the Bible study classes are settled in their work, and it is the commencement of a new year.

Every Chapter in Methodism should make plans to present the Morning Watch at the devotional meeting on that day. The enrollment is not a new organization, nor does it require a separate committee. It is simply an enrollment of members of the Epworth League and other young Christians who will sign a card reading as follows:

COMRADES OF THE MORNING WATCH: ENROLLMENT.

Trusting in the Lord Jesus Christ for help, I will make it the rule of my life to set apart at least fifteen minutes every day, if possible in the early morning, for quiet meditation, Scripture reading, and prayer.

Signature..................
Address..............

Please sign and return to Central Office of the Epworth League.

Many of the young people in the League strive to be regular in reading their Bibles every day; but when the reading is done here and there, with no fixed purpose, and at any convenient time, it is likely to be neglected. The

MORNING WATCH, PERSONAL EVANGELISM.

Morning Watch suggests a time, supplies a definite purpose, and makes the Bible a living Book.

Some members are doing daily Bible study in the regular Epworth League Bible courses. All such members, and those who are doing no study at all, should become comrades of the enrollment. To sign the card gives definiteness and fixedness to one's purpose, gives the movement the strength and inspiration of numbers, and puts the signer in a position where he can consistently urge others to make a habit of daily Bible study and prayer. The devotional meeting at which this subject is presented should be in charge of the First Department.

The following suggestions may prove helpful to the committee in presenting the enrollment, and in making as much of the day as possible:

1. The First Vice-President should order at once, from the Central Office, Chicago, a supply of Morning Watch circulars and cards.

2. At the meeting several speakers should present such topics as the following: "The advantages of keeping the Morning Watch," "The value of meditating on the work of God," "The Morning Watch for personal spiritual growth," "The place of daily Bible study and prayer in the life of the young Christian."

3. Where there are regular Bible study classes, the members of these classes should give short testimonies concerning the value of daily Bible study to the spiritual life.

4. A prominent place should be given to those who are already "Comrades." Their testimonials should be so framed as to induce others to enroll.

5. Ask the pastor, in a few words, to endorse the enrollment and make prominent several points, viz.: That the enrollment is not an inflexible pledge; one can withdraw from it at any time; that there are no dues nor taxes; that each one can decide for himself how he will spend the time each day.

6. At the close of the meeting the cards should be passed, and after a few moments of silent prayer, should be signed by all who desire to do so. The cards should then be collected and forwarded at once to the Central

THE EFFICIENT EPWORTHIAN.

Office of the Epworth League, Chicago. The cards are filed and acknowledged by the bureau. Each signer receives a neat covenant card for his own use. This covenant card should be signed and placed in some conspicuous place where it can be seen each day.

7. The campaign should not end at this meeting. It will be but a beginning. A personal canvass of the whole Chapter should follow. This cavass can be made by the members of the Spiritual Department, or by a specially appointed committee.

8. In all the plans for this day there should be much prayer by all concerned. The speakers and the music should be selected with great care. The meeting should be characterized by no mere temporary enthusiasm, but should be pervaded by an intense, quiet, heart-searching spirit.

The Elements of the Morning Watch.

Prayer.—The secret prayer is the sense of relationship. If we are God's children, prayer is not only essential, but natural to us.

"Prayer is the Christian's vital breath,
The Christian's native air."

Whatever scoffers may say, and whatever may be the claims of science regarding the uselessness of prayer, we have one sufficient answer. These nineteen hundred years attest, through the experience of myriads of God's saints, that prayer is a real force and must be reckoned with. That is a good enough answer for the critics. For the Christian himself there is a more vivid proof. In the measure that he has been a praying Christian he has been a successful Christian. There are many causes of backsliding, but none are so certain to produce that effect as the neglect of the prayer life.

Prayer at the day's beginning is likely to fix the level of the day's living. It is a confession of allegiance, and going from the presence-chamber of the King to a day of sinfulness is not possible, continuously. Either the sinful day must be abandoned or the morning prayer will be.

Prayer at the morning hour works its most potent spell

upon our own lives. There is a mighty reflex power in prayer. It reacts upon ourselves. The morning finds us rested. Our minds are clearer than at a later hour. The day has not yet written its marks of care and preoccupation upon our faces and our hearts. God has the first opportunity to bring moral and spiritual forces to bear upon us. It gives God the first fruits of the day, the right of way in our lives.

Meditation.—Meditation is an old-fashioned exercise. It is not popular in the nervous new civilization of our time. It looks like laziness. It seems to be a waste of time. In the city we must read the morning paper at breakfast, finish it on the way to our work, and find something to be busy with after coming home at night. In the country the methods are different, but the purpose is the same. We dislike to shut ourselves in with our own thoughts. Sometimes we are afraid of ourselves, afraid of what we will think about ourselves when we are forced to think, afraid of the direction in which our thoughts will lead us. Nevertheless, meditation is an exercise full of undeveloped possibilities for good.

It is good that we should think about ourselves. The exercise is not flattering, perhaps, but it is wholesome. A ten-minute meditation every morning may show us flaws in our Christian living which need only right attention to be corrected. The moments of quiet thought may readjust all our notions, and save us from humiliation and wasted powers in the later hours of the day. They make for righteousness at the very springs of life.

It is good that we should think about God, what He is, what His providences are, what He is seeking to teach us by our daily experiences, what His great salvation means to us, and what we can make it mean to others. In a peculiar sense God is our Father, for we have been born into the family of God. That means that He has claims upon us, and that we have claims upon Him. The Morning Watch may be made the communion hour in which, besides the formal prayer, there shall be sweet and holy communion between the soul of the Christian and his Father in heaven.

THE EFFICIENT EPWORTHIAN.

Bible Study.—This is the practical link that holds the Morning Watch to reality. Prayer may become a form, and meditation a mere dreamy dozing, or a quiet thinking about business problems which nobody will interrupt. The Bible is not understood as it should be, because it is not rightly used. We go to it for proof-tests; for historical, geographical, biographical, and even theological facts, but we do not use it sufficiently as a manual of devotion. There is much in the Bible that has charm and depth of meaning only as it is read in the prayer spirit.

The Morning Watch is a thing of faith. The Bible is the foundation of truth on which the structure of faith can be built. The Bible is here. It is available, acceptable, inspiring, as well as inspired. It asks only to be used. The Morning Watch furnishes the opportunity. If fifteen minutes to half an hour seems too short, remember that it is more than the time that would otherwise be spent, haphazard, in Bible study.

Then, Bible study brings to us the Christ we need for our meditation. Without it He is a vague, shadowy figure, half myth and half tradition. With it He appears as the Son of God, the revelation of the Father to the world, our Elder Brother. In its pages we find Him speaking to us, His latest disciples, and saying to us, "Henceforth I call you not servants, but friends."

A Practical Method of Keeping the Morning Watch.

Be Alone.—That is your right, and you need such complete solitude that you will be away from all but God. "When thou prayest enter into thy closet, and when thou hast shut the door, pray." Get away from all consciousness of the presence of others. If you can not do that in the morning, change the hour of your secret prayer rather than miss it altogether.

Pray.—"When thou hast shut the door, pray to thy Father which is in secret." Begin the watch with communion, that the consciousness of God's presence may be felt at once. If you are out of hearing of the rest of the family, pray audibly. There is usually less difficulty in concentrating attention on the prayer if it is spoken.

MORNING WATCH, PERSONAL EVANGELISM.

Read.—This is the time for devotional Bible reading. Perhaps your prayer has suggested a passage to be read. A good plan is to lay out a course of devotional reading, if possible linking it with your work in Bible study, omitting those elements of the course that are not distinctly devotional. Read aloud, and read the passage twice or thrice.

Think.—Before you go about your business, face the day's life from the viewpoint of this place of communion and worship. Many a time you will be able to avoid temptation and to see opportunities for quiet helpfulness. You will go out to the tasks of the day girded with a strength not your own.

Getting Ready for a Day's Work—A Morning Watch Meeting.

This meeting is intended to promote the Morning Watch Enrollment. But first and most important, it is intended to promote habits of prayer, Scripture reading, and quiet thinking. These are simple habits, but the forming of them is all that many people need in order to find the religious life full of a joy and power they have not yet discovered.

We do not pray enough. We do not pray aright. We do not give God's Book a fair chance at our lives. We do not think enough on the things that concern our spiritual life. All these are facts which everybody knows.

But how may we mend our ways? Not by confessing our folly; not by reading new literature about these things; not even by resolving to do better. There is a short road, a royal road, out of our neglect and weakness. And this is it: Begin this very day to pray and read and meditate, and hereafter fight against any influence that would prevent your taking this holy exercise every day that dawns.

Therefore, the Morning Watch! Not a new organization, but a new faithfulness. It means exactly what the theme suggests: secret prayer and the devotional reading of the Bible at a set time every day. Usually the morning is the best time.

THE EFFICIENT EPWORTHIAN.

Morning Watch Interrogations.

What? Prayer, Bible reading, meditation.

Why? That I may know myself. That I may know God. That I may know the Book. Because we do not pray enough. We do not pray aright. We do not read enough. We do not read aright.

When? In the morning. Then the soul is more open to realities. The day is young. The world is still. The cares of the day's affairs have not been taken up. The Morning Watch is the putting on of the armor. If we wait for some other time, we may get no time at all.

Testimony Hints.

If you have been a Comrade of the Morning Watch by custom, whether enrolled or not:

Tell how good the Morning Watch time has been.

Tell how it has helped to interpret the Book and make it personal.

Tell how it has put new vitality into the life of prayer.

Tell how you have managed to keep up this daily exercise of the soul in spite of hindrances.

Then recommend the good custom to those who have not tried it.

If you have never yet begun to observe the stated time of prayer and quiet thinking:

Tell why you have not begun it.

Tell how you have longed for it.

Say that you will begin it now if you can.

Admit that you can do it if you will.

Then enroll yourself, and start now.

What Says the Scripture?

Prayer and uplook in the morning. Psa. 5:3.

Prayer that "goes before" God in the morning. Psa. 88:13.

Prayer for communion in the day's beginning. Psa. 143:8.

Strength from the morning's waiting before God. Isa. 33:2.

MORNING WATCH, PERSONAL EVANGELISM.

The command of Jesus as to secret prayer. Matt. 6:6.
The Master's Morning Watch. Mark 1:35.
The pledge of communion. Psa. 145:8.
The place of help. Heb. 4:16.
The promise of fellowship with Christ. Rev. 3:20.
A combination of power; with Word and prayer. Eph. 6:17, 18.
Treasuring the Word of God. Deut. 11:18.
The power of the Word of God. Heb. 4:12.

REASONS FOR PERSONAL EVANGELISM.

Why should Christians be told that they must be eager to make Christians of others? We understand why a grocer asks his customers to secure other customers for him, or why a newspaper asks its subscribers to help increase its circulation. That is advertising with the hope of profit arising from it.

But is not religion a different thing? Are we not dealing with something too delicate and too sacredly personal to justify our interference? The inner life is a secret and private concern. Why should we invade the seclusion of a man's soul when we would scorn to venture, unbidden, into his home?

The answer has four forms.

We *would* venture unbidden into a man's house if it were necessary to warn him of some great danger. Propriety is all very well, but in time of peril we set is aside. And so, because Christians believe that all who are not Christ's are in real peril, and threatened by suffering more terrible than any earthly calamity could bring, they believe that the unconverted must be reproved, warned, exhorted "to flee from the wrath to come."

Another phase of the answer is that the Christian life is so full of privilege and promise that every real Christian desires others to know its power and blessedness. If propriety permits a good newspaper to be advertised by its readers, or a great remedy to be made public by those who have been benefited, there is a thousand-fold greater reason for seeking to win our friends to Christ. He transforms life. He makes all things new. He implants the power of an endless life in the center of being. It is a marvelous change. It has come to us. We would that it might come to others.

The third reason for personal evangelism is that it is God's plan for spreading the glad tidings. He purposes that Christians shall win Christians. In most cases a direct personal interview will clinch a sermon or a book or a speech, when to preach another sermon or write another book or deliver another speech would result in total failure.

The fourth reason is that personal evangelism is necessary to maintain our own Christian life. Without some attempt to win others to our faith, we can not hope to retain that faith in vigor and clearness. He who can not recommend Christ to others will soon lose his own interest in the Savior.

We are beginning to learn that it is a mistake to confine our attention to the crowd. Religion is so intensely personal and individual that, no matter how general a spiritual movement may be, each person has a separate, distinct relation to it. Every case of conversion is the conversion of an individual. You can not save the masses, or the submerged tenth, or the other convenient rhetorical groups of people. You must save men and women one at a time. This was the method of the Master. His greatest messages, His most careful ministries, and His most successful labors were all for the benefit of the individual.

Peter, Nathanael, the Ethiopian ambassador, and the Roman centurion, all were brought to Jesus by the same simple method. There were great sermons in apostolic times, and great results came from them. But the care taken in the New Testament to record the winning of individuals by individuals has much meaning. The record is for our encouragement and our example. The preaching of great sermons to vast multitudes is good, but it can not be done everywhere, or by everybody, and if it could it is not the ideal way. Faith in Christ is an intensely personal thing. It is awakened by direct, personal, private labor.

Personal Christian work is the best evangelism, therefore, because it is personal. A book can demonstrate the binomial theorem. But the plan of salvation is best com-

MORNING WATCH, PERSONAL EVANGELISM.

prehended when it is emphasized and illustrated by a saved sinner.

Some people come to Jesus Christ of their own accord; but those who do n't must be sought. We are not free from responsibility until we have done all we can to find them.

Where are they? Who are they? They are near; else we could not do *personal* evangelism. They are nearer than we had thought, Andrew's brother, Philip's friend, the evening's caller, the wayside acquaintance, the beggar at the door, the unconverted people of your Church.

All this means that the Epworth League's purpose, to try "to help others attain the highest New Testament standard of experience and life," must be accomplished largely by personal work. Personal Christian work is not easily done. It is, perhaps, the most difficult form of Christian service. But at the same time it is the most valuable form, richest in benefits to the worker and in results. It requires a measure of personal spiritual life that is not so markedly demanded by any other form of religious work. One can do so many things in connection with the Church and the Epworth League without possessing the highest and most definite personal experience. But the work of seeking others and dealing with them face to face concerning their salvation can not be done when the spiritual life is at low ebb. The prayer-life must be unobstructed and the sense of communion with God uninterrupted.

In the first place, then, the personal worker should seek the fullness of the Christian life for himself. Then there must be the most complete and most unquestioning dedication of his powers to this work. With such a beginning the fear of man will become an unimportant thing. The Bible should be studied for its bearing on the matter of personal salvation. Then, here are a few simple rules of approach:

Be natural when speaking of spiritual things.

Avoid denunciation or positive statements concerning particular sins. Leave these to the conscience, as it is enlightened by the Holy Spirit.

Do not be too careful. Prefer an occasional mistake to the missing of an opportunity.

THE EFFICIENT EPWORTHIAN.

As a rule, do not try to do personal spiritual work in a crowd.

Use simple language, and avoid as much as possible those stereotyped phrases which everybody recognizes, but which have ceased to convey any definite meaning.

Do not argue. Seek for points of agreement rather than for points of difference.

Be free to make use of your own experience.

As much as possible, confine your work to those of your own sex and age.

Urge prompt action.

Secure co-operation in prayer. It is a great gain if the unsaved can be induced to pray for himself.

Do not tell any one that he is saved. He will find that out from a better authority than you are.

The beginning of personal work need not be postponed until you have a great number of people among whom to begin. There is some one already near to you whom you know and to whom you can go without need of introduction or special ceremony. That one is the first person to whom your duty calls you.

When decisions have been reached there is great need for care and the following up of each individual case. Do not drop the acquaintance when the first great purpose of your work has been accomplished. You have not only brought a soul to Christ, but you have won a friend. Offer all possible help in the beginning of a new social life. Enlist the co-operation of a few warm-hearted, congenial Christians. Secure your new-found friend as a member of the Epworth League, and set him to work at once at some definite task.

BELIEVE THEY ARE WORTH WINNING.

There is nothing like it for rousing the desire to win people to Christ. So long as we can not see any great gain in it, a thousand things will prevent us from becoming soul-winners. But when we put right values on eternal destinies and on the influences which shape those destinies, hindrances disappear.

MORNING WATCH, PERSONAL EVANGELISM.

God believes in the worth of human souls. His plan to save them is His measure of their value. Our Lord put the divine estimate of a soul's worth into a form we could understand when He gave *Himself* to save sinners.

We say we are profoundly grateful for the personal interest of Jesus Christ in our own souls. But He is no more interested in us than in the millions who have never confessed Him. If our gratitude measures our opinion of what He has done for us, should it not send us to these others that they may share our joy?

Three Methods.

Direct Personal Appeal.—It is the surest way, though often the most difficult at the outset. It was Jesus' way.

The Printed Page.—Much as some people may sneer at tracts, God has greatly honored them in the past, and will continue to do so. The form of the tract has been improved, and sometimes it becomes a full-fledged book. But in any form, wisely used, it will help in the work of soul-winning.

Letters.—When you can not go in person, you can send a letter. Choose the moment of unusual experience, some sorrow, some affliction, or even some advancement and gain, to write a note of sympathy and cheer to the person concerned. That is the mother's way. How often it succeeds!

Ten Pointed Questions, Plus One.

What is the best form of evangelistic work for the needs of the present day?

Is it true that most Christians have never won a single soul to Christ? What shall we do about it?

What is the best way to win souls for Christ?

What is the first requirement of a soul-winner?

Am I willing to go empty-handed into God's presence from my present place of opportunity?

In my present spiritual condition am I fit to attempt personal work?

Considering my present way of life, would any one who knows me be willing to receive spiritual counsel from me?

THE EFFICIENT EPWORTHIAN.

Who is the first person I ought to try to win for Christ?

Would my nearest friends be greatly surprised if I should approach them about their salvation?

Suppose I should try to win somebody to the Christian life, do I know how to go about it?

In view of the answers to these ten questions, what is the first thing I ought to do as a Christian?

How Your Chapter May Begin.

Determine that you *will* begin.

Make the Chapter a "Win One Society," not in form, but in fact.

A passion for souls may be roused by skillful use of the Bible.

No fault-finding; loyalty to the great purpose of the movement.

Agree with two or three others that you will seek the salvation of certain individuals.

Make a record of those for whom some member is specially concerned.

Cottage prayer-meetings afford fine opportunities for personal dealing with individuals.

Never be discouraged.

Real Hindrances.

Inconsistent living spoils the work of many a would-be soul-winner. There is no critic like the unconverted observer of a Christian's conduct. You must not live on his level if you are in earnest about helping him higher.

But the removal of this hindrance is a double gain. A consistent Christian life is in itself a great reward. It means peace, joy, confidence. And it makes possible the greatest service earth knows—the leading of others to the love and presence of Jesus Christ.

Unbelief is a real obstacle. If you do not believe in God, that He can save souls, or in yourself, that you seek souls, or in the unsaved, that they need salvation, you can never win souls to Jesus Christ.

Where is your unbelief? Surely not in God's readiness, if you believe in Him at all. Surely not in the sinner's need, after all you have seen of godless lives. Is it in your lack of confidence in yourself? Get that confidence by whatever means you may. Pray, depend on God, and *begin!* We learn to do by doing, not by doubting or by theorizing. Begin with the opportunity nearest you.

Over-sensitiveness keeps many Christians from the direct work of soul-winning. They are unwilling to attempt such pointed and definite effort. They fear repulse or criticism, or discovery of their own unfitness. Some of these things may be imaginary, but the fear of them is real and a great obstacle.

There is no remedy for it except the acceptance of one's plain duty and the conviction, "I can do all things through Christ." That will come by prayer and quiet meditation, and by complete surrender of life to the purposes of God.

Imaginary Hindrances.

"People resent being appealed to so directly." They do if the approach is made without tact, or by some one in whom they have no confidence. But very few will resent the coming of one whom they respect if there is evidence of genuine feeling and interest.

"I do not know how to argue with unbelievers." It is not necessary. They do not need argument. Most people who have not accepted Christ do not need to be convinced; they need to be convicted. You may be the messenger of the Holy Spirit in doing the work of conviction.

"I have had no experience." Neither Philip nor Andrew was experienced when they won Nathanael and Simon. There is no way to get experience unless you make a beginning. Find your Simon, your Nathanael. They are not far away. You need not many words. Simply: "I have found Christ. You may find Him." That is the heart and art of soul-winning.

"I am too busy to give the time such important work requires." You are not too busy to eat or sleep, or to do any other necessary thing. Only accept the truth that this is necessary work and you will find time for it, even if it compels the giving up of some less important occupations.

"I am not sufficiently familiar with the Bible." That

THE EFFICIENT EPWORTHIAN.

is, in part, a real hindrance, but it is not insurmountable. Soul-winning is one of the strongest incentives to Bible study. Try to win some one to Christ and you will discover a new urgency toward knowing your Bible. But you know at least enough of the Bible to make a start.

The Full Program and the Empty Life.

Adult evangelism is the most difficult evangelism.

We all know of men and women who in middle life have come into real obedience to Jesus Christ. But these instances are pitifully few, and the multitudes of adults who grow day by day less responsive to the Christian appeal are great beyond counting.

Why? Why must it be that one who has missed or refused the call of Christ in youth is doomed to hear it so little in the maturer years?

Because only youth has time enough!

In the noonday a man's program of life is full. He has mortgaged so much to the business of making a living, so much to whatever form of recreation attracts him, so much to treading the beaten track of every day's routine, that he has no place for the tremendous demand on his attention that religion would make.

Try him even on insignificant matters of new concern. Attempt to get the middle-aged man interested in numismatics, or radioactivity, or the poetry of Alfred Noyes. He will say, "I have no time," or, "These things do n't interest me," and he tells the truth. Yet none of them would ask so much time or so great a change in his bearing toward the world as the giving of himself to Jesus Christ.

The tragedy of a mature life without religion is that it has no room for religion. It has no open spaces.

Your friend who is not a Christian is not therefore likely to die a drunkard, or to become a criminal, or to acquire a positive preference for wickedness. He will continue to be, most likely, a good neighbor. He will not lose his position and come to poverty. He will probably vote against the saloon, and stand for good government, and be generous toward those in distress. He will be kind to his family, and true to his friends.

MORNING WATCH. PERSONAL EVANGELISM.

He will lack just one thing. He will be as good as a man can be who is God-less. And he will have become so used to the full program of his life that he will not know how to make room for the thing he lacks.

The urgent reason why every young Christian should seek to win his friend to the Christian confession and the Christian scheme of life is that there will soon be no chance to do it.

Only the young can be attracted by the Christian adventure. The man of affairs is already busy with his own enterprises.

Personal evangelism in the Epworth League is an evangelism of the soul's open spaces, of the mind still at leisure, of the daring spirit which has not yet been quenched. It belongs to the time when there is yet room to get religion into one's program without making a place for it with dynamite. Of course, when the chance offers, and there is no other means, it is even worth while that the gospel should blast its way into the soul, shattering all that hinders it.

But so Christ did not—does not—prefer it. He covets the young, that their lives may grow up, around their loyalty to Him, in perfect naturalness. He desires discipleship that need never know the preoccupations of a program that has no room for God.

Soul-Winning a Glorious Service.

(This is a rough analysis of Dr. J. W. Mahood's book, "The Art of Soul-Winning." The book is abundantly worth studying by all who covet success as soul-winners.)

The soul-winner's motive is the love of Christ. Soul-winning is largely a thing of personal work, rather than of work with the mass. Some of the greatest trophies of the gospel were won by direct efforts at soul-winning, among them D. L. Moody, Colonel H. H. Hadley, Lord Shaftesbury, J. Wilbur Chapman, John R. Mott, and many others.

No one can measure the worth of a soul, as no one can sound the depths that are reached in the death of a soul.

THE EFFICIENT EPWORTHIAN.

But the supreme motive for soul-winning is the love of God in Christ Jesus.

The soul-winner's life must be a life of surrender to God. Before he can win others, he himself must have been won. He must surrender of his life to the leadership and will of God.

He must really know that he has found the joy of salvation.

He must be a praying Christian, given to prayer, believing in it, successful in it.

He must be full of positive faith, implicitly believing God and going about his work without doubting.

He must be a self-sacrificing Christian, denying himself for the sake of his great business in life.

The soul-winner's equipment must be as varied as his work is important.

The Scripture is the sword of the Spirit. It is the soul-winner's best weapon. The more he knows his Bible the more his life will be enriched and his zeal inspired.

There are ways of approach to every unsaved soul, and the soul-winner must search for the best way in every case. That means tact, good sense, adaptability.

But nothing will do without earnestness. If you don't seem to care about my soul, I shall not be impressed by what you say. The eager are the best soul-winners. They *want* to win.

It is easy to get discouraged. But look at the canvasser. If he makes forty calls and gets only six orders in a day, he will try again to-morrow. The thirty-four rebuffs don't discourage him. If ninety-nine souls refuse your help, the one hundredth who yields is worth all your effort.

To feel a great responsibility for souls is all-important. The burden of souls is not easy, but without it no souls can be won.

The supreme equipment of the soul-winner is a personal Pentecost. The Holy Spirit will go with us to seek the lost if we will receive Him. Without Him we can not go at all.

MORNING WATCH, PERSONAL EVANGELISM.

The soul-winner's methods should be "anything to save souls."

Direct approach is for most cases the effective way to begin personal work. It can not be evaded, and if lovingly and tactfully done, it can not be resented.

The consecrated pen can help when direct approach is not possible or wise. A letter written at an opportune moment may turn a soul toward Christ.

Make a prayer list. It has elements of value that can not be told to those who have not tried it.

Be prepared to meet all the common objections of the unsaved. A score of these objections are met repeatedly in revival meetings and in personal work. Get familiar with them and with the answers to them.

No sincere, faithful effort at soul-winning can fail. It may not always produce instant results, but it will not fail, because God and His Christ have put into it all the purpose and power of the plan of salvation.

THE FIRST DEPARTMENT AND HOLY WEEK.

Passion Week is of all weeks the most appropriate for the acknowledgment of Jesus Christ as King.

It opens with Palm Sunday, the day of the Triumphal Entry. What better day than this for any serious-hearted youth to follow the example of the young people of Jerusalem, who welcomed the Christ to His own city?

In thousands of Churches there are special services during Passion Week. These are young people's services as truly as they can be anything else. They all make their central theme the amazing work and personality of Him who, with all His marks of divinity, was a Young Man who loved all youth and coveted it for His Kingdom.

And Easter Day! That should be youth's day, for it is the day that proves life's endless youthfulness.

The Epworth League Chapter that throws itself each year into this opportunity will find a richer reward than the consciousness of having observed Holy Week piously. Its own life will be strengthened and enlarged.

Get your share of the gain of the time by giving your

THE EFFICIENT EPWORTHIAN.

Church and pastor the full measure of service, and your Master the full measure of devotion.

DOING IT BY HAND.

We are beginning to learn that there is no such thing as salvation by machinery. Boards, committees, societies, brotherhoods, leagues, and all the rest are exceedingly useful, but none of them is a substitute for personal service in behalf of the unsaved. No one can escape the responsibility indicated in the story of the Good Samaritan by sending a check to the secretary of the Society for the Relief of Distressed Travelers on the Jericho Road.

Religion is so intensely personal and individual that, no matter how general a spiritual movement may be, each person has a separate, distinct relation to it. Every case of conversion is the conversion of an individual. You must save men and women one at a time. This was the method of the Master. His greatest messages, His most careful ministries, and His most successful labors were all for the benefit of the individual.

The intent of God is that every saved sinner shall be a means of saving other sinners. It is the most natural and simple plan that could have been devised. A sinner saved by grace knows how great a wretchedness he has escaped, and he knows others who are still in bondage. Who could be so attractive to a company of slaves as one of their number who had discovered a way to freedom?"

"If our religion is true," says a wise man, "we are in duty bound to preach it." But it is more than a duty. It is a joy. "To preach deliverance to the captives" is the finest of all occupations, when one has come into the liberty of Jesus Christ.

THE WIN-MY-CHUM MOVEMENT.

In the fall of 1913 a movement was begun by the General Secretary, Dr. W. F. Sheridan, acting on a League effort in Montana that attracted his attention, which was called "the Win-My-Chum Movement."

MORNING WATCH, PERSONAL EVANGELISM.

A week in November was appointed as "Win-My-Chum Week." For a month before this appointed date those Chapters which went into the enterprise were busy with preparation, and then gave themselves wholly to the work in the week set apart.

The Central Office sent out detailed directions, as it will do every year. But the gains of the week were due, as Dr. Sheridan asserted, to the genuine concern and the direct dealing of the young people themselves for and with their "chums."

It will serve the purpose of this special effort to present here some of the outstanding principles of the "Win-My-Chum" philosophy.

"WIN-MY-CHUM" REFLECTIONS.

There may be other ways of serving God in the world to come, but there is only one way in this world—the work of bringing all men into the family of God. All Christian service, of whatever form, must have that as its great purpose. There is no service, otherwise, nor any worship, either.

For service there must be power. God's work will not do itself. Wishing will not do it. Praying will not do it, though prayer will, for real prayer has the power promised to it.

Since all men are related to me, I am in a certain way less free than if I were alone in the world. Robinson Crusoe lost his absoute freedom of action when Friday appeared. Some things I may no longer do. Other things I now must do. I have my brother to consider.

What was it which gave Jerry McAuley his strange power over the wretched outcasts of Water Street? Not learning, nor eloquence, nor logic, nor zeal, but the persuasiveness that grew out of his utter sincerity and his unbounded love toward them. They believed in him, and that made it easy to believe his message. The same thing is true of Harry Monroe, who, at Pacific Garden Mission, to this day preaches a gospel for the lost which the lost are ready to accept because of the preacher's personal influence with them.

THE EFFICIENT EPWORTHIAN.

The Christian does not stop before every action and remind himself that he is about to do something in Christ's name and for Christ's sake. He does it without thinking, because it is the expression of the Christ-life within him. And so he is often surprised when he is reminded of it.

To invest our lives profitably we shall need Christ's estimate of a human soul. He measured it against all things seen—"the world"—and counted the world well lost if the soul were saved.

When a man starts unready on God's work he soon gets tired. That explains the reformer who needs reformation, the preacher who succeeds better in business, the evangelist who has broken down, and the nominal Christian who is taking a permanent vacation from Christian work. These have seen no vision, have felt no compelling incitement, have heard no voice of promise and power. They have not put themselves where God could say, "I will be with thee." And they are failures.

THE EVANGELISM OF A PERSON.

When you were converted, the whole world not only seemed different; it *was* different.

Winning a companion to the Christian life is not the end, but the beginning of a holy task.

It costs sixty dollars, they say, to save a soul in China. Yes; sixty dollars—and Calvary!

To do personal evangelism, first get personal power, and then a personal relationship to the man you're after.

The reason some revival efforts are fruitless is that the people think the effort must end when the meetings close.

If you reported conversions in your Chapter last year, this is a good time to inquire what has become of the young people who were converted.

If personal evangelism really meant in the Epworth League what it may mean, the League could win as many people to Jesus Christ as the whole Church gained last year.

It is better for ten Epworthians to talk to ten of their intimate friends about enlisting in the service of Christ

MORNING WATCH, PERSONAL EVANGELISM.

than for the Chapter to hold an aimless meeting on "Personal Evangelism."

Who Is "My Chum?"

It would be glorious if every Epworthian who has an unconverted friend should win him to the new obedience to Jesus Christ during the week of special effort.

That will not be done; for some Epworthians will miss their chance, and some of the unconverted will turn away from the invitation. It is always so; the seamy side of personal freedom shows plain at times like these.

But some Epworthians will not be content to work for the conversion of one person only. They will seek larger opportunities. And they will count much in the outcome.

Chums are not many; it is not easy for the average young person to have more than one at a time. Then, how can the word be made to stretch a little for the needs of these in the "Win-My-Chum" campaign who would win more than one?

A moment's thinking will show how that is possible.

A chum is somebody you care enough about to associate with on terms of mutual confidence and interest. You choose your chum because you see in him qualities which appeal to you. He responds for the same reason.

Many a time the only thing needed, if you would discover a new chum, is to look at somebody with new eyes. Instead of seeing the commonplace, familiar aspect of an ordinary individual whose personality has no interest for you, you may see, if you look for it, a character worth cultivating, a capacity worth controlling, a life worth influencing. All that, and more, may be included in the time-honored notion that here is a soul worth saving.

But you must look, or this vision will be missed. "Jesus, looking on him, loved him."

To win a new chum, first look with new eyes at some old acquaintance.

A Big Contract—Can I Make Good?

To "win-my-chum" may be harder than taking a city; and more glorious.

THE EFFICIENT EPWORTHIAN.

"My chum" is the closest student of what the religion of Jesus has done for me.

"My chum" has a fair working knowledge of my weak points. He has seen me when I was ashamed of myself.

"My chum" has talked baseball to me, and college, and girls, and business, and books, and dreams of the future—but we have never talked religion much.

That is not bad; it is human nature. Religion is not so easy to talk about as baseball, because it is so much bigger and more sacredly personal.

But now that I *am* going to talk religion to him, the task grows large and difficult. I can't see how to go about it.

If I talk one way, he may think me a prig or a hypocrite; if I try another way, he may be excused for counting me a liar.

I simply can't assume any superiority over him. Nor can I tell him that suddenly I have made up my mind to be tremendously interested in his soul for just one week, after which all will be as it was.

I don't know how to explain conversion to him, or to guarantee just what will happen if he decides to put his life into the control of my Master. His make-up is so different from mine that, honestly, I don't know in the least what *will* happen.

Perhaps the simplest way will be the best way. And the simplest way, it seems to me, is to talk to him about the Lord Jesus—not about myself—to ask him that he will face fairly the questions that must rise in his mind when he thinks of Christ and His claims, and to tell him that I'm not a very good sample of what a Christian should be, but that to see him stand up for my Lord would be the biggest joy of my life, as it surely would be of his own.

That way I shan't need to argue, and there will be little to explain—explanations are not much use at such a time—but just ask him to think honestly about what Jesus Christ would like to do for him and with him.

I have heard that such a method worked with Philip and Nathanael; it worked when the Samaritan woman used only a little bit of it; it worked with Cornelius and—skipping all the centuries between—it worked with Henry

MORNING WATCH, PERSONAL EVANGELISM.

White Warren and with William Fraser McDowell; it worked with F. M. Sayford, and C. K. Ober, and John R. Mott. It surely works!

Maybe, that way, I could win *my* chum!

THE BOOK AND ITS STUDY.

The Christian has a Book in which, together with many valuable but less important things, he may find all he needs concerning the great work he requires in order to accept, to understand, and to tell to others the whole work of God in redeeming man from destruction. It gives the history of redemption, the practical teaching of redemption, and the laws of life which govern those who accept redemption.

Now, if redemption from sin is a great thing, the Bible must be a Book of great practical importance. If our relation toward God and toward righteousness is the supreme concern of life, the Bible becomes a Book we dare not neglect. We can not treat it like other books. There is no urgent need that we should read Shakespeare, and no moral compulsion drives us to the pages of Emerson or Carlyle. But we are not dealing with life, our own life, for this day, but for all the days and the ages. If the Bible is a closed Book to us, God's plan for us is unknown, and our duty to Him is undiscovered. So must we perish!

How shall we study the Bible? What are the best methods? What are the most reliable helps? These questions are asked on every hand. Their right answering is of great moment. Some things may be said that will clear the way for each to find his own answer.

First, then, there are ways *not* to study the Bible. It is not a text-book on any one of the circle of the sciences. It is not a description of the bit of country bordering on the Mediterranean between Asia Minor and Egypt. It is not merely a collection of Hebrew literature. If it is studied for these things, the student will add to his store of knowledge, but he will miss completely the character and aim of the Bible.

"The Bible is one Book, with one Author, one theme, one purpose, and one central and commanding figure." Its Author is God; its theme. redemption; its purpose, to make redemption known to all men; its great central figure, Jesus Christ the Redeemer, the only begotten Son of God. Study it in the light of these facts, and it will become a living Book, for the Spirit of God lives in the Bible.

There are three great subjects the Christian needs to study: First, the historic facts of redemption. What was the course of God's plan to save mankind from sin and death? Such study brings before the student the whole Book, for every part of it is involved in the answer to that question. Second, the practical meaning of the teachings contained in God's plan. What ought a Christian to be? This subject also covers a wide territory of study. It requires the Old Testament as well as the New. It takes the whole Bible to make a whole Christian. Third, the ruling principles of Christian conduct. What ought a Christian to do? And here you have the whole range of Christian activity and life. It includes every form of evangelization, citizenship, and philanthropy; every principle of business and social life. Missions, reforms, politics, worship, are all here.

Is not all this sufficient? Have we not abundant and weighty reason for the reverent and constant study of the Book? Then, let it have its rightful place in our lives, that we may keep the commandments, be doers of the Word, and cleanse our way by taking heed to it according to the law of God.

Bible Study Suggestions.

Compare Scripture with Scripture.

Glean from the marginal readings.

Remember that the Bible is a very old Book.

Interpret the Bible upon principles of common sense.

Be willing to let the Bible mean what it wants to mean.

Keep in mind the purpose of the particular Book you are reading.

Cultivate spiritual sympathy with the Bible, for it is a spiritual Book.

Give the golden moments of the early morning to the study of the Book

MORNING WATCH, PERSONAL EVANGELISM.

Give careful attention to the connection of the passage you are reading.

In reading Moses, Elijah, David, any Bible character, "put yourself in his place."

He who reads the Bible, studies it, loves it, and obeys it, will share its immortality.

The Bible in the heart is a protection against evil, a restrainer of sin, and a source of spiritual energy.

The people who can quote Scripture accurately are not numerous. Is it carelessness, or ignorance, or lack of capacity?

The life that is too busy to afford time for Bible reading and study, is planning for an abundance of leisure when it will be too late.

Remember that every part of the Bible has historical connection with some period of ancient civilization, and read it with a full recognition of that fact.

One book of the Bible thoroughly studied is worth a dozen books superficially read; and each book studied will whet the desire for and strengthen the habit of studying the other books with similar care.

Who should read the Word? The young, to know how to live; the old, to know how to die; the ignorant, for wisdom; the learned, for humility; the rich, for warning; the poor, for enrichment. It is the book for all sorts and conditions of men.

Do n't forget that the Bible is a text-book of service as well as a guide to salvation.

Some Epworthians would still be looking for the Book of Hezekiah if they had n't been in a League Bible-study class.

There's nothing new about Bible study as a form of League work. But your Chapter may find something new in the Bible if you study it.

The Bible is not tested in the scholar's study, but in the world, where men are fighting for their lives. There is not a question of two Isaiahs, but of one sufficient Christ.

There is plenty of prohibition in the Bible, so that no Christian can object to a "Thou shalt not." Nevertheless, the two commandments of the New Testament, on which hang all the law and the prophets, are both "Thou shalts."

Beware of a Bible class that studies about the Bible, but does not study it.

The Bible is the source of all true politics, and of all worthy social reform.

Every Bible student should study in such a way as to prepare him to teach others when opportunity offers.

Do not study the Bible with a microscope. It is meant for every-day eyesight.

Come to the Bible, not because you must, but because you desire to come.

Do not be satisfied with such a fragmentary and foggy knowledge of the Bible as would make you ashamed if it were one of your high school text-books.

If you would solve your doubts, study your Bible.

The more you know the Bible the more you know yourself, and the more you know God. For it is a Book which not only reveals God to man, but man to himself.

Bible Study in the League.

The Epworth League movement is so distinctly a spiritual movement that its interest in an intelligent appreciation of the Holy Scriptures may be taken for granted. The experience of every Christian worker has demonstrated that among the young people in all parts of the Church there is a continual need of a systematic, definite, and connected scheme of Bible study. Our young people need to secure a comprehensive grasp of Bible truth. They need to study the Book, not for its literary value, but as their Book of religion. They must be in a real sense specialists as to this one Book. That this condition has not yet been attained is apparent to every one who has studied the situation with any thoughtfulness. In fact, the Bible, even as history, literature, and sociological material, is to many an unopened Book.

But there are distinct indications that a change is already in progress. Bible study is more largely in the thought and enterprise of authors and publishers than it has ever been. There is a decline in the popularity of controversies about the Bible. The establishment of training schools whose great text-book is the Bible is another sign of the awakening interest in Bible study.

The Epworth League has committed itself to a great and comprehensive plan of Bible work.

Every year there is set apart a Sunday for the special consideration of League studies. One of these will be, of course, Bible study.

The Central Office affords a large amount of genuine help in the League's work of Bible study. It supervises the work of each study class, and furnishes to the leaders, without charge, special assistance and printed helps for the teaching of the lessons.

Organizing a Bible Study Class.

The class may begin work at any time in the year, but in those courses which require twenty-five weeks for their completion, organization should, if possible, take place so that work may be begun early in October. The observance of Bible Study Rally Day will have great influence for good in this work of organization. The whole subject of Bible study may be presented at the Rally Day meeting.

Secure some one who is entirely competent to make a stirring inspirational address on the possibility, value, and importance of Bible study. It should be definite, direct, and devout. It should be the speech of a Bible student, seeking to win others to that study. Then, let the First Vice-President follow with a clear statement of the course which has been chosen, describing simply and clearly the text-book and the plan of study. It will be a help if copies of the text-book are at hand for examination.

An enrollment of Bible students should be secured at this meeting, while the interest is fresh and strong. Each person who enrolls will be expected to do four things: First, to attend the classes regularly; second, to secure a copy of the text-book; third, to prepare each lesson; fourth, to do as much of the special work assigned as possible.

The work of enrollment should not end with this first meeting. A personal canvass of the entire membership should be made, so that every one may have an opportunity of joining the class. No one need be ignored or excluded. It may be necessary in the beginning of Bible study work to do considerable urging, but for the sake of the individual and of the Church no effort should be spared to enroll in the class or classes as many of the Chapter members as possible.

If, however, only a few are willing to enroll, do not be discouraged. A class of two can do successful work. Better have fewer members who are in earnest than a large enrollment of those whose interest dies with the second meeting. A properly organized class will grow, both in interest and in numbers. If fifteen or more desire to take up the work, organize two classes. Ten members are usually enough for one class. Other things being equal, the smaller the class, the better the work. There is not so much personal study done in a large class.

THE LEADER.

The leader of the Bible study class should be selected with great care. Whenever possible, choose laymen for leaders. The pastor has enough on his hands already; apart from that, lay leadership is valuable for many reasons. The leader need not be a proficient Bible student, if he is one who believes in the value of the study and is willing to give much time to his work. These two qualifications are absolutely necessary. The helps provided by the Central Office are sufficiently full and definite, so that any one who has the slightest capacity for leadership, and is filled with the purpose to work, may make a real success of the class. The leader makes the class.

THE MEETINGS OF THE CLASS.

Meetings for study should by all means be held once a week during the life of the course. The time of meeting will be arranged to suit the majority of the members. It is better to appoint a week-night meeting, if possible. Do not let the Bible study class conflict with the Sunday school or with any other of the regular activities of the Church. It certainly should not meet at the Sunday school hour. The best place for the class meeting is the League room

MORNING WATCH, PERSONAL EVANGELISM.

of the church, if there is such a room. If there are good reasons for meeting away from the church, the size of the class will not be so great as to interfere with the use of private houses. The home of a class member is always preferable.

MAINTAINING THE INTEREST.

Let the class secure all the helps it can afford. The best work requires the best of reference works. Many leaders find it a decided advantage to have a reference library at the disposal of the entire class. The leader should note the catalogue of the Central Office, which contains a list of the best reference books at the lowest possible prices.

These books can be secured in various ways. A few individuals will purchase books for themselves; a class subscription might be taken; an appropriation from the Epworth League treasury might be made and the books then become a part of the Chapter library. In some Chapters the money has been secured by holding a "Library Entertainment."

Popularize the work by giving items to the local papers concerning the most important and successful feature of your class work.

Magnify private daily devotional Bible study. The more study of the Word for personal spiritual growth, the more certain the success of the class.

BIBLE STUDY AND THE MORNING WATCH.

These, being two, are one. That is to say, whoso will become a Comrade of the Morning Watch must become a student of the Bible. On the other hand, a Bible student, seeking a stated time for study, will be led in most instances to select the Morning Watch hour.

The arrangement of the daily work in some of the Epworth League text-books lends itself beautifully to the combination of Morning Watch and Bible study. Every Comrade should seek membership in a study class; every Bible student join the Morning Watch enrollment. Each purpose will strengthen the other.

THE EFFICIENT EPWORTHIAN.

The League Meeting on Rally Day.

The thing to be aimed at in this meeting is a Bible study class. If all the talk and prayer and song about the Word of God does not result in a definite movement to study that Word, the meeting will not be a success.

If the meeting is rightly managed it will arouse conviction. Do not let that conviction be wasted. Give it a chance to crystallize into definite action. Start a Bible study class.

Can not the leader provide for a stirring address on the importance of Bible study by one who studies the Bible? Do not get some one who has no record as a student, unless he is willing to close his speech with a confession of his neglect and a resolve to be the first member of the study class.

Sing the choice songs from the Hymnals which bear on the beauties and power of the Scriptures.

Arrange for the testimony of half a dozen people who are daily reading and studying the Bible.

Have a copy or two of the Bible study text-books on exhibition.

Look through the 119th Psalm for texts bearing on the value of and delight in the Word of God. Distribute them for comment in the testimony service.

The First Vice-President should be given at least ten minutes at the close that he may announce plans for the Bible study class and secure the enrollment of members. The plans should be as definite as possible.

Explain the courses. Tell about the scheme for daily study, plans for the harmony, map work, independent research, and other attractive elements in the course.

Begin the Bible study class enrollment at the close of the meeting. Don't let people get away from their newly-aroused convictions.

Distribute the literature of the Bible study courses.

MORNING WATCH, PERSONAL EVANGELISM.

Sample Programs for Rally Day.

I.

Song and prayer service, ten minutes.

The leader speaks: "Why should I read and heed the Word?"

Four brief addresses: "Bible study for my own good," "Bible study as an aid to personal work with the unsaved," "Bible study as related to the work of missions," "The life of Christ the central point in Bible study."

The Bible on Bible study: Selected references.

Personal testimonies: "How I use my Bible," "How the Bible 'finds' me," "Bible study and the Morning Watch," "The things that hinder."

Enrollment of the Bible study class.

II.

Song and prayer service.

The leader speaks: "Bible study as an element in the Christian's self-respect."

Brief addresses: "The direct value of Bible study," "The indirect gains of it," "Bible study for fellow-workers," "Where to begin."

Personal testimonies: "The Morning Watch as a help to Bible study," "What Bible study has meant to me," "The revelations that have rewarded my study."

Address: "Let us begin a Bible study class in this Chapter this year."

Enrollment of members and organization of the class.

III.

Song service.

Brief prayers of thanksgiving for the Word, and of petition for help to use it more faithfully.

Scripture lessons: Psa. 119: 73-80; Phil. 2: 14-16.

The leader speaks: "Why read the Word?"

A member speaks: "The spiritual value of God's Word."

Another member speaks: "The demand of God's Word on your life."

THE EFFICIENT EPWORTHIAN.

Some members testify: "How I read my Bible."
Other members testify: "What my Bible means to me."
Still others testify: "Things that hinder me in my use of the Bible."

The leader speaks again. He recommends the Morning Watch and the Bible study plans of the Epworth League.

The meeting closes with the League benediction, or the repeating in concert of Psa. 119:18, "Open Thou mine eyes, that I may behold wondrous things out of Thy law."

CHAPTER VIII

THE LEAGUE'S WORLD INTERESTS.

THE Department of World Evangelism represents the conviction which has been growing for years that the Epworth League should be definitely committed to a world-wide outlook and a world-wide purpose in its work of training the young people of Methodism for their places of leadership in the Methodist Church that is to be.

The Department of World Evangelism is intended to educate the members of the Epworth League in all the methods and movements of an organized effort at evangelization which touches every land,—our own first, in order that from our own the power and blessing that we have received may flow to all the rest. This involves a study of the various benevolences of the Church, and a study of the work and worth of Christian missions.

Then the department aims to convince all of their relation to the work of world evangelism. This involves the teaching of the truths of Christian stewardship and the insistent claim of all who have need, in whatever part of the world they may be found, upon all those who, by the grace of God, have those things which may supply the need.

Having educated and convinced, the final great work of the department is to inspire all our members with a steady, unswerving, undiscourageable zeal for the work of world evangelism. The prayer cycles and missionary literature are all bent to this end, that every Epworthian may be an eager, earnest, intelligent advocate of the work of bringing the knowledge of Christ to all the world in this generation.

The committee assigned for this department should number not less than three, and may be as large as can be secured. Its members ought to be believers in the idea underlying the department, or at least they should be open-minded with regard to it, and willing to receive all possible light.

The committee should be divided so as to provide for sub-committees to take charge of the various activities of the department. There should be, for example, a sub-committee to supervise each of the following forms of activities: the periodical missionary meeting, the special devotional topics on Christian philanthropies, the mission study class, the missionary library, the distribution of missionary literature, the study of other benevolences, the advocacy and systematic study of Christian stewardship. There is sufficient work here indicated to give each member of the committee a distinct and worthy task. There need be no drones in this section of the Epworth hive.

The Department of World Evangelism will make special effort to magnify and emphasize the monthly devotional meetings given to missions and other great benevolent and philanthropic work. The study classes will require its constant thought and care. It may make large use of a growing and valuable literature in every variety of Christian service. It should stimulate an intelligent study of the benevolences.

It is specially charged with the spreading of the Christian stewardship idea. It may plan and conduct missionary socials, which should be something more than missionary in name. It can help in the Sunday school monthly missionary meeting. It ought to introduce and popularize a definite cycle of prayer. It may make a collection of maps, charts, and other missionary material, which will be found exceedingly useful for display at special meetings.

The Timeliness of Mission Study.

The Epworth League is now a great school for instruction in missions. It is becoming, and will become increasingly, a field from which missionary recruits may be secured.

The most important duty of the Department of World Evangelism is to see that the work of missionary teaching is begun and sustained, no matter what else in the department may be allowed to languish. The reasons for mission study are simple and yet convincing.

THE LEAGUE'S WORLD INTERESTS.

Missions are a necessary part of full Christian living. There can be no permanent or productive missionary sentiment without intelligent ideas on missionary subjects. Foreign missions, with their vast and increasing demands for support, can not be kept going by semi-occasional rhetoric and emotion. Without the missionary idea of Christianity a healthy faith is impossible. Missionary interest is a real and large enrichment of the Christian life. We are debtors to the missionary idea for much of our opportunity of service. Missions furnish the missing link in the chain of Christian work. Nothing but a knowledge of the need of the world can furnish sufficient incentive to the fullest dedication of one's powers to the work of saving the world.

There is a great and adequate literature of missions. There are men and women who have first-hand knowledge, both of the mission fields and of the resources of the Church. Their knowledge is now within reach.

We have a newly increased interest in the subject of missions. It has come to the point of strategic importance in the forward movement of Christendom. It has political and social and commercial bearing on the life of our own land. There is no part of the work of the Church of Jesus Christ more worthy of study than the missionary enterprise.

Why Study Missions.

Because the missionary enterprise is the chief business of the Church. It is not merely incidental. It is not simply an outlet for the Church's surplus energy and cash. It is not a hobby, to be ridden by impracticable enthusiasts. It is the Church's business. For this the Church exists; to make missionaries, to send them, to support them, to reinforce them. If the assertion of this paragraph is doubted, test it by asking and answering this question, "If the missionary enterprise is not the Church's chief business, what is?"

Because knowledge of the missionary enterprise alone makes possible its proper support. It is not now properly supported. The Church is paying dollars for its pleasures, and dimes for its business. A Church which spends $10,000

THE EFFICIENT EPWORTHIAN.

a year on all its activities thinks it does well if it spends $1,000 of the total on gospel-extension work. And yet gospel extension is the Church's business. Spasmodic spurts in giving may occur under the stimulus of overwrought appeals and unfounded prophecies of tremendous movements soon to begin. But such stimulus is soon exhausted, and things are worse than before. If we knew enough of the real situation to give intelligently, we should give more, and not grow weary of the giving.

Because without mission study we can not understand the missionary problem. It is the Church's greatest problem, because it is both the most important and the most difficult of all her tasks. The "open door" is really open, but it opens on opportunity and toil, not on a ready-made harvest. Missionary work is necessarily slow, even under the best conditions. Hereditary instincts and ancient civilizations are not transformed in a day. There are instances in every mission field of faithful work for years without a single convert to show for it. The Christian at home is not likely to be patient, unless he understands how great a task his brethren in mission fields have set before them.

Because without mission study it is not easy to believe in missions at all. "Let every people have its own religion. It may not suit us, but it suits them. Why disturb them?" That is the argument of the uninformed and the unchristian. The national or racial religions have failed. Their excellencies have been corrupted, and some of them have their very origin in vileness. But much of heathenism is fair on the surface. At a distance it seems all that is beautiful and good. It must be studied as it is, and not as it seems, if missionary work is to be sustained. For only such study will reveal the need of Christ, which is the greatest need of every land of darkness and the shadow of death.

Because the missionary enterprise of to-morrow will fail without missionary intelligence. If the problem is great to-day, it is going to be vastly greater to-morrow. Every new advance is a new problem, a new demand on the home Church, a new challenge to Christian faith and courage. The widening borders can not be manned with the resources at present available. There must be a new measure of

THE LEAGUE'S WORLD INTERESTS.

advance in the provision of missionaries and money. The rate of increase is itself increasing. What the Church has done thus far is small compared to what she must do if her very victories are not to be the occasion of her failure. But how can these things be believed while Christians are unintelligent on the subject of mission work?

Because the advance of to-morrow, at home or abroad, depends upon to-day's young people. The number of overworked and wearied veterans in the field is greater than we imagine. Every mission field needs new blood, needs fresh, vigorous, strong young workers. They must come from the young people's societies, from the colleges and high schools of to-day. On the other hand, there is a generation of givers to missions which has about given all it can. Its earning capacity is smaller than it used to be. The young people who are coming to self-support, to the places of profitable work, must replenish the treasury. And, because of the enlarging field, they must have a new standard of giving. But all this will be realized only through a real understanding of the whole subject. All that means mission study.

The League a Producer of Missionaries.

A young woman reader of *The Epworth Herald*, on her way to the mission field, wrote from the steamer to the editor and told how her going has grown out of her work in the Epworth League.

It is a familiar story. Of course, almost every new missionary is an Epworthian, for few young Methodists with the missionary spirit escape service and training in the League. But, more than that, the direct impulse that carries these young people across the line of decision into missionary service comes, with cheerful frequency, from the Epworth League and its work.

The Epworth League is a missionary organization. It is committed to the missionary interpretation of Christian experience. It produces missionaries. If it didn't, it would need either a funeral or a revival. Just now, with the funeral indefinitely postponed, it could well afford to have a revival of missionary dedication.

THE EFFICIENT EPWORTHIAN.

As of old, the harvest is plenteous and the laborers are few. No Epworthian can ignore the obligation which that fact puts on him, to consider what he shall do with his life.

THE ADVANTAGES OF THE STUDY CLASS.

No one can study such a subject as well by himself as in a class. The class gives touch of mind with mind. It furnishes new points of view. It makes each member a helper of the others.

Experts in research work can do their best work alone, but a mission study class is not for experts.

Mass-meetings are not the solution of the mission study problem. They have very great excellencies, but, unless balanced by intelligent study, they give distorted and fragmentary views of missionary work.

A missionary reading circle may be interesting, but it does not set its members at work. It is "too optional."

The study class is responsible for the large gain in mission study which has been secured in the past few years. It furnishes orderly and systematic plans, taking up definite subjects, on which the members can make personal preparation.

The study class stimulates a taste for a higher grade of missionary reading. The missionary libraries, which have had so phenomenal a sale, have been purchased and read by Chapters which have had mission study classes. These books, in many cases, have been the foundation of extensive collections of missionary literature.

MISSION STUDY RALLY DAY.

In September a Sunday is designated as study class Rally Day. If the Chapter purposes to have a class or classes in the text-book, as of course, it should, the Second Vice-President will have the book for exhibition, and the devotional meeting topic will center on the book. The entire conduct of the meeting should be in charge of the Department of World Evangelism.

The chief purpose of the day is twofold: to centralize thought and interest on the general theme, and to make

THE LEAGUE'S WORLD INTERESTS.

possible the organization of one or more successful study classes. In accomplishing these two results, the material and suggestions of this section should be freely used.

The member designated to conduct the work of mission study should have mastered the selected text-book before Rally Day, at least sufficiently to be able to give an intelligent and interesting outline of the work it offers.

It is a fine opportunity for the presentation of facts, plans, and figures, showing what can be done in missionary work by the local Chapter.

Rally Day Suggestions.

The program suggested below may be modified to suit special plans, but it should have substantially the same themes.

Sing missionary hymns. Do n't stop with "Greenland's icy mountains." Be sure to sing "The Son of God goes forth to war," and "O Zion, haste."

Insist on the interest to be found in mission study. Prove it by examples from personal experience.

Set forth in some graphic way "What our Church is doing to-day."

Emphasize the fact that mission study is a tracing of the journeys of our Lord among the nations as truly as a study of the Gospels is a tracing of His going up and down the Holy Land.

If possible, display at the meeting a large map of the field for the year's study. The best is a home-made map with bold outlines and but little lettering or other detail.

A preliminary canvass should be made before the meeting, so that several members may be ready at the first call of the leader to state, "Why I am willing to join the class."

The general invitation may be made more direct if, during the meeting, enrollment cards are passed around among the members.

Do not be satisfied with the enrollment at this meeting. Let the Second Department make a personal canvass for members of the study class.

Begin the class work at once. If only six or eight are

enrolled, never mind. That is enough for a beginning. The main thing is to begin.

If possible, the leader of the class should be selected beforehand. Then, while interest on the subject is still fresh, the class organization may be completed at the close of the meeting, and the time and place of the first class hour fixed.

Suggested Programs.

I.

Selected missionary hymns.

Scripture lessons. (Isa. 52:7-10; Rom. 10:11-15.) Brief comment on the missionary application of this Scripture by the reader.

Prayers. For willingness to know more about missions; that God, through the League Chapters, will raise up an intelligent, eager, praying, missionary Church.

Three-minute talks on mission study. The why of it, the how of it, the when of it, the who of it, and the what of it.

One-minute testimonies on the gains of mission study, from members of former years' classes, or others who know.

Prayers. For the carrying of the gospel to every part of the mission field; for the field itself, that God will keep open the doors of opportunity until His Church shall arouse and enter in; that God may overrule all political and social changes in the mission field, that they may minister to the furtherance of the gospel; for all who are now at work in mission lands.

Invitation to join the study class.

Announcement of time and place of the class.

Benediction. "And He shall speak peace unto the heathen; and His dominion shall be from sea even to sea, and from the river even to the ends of the earth." (Zech. 9:10.)

II.

Missionary song service.

Scripture lessons. (Psa. 72:8-11; Zech. 8:20-23.)

A prayer service; thanksgiving for the missions of the past, of which we are beneficiaries; prayer for willingness

THE LEAGUE'S WORLD INTERESTS.

to learn of the missions of the present; intercession for missions and missionaries; pledge to do our part in making the Church of to-morrow a more intelligent missionary Church.

"Reasons for missionary interest," discussed by the leader in his introductory talk.

The argument for mission study. Two-minute talks by six members on the reasons given under "Why study missions?"

"The advantages of a study class," discussed by a member of last year's class, or by the organizer of the class to be enrolled at this meeting.

"Why I am willing to join the class." One-minute reasons given by those who have already decided.

A general invitation to enroll in the class.

THE WORK OF THE MISSION STUDY CLASS.

There is a large amount of literature ready to hand on the mission study class and its work. Every year this literature grows more abundant, and no mission study plans should be made without having full access to the latest material.

A notice that you purpose to organize a study class in your Chapter, if sent to the Department of Mission Study and Stewardship, 740 Rush Street, Chicago, will bring full information and most helpful suggestions. And all that is sent will have direct application to the particular field or subject which is the current theme of mission study throughout the League.

Other Accessories.—The annual reports of the Missionary Boards, Home and Foreign, contain an accurate record of denominational activity. They will be helpful in furnishing material for special topics and discussions on current questions. They are sent free upon application.

The printed reports of the great missionary conventions will usually be found in the pastor's library, or they may be obtained of the Methodist Book Concern. They contain the best obtainable series of addresses on our Methodist missionary activities at home and abroad.

THE EFFICIENT EPWORTHIAN.

The Board of Foreign Missions publishes a series of booklets designed to give a condensed view of the great mission countries. Booklets on practically every mission field of the Methodist Church are now available.

Special leaflets on the missions in the various fields are published by the Home and Foreign Boards. Catalogues may be secured from the Board's literature departments. See addresses on page 195.

The more prominent papers and magazines are constantly printing articles relating to mission fields which are of great value. Where public, college, or private libraries are accessible, an index of all articles relating to the country being studied might be prepared by some member of the class. The list will be very valuable in the assignment of topics.

Libraries.—Special reference libraries, prepared for use in connection with the several text-books, will be found exceedingly helpful in mission study work. They are essential to a class that expects to do the most thorough type of work. In the outline helps which are furnished to the leader, suggested topics for papers will be found together with special reference to these libraries. But inability to secure the reference libraries should not discourage the organization of a class. Many classes have done excellent work without such help.

It will add to the interest if the members will make a scrapbook of current news from mission fields, reporting each week on the main points. The Church papers are full of such material, and helpful articles will often be found in the secular press.

A good map is indispensable for even a brief study of any country. An excellent map will be found in each of the text-books. A large wall-map of most countries can often be obtained from a local book-store or borrowed from the public schools.

Outline maps of China, Japan and Korea, India, and Africa, printed on paper, have been prepared for the use of mission study classes. These outline maps may be obtained for twenty cents each.

THE LEAGUE'S WORLD INTERESTS.

A missionary map of the world will also be very helpful. Such a map is available; price, $3.50. In size it is 6 x 12 feet. The map is printed on good muslin, and is in seven colors, showing the prevailing religions of the world.

It will be very effective to have made in motto form some of the striking words of missionaries and missionary workers, and to place them on the wall of the study class room. A set of attractive mottoes is listed in the Literature Catalogue of the Board of Foreign Missions.

The stereopticon and the stereoscope offer an opportunity of genuine enjoyment and real profit in the experience of seeing the mission lands while seated in the class or lecture room. For a profitable social entertainment the stereoscope can hardly be excelled, while the stereopticon will be found of great value in public meetings.

Correspondence.—Unless otherwise specified, all correspondence concerning matters relating to the Second Department should be addressed to the Department of Mission Study and Stewardship, 740 Rush Street, Chicago.

THE MISSIONARY DEVOTIONAL MEETING.

The frequent missionary meeting at the time of the regular devotional service calls for unusually careful preparation. If definite planning is neglected the meeting will be dull, dry, and dead. In the missionary meeting, voluntary and extemporary participation will be more difficult to secure than in any other meeting, hence all those who can be enlisted should be instructed beforehand in the parts they are to take. Begin the preparation two, three, or four weeks ahead. For the most part, insist that the members of the Chapter shall provide the program. Do not depend too much upon outsiders. Put the responsibility where it belongs—upon the home Chapter and its members.

Whenever a missionary devotional meeting is scheduled on the topic cards, the leader should at once send to the Department of Missionary Education, 150 Fifth Avenue, New York, for the special helps provided by that department.

The department also furnishes each year a special program related to the mission study theme of the year. This program is particularly effective when presented by the members of the mission study class, although it may be given successfully by any group of Epworthians.

The music of a missionary meeting is an essential element in its success. Some people think that when they have sung "From Greenland's icy mountains," they have given all the missionary flavor to the music that is necessary. But there are other missionary hymns—really great ones—and a little search for them before the meeting will be amply rewarded in increased interest and enjoyment.

Be sparing of essays and readings. If it seems to be best to have some participants read either original or selected material, be sure that the matter is brief and bright, and pertinent to the theme of the meeting.

Use maps and charts freely. If you can not find such material of this sort as you need, there is large room for home-made maps and charts. These need not be elaborate, and excellence of workmanship is not absolutely necessary. The main thing is that they shall be perfectly legible and tell their story briefly and graphically.

Much may be made of the use in public of letters from the mission field. These can be very helpful in a missionary meeting, provided they are not too long and that they are well read. It might seem superfluous to suggest that whoever reads a letter from the field in public should first read it over carefully in private. Missionary handwriting is no better than the handwriting of any other busy people, and some of it can not be effectively read at first sight.

These missionary letters will be of more interest if the Chapter is using the Parish Abroad Plan, formerly called the Station Plan, and the correspondence comes from the field where the Chapter's contributions are being applied. It furnishes the nearest approach to a living link between the home and the foreign field that can be devised. This will also make the letter more interesting to the writer, since he will feel that he is writing to people who are directly concerned in his work, and the letter which interests the writer is for that very reason more likely to interest the recipients.

THE LEAGUE'S WORLD INTERESTS.

SPECIAL THEMES AND PLANS.

Chapters which are so situated as to be able to secure a stereopticon may provide an occasionally welcome variety by utilizing that implement. The Committee on Conservation and Advance has available a list of stereopticon lectures which can be used to great advantage.

Another means of occasional interest is the use of curios and other articles from the missionary field. It is often possible to secure a really interesting collection of such articles, and, if they are not made the main object of interest, but are used to illustrate and make vivid the theme of the meeting, they will be of very great help. But it should be remembered that the curios are merely a means to an end, and that the meeting is not an exhibition of missionary bric-a-brac.

It will be well to hold a missionary meeting occasionally in which the details of the organization and management of Methodist missions shall be given. The Missionary Boards of the Methodist Episcopal Church are great and wonderful organizations. They administer incomes totaling $15,000,000 a year, and the activities of several thousand missionaries at home and abroad. Their work is too little known. A free use of the annual reports and of the admirable tracts and leaflets which are now available will make possible a most interesting and informing missionary meeting.

One missionary meeting which should certainly be held in every Chapter of the Epworth League is a survey of the Methodist foreign mission field. The Board of Foreign Missions publishes a series of maps covering this field, and the annual report will furnish the statistics. Each great division of the field should be assigned to one member of the Chapter, who will give briefly a sort of survey of the work, its workers, its methods, and its history.

Another most interesting missionary meeting may be arranged with stories from the annals of missions. No chapter of the Church's history contains more heroic, thrilling, and pathetic incidents than the story of modern missions. In using this material one word of caution must be spoken. Do not permit any one to read the stories selected.

THE EFFICIENT EPWORTHIAN.

Let them be memorized, as to their main facts, before the meeting, and then told in simple, natural language.

A series of missionary debates can be made both interesting and profitable. A few subjects suggest themselves at once: The question of the value of modern missions; the comparative value of married or unmarried persons as missionaries; the question as to how far missionaries should be engaged in the work of secular education; and the question whether missionaries should receive a regular salary or merely the promise of support,—that is to say, should missionaries be supported like ministers in the home field, or like deaconesses? Many other questions for debate will be suggested as one reads the missionary literature found in our Church periodicals and elsewhere. Indeed, almost any missionary topic may be transformed into a debatable proposition by putting it into the form of a question. For example: the topic, "Educational Work in the Mission Field," stated thus, "Should missionaries provide instruction in secular branches?" becomes a first-class subject for debate.

"Are the native converts loyal?" The records of missionary work are full of stirring incidents which answer "yes" to this question. A search through the missionary libraries will provide more material than can possibly be used in any one evening.

"The rewards of faith" is a suggestive theme. The first converts in many of our mission fields were not secured until years of patient labor had passed, apparently without result. Gather up the story of a few such cases, notably the first Chinese convert, the first Hindu convert, and the first years of work in Japan.

A "report" meeting may be filled with interest. The reports of the Missionary Boards are issued each year. Get them as soon as possible, and use the material they contain to show the progress of the work in the past year. These reports always contain abundant illustrative material, direct from the field.

Charts are easily made, and are very effective. A list of subjects for charts is given elsewhere. Many ready-

THE LEAGUE'S WORLD INTERESTS.

made charts can be had from the Board of Foreign Missions, as will be seen by reference to its Literature Catalog.

A cheap and effective way of adding to the interest by means of maps is open to any one who can get the use of a hectograph or a mimeograph. The map may be traced from a good atlas, and as many copies printed as may be needed. If the map is a simple outline, so much the better, since then the class members may fill in the outline as the study progresses.

Hints for the Missionary Meeting.

Book Reviews.—At each meeting provide for a brief review of one of the books in the Chapter's missionary library, preferably one which bears on the theme of the meeting. This will increase the interest in the library and get its books into circulation.

The Missionary Physician.—Let this meeting be as complete a presentation of the subject of medical missions as can be made. The history of medical missions is full of interesting and convincing stories concerning the great value of this form of missionary activity.

A Question Bee.—Start a missionary question box. Let the questions be handed in at some time previous to the date of the meeting, so that preparation for answering them may be made. The wider the range of questions, the more interesting the meeting will be.

Missionary Hindrances.—There are three great obstacles to the progress of missions—rum, opium, and slavery. These may be vividly presented by means of the material available in every collection of missionary literature.

Studies of Great Missionaries.—The missionary libraries and such text-books as "The Price of Africa," "Princely Men in the Heavenly Kingdom," "Heroes of the Cross in America," and "Servants of the King," offer material sufficient for most interesting studies of typical missionary leaders. A few of these are named here. The list, of course, may be greatly extended: William Butler, Egerton Ryerson Young, Verbeck of Japan, Bishop Thoburn, Mackay of Uganda, David Livingstone, William Carey,

THE EFFICIENT EPWORTHIAN.

Gilmore of Mongolia, John G. Paton, Isabella Thoburn, Adoniram Judson.

The Profits of Missions.—A most striking exhibit of the gain of missions may be made, dividing the subject into these parts: The commercial gains, the geographical gains, the scientific gains, the gains of civilization in general, the spiritual gains.

Missions in Song.—A song service in which the great missionary hymns are used will be a decided success if properly managed. It will be a revelation to a great many people that we have not exhausted the list of missionary hymns when we have sung "From Greenland's icy mountains" and "The morning light is breaking." The following hymns are available for such a service, many of the best of them being found in the Methodist Hymnal:

"Onward, Christian soldiers."
"On the mountain's top appearing."
"Savior, sprinkle many nations."
"Christ for the world we sing."
"Speed Thy servants, Savior, speed them."
"From Greenland's icy mountains."
"Fling out the banner, let it float."
"Forward be our watchword."
"Jesus shall reign where'er the sun."
"The morning light is breaking."
"All people that on earth do dwell."
"O Master, let me walk with Thee."
"Jesus calls us o'er the tumult."
"We give Thee but Thine own."
"Before Jehovah's awful throne."
"The Son of God goes forth to war."
"O, where are kings and empires now?"
"Glorious things of Thee are spoken."
"Lift up your heads, ye gates of brass."
"Ye Christian heralds, go proclaim."
"Hail to the Lord's anointed."
"The whole wide world for Jesus."
"The Church's one Foundation."
"Eternal Father, Thou hast said."
"All hail the power of Jesus' name."

THE LEAGUE'S WORLD INTERESTS.

"Thou whose almighty word."
"Soon may the last glad song arise."
"Tell it out among the heathen that the Lord is King."
"Watchman, tell us of the night."
"See how great a flame aspires."
"Hark! the song of jubilee."
"Kingdom of light! whose morning-star."
"O Zion, haste, Thy mission high fulfilling."

SOME SAMPLE PROGRAMS.

The Methodist Fields.—Ask eight members to represent the various mission fields, assigning one to each. Let each speaker put the case as a native Christian of the country he represents would put it. The extent of the field, the number of workers, the forms of the work, the successes attained, and the unsatisfied needs that press on every hand should be the main points emphasized. The more the speaker identifies himself with the people for whom he speaks, the better. The speeches must be short, of course.

Perhaps there will be an opportunity to push the Parish Abroad Plan as the most practical way for everybody to help answer the "Macedonian call." Write to the Board of Foreign Missions, 150 Fifth Avenue, New York City, for particulars of the plan and ways of working it.

Four excellent methods of conducting this meeting are given below.

The map method. Get a map of the world big enough to be seen from all parts of the room. Mark on it, or otherwise indicate, the location of the great mission fields of the Church. With pointer in hand, some one will give briefly the outstanding facts concerning each field.

The "advocate" method. Appoint members as "advocates" of the various fields. Ask each one to make a two or three-minute plea for the people whom he represents, stating their condition, their needs, their desire for the gospel, and other pertinent facts.

The chart method. Prepare charts which will show the area of each field, its population, number of communicants, number of workers, amount spent for the work, number of converts last year. Use your own Conference as a basis of comparison. For example, a certain Conference has an area of 13,000 square miles. Korea has 84,424 square miles. If a black line two inches long represents the Conference area, a line nearly fourteen inches long will represent Korea. Apply this method to the other details.

The personal method. After one or more of the foregoing methods have been used, let three or four be ready to answer this question, "In the light of the great commission, and of the opportunities available on every hand, what is *my duty?*" Then throw the question open for voluntary answers.

Abundant material for this meeting may be found in the report of the Board of Foreign Missions and in leaflets and other literature published by the society.

Women's Work in the Mission Field.—The great purpose of this meeting is to develop intelligent interest in work among the women of mission lands.

Write to the nearest depot of supplies of the Woman's Foreign Missionary Society for a package of literature. Twenty-five cents will secure a rich variety of fresh and helpful leaflets. The various branches maintain supply depots in Boston, New York, Philadelphia; Baltimore, Md.; Cincinnati, O.; Chicago; Des Moines, Iowa; Minneapolis, Minn.; Lincoln, Neb.; San Francisco, Cal.; Los Angeles, Cal.; Portland, Oregon.

Among the many suggestive themes available are:
"Women under other religions."
"The helplessness of heathen women."
"The ministry of woman."
"Medical missions."
"What Christianity has done for women."

A Missionary Inspiration Meeting.—Have many missionary prayers.

Make them special, not general.

Get maps and charts if you can. If they are not large enough to be seen easily, transfer one of them to the blackboard.

The blackboard work will be more effective, even though rather crude, if it can be done as an accompaniment to the oral explanation of it.

THE LEAGUE'S WORLD INTERESTS.

Ask these questions in calling for testimony: What is the next thing you can do for missions? What can this Chapter do, more than it is doing? This Church?

What one good thing do you know about missionary work?

What is the greatest missionary argument?

What great missionary book have you read? What has it done for you?

What is the real difference between home missions and foreign missions?

How can we know that we have power to do missionary work?

Why is the missionary called to make greater sacrifices than the people who stay at home?

What is wrong with the average Christian's notions about missions?

Is there too much emphasis put upon the question of giving?

What is the net gain to missions from this meeting?

Missionary Socials.

The Second Department can take the old-time social and give it a new lease of life. The social can be undertaken with a purpose which will put it above the level of mere entertainment. It can be made more entertaining than ever, and yet produce results in information, purpose, and power for the benefit of the missionary enterprise.

In planning for missionary socials the missionary libraries will prove invaluable. The material they contain offers almost limitless opportunity for social evenings of instruction and interest. Without going into details, a few characteristic socials are here suggested. The details of their working out will not be difficult, and each subject suggested will furnish the keynote for its own preparation.

Games.—Spend an evening playing foreign games, using the characteristic native games of the country under consideration.

The Curio Social.—This offers endless variety. In nearly every Church there are people who possess numerous mementos of travel, and souvenirs sent from various parts of the world. An exhibition of these, with some comment on the countries of their origin, and other information which will be suggested by the articles exhibited, will furnish an interesting evening's diversion.

The Epoch Social.—Take a period of time—a century, half century, or a decade. Let different speakers sketch the progress of missions within the period selected. Give statistics of growth and development. Tell of the new opportunities for missionary work within the time under consideration. Give the notable events in missionary history. Let this meeting emphasize the rapid march of the Kingdom of God in mission fields.

A Missionary Tour.—Plan a journey to three or four mission fields. Let each mission be represented by the home of one of the members. After a brief stay at the first mission field, and an inspection of whatever material illustrating the work of the field may be available, the company passes to the next house in order, and so on until the tour has been completed. The decorations at each place will be in harmony with the customs of the field represented.

A Founders' Meeting.—At this meeting have brief biographies of the great mission founders, Zinzendorf, Carey, Mills, Butler, Taylor, and others.

A Surprise Program.—A surprise program will bring some desirable results. One or two weeks before the meeting, write a letter to eight or ten of your brightest people. Suggest six or eight parts to be taken in a missionary program, such as telling a story, singing a song, giving a Bible reading or a recitation, reading a poem or a paper. Number the parts, and ask each to designate which he will do. In this way each person will be likely to be exactly fitted. They must not tell what parts they have. Do not announce the parts at the meeting. Give the speakers numbers at the service, and they can appear unannounced in the order of their numbers.

Essay Contest.—Have an essay contest. Limit by age or not, as you choose. High school students will usually enter with zest. Purchase a medal, to be given to the one who writes and delivers the best essay on some mission subject. Make the theme a person, a country, a station, or a

THE LEAGUE'S WORLD INTERESTS.

truth. Count thought, composition, and delivery. Advertise extensively. Name, in a circular, valuable books of reference. Print a few simple rules with the announcement.

The Machinery of Missions.—Few people know how missionaries are sent out, how they live, and how they are controlled. Ignorance in this respect loses support and arouses opposition. Describe in a paper the composition, methods, meeting time, and missionary tests of the General Missionary Committees of the Home and Foreign Boards. It might be well to compare different denominations. Some imagine that much money is used for expenses. Others hold the notion that missionaries receive large salaries and live extravagantly. The "Bishop's Conversion," by Ellen Blackmar Maxwell, is a fine answer to this heresy. The consecration and self-sacrifice of missionaries will touch sympathy and win support.

An Imaginary Trip.—When studying a country, draw a map on the blackboard. Provide cards with the names of stations on them. When a place is mentioned in the study, let some one come forward and stick the card with a thumb-tack into its proper location on the map. (Use the same method in speaking of the missionaries, and place the names of the workers on the map at the stations.) Let a good speaker take an imaginary trip, describing the customs seen and experiences met until he comes to a missionary station. Then an appointed person appears, places the card at the proper place, and tells about the work at that point. The speaker then resumes his trip until another station is reached, when another appointed person places another card and describes the work. So it continues until the trip is completed.

An Information Social.—Large maps showing the mission stations may be hung around the room. If none of these are yet available, ask the young men to prepare them from the maps in the magazines and reports. Four feet by three is a good size. White paper pasted on calico, a brush, and a little ink will not cost much. Colored inks, or diluted aniline dyes, may be used with good effect to show the different districts. Use diagram showing the growth of the missions, the proportion of heathen and Christian population, and the money spent for the work of the field.

Curiosities from the mission fields may be explained and examined. Idols that have been worshiped prove interesting.

Books of photographs, as well as some good missionary biographies, should be laid upon the tables for inspection.

One or two short letters from persons in the foreign field may be read. But they must be lively, interesting, and to the point.

Of course, missionary hymns will be sung, but a hymn in a foreign language copied on the blackboard, and sung by the Music Committee, will add to the interest of the meeting.

A Ceremonial Social.—Spend an evening in reproducing some of the striking social and political ceremonies of various mission lands. It may be wise to limit the ceremonies to one country, or a broader field may be occupied and typical ceremonies of mission countries may be reproduced.

THE CYCLE OF PRAYER.

The world needs to-day more than anything else a constant devotional study of the Bible accompanied by believing prayer. It is suggested that a Prayer Cycle be used in keeping the Morning Watch, which consists in setting aside the first moments of each day for devotional Bible study and secret prayer.

In using such a cycle strive to avoid formality, irregularity, haste, indolence, insufficient preparation, and limitation of our prayers to intercession. Rather let us be fervent in spirit, joyful and thankful, asking for definite things, and believing that our prayers will be answered when we ask according to His will.

It would greatly increase our power in prayer if each person would make a careful devotional study of the Bible with reference to prayer, and thus come to a clear knowledge of the prayer life—its teachings, conditions, promises, and examples. Secure, if possible, "With Christ in the School of Prayer" and "The Ministry of Intercession," by Andrew Murray, each 75 cents, and "The Morning Watch,"

THE LEAGUE'S WORLD INTERESTS.

"Secret Prayer," and "Bible Study for Personal Growth," by John R. Mott, and "Prayer and Missions," by Robert E. Speer.

It is desired that every person adopting one of these Cycles of Prayer be very faithful in the observance of its use, because in united prayer there is untold power.

Prayer and missions are not chance neighbors. They are close kin. No missionary record of ancient or modern times has been without its history of prevailing prayer. And not missionaries only praying, but devout folk, often obscure folk, in the home church.

The mission study books of past years have abundance of material which will illustrate the power of prayer and remarkable answers to prayer in the mission field. Every missionary who has won success will testify that the use of prayer in his work has been the chief secret of its progress.

DIRECT CONTACT WITH MISSIONARIES.

Not every Epworth League can be so fortunate as to secure a visit from a missionary, but almost any League can secure the personal touch that comes through correspondence.

Everybody wants a work of his own, a definite object to support on the foreign field. People like to hear of good done by their gifts. The Board of Foreign Missions, 150 Fifth Avenue, New York City, has worked out the PARISH ABROAD PLAN as a way of securing to Churches, Sunday schools, Epworth Leagues, and to individuals this living link—the direct personal touch with a particular mission field and a definite task.

It is their purpose to secure for each missionary and each district in the foreign field a constituency at home, thus bringing into the lives of our missionaries and native workers those great increments of strength which come from the prayers, the messages, and the love of an organized circle of friends and co-laborers here in the homeland.

Money contributed on the PARISH ABROAD PLAN goes to pay the salaries of missionaries and native workers; to aid in the evangelization of districts and circuits; for the

THE EFFICIENT EPWORTHIAN.

support of native Churches in need; for itinerating, property repairs and maintenance, and all the various items involved in the general expense of a work that belts the globe.

In some cases the Epworth Leagues of a district join in taking the full support of a missionary who is definitely assigned to them, in which case his letters are duplicated at the office of the Board and forwarded to the Leagues concerned. In other cases, the Epworth League will join with its home Church and Sunday school in the support of a foreign parish. In still other cases the League takes for itself a definite piece of work in the foreign field, with which it is kept in touch through correspondence with the missionary or native worker in charge. Full information as to this plan can be obtained by writing to the Missionary Secretaries, 150 Fifth Avenue, New York City.

Many Churches are in the habit of sending gifts to home missionaries on our frontiers, or in the more destitute sections of the homeland. Some Epworth Leagues might like to send a Christmas box or other gifts to the foreign field. Such a box, if filled with wisely selected gifts, would be greatly appreciated. It must be remembered, however, that in many cases there is a considerable duty to be paid, especially in Japan and Korea. Cases have been known where missionaries who could ill afford it have paid more in duty than the contents of the box were really worth to them. This question of duty to be paid should be taken into consideration before the box is sent, and provision made so that this expense may not fall to the missionary.

It happens very frequently that a missionary's family in a foreign land lives amidst the most bare and unattractive surroundings. Luxuries are not to be thought of. Under these circumstances a missionary box from an Epworth League Chapter would be a veritable Godsend. Omit necessities from the box. The bare materials of subsistence will be secured somehow. But the things which the missionary family lacks are the little extravagances in which we indulge ourselves so lavishly, but which to them are entirely out of the question. The missionary may long to buy a few modern books, but where is the money to come

THE LEAGUE'S WORLD INTERESTS.

from? His wife and family may desire to read the latest new story that sells in this country by the thousands. A copy slipped into the missionary box would be exceedingly welcome. Even a little candy of a quality that will stand transportation would be much more enthusiastically received than some people imagine.

Every woman can think of things that a woman likes to have—the little incidental belongings which go to make up the charm in the home, but which are counted in the missionary household under the head of luxuries that can be dispensed with. All these things and many others will suggest themselves to any group of thoughtful people, will make the preparation and sending and receiving of a missionary box a matter of unalloyed delight.

Other Missionary Material.

Do not stop with the reference libraries. They are merely a beginning of missionary literature. Start a missionary library that will aim at one hundred or more vigorous and interesting volumes. Do not be afraid if it rivals or even excels the Sunday school library. Use the missionary periodicals, the missionary reports, and any other available literature.

Make a missionary scrapbook. Some of the best missionary information is found in the current periodicals, and some of the most attractive and interesting pictures are in the same papers. Unless it is captured at the time it appears it will be lost. The missionary scrapbook may be made a most useful and valuable addition to the missionary library.

Beware of antiquated missionary literature. Much of it is not at all suited to present-day needs. Do not put a book on the shelves because it was given to the Epworth League for that purpose. Let somebody of sense and discrimination read the book. If it is morbid or one-sided, or in any way unsuited to the needs of the Chapter, do not use it.

The Department of Mission Study and Stewardship is always ready to send lists of current missionary literature, whether in leaflet, pamphlet, or book form. Make free use

THE EFFICIENT EPWORTHIAN.

of the Department's facilities, which are for this very purpose. And be sure to get its most helpful material on our League representatives in foreign fields.

Charts, especially if they are made by members of the class, have a value entirely distinct from and greater than any other missionary device. Anybody can make a missionary chart. A small sketch may be made, then enlarged to any size convenient. The subjects for missionary charts are well-nigh infinite in their variety.

Suggestions for Missionary Charts.—Comparative statistics: Of population, of giving and spending, of heathen and Christian areas, of proportionate number of preachers to communicants, of proportionate number of preachers to population, of the rate of growth in heathen and in Christian countries.

The reflex influence of missions: On the Church at home, on commerce, on the growth and development of nations, on language and literature, on explorations, on industrial development.

The increase of opportunity, the distribution of languages, the increase of written languages, the increase of Bible translations, doors opened by world politics and civilization.

FREE HELPS FOR THE SECOND DEPARTMENT.

Perhaps there are as many as a hundred Second Vice-Presidents who do not yet know what large provision is made for them by the Mission Study and Stewardship Department of the Epworth League Central Office.

If the hundred will read what follows, they will become enlightened.

This active and most helpful Department will send, to any Second Vice-President or devotional meeting leader who asks for it, special material on *any* missionary subject assigned as a regular topic in the League devotional meeting.

The department will also send, to any leader of a mission study class who reports the fact that such a class has

THE LEAGUE'S WORLD INTERESTS.

been organized, full directions, prepared by experts, for the successful conduct of the class.

Still further, the department invites correspondence on all the problems of missionary education in the League, and will furnish expert assistance in the work of solving those problems.

All this help is free, except that in some cases there is a small charge for booklets and other material, usually less than the cost of printing.

THE MODEL STUDY CLASS.

Divide it like an old-fashioned spelling school. The teacher selects two captains.

The captains choose sides, taking everyone in the class.

Three points of contest are accepted: (1) Any pertinent statement about the lesson. (2) Any proper question on the lesson, to be answered next session. (3) Any right answer to the questions asked.

After the first session follow this order: (1) Answers to the questions asked in the previous session. (2) Any statement concerning the lesson. (3) The questions for the next session. Each side has first chance with questions raised by the other side.

The captain coaches his side; sometimes they meet between sessions. The captain calls for questions, statements, and answers, and keeps the records.

The teacher acts as referee.

The Mission Study Department suggested this, and tried it at some Institutes a few years ago; it worked so successfully that it had much commendation, and many Leagues have tried it, and approved it.

It saves from the lecture method.

It develops the two captains as leaders.

It inspires the students to study.

It causes the owning of books.

It is such a simple method! But it is like play, and the score is worth much to every member.

We recommend its acquaintance to every Second Vice-President in the whole League. Its address is 740 Rush Street, Chicago.

THE EFFICIENT EPWORTHIAN.

More Formal Missionary Entertainments.

The Department of Mission Study and Stewardship will suggest material for missionary entertainments of a more ambitious character than any for whose description there is space in this book. Many popular programs, pageants, and plays are available, and new ones are constantly being added. Every Second Vice-President should be sure recorded as to name and address, with the Department, and should consult it freely for help in the selection and use of such special material.

Material for the Study of Benevolences.

Each of the benevolent societies publishes an annual report giving in detail the work of the society. These are interesting, compact, and complete. The committee should obtain each of these reports each year, and preserve them as part of the library of the Department of World Evangelism. They will be useful as references in preparing programs, for individual investigation of the work of the various societies, and for tracing the development of the work from year to year. They will be sent free of charge to any one making application to the secretaries of the various Boards.

The Year-Book of the Methodist Episcopal Church contains information concerning every phase of our Church work, and should be in the hands of the committee. There is given for each benevolent cause a brief survey of its organization and development, together with a summary of the work of the past year, including some pointed, vital, and interesting statistics. (Price, 50 cents; postage paid.)

Some of the Boards publish official monthly or quarterly papers, which contain contributions from leaders and active field workers, telling of the peculiar part these societies are occupying in the evangelization of the world. These will be especially interesting to the young people. Subscribe for them, and add them to the library of the Chapter.

All of these Boards furnish leaflets and tracts containing valuable facts and attractive incidents and anecdotes. Se-

THE LEAGUE'S WORLD INTERESTS.

cure several copies of each of these and fasten them together to form small booklets, and circulate these as books from your library.

Use a system of pledges for the reading of these different publications in connection with the missionary library work. All literature of this department should be merged in the missionary library scheme.

Secure the circulation of our weekly Church papers, which abound in good, fresh material. Let one copy be bought or borrowed for the library, and get as many private subscriptions as you can secure. Let prayer and facts take the place of the monotonous meeting which you have so often had.

Arrange the collection of material into scrapbooks, folders, or envelopes, alphabetically filed, or prepare a card catalogue with six divisions, one for each benevolent Board.

Information concerning Church benevolences can readily and properly be presented at a regular devotional meeting of the Chapter.

Occasionally the devotional topic will pertain entirely to some one of these benevolences. At such times the First Vice-President might turn the whole service over to the Department of World Evangelism.

Throughout the year many opportunities will arise because of the relation of the regular topic to one or more of these benevolent themes. Instead of the testimony meeting, perhaps it would be possible to arrange for a symposium of interesting facts to illustrate the Scripture lesson and the leader's remarks.

The social meetings of the Chapter may be utilized in co-operation with the Fourth Department. Programs are often arranged with the work of poets, missionaries, and great preachers. When the Fourth Vice-President is looking for something new, let him propose an evening among the colored people of the South, describing their literary and professional schools, and the work of industrial education. In this meeting follow the motto of the famous colored man, to "Do a common thing in an uncommon way," and your evening will be a success.

Plans should be made several weeks in advance for

THE EFFICIENT EPWORTHIAN.

securing material and utilizing every opening which may be found for the imparting of facts concerning the various benevolences.

What One Chapter Did.

It would be a fascinating thing if we could trace every dollar of benevolent money to its final destination. That cannot be done actually, but in imagination we can follow the process.

Here is a Chapter whose members every year give about $150 for the regular benevolences. What has that Chapter done?

It has supported two native teachers, one in India and one in China, who have kept alight the torch of Christian hope in the midst of heathenism, with famine, prejudice, and pestilence all about them.

It has provided windows and doors for a little church in a neighborhood where the gospel of Jesus Christ will be a power long after the givers of the money have gone home to heaven.

It has sent two hundred tracts to a group of immigrants just landed on our shores, greeting them with a Christly message in their own tongue, so that they have felt at once a little less strange in the strange land, and are more responsive to Christian effort.

It has kept a Sunday school in Montana in literature and supplies for a month.

It has paid the salary of a teacher in Philander Smith College for two weeks, during which time four hundred eager black boys and girls have been given a taste of the knowledge they covet so intensely.

It has paid for two weeks all the expenses—how small they are!—of a young man in college who may some day go to that Chapter as its pastor, and be a better man for the place by the amount of that two weeks' schooling.

It has bought twenty Testaments, which a deaconess gave to the hitherto Scriptureless children in a down-town Sunday school. And so, while the Chapter has been jogging along about as usual, it has touched the two most populous centers of heathenism with gospel truth. It has

THE LEAGUE'S WORLD INTERESTS.

stood with the advance guard of civilization on our own frontier. It has taught Sunday school in the Northwest, and given hope and inspiration to a school full of Negro boys and girls in the South. It has been to college with a needy, courageous, self-helping candidate for God's ministry of preaching. It has gone up and down the stairs of Chicago rookeries with a direct descendant of Paul's co-laborer, Phoebe, the first of deaconesses.

And everywhere, teaching, healing, feeding, cheering, it has been busy with the very essence of Christ's work on earth, and has earned his "Inasmuch as ye have done it unto the least of these My brethren, ye have done it unto Me."

WHERE TO WRITE.

As has been suggested in numerous places in this chapter, the greatest source of world evangelism material is the Mission Study and Stewardship Department of the Central Office, 740 Rush Street, Chicago.

Requests for material regarding the various benevolent societies should be sent to—

The Board of Foreign Missions, 150 Fifth Avenue, New York.

The Board of Home Missions and Church Extension, Arch Street, Philadelphia.

The Board of Education for Negroes, 420 Plum Street, Cincinnati, Ohio.

The Board of Education, 150 Fifth Avenue, New York.

The American Bible Society, Bible House, New York.

CHRISTIAN STEWARDSHIP.

While the principle of Christian Stewardship has been fostered by the League from the beginning, it was given official recognition by the Board of Control in the revised Constitution of 1903, with a place in the Department of World Evangelism. The Constitution says: "At least once each year it (the Department of World Evangelism) shall present to the Chapters the claims of Christian Stewardship, and shall seek to enroll the members in the Christian Stewardship Enrollment."

THE EFFICIENT EPWORTHIAN.

The Christian Stewardship Enrollment.

The Christian Stewardship Enrollment is not a new organization; it is simply an enrollment of members of the Epworth League or others who will sign and endeavor to get others to sign a card reading as follows: "I desire to be enrolled as a Christian Steward, who will hold all that God shall give me in trust for Him. I will pay not less than one-tenth of my income regularly and directly to His cause."

The enrollment of all persons who will sign the pledge is kept in the office of the Department of Missions and Stewardship. Already a large number of names are on record in the Epworth League office. The advantage of this enrollment should be faithfully presented at the time of the regular annual Christian Stewardship meeting. The young people should be urged to give this great subject their prayerful consideration and finally should be asked to join its rank.

Why Stewardship in the League?

Our young people of the Epworth League provide unexcelled material for Stewardship promotion in the Church. Passing, as they are, through the period of highest idealism, charged with the enthusiasm and vigor of youth, they are easily awakened to new possibilities of service and quickly aroused to heroic endeavor.

They are quick to respond to a big challenge; they love high adventure; heroism charms them; and if permitted to control their emotions and wills long enough, is likely to enter permanently into their own characters.

The love of money, which paralyzes so many lives at middle age, has scarcely yet secured its strangle-hold, and young men and women of Epworth League age are often better able to estimate the relative worth of material things than are those of more mature experience.

The stewardship of possessions is, therefore, like the stewardship of life, time, talent, prayer, more readily apprehended and embraced, and the larger sacrifices of Kingdom service more promptly and gladly undertaken.

Our young people of the League, moreover, however

THE LEAGUE'S WORLD INTERESTS.

busied or burdened, usually have available much more time for study, reading, promotional activities, distribution of literature, and solicitation of various sorts, than have the older people of the Church.

PUTTING STEWARDSHIP INTO THE LEAGUE SCHEME.

For Stewardship promotion in the Epworth League the Constitution provides for the pastor a carefully selected and specialized helper, the Second Vice-President. This officer shall, "at least once each year, present to the Chapter the claims of Christian Stewardship, and shall encourage the members in the study and practice of Christian Stewardship."

"Once each year"—"*at least.*" If Stewardship is to be really taught, and the world evangelized, the heart of the Second Vice-President must be filled with it, and the principles kept in practice, the year round.

"Shall present to the Chapter"—an "introduction!" A ceremony so well and thoroughly performed as to make Chapter and Stewardship forevermore acquaintances, and in due time intimate friends.

"The claims." Stewardship lays claim to all activities, relations, emotions, affections, powers, possessions of life. A real task has the faithful Second Vice-President.

"Encourage the members." Inspire in them courage—they will need it, if they espouse the cause of Stewardship. Help them—tactfully, sympathetically, intelligently. This requires patience, faith, perseverance, administrative ability of a high order. "Encourage"—impossible unless one has courage, and that means contact with God, stewardship, partnership with Him in the affairs of daily life.

"The Study of Christian Stewardship." It is a big, big subject, not to be mastered in a moment, by a generous impulse, in response to a glowing testimony. It means the mastery of many a Bible passage, many a page of religious experience, many an impulse of self-interest or fear. "Study!"

"And practice." Not only to understand, but to fulfill the will of God in one's life.

The Second Vice-President is thus discovered to be

THE EFFICIENT EPWORTHIAN.

charged with a mission of untold possibilities for the Kingdom, and has a right to expect the loyal and untiring support and assistance of pastor, League President, cabinet, and every member.

Stewardship should be promoted in the Epworth League in both general and special ways.

1. *Special and Periodical.* Every year the League has at least one Stewardship meeting, usually more. This gives opportunity to capture new young people every year for tithing stewardship decision. Here pastor, President, and Second Vice-President may well combine their ingenuity and energies. Lessons, hymns, discussions should be directed to specific phases of Stewardship instruction. Subjects for discussion and testimony may be assigned in advance, especially to those regularly practicing the duties of stewardship. Literature, secured from the League's Department of Stewardship, and the Division of Stewardship of the Committee on Conservation and Advance, should be distributed. Stewardship may often be promoted by the Second Vice-President or someone specially selected, in the ordinary meetings of the League, by pointing out the stewardship implications in the regular lesson. Says an Epworth League leader of national influence:

a. "The young people who accept Stewardship should be enrolled. The decision is highly important. And enrollment is easy. They are accustomed to group-action."

b. "They should be recognized. The signing of a tithe-covenant is as significant as any other Christian decision. It should be given as definite recognition as the others."

c. "They should be followed up. The tithe decision lends itself to instant and constant practice. But it does not automatically produce the practice. You are getting people to form a habit. Remember William James' rule:

TO FORM A HABIT

1. Launch yourself with as strong and decided an initiative as possible.
2. Never suffer an exception to occur till the new habit is securely rooted in your life.

THE LEAGUE'S WORLD INTERESTS.

3. Seize the very first opportunity to act in every resolution you make, and in every emotional prompting you may experience in the direction of the habit you aspire to gain.

"This means such a simple matter as an account book, and brief, clear directions about how to tithe. The fewer complications the better, but the more specific the practice, also the better."

2. *The General Ways of Promoting Stewardship.*
   a. Through the reading of Stewardship literature. Not only literature specially prepared to promote Stewardship, but in *The Epworth Herald,* which every week presents a Stewardship column, and persistently urges its practice in the form of the tithe.
   b. Let them share in the financial activities of the Church.
   c. Encourage your members to find outlets for the tithe, apart from the regular church enterprises. To identify the tithe with "current expenses and benevolences" is fatal. We are seeking not Methodist stewards, but Christian stewards. The tithes will provide money enough, both for our Church and for the world-wide interests of the Kingdom, if we produce enough tithers.
   d. Urge them now and then to check up on the tithe; whether they have more interest in the cause, more intelligence in the general Kingdom work, more inclination to see all life as something to administer rather than something to own.
   e. Give them an outlet for their energies and enthusiasm. If invited, encouraged, and coached by the pastor and the Second Vice-President, they will develop into expert and zealous promoters of Stewardship, in testimony, in the distribution of literature, in the solicitation of new enrollments, and in every form of helpful service.

THE FAILURE OF "THE USUAL WAY."

Jesus was accused of many violations of the ancient law; but none of these who were watching for some cause of offense in him ever accused him of neglecting the tithe.

THE EFFICIENT EPWORTHIAN.

Everybody knows that the usual way of raising money for the Church has something the matter with it.

It makes Christians into coaxers and beggars.

It makes sincere Christians ashamed, that the work of the Church is done on the money of mendicancy.

It puts means above ends; we are forced to give concerts for money, not music; to hold suppers for profit, not sociability; to distribute books for a commission, not instruction; and generally to degrade and pauperize the greatest business on earth.

It makes the money bag the measure of recognition, and mortgages the Church's conscience to its heavy givers.

It uses up time and strength in getting the tools for the work, which ought to be spent on the work itself. (The time used up by Methodist financial ways and means committees in the course of a year is estimated at one man's working time for three hundred years.)

With all its other disadvantages, some people might defend it if it did but work, but it is a self-confessed failure. Like the perpetual motion machine in the Patent Office, it is highly complicated and very ingenious, but it won't work.

The Tithe is the Thing.

Any one who thinks about it knows that the paying of the tithe as a sign of stewardship has nothing whatever the matter with it.

It saves the Christian's self-respect. He need not apologize either for doubtful methods or inadequate results.

It conserves the energies of the Church for the Church's real business.

It puts a stop to the necessity of the Church becoming a peddler of pies, oysters, ice cream, chicken pie, and notions.

It gives the business men of the place a new regard for the Church as a business institution.

It collects itself.

It is a positive means of grace, like a good prayer meeting.

It puts a quietus on all display and self-seeking in one's

THE LEAGUE'S WORLD INTERESTS.

contributions. Nobody can get puffed up over paying his debts.

It makes the Christian's financial relation to his Church a pleasure instead of a perpetual annoyance, and so does a good work on his disposition.

It is the one sure way of proving we are in earnest when we say of God that he owns all we possess.

It links us with God in a real and definite sharing of his work.

It is the plan our Lord approved.

And, every time, everywhere, with rich Churches, poor Churches, city Churches, country Churches, big Churches —it works!

Is the Tithe a Debt?

There is a lot of confusion about this tithing idea; it is the least satisfactory religious idea that I ever hear Christians discuss.

Why? How?

Well, it is so flat-footed, as you might say; "take it or leave it."

You do or you don't. And that's all there is to it. Now, when Christians talk about prayer, they get along beautifully. If one has a notion regarding prayer that is a little different from the other's, it is all right. So with studying the Bible, or going to church, or your favorite hymns. Everybody has his own opinion, and everything's lovely.

Isn't it pretty much the same way about tithing?

No, nor anything like it. If you tithe, you pay a tenth of your income to the work of God. If you don't, you "give," according to some scheme of your own, or as you happen to feel, or what you gave last year, or "about what is right," or "as most other people." But the tither knows, and you know, that the difference between "giving" and "paying" is as wide as a barn door.

But what is the difference?

Dear, dear, the slowness of some people! The tithe is a tenth. The tenth is the part which you put aside for religious uses. It is like rent, or interest. The rate is fixed. You don't say you "give" the landlord his rent. You pay it. Uncle Sam doesn't "give" you the interest on your Liberty Bonds. He pays it.

Yes, I can see that. But why should you "pay" anything for the work of God? Isn't a Christian free from all bondage to the ancient law? Why can't you give as you are able, without bothering your head over rates and words and names?

Because you *are* free. Who freed you? Who is responsible for your prosperity, such as it is? Who really "owns" what you hold, in money or goods? Who is first in your life? Yourself, or God?

Why, there is only one answer. God, certainly. He made me what I am, and would have done better if I had let him. He has the right of way. He is the owner of all. No Christian questions that.

O, yes, some Christians do. But you have the right answer. Now, if God has right of way and is owner of all, how are you going to recognize that? I mean, how will you admit that he really owns what you possess? Uncle Sam admits your ownership of a Liberty Bond, not by thanking you for your help in financing the war. He doesn't give you a button or a medal. That would be nice; but he pays you four and a quarter per cent interest; no more, no less. Same way with your landlord; you don't expect to satisfy him with praises of the house, or compliments on his personal character. You pay him the rent.

But how can you pay God money?

You can't, of course. But God has a lot of faith in you. You are his child. You believe in his plan to save all men, beginning with yourself. And he is willing that you shall take this money of his, and spend it for him, to help carry on this plan of his. Always remembering that the money is his, not yours. And that's where the idea of stewardship comes in; *the relation of one who is trusted to use another person's property for that other person's purposes.*

Very well; but what has all this to do with the tithe? Some poor people would find a tenth too much, and some rich people ought to spend more.

As to the poor, two things. I never heard of a tither who, being poor, complained that the tithe was too much.

THE LEAGUE'S WORLD INTERESTS.

He isn't looking for sympathy. And then it is one of the basic things, like the pay for the roof that shelters him. Up to the point of actual poverty, when the public should step in, every man expects to pay his house rent.

All right; supposing that everybody can afford a tenth. When a man becomes more prosperous, why should he not pay at least a tenth, and as much more as he can? Seems to me I've heard something about "the tithe as a minimum."

You have, and it is one of those phrases which should be banished from the language. There is neither minimum nor maximum to a fixed charge. It is what it is. Would you offer to pay more rent, just because your salary had been raised?

No, because I don't believe in making presents to my landlord.

Right you are. But wouldn't you enjoy making presents to God by giving to his work? And, after you have paid your tithe, that's your grand and glorious Gospel privilege. Go as far as you like, then. It is one of the finest joys of the Christian life.

Maybe so, but what is the practical difference?

All the difference between paying an honest debt, which is a pleasant thing, and being able to offer a grateful gift, which is pleasant in quite another fashion. If you paid no tithe, but considered you owed everything to God, you would always be in debt, and would miss the joy of real giving. The alabaster box of precious ointment would mean nothing to you.

Yes; and why not encourage the larger offerings? Aren't they needed, and badly?

I don't discourage them. But I tell you this, that if one may venture to guess at the purposes of God, he is infinitely more anxious that all his children should admit his claim than that a few should make large gifts. And the proof is, that not enough Christian work could be done in the world to exhaust the tithes of Christians, if all were tithers. The tithe would provide the means for as many workers, as much equipment, as could possibly be used.

Even if the Gospel were really carried to every man?

Yes; all the more. Because, if as soon as a man were

converted to Jesus Christ he began to tithe, he would be providing means for the conversion of others.

That is what my friend "Layman" says on that score, and I agree with him teetotally:

"There would be no calls for money. Church and missionary treasuries would be full to overflowing. All the churches, schools, and hospitals needed in this and other lands could be built and properly equipped. The teachers, preachers, physicians, nurses, and helpers in these institutions could be well supported during active life and cared for when past the working age. Poverty could be prevented or greatly alleviated all over the world, and all this could be done by professing Christians.

"Truly a glorious vision, but not nearly as glorious as if we will look the other way. The *principle* of the tithe preceded the law of the tithe; and the principle never existed and the law of tithing was never enacted or promulgated for the benefit of others, not even for the Church, Jewish or Christian. God intended both for our benefit, for our financial benefit, for our spiritual benefit, to help us build up strong, dependable Christian characters. To bring us into financial partnership with him. To enable us to bring our religion into practical use every working hour of our lives. To make us happier. To make us more useful both to ourselves and to others. Negatively to save us from idolatry which is covetousness, and to keep us from narrowness and stinginess, especially as we grow older."

Then the tithe is really God's sentiment of what it will cost to convert the world?

The tithe is the tithe. It is not a scheme for getting money. It is not to be pushed by a worried pastor as the one way out of his Church's financial muddle. It is not the Church's scheme to get easy money. It is not even the "acid test," as some say, of a man's religion. "Acid tests" are between man and man; God has surer ways of proving his children. It is not anything, first of all, but God's gift of a chance to you, to think about something bigger than money, at the very moment when you are handling the money.

How does that help?

The worst service that money ever does to its possessor

THE LEAGUE'S WORLD INTERESTS.

is to make him think of himself as owner. That cuts him off from partnership with anybody bigger than himself. He boasts that "his money talks." But when he pays the tithe he is saying to himself and to God, "This is sacred money; I will use it for the greatest enterprise in the world."

WANTED: A NEW CREED.

It is time that we came to realize that Stewardship is not a mere precept or practice, but that it is a faith and a life. It stands for a great conviction about God and his purpose for the world, for a great vision of human life and its meaning. It applies to the Church as it does to the individual, to industry and to the nation, to service and prayer as well as to giving. The living Spirit of God is in the world, and he is showing us this larger meaning of Christ for our day. We need a creed that shall express this side of our faith, that shall be not like the memorial of an ancient past but like a banner waving before marching hosts. Here is a stewardship creed:

1. I believe in the Kingdom of God, the coming of a new world of righteousness and brotherhood and peace.

2. I believe in the God of love, who dwells with men and works with men and through men.

3. I believe in man as fellow worker with God, called not only to receive God's gifts, but to know his purpose and to share his toil.

4. I believe that man has no absolute title to any property, but that all human possession is a trust from God for the good of men.

5. I believe in the stewardship of business, that God is to be man's partner in his daily work, that the title to possession must rest upon the fact of service, and that the motive of service must take the place of the motive of gain.

6. I believe that the spending of money, like the making of it, must be a part of God's service, and that this applies equally to what I spend on myself and to what I give for others.

7. I believe in proportionate giving, the setting aside of a definite part of my income so that my giving may be systematic, thoughtful, and effective; and this proportion

THE EFFICIENT EPWORTHIAN.

I regard not as the end of my obligation but as the acknowledgment of God's ownership of the whole.

8. I believe that I should give in accordance with my ability and with the greatness of the need. If the Jews could give a tenth for temple and sacrifice, I may well give that as a minimum for the work of Christ's kingdom; but I recognize that increased ability may mean two tenths or five tenths or nine tenths instead.

9. I believe that I should invest this money for God as carefully as I invest in business, and that study and plan and prayer should go with all my giving.

10. I believe in the stewardship of life, that every calling should be a ministry, and that back of all other gifts should be the gift of my will to God and of my life to the service of men.

11. I believe in the stewardship of the Church, that like her Lord she is here not to be ministered unto, but to minister.

12. I believe in the stewardship of the nation, that as truly as Jehovah once called Israel of old, so the God of all peoples has summoned my country to serve in the family of nations.

What Would It Mean?

What would it mean for the Church to have a generation of Christian men to adopt this creed?

The Church would be set free for the real task of saving and serving men.

We could face a bigger program and have resources to back it up.

We could at once double our forces in city and frontier and foreign field, and the Church would mark the greatest advance of its history since Paul took an empire for his parish.

What would such giving mean for Christian men?

1. It would mean moral victory. There are multitudes of Christian men whom God has prospered who are actually giving a less percentage of their income to-day than ten or twenty years ago. It hurts them to give what they do. Their danger is as real as that of the drunkard or gambler,

THE LEAGUE'S WORLD INTERESTS.

and more subtle. A fixed proportion definitely set aside means a moral victory.

2. It would mean freedom and joy in giving. Benjamin Adams of sainted name wrote on "The Fun of Giving." The Lord loveth a cheerful giver, but there are many people to whom giving is more like pulling a tooth. Set a proportion apart once for all. You will find such freedom and joy in the spending of it that you will want to increase the amount.

3. It would mean a richer spiritual life. There is only one method of spiritual growth. That is fellowship with God. And here is a fellowship in the one thing that is most like God—in giving and loving and serving. Indeed, there is no salvation at all without this: "Except a grain of wheat fall in the ground and die, it abideth alone. He that would save his life shall lose it." I know one man in an Eastern city whose friends have seen his life grow each year richer and stronger, broader in sympathy and larger in vision, because his giving has put him in touch with the noblest spirits and the greatest movements in his city, his country, and around the world.

CHAPTER IX

SOCIAL SERVICE.

Why Social Service in the Church?

Time was when social service was nowhere else. The Church had a monopoly of it. The convents and abbeys and monasteries were the centers of a great, even if unscientific, ministry to the bodily needs of the community.

But that monopoly, happily, is ended. We know now that the Church is not the only institution with a mission to society.

Any American charities' directory reveals hundreds of agencies fighting against poverty, disease, ignorance, vice, greed, and most of them are not organized as departments of Church work at all. Many millions of dollars a year are spent in this country on the many forms of social service—remedial, preventive, constructive—outside of all that the Church in any official way spends at this business.

But all this growing passion for social service is traceable to one source. It is a Christian thing. It has the stamp of Christ's teaching and influence on it in every feature. To the last fragment it is a modern commentary on what Jesus told His disciples they must do if they would *be* His disciples.

We need not be sorry that so much of this work is now done outside the Church. The Church can well afford to give large recognition to every other agency of help and healing, and there is work enough for all.

But we ought to remember that the people who did this work are, for the most part, Christians. We ought to remember that the Church taught the world the secret that makes it all worth doing. We ought to remember that if the Church were to cease its insistence on the needs of the spirit in man all this social reclamation work would begin to be useless and would shortly dry up and disappear.

SOCIAL SERVICE.

Remembering all that, the Church must more than ever give itself to social service. This is no time, when the world has accepted the Church's gospel of brotherhood, for the Church to speak uncertainly about it, or to weaken in the practice of it.

All of which is submitted as a group of reasons why every Epworth League Chapter should magnify its Department of Social Service and adopt a constructive, positive, definite program. Our young people must get the vision and get ready for the task which is the Church's "other" business.

A Chapter in Cleveland, studying the course laid out by Dr. N. W. Stroup, invited an Italian to speak at the meeting. Then the Epworthians discovered a group of Italians living near the church, and are trying to enter into their lives. That's social service!

The Social Service Vice-President who permits herself to raise the funds for her department's work will marry a man who will permit her to chop the wood for her cookstove.

The Chapter which will overlook an opportunity for service more than once needs a new set of eyes—or leaders.

THE THIRD DEPARTMENT AND ITS MEANING.

In 1903 the Board of Control felt that the Epworth League must see the farthest man, and it created the Department of World Evangelism.

In 1913 it felt that the Epworth League must see the nearest man, and it created the Department of Social Service.

There was missionary work in the Epworth League before the Board of Control made a missionary department. In simple truth, it was the missionary work which the League in some places had proved itself able to do that compelled the new department.

And in like manner the League did not wait for the Board to make a new department before showing itself capable of social service. In hundreds of places the young people were busy with all manner of community usefulness before 1913.

THE EFFICIENT EPWORTHIAN.

But the time had come to call for an advance all along the line. Every Chapter, instead of one here and there, ought to be moving itself toward the study and practice of social service.

We had not outgrown Mercy and Help, but Mercy and Help work had forced us to broaden and deepen our conception of what was expected of young Christians in their relation to their fellows.

Mercy and Help had much to do with kindling the new spirit of service which burns in the deaconess work, in the Church's hospital enterprises, and other forms of ministry. Social Service is merely Mercy and Help made positive and preventive, instead of being confined to the patching up of broken earthenware.

"Social Service" is in itself only a phrase, but it is the handiest that offers. It has been defined as *"the application of Christian principles to social life and the realization of the Christian ideal in human society."*

What forms should it take? Why should we of the League lay hold of it as one of our four chief tasks?

These questions have many answers. To the second, the chief answer is that Christianity is a religion which must serve the community as well as the individual. The more real and gripping our religion becomes to us, the more social service we shall want to do. Half of the Ten Commandments are "Thou shalt nots" directed against social sins, and half of the Eleventh Commandment is a "Thou shalt" which requires social service.

The forms of social service to be operated by the Third Department will vary, just as the forms of Mercy and Help have varied.

The new department is greatly needed everywhere. The Chapter which really takes hold of the work now made more accessible will enlarge its usefulness once and yet again.

Social Service—What Is It?

Social service is that form of effort for man's betterment which seeks to uplift and transform his associated and community life.

SOCIAL SERVICE.

There are also some forms of service to the social needs of the individual which may properly be called social service. Social service adds to the effort to help the individual lives of people, the effort to establish proper conditions for the development of those lives. It adds to the relief of the poor and the sick and the prisoner the effort to discover and remove the causes of poverty and disease and crime.

Its goal is social salvation, "the deliverance of human society from disease, poverty, crime, and misery; the development and perfection of the institutions of man's associated life, and the construction of a social order that is the city of God on earth."

HISTORICAL.

The social service movement is no new thing in organized Christianity. The fires of Pentecost kindled a mighty passion to help all human need that soon resulted in organized service. The first Christians met by common action every need of their group, and the organized ministrations of the early Church to the needs of the age was the marvel of Roman historians.

In the ministry of Jesus, much time was devoted to doing good and to the relief of suffering. His opening proclamation announces a mission to the needs of neglected individuals and groups—the poor, the captives, the blind, the bruised. His standard of judgment is that of service to the sick, the poor, the prisoner. His thought of religion is social; it is the Kingdom, the Fatherhood, the brotherhood.

Here Jesus fulfilled the law and the prophets. He was the successor of those men who revealed God in terms of justice and righteousness in the community life, who denounced the injustice and oppression of the rich, who sought to build a community life with God all through it.

Every great awakening in the Church has emphasized the social nature of Christianity by its results in social service. Our modern program of philanthropy and of social and labor legislation was started in the Evangelical Revival.

THE EFFICIENT EPWORTHIAN.

The great missionary awakening of the last generation developed city evangelism, the settlement and the institutional Church. The attempt to minister to the whole life of the people of the slums developed into the wider program of removing those social and industrial conditions which are behind the slum and its imperfect lives.

Then the present social service movement in the Churches was organized with thirty denominations joining together through the Federated Council, behind a common Social Creed, and with organized agencies in the leading denominations co-operating with other social service agencies to develop plans and secure the measures that will carry out this creed.

This means that every Church will be a socialized Church, developing a ministry to its community as well as to the individuals around it, concerned with poverty and disease and delinquency, with civic and industrial conditions. In this socialized Church every department must have a social service program.

What shall be the part and place of the Epworth League?

SOCIAL STUDY.

Service to be successful must be intelligent. To be intelligent it must be based upon a knowledge of accepted principles and methods. The Central Office has arranged for a study course on Social Service. The first year's work is a study of the Social Creed of the Churches, its meaning, and the measures that will carry it out. If it is desired to make a special study of any one particular subject, a selected list of books on that subject will be supplied by the Methodist Federation for Social Service.

Many young people who can not be induced to join a study class may yet be enlisted in a reading course, especially if those who are reading the books in the course are gathered together occasionally for a social hour and for discussion.

Every Chapter should have its own social service library, so that the books may be passed around freely. A list of books can be supplied which can not fail to catch and hold

SOCIAL SERVICE.

the interest of young people, because they deal with typical American conditions from an intimate, personal standpoint.

To supplement this group and class study, a course of five or six addresses can be arranged for the Sunday evening devotional service, these addresses to deal with various aspects of social service. The Methodist Federation for Social Service can supply a list of speakers in almost every State who are available for such addresses.

Another popular form of education which can be made use of is the Open Forum for the presentation of community issues. At this meeting, representatives of various groups in the community may be heard at first hand, and the question-and-answer form of communication may be used to establish a closer sympathy between speaker and audience.

COMMUNITY STUDY.

Any program of social service for the individual or the group must be based upon the needs of the local community. Therefore, these must be discovered. The only way to discover them is to make a study of local conditions, which will outline the field of needed activity.

Before any work is attempted, the Chapter must know also what agencies are already at work to meet the needs of the community and how they are doing it, in order that its efforts may not duplicate the work of other societies, but supplement it.

A chart can be made and placed on the wall of the church showing the agencies which will help in caring for poverty, sickness, or delinquency, or in meeting any civic or social emergency.

It is not advisable or even possible for the Epworth League to make a thorough study of the whole community, especially in the larger centers. In a community of ten thousand and under, however, it may be possible to get a good general view of conditions; but even in this case the effort should be confined to the things in which young people are naturally interested. This will limit the study and activity and concentrate the effort on a few things.

Any Chapter may well limit itself to discovering and improving the conditions of life for the young people of

THE EFFICIENT EPWORTHIAN.

the community. This will include conditions of social life and recreation, conditions of education, conditions of health and housing, and of occupation.

The following schedule of questions will give assistance to the Chapter in studying its own community:

WHAT EVERY CHAPTER SHOULD KNOW ABOUT ITS OWN COMMUNITY.

Poverty and Delinquency.—What charitable agencies exist? Their general efficiency? Any co-operation between them?

Approximate amount spent for relief in one year, and number of cases helped.

What relief work is done by Churches? Is there co-operation between the different departments of the individual Church? With other Churches? With other charitable agencies?

What city, county, or State provision for relief of poverty or sickness is there in the community? Does anybody inspect these institutions for efficiency?

Social Life and Recreation.—What organized recreation is provided? In schools, Churches, Y. M. C. A., etc.?

What amusements are operated for private profit? General character? Any that are flagrantly vicious?

What educational facilities are there for young people who wish to continue their education while working? Night schools? Special classes in Y. M. C. A. and Y. W. C. A.? Lecture courses? Are these facilities efficient?

Health and Housing.—Death rate? Infant mortality? Compared with neighboring communities?

Does the Health Department control contagious diseases? Does it educate the community to measures of prevention?

Is there any section of the town living in unsanitary or congested houses?

What laws relating to such conditions, and how enforced?

Labor.—How many young people over sixteen are wage-earners in the community? (How many, if any, under sixteen?) Where do they work? How many work more

SOCIAL SERVICE.

than ten hours? More than nine hours? Eight hours? How many on Sunday? How many girls working nights?

What are the wages of the lowest paid group? Young men? Young women? Is there a Minimum Wage law in the State, and is it enforced? Average wage in the various industries in the community? How does it compare with the cost of living in that place?

What are the conditions of health in the community's industries? What labor laws in the State? Do they protect the worker, and to what extent? Is there a system of factory inspection, and is it enforced?

What is done to help young people find employment?

Government.—What form of government? Who are the officers? What are their functions and what power have they? What are the forces that really control?

What departments of the local government most vitally affect the welfare of the community?

What co-operation is there between the Church group and these departments?

HOW TO BEGIN.

A good way to begin is for the Social Service Department to make a general study of the community according to this schedule, modifying the schedule to fit local needs, and striking out such questions as are not applicable.

This information should then be classified and worked up in the form of charts, so that it may be presented to the whole Chapter in graphic fashion. The stereopticon can be used to good advantage in this part of the work.

From this general study the members may select that particular condition which appears to call for the most urgent action. When this has been done, a more detailed study of that condition should be made before anything is done to meet the need.

The Methodist Federation for Social Service can give assistance and suggestions in the work of classifying the information and preparing the charts, and can furnish schedules for the more detailed study of the field selected for action.

THE EFFICIENT EPWORTHIAN.

In the case of city Chapters, the district should be defined, and other young people's groups should, if possible, be enlisted in the effort.

MAKING THE MERCY AND HELP WORK CONSTRUCTIVE.

Relief Work.—The practical work of the Epworth League can not be called social service until it becomes constructive and preventive, as well as palliative. Social service is not content to relieve, without at the same time investigating the causes of distress and seeking to remove them.

The very first principle of relief work is co-operation. Co-operation within the Church itself, seeing that one organization does not duplicate the work of another; co-operation with other Churches of the same denominations, and co-operation with agencies outside the Church, especially with the organized charities of the community.

The second principle is quite as important: There should be continuity of service. Spasmodic help will not only do little good, but may work harm. Whatever work may be selected, it should not be dropped until it has been carried through to completion and there is no further need of it. It is much better to select a permanent problem and give attention to that, than to attempt many different pieces of work, doing only a little of each. For instance, if a family is given help, it should be helped continuously until the members are able to care for themselves; not given a basket at Thanksgiving or Christmas time, and left to itself the remainder of the year.

Nearly every Chapter has among its members one or more young women who are able to give a good deal of time to visitation and other relief work. These should be trained as friendly visitors in the community, so that their services may be guided and directed in such a way as will make it doubly valuable. The local charity organization will accept such volunteer help and give the desired training.

If there is no local organization, the young women may study "Friendly Visiting Among the Poor," by Mary E. Richmond, and "The Charity Visitor," by Amelia Sears;

SOCIAL SERVICE.

these will give valuable help. "How to Help," by Mary Coyngton, is valuable.

Work for the Sick.—Where there is a hospital in the community, many small services may be performed for the patients, especially for those in the free wards. Reading matter may be provided, and some one assigned to read aloud a certain amount of time each week. Letters may be written; often in the convalescent wards a program of music and readings will be appreciated.

If there are dispensaries, social service work may be carried on by a system of following up the patients to see that the physician's orders are carried out, and that the patients are provided with the means of procuring what is prescribed, and to improve the home conditions so that further illness may be prevented.

Rural Chapters may provide fruit and flowers for the sick in the city by co-operating with the city Chapters. Express companies will usually carry such gifts free of charge.

Work for the sick, if the Mercy and Help Department is to be made a genuine social service agency, must not end with relief. It must be extended until it looks also to the prevention of illness and to the aggressive advocating of public health measures.

The local Health Department will be glad of volunteer help in spreading knowledge concerning its plans for sanitation and the proper care of disease, in reporting violations of health laws, in distributing literature dealing with public health, in its efforts to eliminate improper housing conditions, and in the effort to enforce the health laws of the community.

The Chicago Health Department is now issuing certificates to moving picture theaters which have good ventilation, and calling upon the public to patronize only those having such certificates. This plan may be followed in any place and may be applied to all buildings used for public gatherings, including churches.

Aiding the Prisoner.—Reading matter may be distributed in the jails, and if this service is attempted it should be systematic and continuous. And such reading matter

THE EFFICIENT EPWORTHIAN.

should be fresh and interesting. Out of date Church papers will not interest the people usually found in jails.

Find out whether the prisoners are given employment. If they are not, insist that they be given something to do for a reasonable number of hours six days in the week. Interest the judges and legal officials in helping to secure modern equipment and modern methods of handling prisoners.

SOCIALIZING THE SOCIAL DEPARTMENT.

In every community there are groups of young people who are not touched or brought into contact in any way with the young people in the Church societies. Every Chapter should make an effort to get into contact with these.

Homeless Young People.—Take, for instance, that increasing number of young men and women in the cities who are away from home, without the restraints of their former environment, and without proper social life in their new surroundings.

Practical help may take the form of finding proper boarding places, and getting these homeless ones invited into Christian homes to spend Sunday, so that they may have a touch of home life. The social hour after Church, at which light refreshments are served, has been used as a weapon against the loneliness and dangers of that hour.

Young People from Abroad.—Then, there are the immigrant young men and women. If America is to care for the new peoples who are drawn in such numbers by the promise of greater liberty, it will be only as the American young people, and especially those of the Churches, see in these groups an opportunity for splendid service.

Race suspicion and prejudice will never be disarmed until the young people meet face to face and find out for themselves the essential unity of the race.

Classes in English and Civics afford a good opportunity of getting acquainted. There are now a number of books designed for the purpose of teaching foreigners in simple, untechnical language, so that any ordinarily well-educated Epworthian may successfully lead such a class.

SOCIAL SERVICE.

The Methodist Federation for Social Service can furnish a list of such books.

The Nation Social, in which the various groups of foreigners furnish the entertainment by appearing in native costumes and giving exhibitions of the manners and customs of their own countries, is another excellent means of getting acquainted. In the cities where these foreign groups have their own editors, singers, and other leaders, these will usually gladly aid in an enterprise of this kind.

Devise your own methods for extending the circle of friendship outside the Church group. The essential thing is to come into vital contact with the young people of other nationalities in the community, for this will open the way to larger forms of service to the immigrant group.

Recreation for All.—Has your Chapter a consistent and persistent program of recreation, or does it merely give a "social" occasionally? A well-planned program, covering the half-year season, will yield far more satisfactory results than a haphazard effort to furnish recreation. The plans should be extended to include every possible group in the community. The fall season may begin with informal "welcome" receptions to the various groups who have been away for the summer—teachers, students, etc.—and the program for this period may take many forms, such as musical and literary evenings.

Education, especially in the city, may be combined with recreation by making visits in groups to various places of interest in the city. This is a particularly good plan in the summer, on Saturday afternoons, when the trip may end with a picnic or social of some kind out-of-doors.

The Rural Chapter.—The rural Chapter has quite as many advantages as the city Chapter when it comes to planning for organized recreation. Here, as in the city, there may be musical evenings, debates, moving pictures, and athletics for the winter season; in addition, the rural Chapter may plan in the summer for such events as the community fair, patterned after the county fair idea, giving prizes for the best flowers, fruits, samples of cooking, handwork, etc., and worked up by the young people themselves.

Combining education and recreation is easy in the coun-

THE EFFICIENT EPWORTHIAN.

try community, for there are less attractions than in the city, and such events when planned are more likely to succeed. The State university and the agricultural schools will usually co-operate in furnishing lectures on various subjects.

The pageant and the festival for National holidays or other times can be used by both city and country Chapter, but the country Chapter will have some advantage over the city group.

City and rural Chapters may work together in planning for fresh-air and summer vacation work. The district may be organized, and a list of the farm houses secured where young people from the city will be taken for short periods at moderate rates. The city Chapter may furnish the names of young people who would be benefited by a vacation on a farm, but who can not afford summer resort prices.

Another plan which can be worked to advantage is for the rural Chapters to organize summer camps by furnishing the place and the equipment for the camp. The city group may pay the running expenses by appointing a club to handle this part of it, making the rates cover the operating expenses of the venture.

The good accomplished does not stop with the individuals benefited; it will establish as well a working acquaintanceship between city and rural Chapters, which is sure to result in further successful ventures together.

Organized recreation, by means of these and other methods, is taking an increasingly large place in the work of the Epworth League. But as the society continues to develop plans for the recreation of its own members and as many others as it can reach, it will discover that the combined efforts of all the young people, and of all the older people even, can not reach all the individuals in the community. There will be groups, especially in the larger centers, that remain untouched.

How is the Chapter to help here? It will first reveal the need of community recreation by lectures, by pictures, by charts, by contact with conditions; then it will work for the broader program of community recreation by means

SOCIAL SERVICE.

of public parks, playgrounds, and social centers, all properly supervised and directed, in the meantime doing its full share of the work of supplying wholesome fun for as many of the community as it can reach.

In this, the society known as Community Service, 1 Madison Avenue, New York City, will give helpful suggestions, as will also the Extension Department of the University at Madison, Wis. On the use of school buildings as social centers, E. J. Ward's book, "Social Centers," will be found illuminating.

Recreation and Social Purity.—No Chapter will be content to provide wholesome amusement without the effort to prevent improper types. And the prevention of improper recreation will lead to the problem of organized vice, for the two are inseparable. The public dance-halls, the amusement parks, and the excursion steamers are recruiting stations for the dealers in commercialized vice.

The first step in prevention is to understand that a segregated district in any community is unnecessary, that it remains only because of the consent of the community. It can not be too emphatically stated that segregation as a policy is no longer considered necessary, or even sound.

This stand is taken not only by the religious forces, but social workers and progressive thinkers the country over. This distinctly new attitude is the result of the scientific investigations made within the last few years by specially selected commissions in various parts of the country.

If there is a segregated district in your community, why should it continue to exist? If it continues it means assuredly that some girls and boys must be sacrificed. The young people of the community should be interested to see that no girls or boys are drawn into that life.

The second step is education in personal standards. Commercialized vice can be rooted out as soon as the community wills. But the only way in which the social evil will be eradicated entirely will be by the recognition of the single standard of morality. The influence of the Church young people should be thrown on the side of the single standard and everything that makes for it.

The Chapter will lend its influence in the suppression

of songs, pictures, and literature that may be suggestive, and will avoid in every way anything which may tend toward evil thoughts. Conscientious young women will avoid extreme fashions in dress, which are usually not only lacking in modesty and utility, but inartistic as well.

Notices should be placed in the public buildings of the community directing young people going into the city to apply for information and direction only to officials in uniform. Chapters in the smaller towns and cities may see that their members who are moving into the larger centers are put in touch with the city Church.

Christianizing Industry.—The modern Church has started on the task of making industry Christian. The young people of the Churches will find their share of this task in endeavoring to improve the conditions under which the young people are now working.

The most pressing need is for legislation concerning the hours of work and the creation of minimum wage boards. If there are no such laws, work for them. Whether the effort shall be for an eight, nine, or ten hour law will depend upon how far advanced your State is, and what the industrial group is fighting for.

Find out where and under what conditions the young people of your community are working—in factories, stores, laundries, telephone exchanges. It is frequently possible, by arousing sentiment in a community, to secure the immediate improvement of conditions by bringing local influence and pressure to bear on employers, without waiting for the slow process of legislation. If satisfactory laws already exist, help to get them enforced.

The rural Chapter may concern itself with the conditions of agricultural labor. The work of women on the farm needs to be made lighter, more attractive, and enjoyable.

The Agricultural Department at Washington, as well as the State Agricultural School, will furnish many suggestions which will aid in making farm life more profitable, as well as more interesting. Community gatherings for the open discussion of ways and means may be made the occasion of social as well as educational meetings.

SOCIAL SERVICE.

GOOD GOVERNMENT.

When the Chapter sets out earnestly to improve community conditions, whether it be in recreation, industry, or health, it will not go very far before it will find that it must work through the government. Epworthians must learn that real citizenship entails a larger responsibility than going to the polls occasionally and casting a vote.

The presentation of subjects in the Sunday evening meetings which will enlighten the young people concerning the local government and its management will, therefore, be of more than passing value.

The Chapter will provide for the public discussion of all measures which touch the community welfare, and especially measures concerning the lives of young people.

A pre-legislation Institute has been worked with success. This Institute consists of a full discussion of all the important measures which are to come up at the pending session of the State Legislature, by prominent men and women who are qualified to speak on the proposed legislation.

In some communities a junior government has been organized, in which a group of young people elect some of their number to fill offices similar to those held in the local government. These junior officers become auxiliaries to the regular officials, assisting them in every way, and using the other young people as auxiliary forces to this end. In aiding the Health Department there has been organized in some places a Junior Sanitary Police to inspect the health conditions of the community and to endeavor to secure the observance of health ordinances.

Every Chapter should have on the wall of its meeting place a directory of public servants—senators, representatives (both State and National), aldermen, county commissioner, member of school board, and others. Then, when it is desired to bring the influence of the members to bear on officials who have certain measures under consideration, the names and addresses will be easily accessible to all.

THE EFFICIENT EPWORTHIAN.

Who Shall Lead the Social Service Study Class?

Miss Winifred Chappell, of the Chicago Training School, discusses this question in *The Epworth Herald* as follows:

"Just now a very real problem confronts the Vice-President of the Third Department—that old department with the alluring new name and the compelling new duties—namely, Who shall lead the social service study class?

"The time is ripe for the organization of the class. Enthusiasm runs high, generated by last summer's institute, or by a series of sermons on service preached by the pastor. Or perhaps a vital book which has fallen into the hands of one member and has passed eagerly from hand to hand has prepared the way for the class—Patten's 'New Basis of Civilization,' or Fiske's 'Challenge of the Country,' or—thrice fortunate Epworth League—Rauschenbusch's 'Christianizing the Social Order.' Then came the devotional meeting of March 15th. Carefully planned in advance, it transmuted the enthusiasm into a definite plan of action.

"The text-book is at hand, too—a dynamic book prepared by a man who knows, for young people who desire knowledge. And the community—it presses in upon the Epworth League, its aching problems crying for solution. It will furnish the laboratory first, and later the field of action, for the members of the class.

"But who shall be the leader? Third Vice-President and President and pastor are knitting their brows over the problem. Upon the leader depends the success of the class. Therefore, the choice is all-important.

"He must be a person with gifts of leadership,—persistence, for it is not easy to maintain a voluntary class in these days of many pressing interests; enthusiasm, for a phlegmatic teacher never begot ardor in his class; and magnetism, that strange, mystic endowment which gives a man power over his fellows; but especially conviction—conviction on the subject of serving one's fellow-men.

"Professed followers of Jesus divide into three classes on the subject of the Church and social service. In the first group—happily becoming small, since, as Professor Rauschenbusch somewhere remarks, the Men and Religion

SOCIAL SERVICE.

Forward Movement made social service orthodox—are those who aver that the sole duty of the Church is to 'save souls,' to 'preach the good old gospel,' that matters of social relationship are 'secular' and to be left to other agencies. In the nature of the case, this group can not furnish a leader for a class in social service.

"The second group consists of those who hold that social service is a legitimate task, one of the legitimate tasks of the Church, *'but'*—always that adversative conjunction. *'But,* we must not over-emphasize service,'—*'But,* we must not let this work detract from the spiritual.' As if the first and second commandments were antithetic instead of complementary! As if Jesus' regard for men's bodies did not lay the best possible foundation for the life of the spirit! From this class also it is vain to look for a potent leader.

"The third group, small as yet, but holding the very destiny of the Church in its hands, is composed of those who maintain that by all that is sacred and good, the Church must serve, must throw herself passionately into the task of redeeming society so that the individuals who make up society may have a chance at life—that abundant life of which Jesus spoke. These know in the depth of their hearts that if the Church perish at the task, perish she must, as her Master did, but the task must be undertaken. From this group must come the leader for the class.

"Somewhere in every community is the man for the place. Let him be sought with diligence and discrimination and induced to take upon himself this important work. For under his leadership the class may be developed into an active force which in time will make large contribution to the regeneration of the community."

THE THIRD DEPARTMENT AND NEW AMERICANS.

The Epworth League studies immigration in its mission study classes, and wisely. For we may as well admit that immigration must be faced and studied, yes, and welcomed.

A bewildering business is going on all over this country, and we are all so mixed up in it that we can't see it unless we take time off from our other work to look at it squarely It is the business of making a Nation, our Nation, which is to have its great place in a still greater federation of nations.

The old notion that the immigrant could be "assimilated" by some sort of magic, which made no account of blunders or blindness, is long overdue for retirement.

As a matter of fact, the immigrant of this generation is doing a great deal to assimilate the people who happened to get here a few years ahead of him.

It is not longer a question of what we shall do with to-day's immigrant, or what he will do with us. Rather it is a question as to what sort of immigrant is to fix the type of American life.

Naturally, most of us think that yesterday's immigrant, meaning our own group—is the one who ought to decide. But there is no "ought" about it.

Just because we happened to arrive first, we have no claim that can stand against the big fact of the other immigrant's presence and power. In many places he is even now much more important, industrially and politically, than the earlier citizens.

One hopeful sign is the passionate patriotism of the second immigrant generation. The public school deserves a lot of credit for that. Who has not observed that the sons of Swedes and Italians and Hebrews are as ardent lovers of America as the sons of Virginians and Vermonters?

That sign is a challenge to the young people of the Churches. Our Churches confess, some with shame and some with shoulder-shruggings of helplessness, that they have not done enough for the immigrant to let him know they are on earth.

The Home Mission Boards spend dollars on fully Americanized communities to the cents that are available for work among foreign-thinking people. Nor can we blame the Boards much. We have no equipment of workers that could wisely use any large funds.

But what a marvel that second generation is! It speaks English, it is youthful, it is ambitious and venturesome

SOCIAL SERVICE.

It will supply its own leaders, if we but capture it. It does not ask for, nor will it follow, leaders who have been provided. And this is much more wholesome than that it should receive leadership that could be wished on it from outside.

Very well; why not, then, a new movement—a movement without officialism or machinery—of the young Americans in our Churches toward these other young Americans? They are here to stay, they are alive to their finger-tips, they can be taught, they can teach us, they are going to share with us the work of making the new America, we are as good as they are—why should we not seek an alliance with them?

How? That is not the most important question. Besides, nobody quite knows how. Something else must come first.

But what does World Evangelism mean, what does Social Service mean, if we can not use their principles in such work as this?

Just as a hint of the possibilities that open up here, think of the classes in English that Epworth League Chapters might maintain; of the socials for languages and nationalities we might have; think how a score of such activities are available to give largest possible expression to the unselfish ideals of the League, and do it in a way to produce lasting and far-reaching good.

The thing will not be done easily. There are prejudices to be overcome, and, what is sometimes more difficult to deal with, a sort of "sotness"—the scientists call it "inertia." The foreign-speaking group does not know one group, nor do we know them.

No wholesale, mass attempt will get far. The work calls for patient, retail methods. Your young Aldens and Rensselaers must get acquainted with individual Wilkowskys and Panorellis, and must really see in them the possibilities of a new sort of fellowship.

And there must be no hint of patronage or superiority. The discovery of these fellow-adventurers for a new America is not a slumming expedition. There must be the same give and take, the same mutual respect, as if you and they were members of a college fraternity.

THE EFFICIENT EPWORTHIAN.

The best avenue of approach, in many cases, will be through acquaintances already formed in High School. Not that all your new friends and potential Epworthians will be High School folk; they are not yet committed to the proposal that all young people should continue through High School, at least, their pursuit of an education.

The big industrial struggle of to-day and to-morrow has for its opposing parties the employees who belong to another. They show little sign of coming to an understanding by any method that either side is willing to accept from the other.

If the young people of both sides were to come together in ways which would make plain their identical interests, they would do much toward mortgaging the future to industrial peace.

To put it definitely, the Church's young people of the older American strain and the young people of the new immigration must mingle socially and democratically. Nor should there be any difficulty about it. The spirit of democracy is in our Methodist blood. Besides, the beginning of all evangelizing is in social fellowship.

Our Churches must become social centers—that is, centers for the bringing together of all the elements that make up the community. Who should object, for example, if some Epworth League Chapter succeeds in getting a group of Italian young people to cross the League threshold for a celebration of the twentieth of September?

Industrial democracy will not amount to much unless we have social democracy to back it up, and social democracy itself needs to be buttressed by democracy in religion.

So with the other great social matters. In every one of them the young Other American's aid must be had, or not much will get itself done in the next twenty-five years.

He it is who must help to do away with Sunday work and child labor and the sweat-shop and the syndicating of vice. He must work with us for the living wage, the shorter work-day, and safety while at work. It is he who must join with the idealists in politics, believing on election day in righteousness and brotherhood and faith. And he must feel the larger patriotism, which finds compatriots under every sky where man works unselfishly for man.

SOCIAL SERVICE.

In a word, the Other American and his wife are the most problematical personalities on the continent to-day, and their children are the most interesting, the most promising youth in the world.

The mission study class which gives ten weeks to the study of immigration should come out of the experience with a sense of having dipped its ladle into the ocean. But there will be some gain in discerning that it *is* the ocean, wholesome, vast, salt, and often stormy, and not a roadside mudhole.

LOCAL WORK.

No matter where the Chapter may be, it should take up some work of social service in its own neighborhood. Not one Chapter in a thousand is so situated that there is no need of this work. As a part of the larger social problems, every community has its quota of sick and needy, of sad and discouraged, of weary and tired folk. They may not be destitute, but they are none the less in need. The Epworth League need not wait until poverty or extreme physical distress calls for assistance. These other things, while less apparent to the thoughtless onlooker, are occasions for important and resultful service.

When a new administration takes hold of this work, it will be found profitable to hold a meeting of the committee, giving an entire variety of work which might be undertaken in the community by this department. Determine which of those that are possible is most urgent and most nearly within the limit of the Chapter's ability. Then select one or two or three of these avenues of activity. It is better to concentrate the work of the department on a few forms of work than to attempt to cover the entire field.

That Deaconess.—One of the most practical forms of service is to secure a deaconess to help in the work of the Church. Let the Chapter assume her support and in every way stand by her work. She will be worth all the money the enterprise costs in discovering ways and means whereby the Church and the Chapter may become real forces in the life of the community.

THE EFFICIENT EPWORTHIAN.

Third Department Money.—With the beginning of every year a budget of the expenses necessary to run the Third Department should be made. Do not stint the work. Resources should be provided, if possible, according to needs. Whenever the committee can find real work to do, it should have abundant means with which to do it. Better economize anywhere else than here.

A plan used by some departments is to make a collection in the Sunday evening meeting occasionally. In other places, one-tenth of the entire Epworth League funds for the year is put at this department's disposal. One-tenth, however, is a very small allowance; one-fourth would be very much better in most places.

Publicity.—One difficulty about the work of this department is that it has not had sufficient publicity. Once in a while hold a public conference for others besides your own members. Plan it and advertise it in such a way that you will be sure of a good attendance. Then, when you have your crowd, describe your work. Give details and incidents that have grown out of the activities of the various committees. Discuss the forms of work which are desirable in your own community. And take a collection. There will be a generous response.

Systematic Visiting.

This work requires an amount of tact and wisdom largely in excess of that demanded by most other forms of personal service. The emphasis must be placed upon the systematic character of the visiting, and yet it must have all the warmth and spontaneousness of personal and interested concern for those who are visited. It will be advisable in most cases to district the community and to hold each member of the visiting committee or committees accountable for prompt and sustained work in his or her particular district. Perhaps it may be found advisable that visitors go two by two, rather than singly.

The great requirement of a good visitor is naturalness. The great temptation in the systematic visiting of the Epworth League, or of any other organization, is to make

SOCIAL SERVICE.

it a perfunctory or formal, and therefore very unprofitable, affair.

The ordinary call should be brief. No matter how the patient may urge visitors, it is usually best that the strain of receiving visitors be ended before it is likely to do harm. Of course, there may be cases where the illness does not forbid long calls.

A call in cases of sickness is largely enhanced in value if it is promptly made. The weary days drags themselves slowly along, and as day after day passes without any sign of interest from the people of the outside world, the invalid is inclined to feel that all interest in him ceased when he became helpless. As soon as you know of a case of sickness, notify the pastor. Arrange matters with him so that if he learns first of any case he will notify the Chapter's Visiting Committee. Except in cases where the nature of the sickness makes visiting unwise and undesirable, it will be a kindness to the friends of those who are sick, and to the sick ones themselves, if the information of the illness is passed around the circle.

As the patient recovers, draw him out to speak of himself and his attitude toward the things that really matter. Gather papers, magazines, and helpful books to loan. Learn from the nurse whether the patient can have fruit or any other luxury, and supply it.

When recovery is complete, the impressions that were made during the visits of the days of sickness may be deepened and strengthened if the case is followed up. Do not give any excuse for the notion that your interest in people begins only when they are sick, and ceases when they get out of bed and become ordinary people once more.

A word of warning should be spoken concerning contagious and infectious diseases. It may seem brave and self-forgetful to go where such diseases are. Moreover, it may seem cruel and unfeeling to stay away. But the safety of the many ought to be considered before the feelings of the individual, and for the sake of other families and of the community at large, all who are not directly concerned should be kept away from cases of contagious disease.

THE EFFICIENT EPWORTHIAN.

Hospital Visiting.—The increasing number of hospitals under the supervision of Methodist organizations makes it possible for many Chapters to do beautiful Christian work in visiting the patients under treatment. Many hospitals arrange for regular visits of this sort, sometimes on Sunday afternoons, when a religious service can be planned for.

In such cases the department should secure the attendance of a number who will take part in the service—some who will sing, and one or two who will speak briefly. At the close of the more formal service, which will probably be attended by all the patients who are able to be brought into the general meeting place, the workers may make brief personal calls at the bedsides. Many a man and woman are nearer to decisions that will change the whole direction of their lives in time of sickness than at other times, and the earnest, loving presentation of the Savior, who heals the sorest of all sickness, the sickness of the soul, will very often result in genuine conversions.

The Stranger in Your Town.—In visiting strangers it is possible to make the call a real pleasure to its recipients. Do not try to disguise the object of the visit. Let it be understood that you came, first, because these people are strangers; second, because you believe that your Church and Chapter can be of some service to them. Very few people will resent a call made thus frankly. Most people, indeed, will gladly and gratefully welcome visitors. By tactful and considerate inquiry, learn a few facts about new-comers. For example, are they regular Church attendants? If not, do they attend Church occasionally? Where? Are the children of the home in the Sunday school? Are the older children also in the young people's society? If not, can they be secured? Is there any sickness in the family? Are there any needs which can be supplied by the officers of the Chapter? The information will give you your bearings. It will disclose the conditions surrounding the newcomers.

Getting Acquainted.—It is sometimes difficult to know how to make the approach when calling upon strangers. It must be confessed that the house-to-house method, ex-

SOCIAL SERVICE.

cept in small communities, where the people are well known to each other, is not a great success. In the first place, it advertises itself as a wholesale method of doing business, and people do not like to be dealt with by wholesale. The sight of two visitors, plainly official, parading solemnly up one side of the street and down the other, is sufficient to dispel all feelings of welcome from the hearts of those who live on that street.

But, fortunately, it is rarely necessary to resort to this mechanical method. On nearly every Sunday strangers may be found in every church in a town of any considerable size. A greeting at the close of the Church service gives an admirable opportunity for the expression of a desire to call, if such attention would be appreciated.

It may be that there are children in the Sunday school whose parents do not attend any Church. In such a case the children's relation to the Sunday school will furnish a natural and sufficient introduction.

Common sense can often bring together Church people and the people they are seeking to help. The pastor may have been notified when Church members changed their place of residence. Of course he will call, and he may furnish the name and address to the Visiting Committee. In such cases, the simple statement that this has been done will be sufficient introduction.

Do not visit the members of other Churches in any sort of official fashion. You may disclaim all intentions of influencing them, but you are almost certain to be misunderstood, your actions are likely to be misinterpreted, and not much, if any, good can be accomplished.

Necessitous Cases.—The League is not an organization for the relief of paupers. It should avoid in every possible way the suspicion that it is a mere charitable society. And one of the things that must be especially avoided is the taint of professional poor-relief. Leave the word "poor" out of the vocabulary of the Third Department. "Poor boxes" and "dinners for the poor," and "clothing for the poor," and all other things bearing such special labels are disastrous and spoil the work. This is not saying that people who need money and clothing and food are to be overlooked, but they are to be treated, not as "poor," but as members of the family of God, brethren and sisters of our common life.

Perhaps the most difficult work of visiting is that undertaken in behalf of those who are in need of material help. Usually those who are the most deserving are the least willing that their needs should be made known and the most reluctant to advertise their needs in person. The utmost tact and judgment are required to make such visiting successful, and yet it is perhaps the most important form of visiting that many Chapters can attempt. Put friendliness and Christian interest first. Let it be understood that your offer of material aid is prompted not only by the existence of need, but by your own personal interest in the matter.

The Epworth League is not a charity organization. Its members are not unofficial poor commissioners. The whole movement is a religious one, and the great claim which the poor have upon you is not simply their poverty, but their relation to our common Lord. They are, or may become, brothers and sisters in the family of God.

Visiting Between Chapters.—The department may arrange for a series of inter-Chapter visits that will strengthen and emphasize the connectional bond of the Church. Assignments may be made so that two members shall go each week to some other Chapter, especially in cities or towns where Chapters are numerous and within easy reach of one another. It may even be possible to arrange a plan of inter-Chapter visitation by which an entire scheme covering six months or a year may be reduced to a schedule. These visits will accomplish much good. Each delegation will see the work of another Chapter moving under ordinary conditions. The plan cultivates the spirit of fellowship and of sympathy with the difficulties and obstacles which are found in large or small numbers in every place.

This inter-Chapter visitation will be found a great help also to the backward ones among the members. It may be easily possible that a member whose voice has never been heard in the home Chapter will learn to speak in a religious

SOCIAL SERVICE.

meeting by standing up in a strange place as representative of the Chapter from which he or she has come.

All this work of friendly ministry is worth all it costs for its own sake. It is a beautiful and Christly thing to comfort the sorrowing, feed the hungry, heal the sick, relieve the distressed, clothe the naked, and raise the fallen. This, like every other form of social service, is its own reward and needs no other. But there is another.

Wherever such work is wisely and unselfishly done, it reacts on the League, the Church, and the Kingdom. People who have come under the gracious influence of the Mercy and Help work are more ready to be won for Christ than at any other time. This work, rightly done, should be a constant feeder of the Chapter and the Church. It should be a steady help the year round, and especially effective during times of revival.

The Regions Beyond.

The needy are in one place; those who lack nothing are in another. That is a fact of modern life which must be reckoned with. In some places there are unnumbered populations incapable of bettering themselves without help. In other places there are those who have abundance of possessions and access to many forms of ministration.

One great problem of our day is the problem of bringing the Good Samaritan and his "neighbor" together. They do not live in the same part of the town; perhaps not in the same part of the State. But for the sake of both, they must be brought together.

The chief means by which this can be done is the encouragement and support of the work being carried on where the need is greatest.

Hospitals.—Our deaconesses and other workers control each year an increasing number of hospitals. These are of the most useful sort; much of the work they do is entirely free, because the patients have no money with which to pay for treatment. Therefore, the hospital must depend for its support largely on people other than its patients.

Rural Chapters and those city Chapters remote from the hospital should have a share in this work.

THE EFFICIENT EPWORTHIAN.

The needs of a hospital are almost infinite, but money will satisfy most of them. Some Chapters are so situated that they can provide supplies of various sorts, and there is no better place to send them than to a Methodist hospital. The products of the farm and garden, of work done by devoted hands, and miscellaneous gifts of many sorts are always welcome. But money is the most welcome gift of all. A barrel of potatoes is good, but it affords no help in paying last month's gas bill, which may sometimes become a more important question that the potato problem. These remarks apply with equal force, of course, to all forms of the "donation."

Concerning the donation idea, one caution will apply to all its varieties: Do not purchase in the open market the things you give to charitable institutions. The same money can be much more wisely expended by those in charge of the institution. They are entirely trustworthy, and their knowledge of the situation means much. There are times in such an institution when a silver dollar is worth more than ten gallons of pickles.

If gifts other than money are more accessible, be sure that those who are in charge of the institution are consulted before anything is sent to them. Give them a chance to inspect the larder and linen closet and to make a statement of the sort of gifts they need. *And always pay the freight.*

Homes for the Aged.—The foregoing paragraphs of this section also apply very largely to the help which may be afforded to Homes for the Aged. In addition to the regular supplies, these homes have constant use for the little "homey" things that old people enjoy, and yet which do not come under the head of absolute necessities. Every family which is fortunate enough to possess grandparents has discovered the amiable and simple whims which cost little, but which mean much for the convenience and comfort of elderly people. Their rooms are furnished, it is true, but a flower, or a picture, or a work-bag, or a pincushion, or a book-shelf, or a newspaper holder, or slippers, or any one of a hundred other things would make those rooms even more like home than they are now.

SOCIAL SERVICE.

Children's Homes.—We are learning that the child is entitled to a home. If it has none, and comes into Methodist hands, we have in part accepted the duty of finding a home for it.
The ideal home is the one which shelters a normal family, with father, mother, and children of the same blood. When a child has missed or lost such a home, he ought to have the best possible substitue for it. And because it is after all only a substitute, we should "make it up" to him in every way possible. As in other cases, the managers of our Children's Homes are always in need of money. The work is pure charity, with no productive resources to provide an income. It must be supported from without.
Many Chapters can best share in the work of these Homes by determining to make an annual offering to their support. After the money has been provided, nothing that children eat, wear, or otherwise use comes amiss in such a home. Soap, stockings, sugar, salt, sheets, are a few things which one letter of the alphabet suggests, and the other twenty-five will help to make a long and wonderfully suggestive catalogue.
There are many other enterprises which deserve, and indeed must have, such support as has been indicated here. The institutional Churches of the cities, the homes of the Woman's Home Missionary Society in various parts of the South and elsewhere, the neighborhood settlements, the deaconess homes, and all the other forms of Christian ministration are not and can not be self-supporting. But they must be supported. And in many cases the one agency best fitted to help in their support is the Mercy and Help Committee of the Third Department.
"First catch your hare." Select the institution you desire to help. If you have no choice, get the Year-Book of the Church and the reports of the various institutions. The Year-Book will tell you where to secure the reports. In selecting your institution, bear in mind these four things:
1. Other things being equal, help the one nearest you. That reduces freight bills, as well as secures greater interest in the work.
2. Consider any special resources at the command of

THE EFFICIENT EPWORTHIAN.

your Chapter. You may be able to help a hospital more readily than an orphanage.

3. With due regard to other considerations, seek to help the institution whose needs are greatest and most urgent.

4. Institutions or individuals, perhaps remote, but so situated that local aid for them is insufficient or unattainable, should be especially remembered. In this class are immigrant homes, homes and schools in the South or among specially needy classes of people elsewhere, hospitals and other institutions in the congested centers of the great cities, not forgetting the heroic preachers and other workers on the picket-line of the Church's work.

A Few General Suggestions.

Don't send a check or give a dollar when you ought to go yourself.

Many districts are taking up fresh-air work, the city and the country Chapters co-operating.

A good thing for a country Chapter to undertake is the repair and maintenance of the parsonage.

There is a box in one church vestibule marked "Mercy and Help." It is as good as the old poor-box, and the name is more thoughtful.

One Chapter spent $30 on an invalid chair, and loans it to those who would otherwise be shut in. It is a paying investment.

One Third Vice-President spent four weeks in one home nursing, and three in another caring for the children while the mother was in the hospital.

Call on the well-to-do, as well as on the poor folk. Some people in good circumstances are in need of you quite as much as the so-called "unchurched masses."

It is an evil sign when we discover that our own interests interfere with our duty to others.

It is not always prudent to help folks, but it is always Christlike.

Every opportunity to be a true neighbor is God's invitation to honor Him.

To be a Good Samaritan you must know how to deal with people whose need is "none of your business."

SOCIAL SERVICE.

The Epworth League Chapter which is too busy with the devotional meeting to take up social service work should elect the priest and the Levite as honorary members.

Be careful how you begin to help folks. For, having begun, you must keep it up until you have done all you can.

The priest avoided defilement, and the Levite spent no money, but the Samaritan the next day was the holiest and the richest of the three.

The best thing about the Samaritan was not his means nor his skill, but his sympathy.

Jesus Christ is our Neighbor; "He that had mercy." And we must be like Him, or we may not claim Him.

If you can not find some one to neighbor, there is something the matter, not with your eyes, but with your heart.

There is need just now in this country of a million Good Samaritans, and yet many more than a million Methodists have gone Sunday by Sunday to Church and confessed that they are Christ's disciples.

Once in a while—even oftener—it is fine to do a piece of Christly work that does n't fit into any statistical blank.

The country Chapter which wants to do a really up-to-date and helpful bit of service should send to the Wisconsin Experiment Station, Madison, Wis., for Circular 29: "A Method of Making a Social Survey of a Rural Community."

Some so-called social service is a process of waking up the community so as to give it a sleeping-powder.

The reason social service is better than mercy and help is just this: a pure milk supply will keep more babies well than a free dispensary could restore after bad milk was brought into the neighborhood.

On one district some country Chapters which had few calls for relief work sent boxes of clothing in to a city Chapter, which knew just what to do with them.

Money for relief work is raised in one Chapter by the earning of a minimum of fifty cents on the part of each one who can be interested in the work. The usual experience social adds zest and brightness to the plan.

The committee which has three or four people ready and willing to sing at funerals will be a blessing to the

THE EFFICIENT EPWORTHIAN.

pastor, especially if he has many funerals to conduct among people who are not connected with the Church.

During the scarcity of vegetables one fall there came a plea for some help from the Omaha Methodist Hospital. One Chapter held a "vegetable sociable." Price of admission, vegetables. A four-bushel barrel was filled without difficulty.

The Mercy and Help Committee of a Rhode Island Chapter called on a happy veteran preacher on his eighty-ninth birthday. The pastor went also, and what with prayer, song, and a few birthday reminders, the call was a most delightful event.

An Illinois Chapter, when it sends in its annual *Epworth Herald* club, adds the names of two or three people in town who do not get many papers, and sends a Christmas card notification to each person "with the League's love."

The flower-mission work is worth all the money it costs. But it can be extended and managed at less expense if the Chapter can plan for a flower garden or a greenhouse of its own. Plants can be loaned from this greenhouse and returned to be ready for further service.

One Junior League keeps the church lawn in order. In the center of the lawn is a circular flower-bed, in which foliage plants are arranged in the form of the League badge. Around this design is a collection of plans which furnishes flowers for the Visiting Committee.

A group of Epworthians drove out to the country one summer afternoon to a "fruit-canning." The fruit was donated by the host, and the cans furnished by the Chapter. The afternoon was delightfully spent, refreshments being served after the serious business of putting up the fruit was over. The nearest Methodist hospital was enriched by a goodly shipment of most acceptable fruit.

A school for colored children in South Carolina was sorely in need of a library. It had three hundred students and no books. The facts came to the knowledge of a Chapter in Wisconsin, and the gift of one volume or more from each member of the Chapter formed the nucleus of what

SOCIAL SERVICE.

will shortly be a fine library. That is fruitful home missionary work.

One committee circulates subscription cards among the business men, asking an annual subscription of goods from their stock. When need for any of these supplies arises, the subscription card is presented by the chairman, and the amount of goods supplied is entered on the back of the card. This is a simple and satisfactory way of keeping the account.

The hardest day in almost every home is Saturday, when all the little folks are out of school and the mother finds much work and worry. Her cares would be lightened if a few young people would give a little time to the children. Gather them in the church vestry for two hours for their amusement. The time will pass pleasantly for the little folks, and may easily be made helpful and instructive. How much it will mean to the overburdened mothers only they can tell.

A thoughtful Third Vice-President provides a supply of quilts and bed-linen with which to supplement the stock in homes where sickness has made unusual drafts on the linen closet. The quilts for this purpose are pieced by old ladies, who are glad to find a way in which they can be of service. The friend who has tried this plan says: "I have been out on two cases of typhoid fever where I took this course. I always carry a few delicacies for the sick, and some flowers, which speak words we never know how to say."

Keep a directory of places where various sorts of gifts will be acceptable and wisely used. For example, discover where cast-off clothing can be used; where pictures, magazines, Sunday school cards, canned and fresh fruits, flowers, and hospital supplies are desired. There are scores of institutions within reach of many Chapters which would be delighted to secure one or more of these forms of supplies, and most of these things are within easy reach of the Chapters themselves.

This committee can do a much-appreciated work by subscribing for *The Epworth Herald,* the *Advocates,* and other papers, in behalf of members who are not able to

THE EFFICIENT EPWORTHIAN.

subscribe for themselves. Subscriptions that will carry blessings with them may be made in behalf of frontier preachers. If the Chapter is helping to support a missionary, a subscription to *The Epworth Herald* in that missionary's name will be a delightful and appropriate gift.

Much has been said about carriages for the aged on Old Folks' Day. This plan of getting out the aged persons in the community is a good one. Why limit it to Old People's Day? Start an Epworth League carriage for the special benefit of the aged Christians. Let it be in operation every Sunday morning, gathering a few who could not otherwise come to the sanctuary. In many places this can be done without expense, if the members of the Chapter will take turns in playing coachman, and if the work is planned systematically so that the burden does not fall too heavily on a few. A variation of this method in the case of down-town Churches is the use of a Sunday school wagonette, which gathers up the smaller children from the remotest homes and carries them to and from Sunday school.

Another mode of gracious helpfulness in connection with the Church service is the Epworth League nursery. If there is a room somewhat isolated from the auditorium, two or three members of the department can fit it up simply so that they may take charge of the smaller children who are brought to church. Simple kindergarten work may be done, or interesting stories told. Even the babies can be taken care of with a little planning. This idea makes it possible for mothers to come to church who could not think of coming if they had to face the ordeal of caring for the little ones throughout the Church service, and who have no facilities for leaving the children at home. A variation of this plan sends a committee from the department to the homes where there are small children, just before the evening service. Then the parents, neither of whom care to go to Church without the other, can go with quiet minds, leaving the Epworthians in charge of the home. The children can be put to bed, or if they are old enough, they can be entertained until the parents return.

Many people who can not come regularly to Epworth

SOCIAL SERVICE.

League or Sunday school would be glad to use the libraries of these organizations. Let the Mercy and Help Committee manage the circulating feature of the library.

Provide a fruit-cellar for the use of the committee. A canvass of the housewives at canning-time will, in most cases, secure the promise of one-tenth of the fruit for the Lord's work. Gather it up, put it in a safe place where it will be available through the winter as needed.

There may be a boy or girl in your neighborhood who ought to go to college, and who could go if only the hard pull at the start were safely over. The Third Department might start one of its members to school without giving offense to the most sensitive feelings, if it were done as a co-operative effort. Make it a partnership affair. Insist that you are going to get as much good out of it as the direct beneficiary. Then pack the trunk, or provide some of the things that, while necessary to the beginning of college life, seem to be out of the reach of the prospective college student.

The public institutions of the city offer an inviting field for work. The various charitable homes, the hospitals, the prisons, the orphanages, are so many opportunities for League work. Of course, if this work is attempted, it must begin by securing the cordial co-operation and support of the authorities. Religious meetings may be held, personal work done wherever possible, and the more material side of the League's work put into play as opportunity offers. For instance, in visiting a hospital, flowering plants, small yet beautiful, may be secured for each patient. At the holidays—Christmas, New Year's, Easter, Thanksgiving—simple but tasteful cards may be provided for all the residents of the institution. The work is not out of place nor morbid, even when done in connection with jails or prisons.

Of course, in such cases sensible Epworthians understand that it is neither patriotic nor religious to express sympathy for the afflictions of the wrong-doer while losing sight of his moral condition.

The country has large opportunities for special service. The comparative cheapness and availability of fruit and produce make such gifts easy to the country Chapter. In the late summer and early fall, by co-operation with city Chapters, shipments of fresh fruit may be sent to those to whom it will be an unwonted luxury. A hen and her brood may be cared for through the summer with Thanksgiving and Christmas dinners in mind for those city dwellers, discovered by the Chapter in town, to whom the provisions will be a grateful and much-needed surprise.

Canned fruit may be prepared for hospitals, for deaconess homes, and other institutions which have large need of such provisions and small incomes. Many of these institutions will provide the cans in any quantity.

A word as to shipment of such fruits. Let the shipper pay the freight. Sometimes a barrel of fruit, coming to the city hospital whose finances are sadly overtaxed, is an embarrassing gift because the freight charges are not easy to pay.

In cases of sickness the Chapter may occasionally do good service by providing voluntary nurses and watchers. But there are many cases where a professional nurse is greatly needed while the family pocketbook will not provide such a luxury. Then the Chapter can be especially useful. In the same way a doctor may be secured when otherwise medical help would be out of the question. Doctors and nurses will usually be glad to make special terms in such cases and to share the privileges of service with the people's society.

Fresh-Air Work.

Fresh-air work is the most practical form of Christianity that can be attempted in a great many places during the summer months. With a little planning the work may be done, easily and effectively, by hundreds of Chapters in every part of the country wherever there is a city large enough to have a considerable population in congested areas. The raw material for fresh-air work is present in large abundance; children whose only playground is the street, and who know nothing of the delights of the open field, the clear sky, and the free life of the farm. About these cities there are great stretches of God's country, with small towns, villages, and farms radiating in every direc-

SOCIAL SERVICE.

tion from the populous center. The territory within a hundred miles of any of these cities is available for fresh-air work.

The proper prosecution of fresh-air work requires the co-operation of one or more city Chapters with one or more Chapters in the country. The work is especially adapted, on the city side, to city Epworth League unions, whose officers can direct and supervise the work. The city Chapter's work is twofold—to find the children who need the outing, and to find the money for their transportation to and from the country. Incidentally, of course, the city Chapters will provide one or more guardians for the journey. The country Chapters have their share of work in finding homes at which the city children will be welcome for one or two weeks as guests. Then, after all arrangements have been completed, and the children have come, the country Epworthians will meet them at the station and distribute them to the homes that are waiting to receive them. At the close of the specified period the children will be gathered together and escorted back to town.

This process may be repeated two or three times during the summer months. It is best, when possible, to provide a new list of homes for each batch of children, lest the work prove too burdensome on a few. Circumstances in individual cases will determine how much or how little supervision of the children is necessary after they have reached the homes provided for them. In some cases nothing else will need to be done. In others the Chapters may find it wise to have picnics, entertainments, and other diversions for the children.

A variation of the plan is possible where there is a community which possesses available vacant houses. Let one of these houses be cleaned and provided with the simple furniture needed. Canvass the neighborhood for these articles. They may usually be secured from members and friends for the period covered by the outing. Where this plan is adopted a guardian should accompany the children from the city, and members of the country Chapter will take turns in helping the children's guardian to care for her lively and irrepressible charges.

THE EFFICIENT EPWORTHIAN.

The correspondence between the country and city Chapters interested in this work should begin early in the season, and everything should be fully planned before the actual work begins. A careful record should be kept of every child who is to go into the country, giving name, sex, date when the trip is to begin, destination, and length of the stay. At the same time a careful canvass should be made by the country Chapters of all the available homes within reach, noting name, address, nearest railroad station, number of children who will be received, age, sex, number of days they will be cared for, date of beginning of their stay.

In the canvass for money to pay railroad fares, the Chapters remote from the congested districts of the city should be given their full share of the work. Do not leave that burden to the down-town Churches and the missions. It is as important to the remotest Churches that this work should be done as it is to those down-town, and the entire problem ought to be attacked by methods which are in the highest sense co-operative.

Distributing Literature.

In the distribution of magazines and papers, a little system will be a great help. The work will not continue more than two or three weeks unless some system is adopted. A corps of carriers should be organized. Use the Juniors for this work.

First, let them canvass the community with a card containing a question something like this, "Will you permit the carrier from the .... Epworth League Chapter to leave a paper or magazine with you each week?" or month, as the case may be. On the lines underneath this question the persons canvassed are asked to write their names and addresses. Arrange these cards into routes. Give each carrier a dozen or so, and ask him to do the work on Saturday or Sunday afternoon. Get a rubber stamp and use it on every piece of literature sent out. Let it read, "With the compliments of .... Epworth League Chapter." Then there will be no question as to the source from whence this literature has come, and you

SOCIAL SERVICE.

will impress the existence of your Chapter upon the minds of those who might never hear of it in any other way.

Literature of many sorts is very acceptable, not only in homes, but in public institutions and other places where many persons are compelled to spend much time. Hospitals are glad for literature for the use of their convalescents. Sailors' homes, rest rooms for street-railroad men and other classes of workers, find a constant demand for almost any kind of literature. Then the charitable institutions of various sorts, and even the prisons, are constantly calling for decent reading matter. But it need not—must not—be confined to sermons, tracts, and reports of religious organizations.

The barber shops of a community are sadly lacking in good literature. They have altogether too much of the other kind. Current issues of *The Epworth Herald* and other papers of like character would do much to counteract the influence of the stuff that is usually found on the barber-shop table.

There is need of a reform in the matter of providing literature at railway stations. Oftentimes the newspaper pocket which hangs so invitingly on the walls of waiting-rooms is entirely empty for weeks together. At other times it contains a beggarly supply of unattractive material. Change all that. Keep the wall-pocket full if it takes three visits a week to do it. The oftener it is emptied, the more certain you may be that it is doing its work properly. Put good, wholesome reading into the pocket. Satisfy yourself, whatever this literature may be externally, that at heart it is positively on the side of Christianity and the Church.

The Redemption of Holidays.

A great social service work can be done in the redemption of our National holidays from popular degradation.

For example, a new Fourth of July is urgently demanded. It is not possible and not really necessary to do away with the noisy, semi-barbarous celebration so dear to the heart of the small boy. But the Fourth of July is an ideal day on which to emphasize and encourage such things as the temperance enterprise, the cultivation of true and vigorous patriotism, the setting up of Christian standards and ideals in political life, and the recognition of a dependence upon God in National affairs.

In attempting this redemption of the Fourth of July the Social Service Committee should begin early and plan for a really great celebration. Nothing small should be attempted for the National birthday. It would be a foreordained failure. And do not omit the holiday features. Recognize the fact that it is a day for play, as well as for public profit. Unite with other Chapters to make the day a notable one. Provide for banners, for the very best speeches that can be provided, and for games and innocent refreshments.

If there is any important measure pending before any legislative or executive body, this Christian Fourth of July affords a splendid opportunity for the circulation of petitions. Usually there is no taint of partisan politics in the air. The fall campaigns have not yet begun, and the thoughts of most men turn easily to ideas in harmony with the hope and prayers of the fathers of the Republic. Detailed plans will be found on pages 352-3.

Another day which may be made valuable in the work of Christian citizenship is Thanksgiving Day. It is something more than the day of a big feed. It has both a political and a religious significance. If the Church has not already planned to observe Thanksgiving Day, let the Chapter take the initiative. Get on the good side of the pastor. Win his consent to hold a Thanksgiving Day service at eleven o'clock in the morning. Tell him that you will see to it that he has a congregation. It would be a strange preacher who would refuse to preach on Thanksgiving Day if his congregation were assured.

The difficulty with most Thanksgiving Day services is the absence of the people. The Chapters can remedy that if they will, and if they do the preacher will be glad to do his utmost.

Of course, when the Epworth League takes the initiative the pastor will be less inclined than ever to deliver a pessimistic, gloomy, doleful wail, and miscall it a Thanksgiving

SOCIAL SERVICE.

sermon. Instead, he will see the bright side, he will discover the good things that are to be found in the history of the Nation, he will emphasize the duty and the spirit of Thanksgiving, and he will bear profoundly on the divine mission of the American people. For more detailed discussion of Thanksgiving Day observance, see page 372.

Holidays like Labor Day, Washington's Birthday, Lincoln's Birthday, and others are especially appropriate for the holding of Epworth League rallies. The patriotic idea has always been appropriately linked to the religious idea, and both ideas are the gainers of the process.

The right of petition is guaranteed by the Federal Constitution. Some people have an idea that petitions do not amount to much. They are mistaken. Petitions of the right sort, presented at the right time, have often influenced legislators to vote the right way. A legislator is a susceptible individual. He is remarkably sensitive to public opinion. Some petitions reflect public opinion. Others do not. If the Epworth League commits itself only to the sensible and timely petition, its influence will be recognized wherever men meet to make laws.

MAKE A DIRECTORY OF PUBLIC SERVANTS.

Who's your United States senator? Congressman? State senator? Representative? Alderman? County commissioner? School Board member?

Not many of us could stand an examination in this branch of knowledge. And yet, if we count ourselves citizens, what knowledge is of more practical usefulness?

Don't you see? Every little while a question comes up for public consideration. The pastor, or the Third Vice-President of the League, or the visiting reformer makes an appeal, asking everybody to write to the official whose influence is desired on our side—which, of course, is the right side!—of the question of the hour.

At the moment we are all interested; perhaps indignant, or enthusiastic, or desperate, as the appeal may have stirred us.

But when the meeting is over, who knows where to write? And it is too much trouble to find out, or perhaps

THE EFFICIENT EPWORTHIAN.

we do n't know even how to go about the task of finding out.

Hint to the Third Vice-President, from A. F. Patterson, of Newport, Wash.: If you would do a bit of practical social service, prepare a directory of those public officials who are likely to be involved in the decision of questions affecting the public good. Then post the list in the League room or, better, in some place where every Church attendant will be able to see it.

Then, when we are asked to send a telegram or a postcard to some official who needs to be encouraged or informed or warned, you can add, "His name and address will be found on your 'Directory of Public Servants.'"

A Large Job for the Third Department.

The job begins by the department's seeing its opportunity to remind the whole Chapter that Prohibition is now in the basic law. Enforcement is no longer a debatable question.

The job continues by giving the department a good excuse for telling the Chapter that Prohibition is not self-enforcing.

The booze business has not disbanded. It is organizing more desperately than ever. It has lost its gold mine, and it does not care what crimes it may need to commit in order to get its gold mine back again.

The whole nation is now going through experiences which Kansas and other states had in the first years of state Prohibition.

The most accomplished liars and statistics-jugglers have been hired to show up the "horrors" of Prohibition, and the most versatile press agents are spreading the joyful news of every successful dodging and breaking of the law.

The job of the Third Department, after it has stirred up the interest of the young people, is to make an alliance with "Old Man Specific"; in a word, to Do Something.

Praise the local newspaper when it supports the law. When it commits the moral mistake of belittling Prohibition or misrepresenting Prohibition, tell it that you rep-

SOCIAL SERVICE.

resent a fair-sized public which actively dislikes that method of defacing good white paper.

Tell each interested official of your community, in the name of the Methodist young people, most of whom are voters, that you are watching him so that you can praise him when he honors his oath of office, and prompt him when he appears to be forgetting his part, and publish abroad his unfaithfulness when he violates his pledge.

Set aside a part of the department's budget as a contribution to support of the organized temperance forces. These organizations helped us to get the Prohibition Amendment, but their work is far from finished, and they can't win this year's battles by pawning last year's Distinguished Service Medals.

Ask for a fifteen-minute prayer service some Sunday night, as part of the devotional meeting. Spend the time in real and definite prayer, united and believing that God, who has given us what victories have been won, will give us courage and loyalty for the duration of the war.

Beating the Old Saloon on "Service."

Before the saloon was banished we were hearing a great deal about the "social values of the saloon." Liquor dealers grasped it as the final straw of self-defense; forward-looking social workers recognized it as something to be provided for with the coming of Prohibition. In 1915, college orators were roundly denouncing the evils of the liquor traffic, but by 1916 and 1917 the best accepted orations had for their subject "After Prohibition—What?"

Prohibition came, and the question was forgotten. The law was passed, and the American public went fishing. But until that question is answered, hope for complete enforcement of the Eighteenth Amendment is vain.

As far back as 1901 there appeared a book, entitled, "Substitutes for the Saloon." It was written by Mr. Raymond Calkins, as a report of an investigation in behalf of the "Committee of Fifty for the Investigation of the Liquor Problem." The far-sighted point of view in this book will be clear from the reading of this extract from the introduction:

THE EFFICIENT EPWORTHIAN.

"An essential part of any sane and safe temperance movement is to supply by such method as is most applicable to the conditions of a community, adequate substitutes for the saloon. The thirst for relaxation and companionship must be satisfied if the thirst for drink is to be overcome. . . .

"Here are these brilliant windows and inviting lights, these lines of leisurely patrons at the bar, and these groups of gossiping neighbors at the tables. These are not members of lodges who have other resorts, or lovers of nature who will scatter to the woods, or pious folk who are at home in Church sociables, or domestic fathers who are inclined to sit at home and rock the baby. What is to become of them? . . .

"It is evident that the vacuum must be filled just where it is, and that both sedatives and society, free from harm, must be substituted for the same resources now so intimately associated with wastefulness and crime. How to accomplish this substitution in ways that make it genuine, adequate, and effective is the next problem in temperance reform."

In the files of *The Epworth Herald* there is an unpublished manuscript, entitled, "Sensible Substitutes for the Saloon." It was written by Dean Frank C. Lockwood, of the University of Arizona. Dean Lockwood says, "In a 'wet' town a man could step into a saloon in almost any block at almost any hour of the day or night.

"He did not have to knock; the door swung open at his touch. Within he found a city directory if he wanted to look up an address. The bartender was willing to give him any information that he might be seeking. He found toilet conveniences. He found a warm room in winter and a cool one in summer. He found a cheap yet savory and well-served lunch. He found congenial companions, and games, and newspapers.

"If he was a regular frequenter of the saloon, he found in the saloonkeeper a genial friend possessing a great local influence. Indeed, the saloonkeeper was a sort of institution in himself. He knew the latest and best (or worst) story, and he could tell it well. He was on confidential terms with the ward political boss—if he was not himself

SOCIAL SERVICE.

chief boss of the neighborhood. By virtue of his political leadership he could secure this one a job; get immunity for that one; and give or lend a ten dollar bill to another in time of distress.

" . . . Divorced from the drink habit and the degrading attractions of the saloon, almost everyone of the attractions mentioned are in themselves humanizing and enriching. The community that does not have some means of simply and graciously supplying these natural physical and social desires is deficient."

Granted that community houses and recreation centers are more common than they were before the war, granted that many former frequenters of the saloon are now finding social desires satisfied at home or at a moving picture show, have we reached the point where we can honestly say that there is a moral equivalent for the social values of the saloon?

A revised edition of "Substitutes for the Saloon," earlier quoted from, was published in 1919. The preface to this edition was written by Dr. Francis G. Peabody. From it the following extracts were taken:

"There remains much for enlightened sentiment and public spirit to do in making provision for certain opportunities which hitherto have been offered by the liquor saloon.

"The saloons have always served the public by being often the only place where a glass of water could be asked for and received without fear of intrusion. Certainly each community should now exercise renewed care in the provision of an ample number of well-placed drinking fountains. . . .

"The community has a certain responsibility to furnish public meeting places for its citizens. . . . Portland, Oregon, has its community houses for both men and women, which might well be studied as models for imitation in other cities. . . . and Portland, Maine, by installing a great municipal organ in her new city hall, with a municipal organist of national reputation giving free public concerts, has opened a new chapter of legitimate effort toward the provision of fine entertainment for the people. . . .

"The time has surely come also for a wider use of school

THE EFFICIENT EPWORTHIAN.

buildings. This reform for the use of these great educational and civic plants for the welfare of the people as a whole, can now be no longer delayed. . . .

"Finally, it seems certain that the provision of proper and wholesome recreation for the people cannot be secured short of the creation in all of our municipalities of a community recreation department of the city government. The situation, especially with regard to the moving picture houses, and to the dance halls, and to burlesque theaters, which now offer the people dramatic entertainment, providing dancing, color, and music at prices within their reach, but under conditions which are often simply deplorable, cannot adequately be controlled without direct municipal interest and supervision."

The development of the community service idea during the war proved that a social program can be devised to meet the extraordinary strain of war time for men far from home. Shall we admit that we cannot do as much in the days of peace?

Social and recreational programs can stand on their own merits. But at this time there is an extraordinary justification. The status of the Eighteenth Amendment makes imperative an adequate provision for the social life of a community.

We have no love for John Barleycorn or his immoral associate, the licensed saloon. We have said that we will have none of either. But if Prohibition is regarded merely as a matter of law enforcement with no attempt to solve the social problems involved, it will fail.

The final fate of Prohibition in America depends on her ability to provide a moral equivalent for the immoral saloon!

Have we gone too far with Prohibition? Put it the other way: Have we gone far enough? Have we adopted that surest method of law enforcement? The removal of those conditions which provoke its violation?

The League Can Help at Election Time.

The Eighteenth Amendment is worth fighting for; what can the Epworth League do to help?

SOCIAL SERVICE.

The enforcement of the Volstead law and state legislation in harmony therewith depends entirely upon the character of the men in public office. In the first place, the men who voted for enforcement laws must be supported for re-election, as the "wets" are trying to enact beer and wine legislation and have candidates in every district for Congress and the state Legislature. Next, judges, members of the county board and sheriff are to be elected this year. It is worth fighting to get men who are in sympathy with the law and have the character to enforce it.

Now, the thing the Epworth League can do is this: First, divide the League into two equal divisions, and let each division elect a captain. Divide each division into squads of five each with a corporal. Divide the church membership equally between the two divisions.

The object is for each division to contest with the other to get the largest number of signatures pledging to register on the appointed day and to vote in the primary for candidates pledged to the enforcement of law and endorsed by the Anti-Saloon League of your State.

Let the district presidents work out a system of points to be reported at district rallies—a banner in each district to be awarded to the church having the greatest number of points to its credit.

The wets have well-financed organizations determined to bring back beer and wine, the entering wedge to the whole liquor traffic; some good people have been impressed with their arguments, and it is necessary to be up and doing to prevent them from winning any point of vantage. Beer and wine in the home would mean that the home might be over or in the rear of a saloon, and that the saloon would be supplied directly or indirectly with beer and wine and become a blind tiger for stronger drinks. This program has been tried out in some states, and it does not work. Eventually it would destroy the Eighteenth Amendment.

The Epworth League can render a patriotic service at this time and incidentally save many lives and much suffering by helping to nominate men of character for re-

THE EFFICIENT EPWORTHIAN.

sponsible office who will sustain our laws. This is as great a patriotic service as any rendered in the time of war.

Christian Citizenship.

The Epworthian should be really and positively a citizen. Not merely a voter, but a 365-day citizen in his precinct, ward, township, city, county, State, Nation. He will not be so absorbed in the contemplation of heaven as to forget the claims and importance of this present world.

The Epworthian loves his country with a real and vital patriotism. For that reason he will be all the more ready to rebuke unrighteousness in public affairs.

The Epworthian will be honest in his citizenship. If he has property he will pay taxes on it. If he brings dutiable goods into the country he will pay the tariff charges. If he works for public pay he will give the full measure of service for his salary. If he has a vote, he will cast it as a Christian. If he has no vote he will use his influence as a Christian with those who have.

The Epworthian, besides keeping the law himself, has a right to insist that others must keep it. The people who do not want to keep the law are the very ones who most need law enforcement. It is folly to advocate good laws and then be careless about their enforcement. Moreover, it is folly to expect that laws will be enforced unless the law-keeping folk are as much in earnest about maintaining the law as the law-breakers are in trying to evade it.

What is Christian citizenship? Why should the Epworth League be concerned about it?

In the first place, it is gospel government, the choosing of Christians to make and interpret and administer the laws. It stands for righteousness in legislation, in the courts, and in every executive office so that the multiplied activities of public life shall be carried on without corruption and partisanship.

The acceptance of Christian citizenship as a part of the League's program of social service is a confession. By that acceptance we admit that there is need for agitation, education, and combination, to lift the standard of citizenship in this country from the low level of self and party

SOCIAL SERVICE.

to the high plane of Christian duty. But if it is a confession, it is also a resolve. It is a distinct purpose to antagonize the saloon element, the lawless element, the willingly ignorant, and the willingly wicked in our social life. There is in it abundant inspiration. It calls us to just such service as the young and eager have longed for.

But Christian citizenship is not first of all a campaign. It begins as a personal readjustment. The Epworthian must himself be a Christian citizen before he can wage warfare against the unchristian element in the city, State, or Nation. That means Christianity in business. That means Christianity made practical on election-day. That means Christianity in every-day work. It means Christianity in every place, high or low, where the citizen has opportunity to put the stamp of his sort of citizenship upon the life of his community.

To many of us Christian citizenship is a challenge. It says, "First cast out the beam out of thine own eye, and then shalt thou see clearly to cast out the mote out of thy brother's eye."

In order to accomplish anything for Christian citizenship it is necessary to believe that the thing is possible. We must believe that machine politicians and the supporters of pro-liquor lawlessness, and those who rule the ignorant and drive them to the polls like sheep, can all be successfully opposed.

But successful opposition must be organized. Usually the forces of evil are compactly arrayed. They know what they want, and, as a rule, they know what is necessary in order to get it. The Christian citizen must have the same sort of wisdom. Agitation which does not lead to combination for actual results is likely to make theoretical reformers and practical hypocrites by means of the very movement which seemed to promise so much for better things.

Christian citizenship is efficient citizenship. The failure of many reform movements may be directly traced to the fact that the reformers want to furnish good government, but do not know how. So the great need is that Christian citizenship shall be made a matter of training. The subjects concerning which everybody needs wider and more

THE EFFICIENT EPWORTHIAN.

definite education are almost innumerable. For example, a young people's society in New Jersey, in its declaration of principles, indicates the thing that Christian citizens need to know: "The union shall strive to remove from the city all temptation to vice not lawfully permitted. It shall attempt to check the purchasing of votes and other abuses connected with the ballot-box. It shall urge Christian people to attend the primaries of their parties, and insist upon the nomination for office of men who are in sympathy with the object of this organization. It shall submit to the proper authorities evidence to convict officers who are recreant to the trust committed to them by the people. The union declines to embrace a political party or support any individual nomination for office. It hopes to accomplish these results by no hasty or spasmodic efforts at reform, but by arduous caution and relentless effort, and requests the aid of good citizens in the furtherance of its principles."

Christian citizenship is gospel pity. Because we are Christians, the lame and the halt and the blind are in a special way our responsibility. The work of caring for them is a sacred business. It can not be done by the chronic office-seeker, or by the selfish politician. The helpless element in the population needs compassion, tenderness, and patient care. Only Christian citizens can provide these things. Christian citizenship is gospel courage. There are always evils which desire to live, but ought to die. To attempt their destruction requires courage. It is easy to say, "Let it alone," but it is also cowardly, and a coward is next door to a traitor.

The Epworthian is under compulsion about all these things because he is a Christian. The Christian gospel insists on right government. It insists on justice, and it insists on fearlessness in the discharge of duty.

All Are Citizens.

Many Epworthians are under twenty-one years of age. But they are citizens. And they will soon be voters as well as citizens. So this subject interests every member of the Epworth League.

Young women may count largely in all work of higher

SOCIAL SERVICE.

ideals of citizenship. Their work may not be so public, but it can be positive and potent.

Who can count the gains secured for righteousness in public life through the labors of the Woman's Christian Temperance Union. Few of its members could vote until recently. They have had no direct political influence. But indirectly they have been a tremendous power for good in the last forty years. Ask any congressman.

The late Colonel Waring, when he was street commissioner of New York, did a great work for good citizenship. He won the school children to his side. They organized volunteer street-cleanliness brigades. They were active helpers in keeping the city's streets free from the litter of paper and fruit rinds and other accumulations. A clean street is one step toward better citizenship.

Women can render invaluable service in connection with the schools. Thousands of Epworthians are teachers. Each of them has more opportunity than a dozen voters to work for Christian ideals and Christian purposes in the citizens of to-morrow.

And, after all, the home is the chief place where good citizenship must be taught, and the effects of bad citizenship counteracted. True, the work of the home is often fearfully attacked by outside influences. But if the home did not stand for Christian citzenship, how long would the other forces be able to keep at work?

THE CHRISTIAN CITIZEN.

The Christian is the only full-fledged citizen. He owes allegiance to a greater country than this. "Our citizenship is in heaven." But the greater includes the less; a man who is a good citizen of the United States must of necessity be a good citizen of Ohio, if, for example, Ohio is his home. A man who is a good citizen of heaven is always for that reason a better citizen of earth.

The Christian will exercise two kinds of power as a citizen.

1. Negative power. He will always and everywhere veto whatever conflicts with the Constitution of the United

THE EFFICIENT EPWORTHIAN.

States and constitution of heaven. And sometimes v-e-t-o spells vote!

He will not vote to expel Christ from Gadara, even though he is interested in the swine industry. He is more interested in men.

He will not think that his work as a citizen is all done on election day or ratification night.

He will not accept his political issues from the saloon, the spoilsman, or the demagogue. He will help to make issues.

2. Positive power. Some things the Christian citizen will always urge and promote by every means in his power.

He will insist on the recognition of the Christian ideal for the State. When he needs to vote as a Christian he will not ask what party emblem adorns his ticket. There are some things on which Christians can not divide—and stay Christians.

He will urge the need of civic righteousness. He believes that the laws of Christ can be applied to National and State and municipal affairs. He believes that the community, as well as the individual, should be set apart as sacred, "sanctified."

He will put righteousness above all tariff questions, and the law of God above the politician's law of expediency.

He will always accept the supremacy of conscience where questions of moral are involved.

He will veto all selfish attempts to enrich the individual at the expense of the State.

That will put him against every form of law-evasion, and will make him a positive factor in supporting the enforcement of all the laws, with no favors to any law-breaker.

It will put him against every form of anarchy, such as bribe-giving and bribe-taking, corrupt legislation, inefficient men in public office, the use of office as a road to wealth.

He will veto all that endangers the Sabbath by making it merely a weekly holiday. That attitude lost the Sabbath in France, and is threatening it here.

He will not vote for immoral men to represent him in any place of public trust.

SOCIAL SERVICE.

Some Things to Emphasize.

The politics of this world will never be purified by the ungodly.

A Christian has the same rights as any other man at the ballot-box, but he has higher obligations.

It is easy to be fervent in advocacy of Christian citizenship on Sunday, but Christian citizenship is most needed when the churches are not open.

Do not be willing to take election issues from the public utilities, the office-seeker, or the politician. The office-holder is a minister of God as much as is the preacher. He ought not to complain when he is reminded of that fact. The Christian's besetting sin is his once-in-a-while-ness. He thinks that one election carried for reform is to usher in the millennium.

Preachers ought to keep out of politics if they can. But most of the time they can not, if they are going to be true preachers.

There is a great difference between citizenship and partisanship.

Do not be discouraged because the evils you attack seem to grow. Remember the slave business, and how it finally died.

Sometimes ask yourself the question whether it is part of a citizen's duty to enforce the laws.

CHAPTER X

CULTURE AND RECREATION.

The Fourth Department is quite as important to the sustained life and usefulness of the Chapter as any other. A group of Methodist young people which ignores both its own intellectual and social demands, and those of the community, will become narrow-minded, biased, and, if the group holds together long, which is quite unlikely, it will become a positive detriment to the Church.

Our religion is essentially one of intelligence and fellowship. Christianity quickens all our powers, and enlarges all our capacities, these quite as surely as any others. So the provision for their nurture and guidance is an eminently proper part of the Epworth League scheme.

In 1913 the Board of Control changed the name of the Fourth Department from "Social and Literary Work" to "Culture and Recreation." The change was significant of the enlarging recognition being given to recreation as a positive element in the religious training of young people.

On the intellectual side the department seeks to make our denominational relation one of intelligent loyalty. It puts the doctrines, polity, and history of the Methodist Episcopal Church understandingly before its members. It would develop a proper denominational self-respect, as far removed from pride as it is from the attitude of apology and servility.

Then, the abounding mental life of the young people is provided for, in lectures and lecture courses, libraries, reading-rooms, literary exercises, debates, study classes, reading circles, and other popular and appropriate ways.

The social side of life is given full recognition. All forms of proper pleasure and amusement are welcomed, and the department must strive to emphasize the social nature of the Christian life by all possible means.

CULTURE AND RECREATION.

Then, there are duties which must naturally fall to the share of this department: the seeking of new members, the welcoming of strangers, the musical work of the Chapter, flowers for Church and League room decoration, ushers for the Chapter meetings, badges, banners, and general decorations.

The department is properly charged with the work of circulating *The Epworth Herald,* which is the official magazine-newspaper of the movement, and whose wide circulation is one of the essential elements in the enlarging of the Epworth League idea.

Then the Fourth Department may be a means of interesting and winning new people. We have not done enough when we have encouraged and nurtured the social and intellectual elements in the lives of our own young people. The work of this department may accomplish a notable spiritual service by attracting the unsaved young people of the community to associations in which it will be possible to lead them to Christ.

And, before we can do great things, even for the young people already associated with the League and the Church, we must provide social and intellectual opportunities that will satisfy them and keep them from venturesome excursions into doubtful territory in search of the life which they crave and which is their right.

The Fourth Department can do all this. It can provide an entirely normal and delightful social atmosphere, and minister to all the mental longings and aspirations of young life. It can recommend the Christian life as a life of joy and gladness; a life of intellectual as well as spiritual growth; a life in which every right desire and worthy ambition is satisfied and encouraged. Thus our own young people will be held for Christ and the Church, and those that have thus far been on the outside may discover the beauty and winsomeness of the life that is in Christ.

CULTURE.

If the Chapter has a regular monthly meeting and provision is made for literary features in connection with it, the preparation of each month's program is a matter of much importance. There is more difficulty in beginning to make a program than in finishing it. No such thing as slipshod work can prosper. Numbers put on the program as stop-gaps or time-killers will kill interest and stop attendance.

As nearly as possible, this department should utilize the talent of every member. Few people can do everything, but everybody can do something. Some are more capable than others, but the others need all the more encouragement. The department is not an entertainment bureau alone. It is a training school.

There is scarcely a Chapter in the entire League without a large amount of undeveloped musical ability. It is better to develop this one talent than to go outside for better music.

Build programs on themes of living interest. An Epworth League literary meeting is no place for dreary essays or technical discussions. The more nearly you can come to the daily life and thought of your members, the more surely their interest in the work will be maintained.

An effective plan for enlarging the number of available books at the disposal of the Chapter members is suggested by the work of a Methodist preacher who died a few years ago. He made a catalogue of his private library, and extended the use of the library to all the members of his Church, guiding them in their choice of books, recommending the best new books, and in every way encouraging them to more and better reading. Why could not the Chapter members "pool" their own private libraries, and prepare a catalogue of the general library thus made available? Each member, no doubt, will have many books which others would be glad to read. By the pooling arrangement, all who go into it will be at once borrowers and lenders, and by the use of a simple system of records it will be easy to keep track of the books. Ordinarily, the loan of a book is not recorded, and few people would care to make a record of the fact that they had loaned a book to a friend, especially if the friend knew it. But, by the joint arrangement, everybody will recognize that a record is necessary,

CULTURE AND RECREATION.

and fewer books will be forgotten or their return overlooked than by the haphazard method.

A Reading College.—The Chautauqua system and other like plans of consecutive reading have made us familiar with the advantages of this method of study. But many people hesitate to commit themselves to a long course, or to a course involving a large number of books. And yet these same people would be glad of some concerted plan of systematic reading. Why not use their interest as a feeder for Epworth League activities and at the same time help the individuals themselves? There are many ways of doing this? A simple one is as follows:

Make a list of available books worth reading. Either through a library census of the Chapter, or by a request from the pastor or some one else, endeavor to discover in the possession of members or friends books which will be gladly loaned to the "college." Require each member to read at least four of these books during the year. This is the smallest number which should be set as a standard, while the more ambitious members may read as many more as they choose. This plan does not require that the college shall hold regular meetings. It is merely a method of providing every member with reading that is worth while.

Include every member of the Chapter in this arrangement. Make it so flexible that every member can be suited. If there are no books on your list to satisfy some particularly exacting member, find out what he wants and get the books in some other way. Do not give up the plan until every member of the Chapter has been enrolled as a member of the college. In order to keep up the interest, take five or ten minutes at the monthly business meeting to ask the question, "What are you reading?" Vary it sometimes by asking, "What have you read this month that has particularly impressed you?" Call the time given to this exercise at the business meeting, "Reading College Moments," or some other appropriate name. Toward the close of the season have a Commencement of your reading college as one of your Chapter socials. Some of the features of a regular college Commencement can be copied in these exercises. Have a salutatorian, a valedictorian, and two or three brief orations. The speakers, of course, will use their winter's reading as a basis of their addresses. If a certificate of a year's work in the college is thought desirable, it can be arranged easily, and copies of the document given out after the fashion of diplomas at the close of the Commencement exercises.

The Book Club.—The book club is admirably adapted to Epworth League work. It does not require any specified number of members. A little group of people who desire to read certain books, but do not care to purchase them, can agree among themselves that each one will buy one book on the list. Then each member of the club has the privilege, after having read his own book, of reading in turn the books of the other members. This same plan can be adopted in the case of magazines, so that each member may have the opportunity of reading a half-dozen magazines while spending money for a single one. One essential requirement of all such work is that each member shall be loyal to the plan of the club, respecting the rights of the other members, observing the time limits carefully, and practicing the Golden Rule in every detail of the club's work. If a slip of paper is pasted on the inside of the front cover of the book or magazine, a record of readers can be made without trouble. Put on this slip the names of all members of the club. Each member will check his own name when reading the book, and will then pass the volume on to the next one in order. The last reader on the list will check his name after reading, and will return the book or magazine to its original purchaser.

Informal Reading Circles.—In every Chapter there are groups of people who are interested in the same general subjects. The reading done by these groups can be made to link them and their work to the Chapter. Whatever the general subject of their reading, they will have some flexible system about it, and members of the group only may be designated as readers, and recorded. If persons who are not members of the Chapter are interested in these voluntary reading circles, use this seemingly slight link that binds them to those who are members as a means of winning them to the Chapter itself. Unless there are insuperable

CULTURE AND RECREATION.

difficulties growing out of other religious affiliations, seek to enroll all the members of these voluntary reading circles in the Epworth League Chapter. You have already found one point of common interest, and others will thereafter suggest themselves almost unawares.

Reading Rooms.—There are many Chapters so located that a room which will combine the uses of parlor, library, reading and writing room, would be of the greatest possible usefulness. When such a room is set apart, a committee of the Fourth Department should be put in charge of it. It can be provided with magazines and newspapers at very small cost. Members of the Chapter or of the Church will gladly give the current magazines, if the Reading-room Committee will wait a week or so after the magazines are issued before calling for them. A table equipped with writing materials; a couch, and an easy-chair or two would give the room a homelike and restful look. In these days when reproductions of great pictures are both cheap and good, the walls need not be bare.

When a room is furnished and equipped, throw it open to the young men of the town. Advertise it. Make it a popular rallying place. Do not devise too many rules, the only important one being that each one using the room must respect the rights of all the others. A member of the committee should be assigned to have charge of the room each evening, different ones taking this responsibility turn and turn about. Properly managed, this Epworth League reading-room will prove in many places one of the most attractive features of the Literary Committee's work.

CULTURAL ACTIVITIES.

A Home Assembly.—The summer assembly idea is probably permanently fixed in the minds of the American people. To read the list of such assemblies, one would suppose that everybody in the whole country attended one or more of these gatherings every summer. But, as a matter of fact, the great majority of people do not yet go to the Chautauquas. For the benefit of the stay-at-homes, an assembly in the home Church may well provide a very profitable form of summer activity in the Fourth Department. Ar-

THE EFFICIENT EPWORTHIAN.

range for a ten days' session, modeled on the regular Chautauqua plan, except that in most cases day sessions will need to be omitted. It is a popular delusion that people will not go into public gatherings during the hot months. It is perfectly true that they will not go into a stuffy, badly-lighted, poorly-ventilated church. But the church need not be stuffy, nor badly lighted, nor poorly ventilated, and when care is exercised in this regard, a church is as cool as any other sort of room. Of course, if an open-air spot is available and free from disturbance, that will be even better. The serious difficulty in arranging this home assembly, of course, is the list of speakers. As befits the season of the year, the program should be largely light and entertaining, rather than solid and instructive. Neighboring pastors and other capable individuals will usually be glad to give one or two days' service in such a cause. The expenses need not be large, and in the general suspension of Church and social activities during the summer months, a home assembly is likely to attract much more attention than it would at any other season of the year.

Lecture Courses.—Many Chapters make an annual lecture course a very successful feature of their work. When properly managed, nothing is more delightful. And nothing adds more to the reputation of the Chapter for ability to manage things and for discernment of the needs of the community than a good lecture course.

Four things are all-important: Really good speakers, a comfortable auditorium, low prices, and vigorous advertising.

The success of the course depends more upon the selection of the lecturers than upon any other one thing. And the selection of the lecturers largely resolves itself into the question of what not to get.

As a rule, avoid lecture-sermons. The lecture will not be spoiled, but helped, by having a definite moral purpose, although an occasional lecture which is nothing more than an hour's innocent enjoyment is greatly appreciated. But the lecture platform is not the place for preaching, and the man who merely takes a sermon and detaches it from

CULTURE AND RECREATION.

its text will not be invited to lecture at the same place a second time.

Beware of lecturers who are persistent blowers of their own trumpets. The lecturer who is a good advertiser is very likely to be an indifferent speaker.

Do not overlook near-by talent. There are people in every neighborhood who would be welcomed and highly esteemed if they were strangers. But, of course, it will not do to sacrifice attractiveness and effectiveness merely for the sake of complimenting some local aspirant.

Avoid the man who bases his claim to an audience upon the solitary fact that he has traveled in far lands. Many travelers would have conferred a distinct favor upon their own community if they had indefinitely prolonged their travels. The globe-trotting bore who can not utter a sentence without prefacing it with "When I was in Rome," or "The last time I saw Mr. Chamberlain," or "Did I ever tell you of my experience in Singapore?" is an unmitigated nuisance. Do not encourage him by asking him to lecture. He will lecture sufficiently on all occasions without being given a special evening.

Steer clear of clowns and buffoons. Pleasantry is desirable, and a good joke is a healthy as well as a delightful rarity, but we may wisely leave the grotesque and the farcical to those who have far more experience with that sort of thing than any Epworthian should desire for himself.

Aim at a course that shall be varied and that shall provide for every taste. If you are to have five entertainments, which is about the average, the course may be divided as follows: Three lectures, one special program by home talent, if possible, and one concert by the choir, or by a group of students from some nearby college, or by local talent.

The matter of the auditorium merits consideration. Most of the entertainments will be given during the colder season, and it is important that the public shall be satisfied at the outset that the auditorium will be comfortable in cold weather. A cold room on the night of the first lecture will kill the course, and it ought to. People may be willing to attend a church which is not properly warmed, because they feel impressed by a sense of duty. But it is nobody's duty to patronize a lecture course unless he enjoys it. Therefore, look well to the heating and ventilating.

In a course of five numbers every effort should be made to keep the price under one dollar for the course. In some places, owing to the cost of talent, it may be necessary to charge a dollar for the course, but many successful courses have been arranged and all expenses paid with fifty cents as the price of the course tickets and twenty cents for single admission. In case two of the evenings are provided for by home talent or by amateurs from some college near at hand, the expenses for these evenings will not be very high. Two or three hundred tickets will provide funds sufficient to pay all incidental expenses and leave a good fee for each of the lecturers. Do not try to make money. A lecture course which is an enterprise for financial profit is too serious an undertaking to be completely successful. It will be sufficient if the committee "comes out even." If the expenses of the course can be paid without drawing on the League treasury, the Lecture Committee will deserve the thanks of the Chapter and the community.

Short Suggestions for Cultural Programs.

A Biblical Hall of Fame.—Shepherd Chapter, of Fairfield, Ill., held a very interesting and profitable literary meeting, at which it created a Hall of Fame composed of ten of the greatest men of the Bible.

Announcements were made two weeks in advance, in order that each member might prepare a list of those he deemed the ten greatest characters, in order of their importance.

At the meeting, nominations were made for first place, and from these nominations by vote the Chapter decided the name that should be placed first upon the list. This plan was continued until the list was complete.

So much interest and enthusiasm was manifested that two weeks later a similar selection of the ten greatest women was made, and later the ten most popular books of the Bible were selected.

CULTURE AND RECREATION.

A "Discipline" Evening.—Many Chapters will find a "Discipline" social a very profitably spent evening.

We know much too little of the Constitution and institutions of our Methodism and of the way in which its affairs are conducted.

Let the pastor, or some other person who is thoroughly familiar with the Discipline, arrange the program.

Questions may be numbered and read audibly, giving a stated time for the answer to each question, to be written on paper. This will create discussion and spread intelligence concerning the things which every Methodist ought to know. Or, if it is a Chapter whose members are fairly well-informed, the spelling-school plan may be used.

Hints for Literary Evenings.—Among the legislators: a talk about the making of laws, by a city alderman, a State legislator, or a lawyer. Close with a question-box.

Notable things in the magazines: half a dozen careful summaries of striking and important articles from the current month's periodicals.

State nights: an evening with the history and literature of your State.

Why I love my country: a symposium on patriotism.

Short story contest: the reading of five or six original stories, written by members of the Chapter. The best story selected by ballot. Vary this by substituting verse instead of stories.

Debates: for these there is constantly provided an unlimited amount of new material.

Favorites of the old readers: an evening of readings from the old Sixth Readers hidden away in attics and secondhand shops.

Quotations: a medley of favorite sayings, giving in each case the author, place of occurrence, and a brief suggestion of the context.

Book reviews: brief descriptions and characterizations of the books newly published, possibly with the reading of extracts from the books considered.

"An Evening with the Bells" will prove a very enjoyable affair. The program explains itself: Essay on bells; piano duet, "Yuletide Bells;" reading, "The Bell of Atri;"

chorus, "Jingle Bells;" reading, "Curfew shall not ring to-night;" solo, "Ring the bells of heaven;" reading, "The Inchcape Rock;" chorus, "Hear dem bells;" recitation, "Ring out, wild bells." A large bell of colored paper over a wire netting, inside of which is a lighted candle, suspended from the ceiling together with some evergreens and plants, will give the room an inviting appearance.

A Congress of Nations.—The speakers representing famous personages of various countries, and making speeches in keeping with the character represented. National costumes may be used.

A Congress of Notables.—The same idea as the above, with the characters taken from the living notabilities of our own land.

The Inside of Big Enterprises.—Descriptions, by people who know what they are talking about, of the inside workings of such enterprises as a department store, a newspaper, a bank, a railway, a steamship, a hotel, an oil refinery, a locomotive works, an electric power station, and scores of others. Utilize the industries near at hand, and enlist the help of experts.

Studies in Methodist Methods.—One or more evenings on our Church, what it does and how it does it.

The Red Cross in Peace and War.—A survey of its beautiful and blessed activities.

The Life History of Familiar Words.—A co-operative program in which several members will give the romance and poetry which is in the story of many of our commonest words.

A Series of Evenings on "Choosing a Life Work."—Get the mechanic, the professional man, the farmer, the minister, the journalist, the drummer to tell why they choose their work and to give stories which illustrate its peculiarities.

The children of Dickens: with readings from "Old Curiosity Shop," "Dombey and Son," "Nicholas Nickelby," "David Copperfield," "Hard Times," and others.

The women of Shakespeare: five or six papers, each discussing one of the poet's famous creations.

Tennyson's religious poems: readings, songs, "Crossing

CULTURE AND RECREATION.

the Bar," and an appreciation of Tennyson as a religious teacher and leader.

The great hymns of the Reformation and the evangelical revival.

Hymns of the ancient Church: their story, their value, and their present power.

Imaginary journeys: to famous places and people, and to historic scenes.

An evening with the newspapers: how they are made, and why.

Shakespeare as a humorist: a study of the lighter side of the dramatist, illustrated by illustrative readings from the plays.

The Romance of Geography.—Give one night to America, others to the rest of the world. Ask various members to tell some unfamiliar things in the story of Columbus, the Cabots, Ponce de Leon, Hudson, Captain Cook, Marcus Whitman, Lewis and Clark, Pere Marquette, La Salle, Coronado, Fremont, and other explorers. The field and its material are both inexhaustible.

Evenings With Experts.—Business men may talk about business, the inside workings of their work. A physician could talk about the care of the health, etc. The lawyer could talk about some of the legal terms used so often, but not understood. The teacher could tell of the work of the school from her standpoint. You could find many others willing to help in this good work. Be sure they are experts.

Interdenominational Evenings.—A series of interdenominational evenings can be made seasons of delightful fellowship. One year arrange a series in which representatives of the various denominations shall explain and illustrate the peculiarities of doctrine and policy which distinguish their respective Churches. The next year have a similar series, but instead of asking each speaker to discuss his own Church, ask him to discuss some other. For instance, ask a Presbyterian to speak on the subject, "What I like about Methodists." The next evening of the series a Methodist can be asked to reciprocate, and so on through the list of available speakers in the community. It is better to emphasize the likable things in other denominations than

THE EFFICIENT EPWORTHIAN.

to exhibit in life-size fashion the things that are not so attractive. It will be found, when three or four representatives of as many denominations have told what they like about each other, that after all there are more points of resemblance than of difference among the great Christian denominations.

Short Studies of Great Businesses.—This can be given in a series of evening gatherings. Have people who know their work tell about it. Let a member of the firm of a department store tell about its inside workings. Other topics that could be discussed might be the newspaper business, an electric power house, a hotel, a bank, a candy store, a photograph gallery, a railway station, etc.

A Congress of Nations.—The speakers representing famous personages of various countries and making speeches in keeping with the character represented. National costumes may be used. Choose characters that can be represented creditably by the talent available. For instance: Paderewski, Kipling, Madame Curie, Lloyd George, Tagore, Marconi, Grenfell, Sir Thomas Lipton.

A Congress of Notables.—The same idea as above; the characters taken from the notabilities of our own land, such as Wilson, Bryan, Harding, Hoover, Henry Ford, "Pussyfoot" Johnson, Jane Addams, Judge Lindsay, Edison, Orville Wright.

Civic Debate.—This is a social service event. Participants should be three of the leading lawyers of the town on one side, and three leading ministers of the town on the other. The question might be, "Resolved, That higher standards of civic righteousness prevail now than a quarter of a century ago."

Hold the debate in a church or a hall, and be sure to advertise the event. You can charge admission, if you choose. This will start newspaper comment and make the public do things along civic lines.

After a general debate of this sort, get down to specific things, and put younger folks on, as well as older ones. Take up such questions as social surveys, the question of vocational schools, public recreation, and other living issues.

(Adapted from "Social Activities," Albert Chesley.)

CULTURE AND RECREATION.

The District Reading Circle.—Prepare a list of from fifty to two hundred books suitable for the Epworthians to read, the list to include religious, missionary, temperance, juvenile, fiction, poetry, and biography. You could call the list "Our Reading Circle Books." Organize a circle, the members of which will be those who take these pledges:

"1. I promise to read at least six out of the list of books during the year, two of them to be religious subjects.

"2. I promise to read a portion of the Scripture daily." This would be most profitable.

The Envelope Library.—Old magazines are used for this purpose. A story or article may be cut out and slipped into an envelope, with the title and author written on the envelope. You can make a large collection of these envelopes in a short time. Include stories, poems, pictures, jokes, etc. They will brighten the sick-room. This is good material for the Third Department, the Visiting Committee.

Subjects for Debate.—That the increase of machinery is a detriment to the working people.

That cultural education is of more value to the average person than industrial education.

That students should have a part in college government.

That small colleges are preferable to large ones.

That the present social unrest is due to removable causes.

That Zionism will restore to the Jews a national life in Palestine.

That poverty is more of an opportunity than a hindrance in the development of character.

That the character of the American people has been improved by the immigration it has received from Europe.

That secret fraternities should be encouraged in High Schools.

That strikes are productive of more harm than good to the workers.

THE HERALD'S GREAT AND GOOD FRIEND.

The Fourth Vice-President is an officer of the Epworth League. But he is also an officer of *The Epworth Herald.*

THE EFFICIENT EPWORTHIAN.

This has always been so, but at Buffalo, in 1913, the Board of Control emphasized it. Into the revised Constitution of the League the Board wrote four major duties of the Fourth Vice-President. One of them was the supervision of *The Herald's* interest in the local Chapter.

The Fourth Vice-Presidents have always done amazingly well. They win new friends and steady the old ones whose allegiance seems to waver. They walk endless miles and display angelic patience rounding up the elusive last subscriber for the club they are organizing. They make up the lists, collect the moneys, buy the drafts, and carry on the correspondence with the Book Concern. And many of them do this again and again for three or four or five years.

For all this highly useful work a Fourth Vice-President gets—what do you suppose? A twenty per cent commission? No. A more or less valuable premium? Guess again. He gets a free copy of the paper for his own use. That's all.

And he is more than likely to pay for his own copy, and to give the free copy to the Chapter, or to the town library, or to the barber shop on Main Street.

As long as *The Epworth Herald* knows how to be grateful, it may be counted on to be the ardent champion of the Epworth League's Fourth Vice-President.

The Epworth Herald as a Trade Paper.

The Epworth Herald is the trade paper of a body of working people.

It knows perfectly well that they can get better pictures, and more complete news of current events, and a few other things, somewhere else.

But it knows also that they can't get better Epworth League help, or more Epworth League news, or clearer understanding of Epworth League life, or surer training in Epworth League efficiency, or quicker sympathy with Epworth League ideals, *anywhere*.

That is what a trade paper is for.

Besides these things, *The Herald* gives attention to

CULTURE AND RECREATION.

important world news and to really big Church news. It prints good stories and general articles; it tells all the good jokes as early as most papers; it has an editorial page that deals with all sorts of subjects which have meaning for young Christians; it prints short but dependable reviews of the newest books; it is a pretty good paper for anybody to take.

But, first of all, and last of all, it is the trade paper of the Epworth League.

The Official Paper.—*Epworth Herald* programs have been used from the beginning. It is to be hoped they may be available and popular indefinitely. The supply of material will not run short, and, in the natural course of things, the quality should improve with every year. Decorate the room with notable cover-pages and other striking illustrations taken from recent issues of the paper. The smaller pictures may be mounted on mats and grouped appropriately according to subjects. The program will be made up of selections from the paper. All departments, of course, should be represented in this program. That is to say, it should have a story, an article of more or less solid wisdom, a bit of the literature of the spiritual life, a poem, a few jokes, an editorial or two, a few personals, some choice bits of Epworth League news, and one or two interesting paragraphs from recent devotional meeting studies. Call each participant an editor. Then the program will be provided by the editor-in-chief, the story editor, the news editor, the funny man, the religious editor, and so on. It is understood, of course, that no program of this kind would be complete or satisfactory without the circulation of subscription blanks and the urging of the time-honored injunction, "Now is the time to subscribe." If your *Epworth Herald* list is woefully short, this is an admirable plan for lengthening it.

A special program for *Epworth Herald* Day (the second Sunday in December) is published by *The Herald* every year, and sent free in quantities to any Chapter which asks for it. It furnishes the material for a remarkable meeting, and gives the Fourth Vice-President the best possible opportunity to secure a large *Herald* club. Requests for the

THE EFFICIENT EPWORTHIAN.

program should be sent to the editorial office by the middle of December.

The Recreational Work.

The recreational work of the Fourth Department is intended to be a feeder for all the other departments, but it ought not to be expected necessary to feed the members.

If the recreational work is carefully, enthusiastically, and judiciously done, every department will feel the stimulus and help it will bring.

The recreational work of the Chapter is by all means *not* to be considered a source of financial profit. It is not the Chapter's bargain counter. It has no function as a money-maker. There may be some profit in some of the enterprises which it undertakes, but the purpose to make a profit should never be foremost. The money-raising work of the Epworth League should be done, as largely as possible, through the Treasurer's Department, and the ideal should be held up before the members continually that direct giving is the only giving, and that the Epworth League can not eat its way into financial prosperity without serious detriment to its social and spiritual life.

In an Epworth League social the social feature should be at least as real as any other. A free-of-cost social is the ideal. It is much more likely to be popular and in keeping with the true purpose of socials, than one to which an admission fee is charged. Any event which has its origin in a purely financial consideration is not a social. The money element may have a place in some occasion of Christian fellowship, but its place will be secondary always.

Any social, so called, but sadly miscalled, which has for its first and important end the raising of the pastor's salary should not be tolerated in any self-respecting Chapter which is willing to have any preacher at all. Such a social degrades the Church, humiliates the preacher, and is usually a financial failure, as it ought to be. When it is a financial success its effect is even worse. The Church which is too poor to pay a preacher is too poor to carry to a successful issue a social for the benefit of the salary fund.

The adoption of the New Testament method of Church and Epworth League support would abolish the whole tribe

CULTURE AND RECREATION.

of melancholy functions whose only social feature is their name, and would make possible real socials—socials to save, without money and without price.

Socials and Sociability.

What are the marks of a good social? Negatively, at a good social there may be noted the absence of certain things which would make it a bad social. There is no stiffness, no coldness, no formality, no groups, no cliques, no reserve, no neglected folk, no talking of shop, no exalting of self. Speaking positively, a good social will have a large freedom of movement. Strangers will be generously introduced. The fine art of conversation will be cultivated. The timid and backward among the company will receive special attention. The little talks will be upon themes of mutual interest. Above all, a good social is a social which has a great purpose, which is inspired by the greatest of all purposes—the purpose to recognize that the social life is a Christian privilege. Emphasis should be placed upon our oneness in Christ Jesus. We are brethren.

The social work of the Epworth League must, above all, be clean. Do not tolerate for a moment any attempt to keep the letter of the Church law on the subject of amusements while violating its spirit. Epworthians can not compete with the theater on the theater's level. If the League's amusement features can not be kept free from suggestions of the play-house, they should be abandoned altogether. Self-respect and loyalty to the ideal of the League demand that we shall not surrender to these tendencies. They are the very tendencies which the League's social work is seeking to overcome.

The suggestions and plans in the following pages by no means cover the whole field. They are the merest hints of what is becoming a very rich deposit of recreational material. The Methodist Book Concern publishes a number of books which give detailed programs and descriptions of recreational activities. Some of them were written especially for the League, and they afford an inexhaustible supply of usable material. Every Fourth Vice-President should have a list of these useful books.

THE EFFICIENT EPWORTHIAN.

Tackling the Other Side of the Amusement Question.

The amusement question will not down, and it will not *be* downed.

The Board of Control of the Epworth League did a brave and necessary thing at its annual meeting in 1913. It put the word "Recreation" into the forefront of the Fourth Department's new name.

By that action the Epworth League was told plainly that it must do something more about the recreational life of its young people.

The League knows what amusements the Church objects to, and makes no attempt to change the law. Dr. Robert Stephens, of Illinois, said, in the great debate on Paragraph 260. at Minneapolis, in 1912, that not a single petition for a change had come from any League organization in the world.

But the changed name of the Fourth Department has put on all Epworthians the duty of filling out and completing the Discipline's famous amusement clauses.

Those clauses said "Do n't." But there is nothing inspiring in a prohibition. It may be respected and remembered and obeyed; it will never be loved. Nobody is really captivated by the obligation of speaking nothing, or doing nothing, or refraining from something, or avoiding something.

Now the League and the Church, too, are getting ready to say "Do." There is good authority for it. When the lawyer went to Jesus with his question about the greatest law of the "Thou shalt nots" in the Decalogue, Jesus met him with two greater laws, both beginning "Thou shalt."

Whenever the Church has spoken its will about the things which determine character, sooner or later it has had to speak positively as well as negatively. It opposes improper amusements and names them, counting them bad because they tend to undermine character; it is seeing now that proper amusements are to be counted good because they undergird character.

Youth is disciplined by its play as well as by its tasks. "Waterloo was won on the cricket fields of Eton."

CULTURE AND RECREATION.

Play—recreation—amusement, whatever you choose to call the thing we are after, gives young folks their chance to lunge out, to put themselves into circumstances genuinely social and genuinely interesting.

The college play—dozens of them are given by students in Methodist colleges every year—the missionary pageant, the tennis tournament, the outdoor games and the indoor games of the several seasons—all are educative in the highest sense, because they develop character and, moreover, test it while it grows.

Youth is the restless time. It loves the intense, the varied, the moving things. It balks at gray monotony. And this is not of the evil one, but of the Lord.

God gave youth its spirit of adventure, and turned it loose in a world that held enough adventure to satisfy it. He made life vivid, "contrasty," dramatic. The rebound from dull, grinding drudgery in school or shop or home is as natural as hunger.

And now the League has a commission, made plainer than ever, to capture the play-life of the young people. It must construct a program of recreation that will offset the many harmful amusements which are beyond its control.

For instance, no one doubts the frequent harmfulness of the moving picture show. But you can not abolish the moving picture show or make the young people shut their eyes to its glamor. To make laws against the show and to issue prohibitions to the young people would be worse than useless. It would be King Canute proposing to stay the tide with the king actually believing himself stronger than the sea.

The real testing time has come. It is easy to say "Do n't." The thing is so simple and so final—if it works. But can we say "Do?" Can the League provide a natural, acceptable scheme of recreation, both attractive and wholesome? Can we make our recreation fascinating as well as clean?

The present writer believes enthusiastically that this thing can be done. He believes the young people of Methodism can play and really enjoy it, without doing any damage to their piety. He believes they can find recreation

THE EFFICIENT EPWORTHIAN.

that will be so satisfying and absorbing as to make any amusement paragraph of merely historical interest, like the General Rule about the buying and selling of slaves.

A Simple Recreation Program.

Every Epworth League Chapter should provide in its work of recreation a program of good, though simple, ways for young people to play together.

That means indoor and outdoor games, but it means more than that.

The "get-together" instinct needs to be remembered and satisfied. In many cases this can be done through the expedient of keeping open-house in the League room one evening a week or a fortnight. With ample opportunity for conversation, a few lively games, music, and, as often as possible, some very light eat-and-drinkables, the League's open-house may become a recognized and much valued institution.

Many a Chapter can build up an entertainment course of three to six numbers, including, perhaps, a concert, a home talent program, some good moving pictures, and some "Evenings with experts."

The dramatic instinct, which the pastor recognizes in his realistic illustrations, and which helps the choir to do so well with the more vivid anthems, may find expression in a pageant once in a while, using local annals, or missions, or Church history as a foundation.

By all means let us do more with and for outdoor sports. The Chapter which has a ball-team has a good thing. Tennis is, in all respects, a profitable sport for the young folks of that Chapter. A "hiking" club and a hockey team will provide forms of recreation which can be used under winter skies.

We must make more of our homes. In all well-regulated families the home belongs to the young folks. Periodical "at homes," then, *in* homes, with the home atmosphere and the normal-temperatured pleasures that leave no bad taste behind. Games there, too, as well as in the League room, but the main emphasis on fellowship, which is, as Steiner says, being a fellow in the same ship.

CULTURE AND RECREATION.

If all this needed to be put into the form of a positive recreational policy, would it not run somewhat after this fashion?

1. We will get the young people of the parish together as often as possible in the League room for good times through good fellowship.

2. We will give the community a series of clean and cheerful entertainments, at the lowest expense, following as far as possible known preferences of the people we seek to serve.

3. We will find ways of giving legitimate expression to the dramatic instinct by arranging representations of people and events worth remembering in connection with our community, our Church, and the Kingdom.

4. We will offer such a choice of outdoor sports that all the young people may have frequent opportunity to play together in the open air, winter and summer.

5. We will invite the young people of the neighborhood to share the hospitality of our homes as often as arrangements can be made.

And we will do all this that we may make real and general those pleasures of youth that bring no sorrow with them.

The Fourth Department's Great Chance.

Every Fourth Vice-President in the League is directly and personally and officially interested in one piece of legislation enacted by the General Conference of 1920. The nub of it is in these words, presented in Report No. 17 of the Committee on the State of the Church:

Wherever a Chapter of the Epworth League is organized and maintained, the Fourth Vice-President of the same * * * may be designated as director of social and recreational life.

In order to provide for other contingencies, the Chairman of the Committee proposed the addition of these words: "Or wherever there is a social and recreational director of the Sunday School, or any other social and recreational director."

The addition is important, because it calls for team work as between all the recreational leaders in the local Church. But there are twelve or fifteen thousand Fourth Vice-Presidents of the Epworth League already at work in our churches, and it is doubtful whether there are one-hundredth part as many other social and recreational directors. So the paragraph needs must mean vastly more to Epworthians than to anybody else.

"You have a Department of Recreation," the Church is saying, "and we might naturally expect you to know what to do for all the community's young people. But *do* you?"

The honest answer, in many of these Chapters, must be, "No; we don't." For we must confess that the League has been content sometimes with small and immediate recreational results. It has had no far-visioned program. It has not seen itself as the providentially privileged leader of decent community recreation.

A great and effectual door has opened to us by this action of the General Conference.

To enter it the League must gird itself for new studies and new attainments. Its Fourth Department must set itself to the understanding of play as a moral and spiritual force.

It must build a program of recreation capable of attracting all the young people of the church and community.

This new possibility of service by the League for the whole Church has in it something to capture the imagination of self-respecting youth.

More than all else, is the fact that the League's recreational work has gained the Church's attention. And now the Church says to the League, "Are you ready for the next advance?"

If we found it necessary to say no, we should deserve that some other should take our crown.

Successful Social "Stunts."

In the paragraphs which follow hints of various helps for the social evening are given. The space at our disposal would be insufficient to describe in full one-tenth of these

CULTURE AND RECREATION.

ideas, but the hints given are such that most Epworthians, by a little personal thought and the exercise of native ingenuity, can fill in the details with entire satisfaction to themselves and the people whose entertainment they have undertaken to provide. There is given much more than enough in the way of hints and suggestions to provide a social for every week in the year.

Charades.—
Attenuate. At-ten-you-ate.
Ingratiate. In-grey-she-ate.
Catering (Kate, her ring).
Commentator. C o m m o n (Irish potato) tater.
Heroes. He-rows.
Tennessee. Ten-I-see.
Penitent. Pen-i-tent.
Necklace. Neck-lace.
Pantry. Pan-tree.
Carpet. Car-pet.
Shylock. Shy-lock.
Welcome. Wel-come.
Horsemanship. Horse-man-ship.
Sack-cloth. Sack-cloth.
Sweepstake. Sweep-stake.
Antidote. Ant-i-dote.
Football. Foot-ball.
Bridegroom. Bride-groom.
Sunday. Sun-day.
Definite. Deaf-in-ate.
Snowball. Snow-ball.

(Adapted from "Indoor Games for Boys," Baker.)

A Comic Orchestra.—An imaginary instrument is chosen by each one present, such as violin, piano, harp, etc. As soon as the leader begins, the others must follow and make a noise and go through the motions which represent the instrument he represents. The leader may be playing a flute. He stops suddenly and plays the violin, then the one playing the violin must take up the flute. The leader may change as often as he likes. Any one failing to make the changes at the proper time must pay a forfeit.

(Adapted from "Indoor Games for Boys," Baker.)

A *Corn Social* in the fall will take well, with ears of corn, corn-stalks, and pop-corn for decorations; corn products for refreshments; a guessing contest as to number of grains on a selected ear, and the recital of Mrs. Allerton's "Walls of Corn" and other appropriate selections.

Candy Making.—The old-fashioned candy-pull still has power to charm, and yet we need not be tied to the one

THE EFFICIENT EPWORTHIAN.

solitary method of making candy. Nearly every cook-book nowadays has an assortment of good candy recipes, and they are all the better, in some respects at least, when made at a social by a large number of cooks. What the candy lacks in elegance and perfection of flavor will not be missed, while the good fellowship and hilarity developed in the candy-making process will be worth more than all the candy that may be concocted.

An Abbreviated Social.—An abbreviated social, in which everything is cut short—medleys, piano solos, and other musical features stopped in the middle; progressive conversations, with changes at unexpected moments; "follow my leader;" unfinished stories, stopping just on the verge of the thrill, and refreshments which when first served are short as to quantity, but which, of course, may be lengthened.

My Native State Social.—This is good for a Chapter where the members are from various parts of the country. Each one invited should be asked to wear something to indicate his native State. For instance, sunflower for Kansas, nutmeg for Connecticut, etc. Each one must deliver a short eulogy on his State.

Have an *Old Members' Social,* including a reunion of those who were active in the work in other days, and the reading of letters from those who are not able to be present in person. Speeches, reminiscent and prophetic, are appropriate at such a gathering.

Of great value are *Students' Receptions* at the beginning of the school year. Decorate with the school colors and banners. Sing school and college songs.

Songs Without Words.—Some one plays snatches of familiar airs, and the guests are to name the songs and write them down. For example, songs like these might be played: "Annie Laurie," "Suwanee River," "My Old Kentucky Home," "Blue Bells of Scotland," National songs, operas, popular songs.

The names of these may be woven into a story, something on the order of "A Musical Romance."

(Adapted from "Games," Jessie Bancroft.)

CULTURE AND RECREATION.

A Tower of Babel Social.—This is good for a city Chapter to use. Give the program in many languages. For instance, an English story, a German song, a French poem, Italian song, Swedish story, etc. "The Marseillaise" might be used for the French, "The Watch on the Rhine" for the German, or some one could read a selection from "Faust."

If translations can be given afterwards, so much the better. Two people who speak the same foreign language could put on an interesting number, one giving the address and the other interpreting it as it proceeds. This would give the audience a hint of the experience many a missionary must go through, and every public speaker who delivers addresses in foreign parts.

The Sons of Ehud.—Everything is left-handed in this social. The programs are cards which open on the wrong side, and they might have the following verse, which was once used with great success:

> "Left-handed greeting,
> Left-handed eating,
> Left-handed compliments, too;
> Left-handed name,
> Left-handed game,—
> I think that's enough, don't you?"

The guests had to shake hands with the left hand, and "grinds" were given instead of compliments. The left hand was used in eating the refreshments. The hostess can think of other schemes in which the left hand may be made more prominent.

(Adapted from "Social Activities," Chesley.)

Scrambled Post Cards.—Take cards or pictures of well-known buildings or persons, and cut them into five pieces. Get as many envelopes as cards, and put into each envelope five pieces. Give each one an envelope, and he must try to match the pieces in his envelope.

(Adapted from "Social Activities," Chesley.)

A Menu of Numbers.—This is a novel way of serving refreshments. Each guest is given a card with numbers from 1 to 10, each number representing something used for refreshments that evening. For instance: 1 is a spoon; 2, paper napkins; 3, toothpicks; 10, fork, etc. Each guest is told to check six articles that he wants. In this way some will get plates, spoons, etc. If some are deprived of the good things to eat, the refreshments can be passed later.

(Adapted from "Social Plans for Young People," Christian Reisner.)

Tongue Twisters.—1. One old ostrich ordering oranges. 2. Two timid toads trying to trot to Tarrytown. 3. Three terrible, thumping tigers tickling trout. 4. Four fat friars fanning flickering flames. 5. Five frivolous foreigners fleeing from fabulous snipe. 6. Six Scottish soldiers successively shooting snipe. 7. Seven serious Southerners setting sail from Switzerland. 8. Eight eager emigrants earnestly examining elements. 9. Nine nimble noblemen nibbling nuts. 10. Ten tremendous tomtits twittering on the tops of three tall trees. 11. Eleven enormous elephants elegantly eating Easter eggs. 12. Twelve tired tailors thoughtfully twisting twine.

Tongue Twisters.—The first player repeats the first phrase. Player number 2 repeats the same and also phrase number 2. Number 3 repeats phrases 1, 2, and 3, etc., until some one breaks down.

1. A good fat hen. 2. Two ducks. 3. Three plump partridges. 4. Four squawking wild geese. 5. Five hundred oysters. 6. Six pairs of Don Alphonso's tweezers. 7. Seven hundred Macedonian horsemen, rank and file drawn up in line of battle. 8. Eight cages of He, Hi, Ho, bibulous sparrow kites. 9. Nine floating fly boats, floating from Fort Manilus to Damascus laden with fruit and flowers. 10. Ten diacaustic, dogmatic, diathetic, parallel propositions proposed to be received by all mankind.

A Barter Social.—A barter social has elements of wholesome fun in it. Each one attending it is expected to bring an article whose value does not exceed a certain specified sum, usually five or ten cents. It may be wrapped in any manner, and the more ingeniously done, so as to hide any

CULTURE AND RECREATION.

indication of its real character, the better. As soon as all have arrived, the trading begins. Each one strives to exchange his bundle for one that seems to hold out greater possibilities. There is no limit to the number of exchanges that can be made, but after a certain time all trading must cease. Then the packages are opened, and the fun will be at its height in the disclosures that are made and the surprises that await the traders.

The Social of the Senses.—This requires five rooms, or five sections of one room. In one the sense of touch is to be exercised. Articles hidden under a cloth may be felt, and their nature and composition determined in that method. In another place the sense of smell has its opportunity. Odoriferous articles are provided, and the composition of each is to be determined by its odor. In the sight section various tests may be applied, as to gradations of color, comparison of length of line and area of surfaces, and so on. In the taste section the articles which are provided are disguised as much as possible, except to the sense of taste. For example, a series of white powders can be provided, each reduced to the same consistency. Flour, sugar, salt, baking soda, and the other harmless substances will provide material for this section.

The Fagot Party.—This social must be held in a place where there is a fireplace. Each guest should be asked to come and bring a fagot, which may be anything from a toothpick to a handle of a snow shovel.

You might first have a musical program. Then light a fire in the fireplace and turn all the lights out. One person should put his fagot in the fire and begin to tell a story of his vacation experiences, or any story or fact, and it should last until his fagot is burned. Then the others will follow. Serve ice-cream and cake.

Musical Evenings, each devoted to a special kind of music, will draw good audiences. From the musical resources available arrange such programs as "Songs of the Old Folks," "Songs of Places," "Songs of the Sea," "The Songs of Yesterday," "Plantation Songs," "Songs of the Nations," "American National Songs," etc.

THE EFFICIENT EPWORTHIAN.

Hold a *Traveling Social*. This may be made a sort of progressive banquet, in which one course is served in one home, the next in another a block or two away, and so through the entire menu. The plan may be varied by considering each home visited as a different country and adapting the decorations, refreshments, and other arrangements to that plan.

A Jumble Social.—The program as given by an Iowa Chapter was a perfect jumble from the first to last. The first number was a piano duet, one player giving, say, Mendelssohn's "Wedding March," the other executing the "Dead March" from "Saul." The pastor gave a ten-minute address on five different topics. Two ladies recited simultaneously, one giving a selection of the general character of the "Charge of the Light Brigade," while the other recited a poem in the "Psalm of Life" class. Jumbled names kept the pencils of the company busy for ten strenuous minutes, at the end of which a big ginger-cookie "jumble" was given to the player who first untangled the name-jumble. Jumbles were the central feature of the refreshments served.

PENCIL, PAPER, AND BRAINS.

Descriptive Initials.—Have a list of noted people and make descriptive phrases, using the initials of their names. Such as, "Always loyal," for Abraham Lincoln; "Tireless Reformer," for Theodore Roosevelt. You can use the initials of some of the Chapter members, or of people of local interest, or names of popular books.

A Word Building.—Use the name of your Church or any other words you desire, of more than twelve letters, containing as many vowels as possible. The player must see how many words he can make out of that word. A good prize for this would be a small pocket dictionary.

Hundred Dollar Social.—Every guest has an opportunity to spend $100. He is presented with a check for $100, and is asked to spend his money. These items will be endorsed on the back of the check. Later on, these shopping lists will be read, and the guests should decide who the spender is by the manner in which he has spent

CULTURE AND RECREATION.

his money. This is merely a start, and many other schemes may be worked out.

The Dry Goods Describer.—
1. A long-haired animal of Peru. Alpaca.
2. A loud noise. Crash.
3. A symbol of worldly sacrifice. Nun's veiling.
4. A material used by painters. Canvas.
5. An amphibious creature. Duck.
6. Hills in Scotland. Cheviot.
7. A rising billow. Storm serge.
8. The grassy sward. Lawn.
9. A dwelling and wove. Homespun.
10. A spotted mountaineer. Dotted swiss.
11. A much discussed waterway. Panama.
12. A musical instrument and a Scotch river. Organdy.
13. A Scotch-English river. Tweed.
14. A fisher's necessity. Net.
15. Paddy's shoestring. Irish lace.
16. What an "ad" gets. Insertion.

(Adapted from "Dame Curtsey's Guessing Contests," Glover.)

Hidden Authors.—
1. A name that means such fiery things one can't describe its pain. Burns.
2. Kind of bonnet. Hood.
3. A high Church official. Pope.
4. Part of a hospital. Ward.
5. What a host said when the meat was tough. Chaucer.
6. Something hard to bear. Payne.
7. A kind of bread and a preposition. Ruskin.
8. A breakfast dish. Bacon.
9. Something on foot. Bunyan.
10. A blossom. Hawthorne.
11. A game and a preposition. Tennyson.
12. Muddy water. Riley.
13. Badly wounded. Alcott.
14. What the fox dreads. Hunt.
15. The name of a river. Poe.

16. A tall chap. Longfellow.
17. Brighter than any humorist. Whittier.
18. A noisy author. Bangs.
19. The giver of kindly help. Ade.
20. The farmer's possession. Field.
21. A throbbing pump. Harte.
22. A measure of literary value. Wordsworth.

(Adapted from "Dame Curtsey's Guessing Contests," Glover.)

Choosing the Cake.—What kind of a cake would you buy for:
1. Sculptors. Marble cake.
2. Dairymen. Cream cake.
3. Milliners. Ribbon cake.
4. Babies. Patty cakes.
5. Lovers. Kisses.
6. The betrothed. Brides' cake.
7. Carpenter. Plain (plane) cake.
8. Idlers. Loaf cake.
9. Pugilists. Pound cake.
10. Brickmasons. Layer cake.
11. Borrowers. Sponge cake.
12. Sweethearts. Angel cake.
13. Ball players. Batter cakes.
14. Those who sample all these too much. Stomach ache.

(Adapted from "Games.")

The Depths of Ignorance.—Pass papers around with this statement at the top, "What We Do Not Know." Under this you can write questions similar to the following:

Here are some suitable for the men—
"How do you make a dinner menu for six, your allowance being $2.50? Give items."
"How do you make and trim a lingerie waist?"
"What is meant by a gored skirt, and what is applique?"
Here are some suitable for women—
"What is meant by double entry?"
"What would you do with a draft for $100?"

CULTURE AND RECREATION.

"What would you do if a rich and poor man should propose to you at the same time?"

The hostess can add others suitable for her guests.

(Adapted from "Dame Curtsey's Book of Novel Entertainments," Glover.)

The Telegram Social.—One plan is to have the guests write the letters of their surname at intervals on the telegraph blanks given to them. Then they must write a message using these letters of the name as the first letter in the words of the message.

Another plan is to take any ten letters of the alphabet and place them on the blank, and write a message using these letters as the first letter of the words of the telegram.

Authors' Traits.—By the statement of the author's characteristic, the name may be discovered. For example:

The oldest author—Adam Smith.
The youngest author—Child.
The healthy author—Hale.
The sickly author—Haggard.
The farmer's author—Field.
The jeweler's author—Goldsmith.
The domestic author—Holmes.
The woodland author—Hawthorne.
The blistering author—Burns.
The breakfast author—Bacon.
The dinner author—Lamb.
The lancer's author—Shakespeare.
The tall author—Longfellow.
The hungry author—Chaucer.
The repellant author—Sterne.
The Roman author—Pope.

The Composite Novel.—Divide the guests into groups of about five or six. Several long sheets of paper should be started, each group having one. One member of the group should write one paragraph of a story, the next person should write the second paragraph, etc., to the end of the group. Later the story of each group will be read.

Another plan might be to have each one present write

a paragraph of a story and have as many stories written as there are people.

Twisted Trees.—Slips of paper should be passed having on them names of trees, the letter in any order but the right one. Here are some; others will be easily added:

Epaml.	Nybeo.	Dwntoocoot.
Kyochir.	Neldni.	Cuthetns.
Liwwol.	Rocyemas.	Onaiglam.
Agohynam.		

(Adapted from "Bright Ideas for Entertaining," Mrs. H. B. Linscott.)

The City You Live In.—These are words ending in "city." Write the description on cards, or let one person read them, allowing twenty or thirty seconds for the writing of answers.

What city is for few people? Scarcity.
For happy people? Felicity.
For chauffeurs? Velocity.
For truthful people? Veracity.
For greedy people? Voracity.
For wild beasts? Ferocity.
For home lovers? Domesticity.
For actors? Publicity.
For wise people? Sagacity.
For hungry people? Capacity.
For telegraph operators? Electricity.
For crowds? Multiplicity.
For nations? Reciprocity.
For odd people? Eccentricity.
For office seekers? Pertinacity.

(Adapted from "Bright Ideas for Entertaining," Mrs. H. B. Linscott.)

Y. O. I. (Your own initial.)—Each player is given a slip of paper. At the top of it are written initials of some one who will be present. Have under this a list of questions which are to be answered. The answer must consist of only as many words as there are initials at the top of

CULTURE AND RECREATION.

the paper, and the words must begin with the initials in their right order. For example: "H. B. B."

To whom does this paper belong? Henry B. Brown.
What is his character? Horrid, but bearable.
What kind of hair has he? Heavy, burnished brown.
Have about twenty questions like these.
(Adapted from "Games," Jessie Brancroft.)

Identifying the Poems.—You can use poems of any author. The questions are given to each guest, and he should put down the correct answer. For example:

Tennyson—
What poem is it that sings down the vale? "The Brook."
What is the poem that honors a friend who is gone? "In Memoriam."
What is the poem whose father is king? "The Princess."

Longfellow—
What poem recalls King David? "A Psalm of Life."
What poem celebrates a rural mechanic? "The Village Blacksmith."
What poem would frighten a superstitious crusader? "The Skeleton in Armor."

Whittier—
What poem is a winter experience. "Snowbound."
What is the poem of a brave woman? "Barbara Frietchie."
What poem is without footwear? "The Barefoot Boy."
Many other lists may be arranged.
(Adapted from "Games," Jessie Bancroft.)

A Drawing Party.—One plan is to have each one present, draw a picture of one Mother Goose rhyme and the others must guess what rhyme is represented.

After this you could have them draw flowers, animals, maps, people, etc., and guess what they represent in the same manner.

Then ask each one to draw a map of the State you live in. Or small outline maps of the United States could be provided, and each player asked to indicate the location of the following cities: Rochester, Cairo, Duluth, Toledo, Memphis, El Paso, Spokane, Cheyenne, Norfolk, Hoboken. Many will miss some of these by hundreds of miles.

A Shakespearean Romance.—Each player is provided with a sheet of paper prepared with the following questions, or the questions may be indicated at the time. Each question is to be answered with the title of one of Shakespeare's plays. The player wins who has the largest number correct at the end of the time allotted for the game. Other questions may be devised:

In whose reign did the romance occur. (King Lear.)
Who were the lovers? (Romeo and Juliet.)
What was their courtship like? (Midsummer Night's Dream.)
What was her answer to his proposal? (As You Like It.)
About what time of month were they married? (Twelfth Night.)
Of whom did he buy the ring? (Merchant of Venice.)
Who were the best man and the maid of honor? (Antony and Cleopatra.)
Who were the ushers? (The Two Gentlemen of Verona.)
Who gave the reception. (Merry Wives of Windsor.)
In what kind of place did they live? (Hamlet.)
What was her disposition like? (The Tempest.)
What was his chief occupation after marriage? (Taming of the Shrew.)
What caused their first quarrel? (Much Ado About Nothing.)
What did their courtship prove to be? (Love's Labor Lost.)
What did their married life resemble? (A Comedy of Errors.)
What did they give each other? (Measure for Measure.)
What Roman ruler brought about reconciliation? (Julius Cæsar.)

CULTURE AND RECREATION.

What did their friends say? (All's Well That Ends Well.)
(Adapted from "Games," Jessie Bancroft.)

The Latest Periodicals.—The programs might be in the shape of a magazine with little pen and ink sketches over the cover. These questions may be written inside, the answers of which are the names of magazines:

1. One hundred years old. Century.
2. Santa Claus. St. Nicholas.
3. Veracity. Truth.
4. One who sketches. Delineator.
5. A prospect. Outlook.
6. What we cling to. Life.
7. Hash. Review of Reviews.
8. Prosperity. Success.
9. Money the trusts want. Everybody's.
10. The suburbs. Country Life in America.
11. What we are proud to be. American.
12. Pertaining to the biggest city. Metropolitan.
13. What influences politicians. Current Opinion.
14. Intellectual pepsin tablets. The Literary Digest.
15. What poor folks would like to be. Independent.
16. A black that makes the newspapers read. Printer's Ink.
17. The last mail of the week. Saturday Evening Post.
18. The work which is done underground. Collier's.
19. A citizen of the world. Cosmopolitan.
20. Something that is never done. The World's Work.
21. What every Church member should be. Christian Herald.
22. What every Leaguer should read. *The Epworth Herald.*

(Adapted from "Dame Curtsey's Guessing Contests.")

Socials for Special Days.

St. Patrick: His Day.—The guests should be asked to come representing some Irish lady or gentleman, and also to be prepared to sing some Irish song, or tell some Irish story. As the guests arrive the assumed name of each may be written on a card and put on his back. For example: Mike McGinnis might go as a policeman; Handy Andy as a waiter; Robert Emmet as an orator; Terence Mulvaney as a soldier.

Readings: "The Bells of Shannon," "The Blarney Stone," selections from "Handy Andy." Songs: "The Minstrel Boy," "The Harp That Once Through Tara's Halls," "The Wearing of the Green."

Refreshments may be wafers tied with green ribbon, olives and pickles, Irish potato chips served on lettuce leaves; green tea and lady fingers tied with green ribbon, and green ribbon candy.

Travels in Tuneland.—The contest method can be well employed for this really worth while and interesting evening.

First, you may have a game of Authors. Ask such questions as: "Who wrote 'O Master, Let Me Walk With Thee'?" A quotation may be given instead of the title. Each guest writes the answers, and the papers are graded with or without exchange.

Naming tunes is very interesting. Your choir leader will no doubt be glad to assist you in this. Have someone at the piano play one of the hymnal tunes until someone names it correctly. Use some of the more familiar ones, such as Old Hundred, Duke Street, etc. The composer of each should be asked.

The history of one of the famous hymn writers or composers might be given, together with the immediate circumstances under which some of his famous hymns were produced.

A Dickens' Evening.—This should be on February 7th, Dickens' birthday. Have the guests come in costumes representing a character of one of his books, or the title of one.

Have the refreshments as English as possible. Have candle light only. Serve individual meat pies, if it is to be a supper; also orange marmalade with seed cakes, rye bread, and there are many other dishes appropriate for this occasion.

CULTURE AND RECREATION.

When the guests arrive take their character names. Later pass around pencils and cards, and the company will guess the characters represented. The prize might be a framed picture of Dickens.

Decorations may be British flags; have English china, if possible, or any pewter you can get.

Some of Dickens' writings may be read aloud.

English prints will help you in planning the costumes.

(Adapted from "Dame Curtsey's Book of Novel Entertainments," Ellye H. Glover.)

Lincoln's Birthday.—In sending out invitations, tell the guests to come in costumes of 1860. Make simplicity the keynote, both in the decorations and the menu. If you serve dinner, use a log cabin for the centerpiece and surround it with a rail fence. The place-cards may be little black china dolls with red and blue checked gingham dresses. Put the quotation, "With malice toward none, with charity toward all," on the place-cards. Drape a flag above the table, and give each guest a little silk flag for the buttonhole or the hair.

The program should include songs of the war period, most of which are well known. Tell some of Lincoln's anecdotes.

During the evening some one may read, "O, Why Should the Spirit of Mortal Be Proud?" Lincoln's favorite poem.

(Adapted from "Dame Curtsey's Book of Novel Entertainments," Glover.)

St. Patrick's Dinner.—Place-cards should be shamrocks and green candles should light the tables. Menu cards ought to be printed in green.

"The Grub:" Mulligatawny soup, emeraud olives, Ould Sod celery, roast pig, Irish potatoes, green peas, spring greens, rye puffs with Dublin sauce, Killarney salad, wafers, "brick" ice cream, mortar cake, Roquefort cheese, saltines, demi tasse, grapes in Cork, Irish mereshams.

(Adapted from "Social Activities," Chesley.)

Washington's Birthday Party.—Have at the top of the invitations a print of Mount Vernon, with the Stars and

Stripes crossed beneath the chandelier. A host and hostess may be dressed as George and Martha. As the guests arrive, give the girls quaint caps like Martha's, with a fichu, both being made from white crepe paper. Each boy may get a cocked hat and a belt and sword.

The rooms, of course, will be decorated with flags. The place-cards may be little hatchets. Souvenirs may be cherry log candy boxes with candied cherries.

Short speeches: "A New Version of the Cherry Tree Story," "Home Life at Mount Vernon As I Imagine It," "If George Could See the City Named After Him," "What He Would Think of His Name State." Take a ballot vote on "What Was Washington's Greatest Quality;" exchange, read, and count.

(Adapted from "Dame Curtsey's Book of Novel Entertainments," Glover.)

Historic Lovers.—This is a most interesting Valentine party. You could have your invitation read thus: "Romeo and Juliet desire your presence at dinner on the night of February 14th, at (hour to be given). Please come attired as Jack. Jill will meet you at our residence." Of course each invitation is worded according to the persons. Others invited might be Paul and Virginia, Dante and Beatrice, Cinderella and the Prince, Punch and Judy, George Washington and Martha, John Alden and Priscilla, Hiawatha and Minnehaha, Ruth and Jacob, Ivanhoe and Rebecca (or Rowena), David Copperfield and Dora, Robert and Elizabeth Browning.

Each lover might write a formal proposal to his companion, and she might write an acceptance or a refusal. The note paper, of course, should be decorated with hearts.

(Adapted from "Dame Curtsey's Book of Novel Entertainments," Glover.)

A Polar Evening.—This is good for a hot day. The invitations can be made very attractive. Show an airship pointing toward a snow mountain where a polar bear stands holding a flag, on which is "North (or South) Pole." On the airship could be printed either Peary or Amundsen, or both.

CULTURE AND RECREATION.

The guests may be fined ten cents (for the Chapter's Social Service Fund) if they mention hot weather. On their arrival serve iced grape juice. Drape the dining-room in white; chairs also. Put a white canvas or sheets on the floor. Get a huge cake of ice to serve as a centerpiece, concealing the pan which holds it with ferns and vines. Serve the refreshments on white china, everything cold, of course.

For program: "My coldest experience"—several actual happenings, told by people previously appointed. "The Wreck of the Hesperus"—a reading. "Sleighing Song," by a quartet, all joining in the chorus. Extracts from "Snowbound."

Parlor snowball: Cotton batting balls, loosely bound with thread, and thrown at various targets, animate and inanimate, sides being chosen and scores kept.

(Adapted from "Dame Curtsey's Book of Novel Entertainments," Glover.)

The Annual Banquet.—Once a year have an inexpensive but carefully planned and attractive banquet. The refreshments need not be—should not be—elaborate. The chief feature of the banquet should bear directly on the work of the Chapter. The banquet may be varied with each year, according to the custom obtaining with regard to wedding anniversaries. There are Chapters which can celebrate their crystal anniversary, while others are but a year old and must begin with the cotton anniversary.

Carnival of Seasons.—This is a good social for the fall, and should be held in a barn. Decorate with autumn foliage. Have four booths for the seasons. Spring should be decorated in green, apple and peach blossoms, if possible. The younger members should be in charge of this booth. Summer booth should have summer fruits and flowers. Fall should have many pumpkins, green and red apples, cornstalks, etc. Winter may have Christmas tree decorations. Articles appropriate to the season can be sold.

A candy pull and games will add to the evening's enjoyment.

Labor Day Celebration.—The guests might be asked to come, each wearing an article indicating his labor. For example, a teacher might come with a ruler, several books, pencil and pads, etc. The banker might carry some bags full of toy coins, bank books; and the druggist could bring some bottles and some patent medicines.

The dining-room may be cleverly decorated. The centerpiece might be a toy washtub with wringer. A small doll could be standing by the tub, washing. A clothes line may be extended to small poles at the four corners of the table, and have tiny garments pinned on the line.

For program many ideas will suggest themselves. "The Village Blacksmith" has several musical settings; Kipling's "McAndrews' Hymn" is good reading, and for the darker side of labor there is Hood's "Song of the Shirt" and Mrs. Browning's "The Cry of the Children."

Adapted from "Dame Curtsey's Book of Novel Entertainments.")

Holiday Cards.—One young woman obtained the names of those who live in homes and institutions where they have no friends, and sent a Christmas card to each one on Christmas Day. This is a small thing to do, but it brings cheer to many a heart.

A Chapter could spend an evening preparing such cards, painting, printing, etc., and make a number of people happy, besides having a good time themselves.

(Adapted from "Dame Curtsey's Book of Novel Entertainments," Glover.)

Hallowe'en Happenings.—When the guests arrive, the house should be but dimly lighted, and a weird and mysterious atmosphere should prevail. Red shades on the lights, or a red screen before the open fire, give a rich glow. The guests may be received by some one dressed as a witch, or garbed in a white sheet to represent a ghost. Welcome should be spoken in sepulchral tones, and accompanied by groans or wails. Some one may play snatches of wild, weird music on the piano, or strike occasional clanging notes from muffled gongs. Jack-o'lanterns peer from unexpected places, and, if convenient, an Æolian harp may be arranged in an open window. The awesomeness of effect

CULTURE AND RECREATION.

will be sufficiently relieved by the irrepressible laughter of the merry guests as they arrive.

The Initial Letter.—Pare an apple in one continuous piece. Swing it slowly around your head three times, and let it fall on the floor. The letter it forms as it falls will be the initial of your future fate. This incantation should be pronounced as the experiment is tried:

> "Paring, paring, long and green,
> Tell my fate for Hallowe'en."

The mirror is another test. A girl must stand with her back to a mirror, and, looking over her shoulder, repeat this charm:

> "Mirror, mirror, tell to me
> Who my future Fate may be.
> Ere the magic moments pass,
> Frame his picture in the glass."

A merry trick is Blowing out the Candle. A boy and a girl may try this at the same time. Each must be blindfolded, and after turning around three times, may try to blow out a lighted candle.

Counting the Seeds is a game all may play at once. Each is given an apple, which is at once cut in two, crossways, and the seeds counted. If two seeds are found, it portends an early marriage; three indicates a legacy; four, great wealth; five, an ocean trip; six, great public fame; seven, the possession of any gift most desired by the finder.

Nutshell Boats make a pretty test of fortune. In the half-shells of English walnuts are fitted masts made of matches and tiny paper sails. On each sail is written the name of a guest, and the boats are set afloat in a tub of water. If two glide together, it indicates a similar fate for the owners; if one sails alone, it means a lonely life. A gentle stirring up of the water will make the boats behave in an amusing manner.

After merry and rollicking games, it is welcome rest to sit down to Fagot stories. The hostess should have in readiness a number of small fagots, or bunches of small dry twigs, tied together with a bit of ribbon. One should be given to each guest. These, in turn, are thrown on the fire, and each guest must tell a story that shall last as long as his or her fagot is blazing.

(Adapted from "Pleasant-day Diversions," Carolyn Wells.)

Write rhymes of four or six lines on thin paper, and place in chestnut shells. Tie together with ribbon, the ladies' in one color, the gentlemen's in another. If there are personal hits in the rhymes, tie the name of the person for whom each one is intended on the outside of the shell.

Hide a ring, a thimble, and a penny in the room. To the one who finds the ring, speedy marriage is assured; the thimble denotes a life of single blessedness; the penny promises wealth.

Have one of the young ladies who knows a little palmistry be the witch of the evening. A short, bright-hued skirt, a gay plaid shawl crossed over her shoulders, a scarf bound about her head, will make a very striking costume, and, with the aid of a little paint and powder, quite an effective disguise. If she is enough acquainted with the guests to give some personal history, she can produce some very "telling" fortunes.

Prepare a basket of rosy-cheeked apples, each with the initials of a name pricked in the skin, which names must be used in counting the apple seeds.

After the supper table has been cleared of all except the decorations and candles, have a large dish filled with burning alcohol and salt brought in and placed in the center. Seated around this ghostly fire, all other lights except the candles having been extinguished, let the guests tell stirring stories rigmarole fashion; that is, some one starting the story and stopping short at its most exciting point and letting his neighbor continue it, etc.

(Adapted from "Bright Ideas for Entertainng," Mrs. H. B. Linscott.)

Outdoor Pleasures.

It is a pity the bicycle is no longer fashionable, but it is no less useful than it used to be. A League run to some

CULTURE AND RECREATION.

place not too remote, with lunch at the objective point and an hour or two of rest before starting the return trip, would be a splendid day's fun for many Chapters. Dress sensibly, wheel at a moderate pace, stop for a bit of breath occasionally, keep an eye out for scenery and incidental happenings, be jolly over the inevitable mishap, and you will come back invigorated. Fifty miles for the round trip is an outside mark for a day's run by a mixed company. Thirty miles would be better, allowing for an average pace of six miles an hour. Do not try century runs. They are for the faddists, who go camel-humped over the route, caring for nothing but to make it in record time. There is no fun in that.

Walk! It is the pleasantest sort of outdoor sociability. Dress for rough tramping, so that you will not need to be anxious about the effect of dust and mud and stony roads. Carry nothing that can be spared. Send the lunch by some sort of conveyance to the point selected—the home of some country member, or a friendly farmhouse. Walk leisurely,—not a bit over three miles an hour. Keep your eyes open as you go. Make a little side-excursion by the way if you feel so inclined. Encourage one another. Sing on the journey. Keep up a merry exchange of harmless jokes. Add each pedestrian's mite to the common stock of outdoor knowledge. The Chapter which by such methods popularizes the Epworth League Pedestrian Club will do much for the health and spirits of its members.

The *Lawn Social* is always available where there are "door-yards" of real grass which will stand a little rough usage. If a porch is properly situated, a bit of a program may be rendered, the porch being used as a platform for the speakers. Or a platform may be improvised from materials lying around the place.

Pedestrian Sociability.—Hiking parties are great fun. Wear old clothes, so that the dust, mud, etc., can not hurt them. Take your time when walking, so as not to get tired. Singing on such an occasion is always delightful. Have a study of birds on one trip, a study of flowers on another, etc. This will increase the health as well as the knowledge.

THE EFFICIENT EPWORTHIAN.

Barn Social.—This is, of course, to be held in a barn. Lanterns should be hung to the rafters—not the paper kind. Appropriate decorations may be used. The guests may be taken to the barn in a hay wagon. A husking bee would be a good addition to the evening's pleasure.

Three Good Picnic Games.—Tennis volley ball or "fist ball." To be kept in air. Teams of any number, two to ten, line up on opposite sides of a net stretched eight feet high. Mark boundaries of field at points agreed upon, side lines being at right angles to net at its end. Put ball in play by striking with palm or fist, sending it over the net. As long as it is kept in the air and returned to the other side of net, it is in play. When it drops, or is hit into net or out of bounds, the other side scores one. Fellow players may toss the ball to one another in order to get it over. Ball must not be caught or held, or struck otherwise than with the hands. In starting the play a ball that touches the net as it goes over is a "let," and is served over. In play if the ball goes over after touching the net, it remains in play. The side which first scores twenty-one wins the game.

Baseball played by kicking a football instead of batting; otherwise same as baseball. Use indoor baseball rules.

Playground ball or "indoor" ball. Everybody knows how to play it.

A Country Dinner.—Plan a meeting at a farmhouse. Have an old-fashioned dinner, with fried chicken, mashed potatoes, cream gravy, hot biscuits, jelly, etc. Have some toasts, such as, "What I know about fishing," "Green fields and running brooks," "School is out," and many others may be thought of.

Sing old-fashioned songs. If the house is far away, you might go in a hay wagon, but go in a crowd.

Rambles.—Make these hiking parties with a purpose. One time the members may study wild flowers, another time birds, then trees, or historical places. There should always be an expert along with the party to describe things. A corn roast may be used on some of these rambles at the right season. On one day let the girls go in one direction,

CULTURE AND RECREATION.

the boys in another, all returning to the church for an evening social, with a few speeches in which experiences will be exchanged.

(Adapted from "Social Activities," Albert Chesley.)

A Community Field Day.—This is an event for every one, children as well as grown-ups. School pennants and flags might be used as decorations. Cheers, "yells," and songs should be planned. If the amusements are interesting enough, no one will have to be made to do things, but they will want to enter into everything. Some good games are volley ball, tether ball, prisoner's base, relay races, captain ball, quoits, corner ball, potato race, throwing ball into barrel, tug-of-war.

Of course, the picnic lunch is very important and should be carefully planned.

Adapted from "Year-Book of Playgrounds," 1908, Miss Cora B. Clark.

Tennis Tournament.—The Department of Recreation can use this idea to good advantage. The tournament may enlist anywhere from six to forty players. If it extends over a number of days or weeks, the spirit grows. Of course, everything must be fair and free from unpleasant rivalry.

The Picnic.—This has been so often a dismal failure that it is not properly estimated by many people. When it is too big and too laborious, it is a most exquisite form of social torture. But it can be made to furnish social resources of the highest order. Do not undertake too much. Do not strain a point to secure a big crowd. Do not make the mistake of dividing up into groups. Have all things in common. If that is not possible, the company is too large or ill-assorted, and the picnic will be only a moderate success. Be sure to include the old but favorite races, the sack race, the potato race, the blindfold race, and the other producers of athletic hilarity.

Camping Out.—No better way to invest some of the vacation time can be imagined than in a sojourn in the woods or by the lake. An Epworth League camp is one of the most delightful of summer resorts. A group of congenial young folk, with two or three older folk for company and counsel, can have a "glorious time" at small cost.

The Holiday Tour.—Travel in a party, properly chaperoned. The English young people's societies do this admirably. True, they have many points of interest at short distances from their homes, but so have many of our Chapters. Some of these English young folks go to the lake district, to Scotland, to London, to Paris, and even to Switzerland, Norway, and up the Rhine. But many of our Chapters are near places of great natural beauty or historical significance. Visit a near-by city, or a Chautauqua assembly, or a camp-meeting. A Chapter which one summer rented a cottage at a camp-meeting for its members found the investment a profitable one in many ways.

Bringing Outdoors Indoors.

Baseball Game of Buzz.—This is the old game of buzz, played in imitation of baseball. In buzz, a number is selected which, with its multiple, is not to be repeated as a company of players count in turn the numbers from 1 up, but, instead of which, "buzz" is to be said. If 4 be the number, the players, seated in a circle, will say, "1, 2, 3, buzz, 5, 6, 7, buzz," etc. In this game the players, who may be eighteen or less, are on two even sides. The chairs for one side are arranged in relative position like the diamond of a baseball field. The other side is seated in a row in a position corresponding to the batter's bench. The man at the bat goes and stands at the "plate." The numbers are now repeated in turn down the bench and around the bases and field, the "buzz" number being selected for each inning by the side at bat. If one of the sides in the field makes an error, the batter takes the next base until he has made a run, which is scored. Then another batter takes his place. If the batting side makes an error, the batter is out, and when three are out the sides exchange places.

(From "Indoor Games for Boys," Baker.)

A Game With Clothespins.—Two sides face each other. A basket which contains twelve clothespins is at the head of each line. Each player must hold the next player's left hand; thus every one's right hand is free for passing. The pins are passed down the line one at a time. If one is dropped, the one who dropped it must pick it up and pass it on. When the last player gets the pin, he puts it on the floor until the twelve are there. Then he starts them back again in the same way. The side which finishes first is the winner.

(Adapted from "Indoor Games for Boys," Baker.)

Screen.—This may be played over a screen in the house, or a fence out of doors. What it is should be high enough so that the players can not see each other. The players are divided into two groups, each side having an umpire, who should keep the score of the opponents. The ball must be thrown back and forth over the screen and must not drop to the floor or the ground. Opponents will score one point if the ball does touch the floor. The winning point is 21. It is a modified form of volley ball. If played indoors, the ball should be very light and soft.

(Adapted from "Games," Bancroft.)

The Stray Sheep.—The players must stand in a circle, and one walks around the outside and asks some one, "Have you seen my sheep?" The one asked says, "How was he dressed?" The questioner describes the way some one in the circle is dressed, and if the one questioned names the right player, the one named must run around the outside of the circle, chased by the one who guessed. He runs to his own place. If caught, he takes the place of the questioner. For example: The description might say he wore a gray suit, red necktie, low shoes, etc. Every one must be alert.

(Adapted from "Games," Bancroft.)

The Indoor Picnic.—Invitations may be sent out on brown paper. Unique plans might be worked out for these. One suggestion is to have the address on the first page of the invitations; on the second page, "Summer Attire," and on the third could be the invitation itself. The girls ought to be asked to bring luncheon for two.

Number the baskets and also the young men, and at

the proper time the girl will find a young man with her basket.

By means of signs, the guests can be directed to a bowling alley, which proves to be a small set of nine-pins; to the shooting gallery, where they will find a rubber tipped arrow. Parlor croquet does the work for the croquet grounds.

Boughs of trees will add to the picnic atmosphere; also a lemonade well, made out of a wash-tub.

The lights can be put out one by one, giving the effect of approaching night.

(Adapted from "Eighty Pleasant Evenings.")

A Parlor Field Meet.—

1. One-yard dash.—Push a penny with your nose one yard across the floor.

2. Tug-of-war.—Tie a raisin in the middle of a long piece of string, and each contestant starts at the end of the string and chews it and sees who can get to the raisin first.

3. Hurdle Race.—Several contestants take six needles and see who can thread them first.

4. Drinking Race.—You must see who can drink a glass of water by means of a spoon and get through first.

5. Cracker-eating Contest (for girls only).—Have ten girls on each side. Each girl has a cracker. Start the first girl on each side at the signal. The winner is the one who can eat her dry cracker and whistle first. The side which finishes its ten crackers captures the prize.

6. Shot-put.—A race in which each contestant puts buckshot into a pill bottle, one shot at a time.

7. Parlor Football.—An extension table, an empty eggshell; the players kneeling, chins on a level with the table; the "ball" to be advanced to the goal by blowing. Two goals out of three decide the game.

(Adapted from "Home Entertaining.")

Three Deep.—All but two players form two circles, one inside the other, both facing inward. The other two players are the runner and the catcher. The chaser tries to tag the runner, and the runner is safe if he can stop inside the circle in front of any couple, thus making it

CULTURE AND RECREATION.

"three deep." In that case, the outside one is the third one, and he is now the runner. He can seek safety in the same way. If the chaser tags the runner, they change places, the runner becoming chaser and vice versa.

(Adapted from "Games," Bancroft.)

Feather Volley Ball.—The players form sides and sit around a table. A little feather is tossed into the air in the middle. The players of each side should have as their aim to blow the feather so that it will rest in the other camp, and not let it settle in their own. This will give every one a hilarious time. Players must not leave their seats.

(Adapted from "Home Games.")

Tennis Tournament Party.—Decorations should be tennis racquets and nets, also red and white flowers. Use small cardboard racquets, on which you will write the invitations. Have a large net stretched across the room and put in this net red and white pasteboard racquets, each one being tied to several yards of red and white ribbon, and tangle them up. The guests should wind up the ribbon on the racquets and get as many as possible without breaking the ribbon.

Distribute cards and ask each to write a tennis pun or joke. You should get several better than these: "Tennis is the frankest of games; it calls love nothing." "A guinea fowl can make a bigger racket than Wright and Ditson." "Why should an expert waiter be a success at tennis? Because there's no flaw in his service." "Why are the king's purse-bearers like a tennis ball in play? Because they must stay in the court to count."

Refreshments may be served in tennis racquets. If in summer, serve lemonade and wafers, and if in winter, coffee and cake.

(Adapted from "Bright Ideas for Entertaining," Linscott.)

A Baseball Party.—This is a dinner party. Nine guests should be present, making the necessary "nine." Each one may be assigned to a place on the "team" and may find his

THE EFFICIENT EPWORTHIAN.

place at the table in that way. There should be small "fans" with the word on them, such as "catcher," "pitcher," etc. There should be nine courses in the menu (innings). Little booklets with "Official Score" written or printed on them may be used as menu cards, putting in simply the ball terms. This is the menu:

First inning: First strike—oyster cocktail. Second inning: Where the losing team lands—soup. Third inning: Caught on the fly—small trout with diamonds of crisp toast. Fourth inning: A sacrifice—lamb chops with potato balls. Fifth inning: A "fowl" ball—chicken croquettes with French peas. Sixth inning: The umpire when we lose—lobster salad with cheese straws. Seventh inning: A fine diamond—ice cream in diamond-shaped slices; cake. Eighth inning: Necessary for good playing—preserved ginger with wafers and coffee. Ninth inning: Everybody scores—the passing of favors.

(Adapted from "Bright Ideas for Entertaining," Linscott.)

Indoor Baseball.—The company is divided into two groups. Play the game with small leaden disks, which should be thrown upon boards two by three feet. Three sides of this board are enclosed by strips so that the disks will not roll off. Have the board marked and the sections named: Home run, base on balls, stolen base, two-base hit, out on base, three-base hit, foul and out, one-base hit, struck out, fly caught. This should be played very much like indoor baseball.

Camp Delights.—A most enjoyable evening in camp may be spent in having an imitation of high school or college Commencement exercises. You could have your orations, camp history, camp prophecy, presentation of gifts, camp songs, etc. The same idea can be adapted to the Chapter room and the Chapter organization. Work at a complete "class day" or Commencement program.

(Adapted from "Social Activities," Chesley.)

LENGTHENING THE MEMBERSHIP ROLL.

A normal Epworth League Chapter is in constant need of new members. In the first place there will be a gradual

CULTURE AND RECREATION.

withdrawal from the active work of the Chapter of those who have been longest connected with it. They will become more and more advisory and, in a sense, honorary members, giving their active service to other interests of the Church. Their places must be filled by the coming in of new members.

In the second place, an Epworth League Chapter is essentially a missionary organization. It is not to be content with interesting and helping those who are already enrolled on its record. Like the Church itself, the Chapter must go out among those who have not yet been reached and enlist their interest and their co-operation, in order that it may win them to the highest standard of Christian experience in life.

Where are the new members to be found? The comprehensive answer is, everywhere. The Fourth Department should let no opportunity escape of learning the name and the location of every probable recruit. Strangers coming into town should be visited at the first possible moment. There are already young people in the community who are frequently at the League meetings, no doubt, but have never been asked to join. Some members, by reason of their association in business or school with other young people, can make out lists of special classes, clerks in stores, the young men in factories and business houses, young women who are in business or domestic service, students of all the educational institutions in the neighborhood, and other classes.

There are two other most important sources of supply. First, the Junior League. The Junior League members are very rapidly growing up. Every year many of them are ready to leave the Junior ranks. Do not let them be lost to the young people's work at the time when they feel themselves too old for the Junior League. It would be a glorious thing if every Junior League Chapter could arrange for annual graduation, and if it could be understood that entrance into the membership of the Epworth League is as much a matter of course as is the going from the Primary Department into the older classes of the Sunday school.

THE EFFICIENT EPWORTHIAN.

Second, the revival. Wherever young people are being converted and forsaking sin and turning to God, there is a fruitful field in which to secure new members for the Epworth League. The great problem of the Church to-day is, "What shall be done with our probationers?" If every young person who becomes a probationer should at the same time become an Epworthian, with a definite place in some department of the Chapter's work, and with all the advantages of fellowship and membership which the Epworth League provides, there would soon be a noticeable decrease in the number of probationers dropped from the rolls. Should the Epworth League be particular concerning the new material it gets? Yes and no. There should be no "rushing" of members, no throwing out of the drag-net merely in order to get as many members as possible. And yet the ideal aim is to secure every young person in the community who is not already affiliated with some other young people's society.

This aim is not to be sought simply to get a big membership list, but in order that the real purposes of the Epworth League may be accomplished both in and through the young people.

The work of canvassing for new members has no special season. It can be carried on continually, although there may be times when a special effort is both possible and desirable. The chairman of the Fourth Department who desires to make a success of this part of the work will look carefully over the territory. Members of the committee will be assigned to such special districts or special classes of young people as may best secure the end desired. Some will be assigned to make a canvass of Sunday schools. Every member of the Sunday school who is of proper age should be in the Epworth League Chapter. Special attention ought to be paid to the young men's class and to the young people who are already members of the Church.

Sometimes good results are secured by asking one member, or a club of members, to aim at securing a certain definite number of new members—three, or five, or ten.

Membership contests have been tried with very excel-

CULTURE AND RECREATION.

lent results in many Chapters. Their use should be safeguarded very carefully, however, in order to prevent the employment of questionable methods during the contest, and a reaction and consequent lack of interest when the contest is over. The usual method of conducting a membership contest is to divide the present membership into two sections, each under the leadership of a captain. A time-limit is set, usually varying from one to six months, and each side strives by every possible means to secure applications for membership. At the close of the contest the section which has secured the most members is entertained by the other section at some kind of a social gathering. To this the new members are heartily invited. The occasion may also be signalized by the proper reception of the new members.

Wherever the pledge is used, let the Chapter be quite as eager to secure associate members as it is to secure active members. Associate members are well on the way toward complete acceptance of all that the League stands for, and it is a mistaken policy to keep down the number of associate members. But, of course, insist that associate membership is not a permanent arrangement. An associate member should not be satisfied to remain such, nor should the Chapter be willing to keep associate members permanently in that relation.

The work is not all done when the new members are elected and have signed the Constitution. They are yet to be "broken in," and on the experience of their first few weeks in the Chapter will depend very largely their enjoyment of the new relation and their usefulness in the Chapter's work. The very best place to complete the work of strengthening the Chapter's hold on its new members is the devotional meeting. In that meeting the fellowship fact must be abundant, and opportunity must be tactfully given to the new members for participation. When necessary, this may be done gradually and by indirect methods. Do not make the mistake of asking an inexperienced and shy new member to take the entire responsibility of conducting a devotional meeting the week after he or she has been received. Use such methods in the devotional

THE EFFICIENT EPWORTHIAN.

meeting as will make it possible for the more backward and bashful to take some part at the very outset.

An important element in making new members feel at home is that they should be provided with some definite share in the work. No person who is satisfied to be a member of the Chapter at all need be without a congenial and useful share in its activities.

The new members will be a little hesitating at first. No stranger enjoys making advances toward better acquaintances. The Chapter members must see to it that there is prompt and cordial recognition of new members at every possible opportunity. The welcome which they receive at the various meetings should be, if anything, a little warmer than that which is accorded to the older members. If possible, little distinctions and marks of special consideration should be shown until they begin to feel thoroughly at home in their new relationship.

The Chapter misses a great opportunity if it neglects to make due recognition of the new members when they are received. By all means have a formal reception. It need not be elaborate, but it ought to be impressive. There is no place, of course, for the exaggerated symbolism or the boisterousness which characterizes some initiations. But there is room for a dignified, impressive, and memorable service.

Winning the School Folk.

The Epworth League is fairly ready to take John Wesley's advice and make much of the great occasions. But always there is room to do more of it. Some Chapters pay particular and successful attention to the important days of the school year.

The details are not important, but the idea is. It can be adapted to every town in the country, for every town has schools and Commencements and graduates.

And it should be. The Epworth League must ever say, "I am for youth, and nothing that concerns youth is foreign to me." Besides, the young people of the schools are the very people who own the League. They are young, and they are learners. What other qualifications do they need to give them title to the Epworth League's ministry?

CULTURE AND RECREATION.

When the League has served them, it can with entire appropriateness invite them to accept its Master and to serve Him. But attraction must come before invitation, or the invitation will have small success.

And in every place where young people come together to study and to work at a common task, there is an Epworth League opportunity.

Make much of the young folk of the schools!

THE CHAPTER AND THE ELUSIVE YOUNG MAN.

What do the boys and young men of your Church think of the League.

Are they in it as actual, not nominal members?

Are they inclined to sneer at it, and to make fun of it, and to consider it a milk-and-watery affair?

Do they love it, or respect it, or patronize it, or belittle it, or ignore it?

If there is anything unpleasant in the young-man attitude to the Chapter, there's a reason. And it is better to find the reason than to scold the young fellows.

A young man of sixteen years and upwards—he *is* a young man, you know—is a strange new creature. He has intense likes, and intenser dislikes.

If he has not been forced into a mold of unthinking credulity, he prefers reality to second-hand orthodoxy.

He does not care for religious "exercises." He will do religious deeds, when the thing appeals to him, but he has a profound scorn for pious pantomime. That is the reason he hates clippings and essays and the whole list of artificial expedients employed in some devotional meetings.

Very few young men will go into any plan of study unless they can be shown the good of it. And they do not reckon as anything particularly good the padding of the Chapter's study class record.

He is an unusual and not in every sense wholesome young man who excels in the ordinary forms of "mercy and help" work. The average young chap is awkward and self-conscious when he tries it, and he does not try it for long. But he has some affinity for many forms of social service.

THE EFFICIENT EPWORTHIAN.

To rouse young men's enthusiasm for recreational work it must be vigorous rather than æsthetic, physical rather than intellectual, and amusing rather than instructive.

Very well; if your Chapter is failing to win and hold its fair proportion of young men, the reason may perhaps be found in one of the preceding five paragraphs. What then?

It is not a question of wanting or not wanting the young manhood of the community; of course the Chapter wants it. And so the Chapter's program must be framed with that in mind. To frame it is largely the Fourth Vice-President's work.

At every possible point, seek first to masculinize the Chapter's plans and work. Get expert help; a Young Men's Christian Association man of sense will be an invaluable counselor.

Don't be afraid of overdoing it; that danger is small. The young women are more ready to work in the Chapter with manly young fellows than with the other sort. And, once the young women fairly see this situation, they will be heart and soul devoted to making the Chapter's work as attractive to young men as it is to themselves.

There is enough big work, adventurous work, and alluring work to be had in the Epworth League as it is now constituted to give every normally decent and human young man within its reach a chance to be religious without being affected, and to render Christian service without being self-conscious.

Provide for the young man!

The Evil in Membership Contests.

The thing that makes a membership contest bad is the ending of it.

To end it on the night when the final scores are made, or on the night of the "banquet," is to spoil it.

The purpose of a membership contest is not points, nor the winning of a race, nor something to eat, but *members*.

And when you have gained a member, your work is not finished; it is just begun.

A member is sought for what the League can give him,

CULTURE AND RECREATION.

and for what he can give the League. Neither of these processes can begin until the contest is over; they ought to continue as long as either party has need of the other.

Many a membership contest has done much harm from the failure to think through what it ought to mean. It has been a dismal failure because of a mistake which was first made some time before League membership contests were invented—the mistake of considering the means more important than the end. That is one of the world's favorite blunders. It has led to strifes and wars. It has overturned dynasties and ruined empires. It has retarded civilization and delayed the gospel.

To become more interested in processes than results, and to count the machinery as more valuable than the output—all this is no new thing. But it is just as bad as if it were a sort of folly first discovered and practiced by the young people of the Epworth League.

We shall not need to be troubled about the methods by which members are gained if we do but keep in mind the one worthy motive for seeking them.

Nobody will think of "gambling" in connection with a membership contest if both sides are keenly alive to the problem of what to do with the new members, and what to do for them.

Nor can there be any danger that the new members will suffer neglect at the close of the contest if the Chapter really understands that the relation it has sought to establish has but now begun.

CHAPTER XI.

MAKING THE RECORD AND FINANCING THE WORK.

The Epworthian Scribe.

The Epworth League Secretary may easily be a mere functionary, doing routine things in an indifferent fashion. But if he will rise to his privileges he may be brain and nerves to his Chapter.

To him will come the experiences and needs of the departments to be transformed into plans, reminders, opportunities, and permanent achievements. So may he be miles above "only the Secretary."

He is the Chapter's recorder, historian, letter-writer, reporter, bookkeeper, statistician, custodian of supplies, advertising agent, and generally indispensable official. The officers in other departments may be but moderate, respectably ordinary people, without absolute ruin to the work, but the Secretary's place demands genius. Not the skyrocket kind, but genius for plodding, for detail, for exactness, for promptness, for general alertness, and uncommon common sense.

These qualities, not always inborn, are attainable by any one who desires them sufficiently, and so are presupposed as present or on the way in the case of every Secretary who reads this Chapter. It should not be necessary to say that the Secretary must be a Christian. Else how can he be a good Secretary in an organization whose vital principle is the extension and intensification of the Christian life?

Supplies.—The Secretary will be wise if, immediately upon his installation, he gets all the supplies he needs for his department and for the Chapter. He will require for his own use record books of one or two sorts, scrapbooks,

RECORDING AND FINANCING THE WORK.

and stationery. He is the proper custodian of the Chapter's stock of pledge cards, topic cards, report blanks, transfer cards, and the like. These things should not be allowed to get out of stock. They are as cheap before they are needed as two weeks after the last one is gone, and their presence is a wonderful preservative of patience.

Committee.—The Secretary should ask each of the four Vice-Presidents to select one member who will be the connecting link between that department and the Secretary. Then, with an additional helper, to whom it will be safe to intrust the advertising work, the Secretary's committee is complete. So far as possible, all work with the departments should be done through the members who represent them on this committee.

Membership Record.—This ought to be complete, and frequently revised. The first revision will probably be needed the day the book comes into the Secretary's hands. Eliminate every name that does not stand for a known and definite membership. Read and apply to local conditions Bishop Vincent's tract, "Wayworth Chapel Records."

To be complete, the membership record should have every member's name and address, date of election to membership, Church relation, and department to which the member is assigned. If the Chapter uses the pledge, "active" or "associate" will be a necessary notation for each member.

The record will be all the better if it includes an attendance register. Some Secretaries keep track of the Church, prayer-meeting, and Sunday school attendance of their members. A list of the members, arranged by departments, is a most useful thing, especially if it is posted conspicuously in the League room. Another list, not, however, for conspicuous posting, may well be kept, containing the names of chronic absentees or otherwise unsatisfactory members, whose shortcomings may properly be noted by the Secretary. These names should be referred to the Cabinet or the Department of Spiritual Work, and the results of any special attention should be quietly noted.

The Secretary will always "go armed." That is to say, he will have his membership record with him at every

THE EFFICIENT EPWORTHIAN.

League meeting. It will be needed nearly every time to answer some more or less important question.

As there are always some folk "almost persuaded," there is always need of a list of prospective members. Glean these names from every source. Keep a keen eye on the stranger within the gates. Get the names of the young people who are friendly to the League. Make a list of names of clerks in stores, young men in the shops, young women in service or in business, high school students, telegraph employees, and of the people whom some special industry brings into the neighborhood. And, having these names, use them. The First Department can seek to interest these people in the Church and Chapter; the Second can use all the recruits it can get; the Third may be able to help them in some time of need; the Fourth will always be glad for the names of people to whom can be given invitations to lectures, classes, socials, and entertainments.

When a new member is secured, get the correct name at once. The Constitution of the League will have been inserted on the first pages of the membership record, and a place provided there for new members' signatures. Then each one should be given a copy of the Constitution for his own use. As soon as he is assigned to a department, note that fact in the record, and all the other necessary facts concerning him, just as soon as may be.

When a member moves away there is a chance for the Secretary to do him and the Church a simple but important service. First, make out a transfer card and give it to him with the Chapter's love and hearty good wishes for the future. Then, write to the pastor of the Methodist Church nearest his new home. A Methodist preacher gets so little of this sort of help that he will be correspondingly grateful, and for very gratitude he will fairly bubble over with welcome to the young stranger. The half-hour which the Secretary might need to accomplish this result would save to God and the Church practically every case—and their number is distressingly large—which now is reported, "He moved away and we lost track of him."

For a permanent membership record, which will be of ever-increasing value, and which can never be outgrown, a

RECORDING AND FINANCING THE WORK.

card catalogue is the best thing obtainable. The single card for each member, on which is written his name, address, and other personal notes, may grow to two or three more cards full of interesting facts of his League, Church, and public life as the years go by. The catalogue may be elaborated into a sort of biographical dictionary of the Chapter, and it is so simple of operation and so instantly accessible for consultation, that for historical purposes alone it is worth ten times what it costs. A card outfit large enough to begin with can be had for as little as $1.

Business Records.—The one indispensable requisite of business records is accuracy. Rhetoric and elaboration are not needed. A plain handwriting, free from flourishes and original abbreviations, is better than a florid imagination and impossible scroll work.

Keep the records up to date, entering them on the permanent book as soon as they are approved. Usually it will not be necessary to enter everything which has been discussed in a meeting, though the rule which says that motions not carried are not to be recorded may often and wisely be broken. There are times when it is well to have a record of what the meeting did not do. Show the general direction of discussion in important matters.

Paragraph freely, being especially careful to give every separate item its separate paragraph. Require long or important motions to be furnished in writing, and transcribe them literally. Use sub-heads, as in this chapter, or, what is better for the Secretary's purpose, writing them in the margin, well out beyond the body of the record. So simple a thing will make the record fourfold clearer and easier of reference.

The recording of elections and of the names of committees appointed does not end the Secretary's duties in the premises. Every member of a committee should have definite notice of appointment, with a plain statement of the work expected of the committee. Every officer-elect should be promptly apprised of the honor conferred. Do not permit any hitch in committee work, or any vacancy, however temporary, in official ranks, because it was thought that everybody knew all about it. Tell them beforehand.

THE EFFICIENT EPWORTHIAN.

In the Cabinet meetings and general business meetings, the Secretary is the one indispensable element. He has the business of the evening at his fingers' ends. He is at the President's elbow, alert to prompt, suggest, untangle snarled threads of business, and quick to refer to the subject in hand.

And, with all this, he has the minutes of the meeting written up to the minute. It does n't take rare ability to do these things; only attention, sense, and a proper valuation of spare moments.

Many special records may be kept. The committee member from the First Department may make a simple but very useful record of the devotional meetings, noting the names of leaders, the attendance, and special features. From the Third Department will come reports of surveys, study classes, and social service campaigns; accounts of calls made, tracts distributed, people helped, and results accomplished. From the Second, Third, and Fourth Departments will come descriptions of literary and social gatherings, reports of reading and study done, programs, and other material of permanent interest. These records will be fuller than the monthly department reports, which are usually brief summaries in statistical form.

By cultivating an appetite for complete records of these things, using the members of the committees in getting what is wanted, material will be provided for some exceedingly profitable correspondence, as will be noted in a later paragraph, to say nothing of the value of such material to the local Chapter.

Of course, the Secretary will insist on written monthly reports from the departments, whether the monthly business meeting is held or not. By furnishing blanks to the various Vice-Presidents, the reports as they come in can be perforated and bound in "volumes" of one year each by the use of paper fasteners. Make a neat title-page for each volume, bearing a sufficiently complete inscription to indicate the contents at a glance. If the Chapter can not afford or does not care to use the regular report blanks, furnish the Vice-Presidents with paper of uniform size, so that the reports may be bound as suggested.

RECORDING AND FINANCING THE WORK.

Co-operation With the Treasurer.—The Secretary should keep a record of all bills brought before the Chapter, showing their date, amount, for what incurred, the action of the Chapter, and the date of the orders on the Treasurer, and have them signed by the President, using a regular form and keeping a record on the stubs of the order forms.

Correspondence.—The Secretary is the connectional officer of the Chapter. He holds it in the organized relation to the District League and the Central Office. None of these can do anything with or for the local Chapter if they can not get in touch with it. It should be written in bold letters over every Secretary's table, "Answer promptly every official letter which requires an answer." If the letter calls for information which can not be furnished at once, write an acknowledgment of its receipt and indicate a date when a complete answer will be sent. The observance of this simple rule of business ethics in the local Chapters would make some District officers renew their youth amazingly.

The first official duty of the Secretary may be to send the names of the newly elected officers, including his own, to the District Secretary and to the Central Office. How otherwise could those two useful institutions, the District League and the General Secretary, be in a position to serve the local Chapter, for whose service they exist?

There should be no hesitation in originating official correspondence. If there are new plans to describe, hard questions to ask, or difficult problems to solve, write, briefly, but clearly, to the district or general officer who is most especially concerned.

A list of all the Chapters in the district is a valuable possession, or a new plan of work, a copy or a description may be sent to a few of the Chapters, with the request that the courtesy be reciprocated when occasion offers. Send to a new list of Chapters each time until the district has been covered by the correspondence. Then branch out and send letters into the larger field. This method will spread good material in places where it will be appreciated, and a steady return current of helpfulness will set in toward

THE EFFICIENT EPWORTHIAN.

the originating Chapter which may easily pay a per cent on the investment.

If there are any philanthropic or charitable institutions, settlements, deaconess hospitals, or the like within reach of the Chapter's help, write to them and learn what service can be rendered. Then the matter may be referred to the Department of Social Service. Or the list of such institutions may be furnished to that department for its attention.

When a member of the Chapter goes away for a protracted stay, say to college, or to work in another place, a correspondence circle may be organized in his behalf. The Secretary need not do it all. Others should write; not all at once, of course. Let there be an occasional letter of friendly interest and League and Church news. It will hearten the absent one and keep him in sympathetic touch with the home work. When he comes back he will not need to be broken in again, but will go straight to work as though he had not been away.

Statistics.—Errors in spelling are not fatal; errors in figures are without remedy. Be accurate. Do n't estimate; most estimates exaggerate. A count of heads in a congregation is an amazing reducer of immense audiences.

Keep all the Chapter's statistics that there is opportunity to get. More is better than less. Count the members, the attendance at League meetings, the Christian Stewardship enrollment, *The Herald* subscribers, the Comrades of the Morning Watch, the study class members, and all the rest. Every six months summarize these statistics, and insert them on a page of the record. Compare with the preceding six months. Show the figures to the department leaders who are concerned; make the statistics exert a helpful influence on the work of the Chapter. When *The Herald* canvass begins, furnish the names of present subscribers to the canvassers, and help them in their work.

Scrapbooks.—Get one. Still better, get two. Into them put every bit of printed or written matter which can be found having any reference to the Chapter or the general League work. One scrapbook will be filled with local memorabilia: programs of special gatherings, newspaper notices, the reports borne by delegates to the various con-

RECORDING AND FINANCING THE WORK.

ventions, of convention proceedings by the same delegates, the news items sent to *The Herald* and the *Advocate,* and all the large variety of valuable but fugitive material, historic and inspirational, which will never be of any use unless it is promptly put into permanent form.

The other scrapbook should be for methods, plans, suggestions, and programs, clipped from *The Herald* and other papers.

It may well include Board of Control matters, official answers to questions, interesting bits of League history, and the like. One we know of has two hundred and fifty pages the size of *The Herald's* page. It contains practically everything on League methods that has been printed in the official paper from the beginning. It is a League encyclopedia. One so large, of course, is arranged in sections, a section for each department. Perhaps the department leaders may be induced to make their own scrapbooks, but if they do not, the Secretary should certainly see to this work. It puts years of experience at the disposal of the youngest Chapter of the League.

Advertising.—This is a field with almost unbounded possibilities. A vast amount of dignified, clean, and attractive advertising can be done by every Chapter Secretary. Get "Handbook of Church Advertising," by Francis H. Case, and note how many effective methods can be utilized to make the Chapter and the Church known to the entire community. Let one member of the Secretary's Committee have this as his exclusive work. It will not be a sinecure, but if well done it will bring real results.

The Secret-ary.

That is some people's idea of his business; he is a keeper of secrets. Secrets are entrusted to him with the confident assurance that wild horses could not drag them from him.

A few Epworth League Secretaries appear to hold that theory of their functions. Information by the ream comes to them, but precious little of it ever sees the light again. They remind one of that time-honored college conundrum: "Why ought ...... College to be the most scholarly insti-

THE EFFICIENT EPWORTHIAN.

tution in the country?" "Because the freshmen bring abundant knowledge to it, and the seniors never take any away."

Such a Secretary is missing a great opportunity. Nobody wants to prove that a Secretary can keep a secret. What is desired is that the Secretary shall be, not a reservoir of facts, but a channel, conveying to the proper receptacles the information which finds its way to him. All Secretaries who read this book are asked, at the suggestion of the General Secretary, to adopt these brief rules for the conduct of their work, and to obey them:

1. Know all that is possible to be known about your Chapter.
2. Answer to-day every letter that needs an answer.
3. Give the exact facts, as far as you know them, not general statements.
4. Tell all you know to whomsoever has the right to ask.
5. Do not always wait to be asked.
6. *Answer to-day every letter that needs an answer.*

Whoso makes these rules his own, and heeds them, will not be the *secret*-ary, a mine of inaccessible facts, but The Secretary, a mine of inspiring and refreshing information.

Publicity for League Work.

The Publicity Secretary, or whatever other name is given to the member in charge of the Chapter's advertising, is the link between the Chapter and the outside world. He can do a great variety of helpful things, which will have a large share in creating and maintaining public interest in the Chapter's work. And yet he will not be given to boasting or to any form of press-agent work which does not grow out of the honest effort of the Chapter to count for good in the life of the community.

Here are some sensible hints for the Publicity Secretary.

As to the newspaper: Get acquainted with the newspaper people, and by all reasonable means seek to keep on good terms with them. Find out when the editors want the news, and be sure to get it to them a little ahead of time. If there is more than one paper in the town, prepare separate "copy" for each paper, phrasing the matter

RECORDING AND FINANCING THE WORK.

a little differently each time. Editors have a prejudice against printing matter which they know is to appear in identical terms in another paper.

It may seem unnecessary, but it is n't, to insist on good "copy." That means typewritten copy, or very plain penmanship; black ink on white paper; writing on one side only; paper folded, never rolled; items brief and to the point, omitting all pious platitudes and mere rhetoric; and a signature, "not necessarily for publication, but as a guarantee of good faith."

Perhaps your friend the editor will let you provide an Epworth League column once a month. That is a serious responsibility, as well as a favor. Do not ask for it unless you are willing to work at the task of filling that column worthily every month. But if you are willing, you can do the Chapter a great service through that newspaper. Or perhaps the editor will print, among other League items, a very brief exposition of the devotional meeting topic every week. The pastor may be just the man to write this, and it will be profitable work, both for him and for the paper.

Other forms of publicity must not be neglected because the newspapers are accommodating. Set up an Epworth League Bulletin Board in some conspicuous place. Keep it up-to-date. Put on it all the notices of League events, legibly written in a large hand on stiff paper, and then tacked to the board. If the Church prints a weekly leaflet of notes and notices, pre-empt a corner of it for League purposes, and keep that corner filled. Some Chapters manage the details of the Church leaflet themselves, giving all the societies and activities of the Church their proper recognition.

Send an occasional brief note to the official Church paper for your territory. A postal card will do, in most cases, and the editor will print such an item more readily and more gladly than a longer one. It is a mistake to suppose that editors like lengthy news items.

The Herald is entitled to the news of your Chapter, and you are entitled to see it in *The Epworth Herald* if you send it in. But it must be sent. *The Herald* is not able to print what you might have sent but did n't.

THE EFFICIENT EPWORTHIAN.

Do not send any paper a clipping from some other paper, except for the editor's information. It is unreasonable to ask him to dig out from the clipping such facts as you desire him to use. And it is unfair to the Chapter. The clipping is unusable as it stands, and, in making it over, the very thing which was intended to be emphasized may escape altogether. Pick out your own plum. Maybe the editor might not recognize it as one.

Sometimes a Methodist editor gets clippings taken from other Methodist papers, with the request to reprint. This is a double breach of good manners. It assumes that the editor has not seen the item in the other paper, and it expects him to print stale news in the exact form in which it was given two weeks before. No editor will do such things if he can help it, and usually he can.

The Epworth Herald has established a Poster Service which is intended to provide a regular and attractive supply of advertising matter for the Chapter. Posters are a tested and proved form of publicity, and it is now possible for every Chapter to secure good posters, with constantly varying treatment and subject, at a cost far below the expense of having them made locally. Write to the Editorial Office of *The Epworth Herald,* 740 Rush Street, Chicago, for the details of its plan. It can be used by any Chapter, anywhere, if only the Chapter maintains the weekly devotional meeting. If one of the Centenary bulletin boards is available, it will be found very handy, but the poster service can be used without it.

The Exodus of John and Mildred.

It was on a Kansas farm. Four boys and the new boy were talking. The new boy had come from New York, and only two of the others had ever been as far from home as Topeka, forty miles away.

To those two, Kansas Avenue, Topeka, was a magnificent thoroughfare—broad, long, lined with luxurious stores.

Even the new boy was impressed. He had not seen any Western towns, except from the car window, and he was unsophisticated enough to think that perhaps the Golden West he had read about could produce cities whose main streets were no mean imitation of Broadway.

RECORDING AND FINANCING THE WORK.

That was long ago. But before and since that day, when boys talk together on the farm, they turn soon to the thought of the city. Those who haven't come from it want to go to it.

It avails nothing that, in the evening around the piano, they sing, "Don't be in a hurry to go." They have heard the call of the city, and many of them will answer.

It is good for the city that it gets so many country boys and girls; it could not last long without them. And it may be—maybe—good for the boys and girls themselves.

But they get lost so easily.

Not many "go astray" in the sense the city missionary means, though the number of those who do is a dreadful total. They just get lost.

Think of the young folks from your town who were leaders in the League and Sunday school: bright, useful, happy. Then think of those you know who are showing these same qualities in their transplanted life.

Where are the others?

The fall is especially the time to think seriously about these things. Harvest time is on; one crop after another is gathered in. The school doors will open to some; the farm will be good enough for others; and some will give themselves up to the lure of the city.

Before they go is the best time for them and the home Church to fix their bearings in the new life. The pastor will do his part. But for the League's own members, why should not the League Secretary do something?

These boys and girls have been good helpers at home; they will be worth just as much in the city. Give them real letters of introduction, not just certificates of membership, so that the city pastor and the city Chapter will have some notion of their value and individuality.

For instance:

> This will introduce John Millholland, First Vice-President of the Epworth League Chapter at Farmington. He has done good work, and is good for more. He was the leader of our Bible study class last winter, holding a group of fourteen to the end of a three

THE EFFICIENT EPWORTHIAN.

months' course. We hope he will find himself welcome in the Epworth League to which he brings this note.

Frank H. Prescott, President.
Marie Carmody, Secretary.

Or this:

The bearer is Miss Mildred Chamberlain, a member of the Epworth League at Connors Glen, who comes to the city to take a business course. She has served for a year on the Fourth Department Committee, and is a teacher in the Junior League. We are sorry to lose her, and can only hope that some city Chapter will discover how devoted and useful she is.

Do you question whether the young pilgrims cityward would make use of such messages? We don't.

But if any doubt is raised, there are more ways than one of sending a letter to the city. All you need is a little sanctified ingenuity, a little persistence in asking questions, a little persuasive extraction of information.

And what of the outcome? Both John and Mildred will find themselves among new friends in the very days when the city might do its worst for them if they had no place of anchorage.

At any rate, the Epworth League has lost so many young people in such transition times that a great deal of work is justified in the attempt to stop so costly a leakage of life.

The Chapters of the city might do more, but their first handicap is that they do not know the strangers, or hear of their coming.

The Chapters of the home places *can* do more, because they know all about the exodus of their Johns and Mildreds. And they are really unselfish enough, if they only thought about it.

This is written for the Secretaries of those Chapters. Suppose, this year, you think about it!

SIDE LIGHTS FOR SCRIBES.

Put life and wisdom into the minutes. They may go to make up a record that may be read in twenty-five or fifty years from now. We should avoid sameness in minute-

RECORDING AND FINANCING THE WORK.

writing. Intelligence, brightness, and originality should sparkle on every page of your minute book.

Have a book where members of the Chapter may enter their names and addresses. Have every new member sign this book.

Post a membership list in the Epworth parlor or in the room where the Chapter meets, so that all can see who are members. It might stimulate some one else to join.

Notify members of their election, and ask their hearty co-operation in the work of the Chapter.

Ask the Cabinet officers to hand in a written report to the business meeting.

Bombard absentees with postal cards. Keep a record of those present at the devotional meetings. Then send a card to all absentees as soon thereafter as possible, urging attendance. Give names of absentees to the Department of Social Service, who should call upon them this week.

Write absent members who are at college or who are off on a vacation. Give them a word of cheer. An appropriate Scripture passage, a hearty "hello," might keep one from neglecting his Christian duty.

Ask that those who may be invalids and who are members of your Church be assigned to your department. If possible, get them to write letters to each other and to those who are away from home.

A letter from these shut-ins to their unconverted friends is practical. The testimony of a faithful Christian for Jesus from the sick-room has great influence, and might lead some soul to Christ.

Do not fail to answer or give attention to all communications regarding League work that may be addressed to you, whether letters or circulars. Do this promptly.

Keep thoroughly informed of the advancement made in the League work throughout Methodism, and with the young people's work generally.

Insist on monthly reports from officers, and file them away in such a manner that they will be preserved as a part of your history.

Have a thoroughly revised membership roll, and have

THE EFFICIENT EPWORTHIAN.

a list of your committees neatly printed, framed, and hung up in your Chapter room.

Insist on a variety of plans in the work; not sensational ventures, but thoroughly ingenious plans. Keep the curiosity of your membership aroused, and then satisfy that curiosity.

Acquaint yourself, as far as possible, with all the members in your Chapter. Know them not only by sight and by name, but study their dispositions, investigate their environments.

Do n't be tempted to over-elaboration. From these hints and from your own experience arrange a scheme for your department. Plan your work thoroughly, but not beyond your means. You can master a simple plan, and work it; a cumbersome one will master you and will give you constant trouble. And your successor will be sure to drop it, thus breaking the continuity of the department's work, and perhaps seriously affecting the whole work of the Chapter.

Have a pocket notebook for that bright idea which just popped into your head. Then you can catch it before it pops out again.

A supply of postal cards, having the Chapter name and the Secretary's name and address, printed or stamped as a heading will lighten many burdens of correspondence. For some uses a postal card is as good as a letter, and it has the advantage of being so handy that it invites use when a letter would involve so much trouble that it would never be written.

If three Chapters in ten have a sufficient supply of League literature, we will guess again and say four. But that's the outside figure. Take stock of *your* Chapter's supply, and then stock up. Good printed matter is too low in price for any Chapter to muddle along without it.

The first thing a newly-elected Secretary should do is to send a completely revised list of the Chapter's officers to the Central Office at Chicago.

Consider the Socialist, O Epworthian! In Milwaukee he puts one-tenth of his income into literature, and every Sunday morning, fifty-two times a year, there are three hundred of him putting polyglot pamphlets into the homes

RECORDING AND FINANCING THE WORK.

of the people. Victor Berger says that the devotion of those who prepare and distribute this literature rivals that shown by the early Christians when the Church was on the way to the conquest of the Roman Empire. If we of the Epworth League are not above learning from the Socialists and the early Christians, we can make the Church and the community pay our work at least this compliment, that they will take notice of it. After that, it depends on what's in the literature—and in us!

Use neat, businesslike stationery. If you do much letter writing—as you should—get printed stationery. It is not expensive, and it is worth your while just for the impression it makes, aside from its convenience.

Chapter Supplies.—Some of these are for the Secretary's use; others are to be kept on hand for the use of the other departments. All of them may be had from the nearest branch of the Methodist Book Concern, except the blank for the Secretary's report to the Central Office, which is furnished free on application to that Office, Chicago. A complete list will be furnished by the Central Office.

THE CHAPTER'S FINANCIAL MAN.

The importance of the Treasurer's work is usually far underestimated, never overvalued. It is vital to the success of every department. The Chapter can never be efficiently conducted without money, and the lack of a trifling amount often defeats the most important work. It is also absolutely indispensable that the revenue be reliable if plans are to be made in advance and carried forward to the highest success. This department, therefore, should assure an adequate revenue and gather it with dependable regularity.

As soon as possible after entering upon your duties, from your predecessor's experience and from a survey of the resources of the Chapter, determine and report the available income, that the Chapter and the Cabinet may plan accordingly. With this report, make whatever recommendation you think best for improving the financial policy.

When the members are assigned to the various departments, secure a good committee. Then assign its work and,

THE EFFICIENT EPWORTHIAN.

both by example and all necessary insistence, see that your financial plan is promptly, untiringly, and thoroughly carried out. Never admit an apparent necessity for resorting to those financial methods that burden and cripple the Fourth Department and discredit the Church before the world. Success by right methods will avoid reproach, and train your young people to ideals and habits that will bear valuable fruit throughout their lives and the lives of those they influence.

Your most valuable service will be achieved in promoting, with the Second Vice-President, the study and practice of Christian Stewardship. Together you should be unremitting in its promotion. This faithfully accomplished, your remaining duties will be easily but far more successfully performed. Look through the pages of this book devoted to that subject.

Money is more easily spent than raised. Therefore, study more how to get money and how to save it, than how to spend it. But when money must be spent, do not hesitate, do not be niggardly. Recommend generous expenditures where they are justified by the existing situation.

The most generally satisfactory method of securing a revenue for the Chapter is by securing monthly contributions, voluntary in amount, from each member. It should be subscribed immediately after joining. When each member contributes, a small amount from each that will in no degree interfere with his obligations to the Church will suffice. Do not permit any through false pride to assume what we will regret and perhaps evade with moral harm to himself.

Keep neat, accurate, and complete records. Give and take receipts for every cent received or paid, and require it of your committeemen. Preserve all the receipts you receive and the stubs of those you give. Write the entries of your transactions promptly, never waiting to write up a lot at once, or the only certainty about your records will be their uncertainty. Keep every fund separate. Have an account with every fund.

Never accept the records of your predecessor until the Auditing Committee has examined them, verified his final

RECORDING AND FINANCING THE WORK.

financial statement, and entered these facts in the record. Then require him to transfer immediately the cash on hand according to that statement, taking your receipt. Pass your records and cash to your successor in the same manner. No distrust is implied; these are simply good business methods. Our young people need to acquire them.

The Treasurer should keep a memorandum of all proposed expenditures, and by foresight enable the Chapter to guard against any avoidable congestion of liabilities that might embarrass the Chapter or injure its credit.

The Treasurer, not later than the day after Anniversary Day of each year, should remit to the Central Office of the Epworth League, Chicago, Ill., for the administrative expenses of the Central Office, ten cents for each member.

Collect dues from everybody if your Chapter is financed by dues. Do not confine your activities as a collector to those who volunteer their dues. Call on every member of the Chapter for the small amount which may have been promised, and keep calling until the amount is paid.

But when the Chapter has adopted the Twenty-four-Hour Day, dues as such are not necessary. The Treasurer should become familiar with the plan, as given on another page.

When collections are taken at a public meeting, get some one to help you count the money, that there may be no question as to the accuracy of the report.

Bills that are regularly incurred for some fixed expenses may be ordered paid by the Chapter as they fall due. For such bills a new order every month is not necessary.

Discourage doubtful money-raising schemes. The best way to do that is to be a successful collector of the funds which are raised in the ideal way, by personal and direct payment from every member according to ability. One of the objects of the League is to prove by deeds that there is a better way of raising Church and League funds. The Chapter whose Treasurer collects dues and subscriptions faithfully will have small excuse for going into the ice-cream business to pay its debts.

In some cases a fixed sum will be named as "dues." This is not so good as the entirely voluntary and flexible subscription. It makes no account of differing financial

THE EFFICIENT EPWORTHIAN.

ability, and savors of the club or fraternal order, into which you put a certain sum, which is regulated by the amount of benefits which you receive or may expect. That is not the League ideal, which is better expressed in this ancient saying, "From each according to his ability; to each according to his need."

But weekly, monthly, or quarterly dues are better than any form of haphazard finance. If the Chapter can do its work at small outlay, there may be but little objection to uniform dues.

The Epworth League Budget.

Prepare a budget!

Discover what each department ought to do this year, and what it will cost—how much for topic cards, and reference libraries, and mercy and help work, and extra *Herald* subscriptions, and free socials, and advertising, and the special work you surely must do.

Do not make niggardly estimates. Your Chapter can pay for all it ought to undertake, whether by dues or subscriptions or collections. By one or more of these methods provide for enough money to cover your estimates, with a little margin. Then you have a budget.

A budget is sensible. It is Scriptural (counting the cost and laying by in store). It is scientific. It is the one self-respecting method of dealing with Epworth League finances.

Its advantages are better discovered than described. But they are real and large and lasting.

Prepare a budget. And stick to it!

The Twenty-four-Hour Day Plan.

The term Twenty-four-Hour Day plan means the support of a program in operation somewhere for the entire course of the day. Our activities are going on on the other side of the world when on this side we are in darkness and slumber; so that, during the whole round of the clock, our interests and our activities both are linked together somewhere.

In a word, this is the method: Any Epworth Leaguer

RECORDING AND FINANCING THE WORK.

who accepts the Twenty-four-Hour-Day plan thereby promises to put into the envelope furnished for the purpose, without cost from the Central Office, at least two cents a week in the pocket designated "World-Wide Work." In another pocket marked for the "Home League" he may deposit his weekly amount agreed upon by the local Chapter for the support of local interests, whether they are Chapter dues or some form of benevolent or other interests.

Getting Started.

First, in your business session, or in your devotional meeting, have the plan explained to the Chapter, but let the approval be official at a regular business meeting.

Second, gather the names of all who enter into the plan and record in the Treasurer's book; then forward the number of those accepting the plan to the Central Office of the Epworth League, 740 Rush Street, Chicago, Illinois. Upon receipt of this the Central Office registers the Chapter as Twenty-four-Hour-Day League if at least twenty-five per cent of your total membership has become Twenty-four-Hour-Day Leaguers, and boxes of envelopes covering the number will be forwarded at once to the officer designated to receive them.

Third, patiently cultivate the habit of regular payment and have your Treasurer remit quarterly. The vouchers are returned at once, in duplicate, one for the Chapter and the other for the pastor, so that the total of your payments for the year may be reported in the Epworth League column of the Conference Minutes, thus giving to your church credit for all moneys raised for Epworth League work by your chapter.

The Plan and the Whole League.

Is the plan limited to one-fourth of the membership? NO. There is a way by which the whole League may share in the privileges and benefits of the arrangement. Here it is: The first twenty-five per cent of the members of a Chapter subscribing, thereby make their Chapter a Twenty-four-Hour-Day League, and the quarterly remittance of their money to the Central Office contributes to the general promotion work of the organization. The young people's headquarters at Chicago is open during the

THE EFFICIENT EPWORTHIAN.

entire year, where busy departments with clerks, stenographers, and helpers of various kinds are kept going to meet the requests from the field for free literature and for assistance of every kind; where touch is maintained with nearly 25,000 Chapters; where the General Secretary and department heads do their work; where plans are worked out for assistance to the more than one hundred Epworth League Institutes planned for each summer; where training conferences are planned and provided for; where arrangements are made for the meeting of important committees like those which have to do with the selection of the League topics; the year's program; Win-My-Chum week; conference anniversaries; conventions, and for the maintenance of our relations with the Boards and organizations of the Church and interdenominational agencies with which the League has a vital kinship.

Suppose fifty per cent or one half of the members of a Chapter desire to enlist in the Twenty-four-Hour-Day plan? Very well. Then this additional advantage accrues to such a Chapter, namely: it may, by vote, request that the funds from the second twenty-five per cent of the enlistment be returned for League work within the Area.

Where three-fourths of the members of a Chapter expressing a desire to enlist in the Twenty-four-Hour-Day plan, they may, in addition to the support of general promotion, and having their money returned for work in the Area, designate the money from the third twenty-five per cent enlistment to be devoted to the support of an Epworth League secretary in a foreign field.

Any Chapter with an enlistment of one hundred per cent of its members by the payment of an amount equal to or greater than two cents per week for each and every member, may select any Epworth League objective from those listed at headquarters for all its money above the second twenty-five per cent.

By this plan, calling for only two cents a week for the world-wide program of young people's work for young people, no Epworth Leaguer who has made his individual subscription to the church needs to feel that his ability to discharge that obligation is imperiled in the slightest degree by the payment of only two cents a week.

CHAPTER XII.

THE LEAGUE'S RED-LETTER DAYS.

THE Epworth League should make much of the red-letter days in the calendar. They offer opportunities for such observance as young people have time and inclination for, and their recognition is a distinct service to the community and the Church.

The following schedule shows the special services provided for by the General Secretary:

JANUARY.   *First Sunday,* Morning Watch Enrollment.
APRIL–MAY.   Institute Sunday.
MAY.   *Second or Third Sunday.* Anniversary Day.
JUNE.   Junior League Day.
JULY.   *First Sunday,* Christian Citizenship.
SEPTEMBER.   Rally Day.
              Studies Promotion Day.
NOVEMBER.   Win-My-Chum Week.
DECEMBER.   *First or Second Sunday,* Epworth Herald Day.

The material for many of these days varies from year to year, and can be found in the pages of *The Epworth Herald* and the other Church papers, or it may be secured direct from the headquarters of the organization more directly interested. This statement applies especially to the missionary programs, Lincoln Sunday, Anniversary Day, Church Extension Sunday, and the Sundays devoted to special forms of League work. Material for these League days may also be found in this book, under the proper department headings.

General suggestions for recognizing some of these special days, and for the observance of secular holidays, are here given, and also in Chapter X, in the hope that more general attention will be paid by our Chapters to the high days of Church and State.

Lincoln's Birthday.

Make this a patriotic observance of the true sort. In remembering Abraham Lincoln we need no spread-eagle oratory, no stump speeches. The lesson of his life means most when it is given simply and allowed to make its own impression.

Decorations: The flag, "with every star in place;" a bust statuette or picture of Lincoln.

Congregational singing: "Star-Spangled Banner;" "Battle Hymn of the Republic;" "America."

Special music:

"If you can not, on the ocean,
Sail among the swiftest fleet."
(One of Lincoln's favorite songs.)

Recitation: Lincoln's speech at Gettysburg.
Whitman's "O Captain, My Captain."

Some Lincoln stories, illustrating his kindness, his devout nature, his devotion to the Union, etc.

Brief addresses: "Lincoln, the Boy;" "Lincoln, the Citizen;" "Lincoln, the President."

A longer address: "To-day's Need of the Lincoln Type of Patriotism."

Washington's Birthday.

February 22d is almost as familiar a date in American thought as July 4th, and for much the same reason. It is the birthday of the man who, more than any other, made possible the birthday of the Nation.

It is the fashion nowadays to make Washington's birthday more of a social than a serious celebration. The old customs and the old costumes are revived, and the cherry tree and hatchet figure largely in the decorative scheme. There is no harm in all that, but none the less we need to remember Washington and the men of his time with vast reverence for their great work, not forgetting, but not emphasizing, their weaknesses and limitations.

THE LEAGUE'S RED-LETTER DAYS.

For the more formal and thoughtful observance of Washington's birthday an outline program is suggested here:

Decorations: The National colors; a reproduction in colors, if possible, of the Washington coat-of-arms (see any good history or a life of Washington); a portrait or bust of Washington; a picture of Mount Vernon; pictures illustrating scenes in Washington's life (crossing the Delaware, at Valley Forge, receiving the surrender of Cornwallis, saying farewell to his officers, taking the oath as President, etc.).

Singing: "America;" "God of our fathers, known of old" (Kipling's Recessional—effective as a solo or a quartet); "God of our fathers, whose Almighty Hand;" "A Mighty Fortress is our God;" "To Thee, O God, whose Guiding Hand."

Recitations.

Addresses: "George Washington's message to our time;" "Washington's preparation for greatness;" "The eighteenth-century idea of patriotism;" "Washington—a study in self-mastery;" "Washington, the Christian man in public life."

For the Sunday Nearest Washington's Birthday.

Song service.
Prayer, by leader or pastor.
Scripture lesson.
The leader speaks: "The Christian Citizen."
Hymn.
A member speaks: "George Washington's influence on the National life of to-day."
Another member speaks: "What can we do for the cause of Christian citizenship in our own community?"
Testimonies: "How my religion and my patriotism help each other;" "My idea of Christian duty in public affairs;" "What can I do to help make this a Christian nation?"
Brief prayers.
Hymn, "America."
The League benediction, or this:
"Render therefore to all their dues; tribute to whom

THE EFFICIENT EPWORTHIAN.

tribute is due; custom to whom custom; fear to whom fear; honor to whom honor. Owe no man anything, but to love one another: for he that loveth another hath fulfilled the law." (Rom. 13: 7, 8.)

The prayer service at the close of the testimonies may be made very helpful. Encourage general participation. Call for prayers of thanksgiving, of confession, of petition. We have much to be thankful for—National and personal blessings, freedom, and the privileges of citizenship. We have much to confess—National and personal failure, indifference to the highest needs of our community, State, and Nation; the widespread commercializing of civic ideals. We have much to ask—for a sounder Christian patriotism, for courage to carry Christian principles into public affairs, for grace to urge the claims of Christian citizenship on all who bear the Christian name. If possible, at least fifteen minutes should be given to this part of the program.

Get a soloist or quartet to sing Kipling's "Recessional." It can be found in "Gloria Deo," or the Christian Endeavor Hymnal. Other appropriate hymns are: "God bless our native land;" "America;" "To Thee, O God, whose guiding hand;" "God of our fathers, known of old;" "A Mighty Fortress is our God;" Battle-hymn of the Republic."

ANNIVERSARY DAY.

From the first the Epworth League has made much of its birthday. May 15, 1889, will always be an epochal date because of the far-reaching work which was completed on that day. To keep the day in remembrance, the custom has been established of observing May 15th, or the Sunday nearest it, as Anniversary Day.

Most Chapters observe the day on the nearest Sunday, and the special program which is prepared every year is arranged with this fact in mind. Let it be set down here, then, that one important element of the celebration—the Anniversary Program—is always within reach of even the smallest and weakest Chapter. The program is usually sold at a small price in quantity sufficient to supply the whole audience, including the necessary supplements. The theme of this program is changed with succeeding years,

THE LEAGUE'S RED-LETTER DAYS.

but it provides a most convenient and interesting aid to the proper observance of the day. And it is planned so as to be within the powers of any Chapter of the League.

Anniversary Day in many places has come to be fully recognized as Young People's Day, and the exercises of the whole day are arranged accordingly. The pastor usually throws himself heartily into the work and gladly avails himself of the opportunity to render special service to the Chapter. For it is not only a kindness to his Epworthians, but it is an enlargement of his own sphere of influence, and in almost every case he takes this view of it.

The celebration of Anniversary Day should begin early in the morning. If there are Comrades of the Morning Watch in the Chapter, they should arrange to observe the Watch together, inviting all others who will to join them. This is not a new plan, of course, being simply a variation on the idea of the Sunrise Prayer-meeting, but it links the service to an organized movement within the League, and affords a means of extending the usefulness of that movement.

For the early service ought to be such that it will recommend the Morning Watch to many who have not before adopted it. If there are no enrolled "Comrades" in the Chapter, hold this service nevertheless.

The Chapter may properly ask the pastor to make his morning service bear directly on some phase of the young people's movement. There should not be the slightest attempt to interfere with the pastor in the treatment of the theme, but if he is willing, as of course he will be, to prepare a special Anniversary Sermon, the Chapter should show its appreciation by attending in a body. Perhaps a special section of the Church may be reserved for the young people.

The preparations for the evening service should begin at least a month before Anniversary Day. The special program should be secured in sufficient quantity to supply all who are likely to attend. Supplements will provide the material for the various speakers, and the program proper will contain the special music.

The proper Program Committee for this Anniversary

THE EFFICIENT EPWORTHIAN.

Day is the Cabinet. Call a meeting as soon as the programs arrive. Plan the work promptly.

The speakers' parts should be memorized. This can not be emphasized too strongly. The difference between memorizing and reading makes the difference between a good program and a failure. People can not be interested in a program which is read.

Most of the songs provided in the program will probably be new to the Chapter, and several rehearsals will be necessary. Organize a choir for this purpose if you have not a League choir already.

The Fourth Department will have seen to the decorations, which, while they need not be either expensive or extensive, should be really decorative, and in the best possible taste.

During the evening there should be opportunity given for a summarized report of the work the Chapter had done in the past twelve months. The President should make this report.

An offering should be taken, of course. The money will be used for one cause this year, and for another cause next year; but it should be gathered. That is a necessary and highly appropriate part of the day's observance.

The day ought not to be closed without an earnest and personal invitation to all of the young people of the Church to identify themselves with the Epworth League and with the work which it is doing. Oftentimes membership application cards may be used to excellent advantage.

After the installation, the members of the Chapter will join the officers at the altar, and, kneeling, will sing some hymn of consecration. This should be followed by the dedicatory prayer, offered by the pastor or some member previously appointed.

The pastor or Chapter President should have charge of the service of dedication, except where the installation of officers precedes the dedicatory service. In that case the pastor alone should have charge of both services.

Signalize the day by the inauguration of some new enterprise, as suggested in the paragraphs which appear under the heading, "Some New Departure," on pages 355-7.

THE LEAGUE'S RED-LETTER DAYS.

The beginning of some new and really necessary work by the Chapter on Anniversary Day will save the day from being a mere "hurrah" time, filled with nothing more abiding than frothy enthusiasm. And the new work will have the advantage of a good start, widespread interest, and the backing of the Chapter, the Church, and the community.

IF NOT THE SPECIAL ANNIVERSARY PROGRAM?

If, for any reason, it does not seem best to use the special program prepared by the Central Office, there are several other ways of emphasizing the importance of the day. The idea of ignoring the day should not be entertained for a moment. Perhaps the pastor may be willing to devote the evening service to a consideration of the young people's work, preaching a special sermon to them, or traversing the ground suggested by the material on page 344.

As a part of any work decided upon, the Junior work, the report of the Chapter for the retiring year, and the program of the new year's work should be introduced.

In many places it will be possible to secure a member of the District or State Cabinet to give the address of the evening; or some near-by minister may be secured through the co-operation of two Chapters in the exchange of pastors for the evening.

When any of these plans are used, let the regular Epworth League meeting be dispensed with, and all energy and interest concentrated on the public service. Emphasize in every possible way that it is an Epworth League meeting. Simple but attractive decoration should be used, and the League colors should be prominently displayed. The program may be utilized to secure new members. There is no better time for this than an hour in which the value, dignity, and helpfulness of the Epworth League is being especially emphasized.

It may be found practicable to present a statement of the special work now being urged and prosecuted in our Epworth League Chapters. The various activities which have been so profitable in so many places may well be emphasized at this time. Speak of the great progress made

THE EFFICIENT EPWORTHIAN.

in Bible study; the remarkable spread of the mission study movement; the work of individual evangelism through the "Win-My-Chum" movement; the Morning Watch; the Christian Stewardship enrollment; the study courses in Christian Experience, Personal Evangelism, and in Social Service; the work done in the Social Service Department, and the Chapter's recreational and cultural activities.

Ask several members to sum up in brief papers the work of the year in your Chapter. Subjects such as these will give opportunity to show the progress of the past twelve months: "The year's gain in Bible study;" "What we have learned about missions;" "The Chapter's aid in our spiritual growth;" "How the Church has helped us;" "What we have done for the Juniors;" "Our Social Service;" "The Christian Stewardship revival;" "Our influence on the community outside the Church;" "The advance in social helpfulness," and "The intellectual profits of the year."

The report of the Chapter for the past year should be read by the retiring President. The program of the new year's work should be outlined by the President who has just been installed.

The pastor will install the officers, when the installation is made a part of the program. He should also have charge of the service of dedication, calling the members of the Chapter around the altar just before the singing of a dedication hymn, and leading in repetition of a dedication prayer. Make this part of the exercises as simple as possible. It should be profoundly effective if reverently done.

The following program will serve as a foundation for the exercises. Of course, the more variety that can be introduced, the better, if it does not destroy the unity of the service:

Song service.
Prayer.
The leader speaks: "Our Chapter—its purpose and work in the past year."
Prayer.
Brief addresses by members. (See subjects on this page.)

THE LEAGUE'S RED-LETTER DAYS.

Installation of officers.
Dedicatory service.
The League benediction.

In a small Chicago Chapter, where many of the members are young and have not yet learned to take much active part in the meetings, the Cabinet decided to celebrate Anniversary Day by having an "Encouragement Meeting." On the previous Sunday it was announced that every one was expected to bring something in written form, telling how the Epworth League had helped him during the past year. In order to give the members some idea of what was meant, a list of suggestions was read, as follows:

Would your life have been different if there had been no Epworth League Chapter in this Church? How?

Has any particular meeting helped you especially?

Has any meeting helped you? How?

Has any one of the library books helped you?

Have you stopped any bad habit or started any good habit because you have attended the League?

The papers were not to be signed, but they were collected, shaken in a hat, and then re-distributed, so that each one would read another's paper. The plan worked very well, and many who had never before done anything more than recite a verse of Scripture wrote something definite about themselves. Such papers as the following were received:

"One of the members helped me to give up the cigarette habit."

"I want to tell you that I have started to be a Christian"—from one of the most bashful girls in the Chapter.

"The song, 'He holdeth the storm in His hand,' has cured me of a terrible fear of thunder-storms," etc. The other responses were quite as practical.

WHAT ARE WE GOING TO DO ABOUT IT?

The Church could not spare the Epworth League. But it can not endure that the League shall rest on any record and be proud merely of what it was and what it has come to be.

The League must be a bigger institution, and a better

THE EFFICIENT EPWORTHIAN.

one, if it is to hold its place and do its work in the Church. There are plenty of agencies outside the Epworth League through which the Church can operate unless the League shall continue to prove itself the most effective agency for the task in hand.

What is that task? Anniversary Day is a good day for the asking and answering of that question.

Well; it is not the mere getting up of steam. Let it be admitted that the hurrah days are over. We have more need for enthusiasm than ever, but it must be enthusiasm which has motive and direction and purpose.

Nor is it the League's task to make the young people of Methodism a class-conscious company. The League is not an order, like the ministry, nor an exclusive company, like a college fraternity, nor a society of experts, like the Brotherhood of Locomotive Engineers. It is the youth of the Church enrolled during the brief years of youth in the vocational, manual training school of the Church.

The League's task is not the production of more or less devoted Methodists. It seeks to develop intelligent Methodist Christians, and risks their loyalty on their intelligence.

The League's task in the years to come—*beginning now!*—is to train, to inspire, to employ the young life of the Church—to train for efficiency; to inspire for dedication to Jesus Christ and His ideals; to employ on the principle that every Christian needs a place of Christian service, and the Church needs *him*.

All this can not be done by good intentions or by haphazard. Never was a time when God so required and so honored the carefulest, most painstaking thoroughness in the preparation of His servants. The mature Christian of to-morrow must specialize in religion in all its branches, and he must get ready for his specialty.

That is the task of the Epworth League. It is a technical school. It is to give its students confidence in their work, humility in their mutual leadership, the spirit of sacrifice in their service, awareness as to the facts of life and their bearing on Christian faith, and an open-eyed optimism concerning the program of Jesus Christ for the Church and the world.

THE LEAGUE'S RED-LETTER DAYS.

Called—Expected—Trusted—An Anniversary Day Homily.

The Epworth League is a company of people that are called. It is not perfect or it would not exist. It is a group with unmeasured possibilities. The people of middle life will live out their lives on their present level; you know what they will do and what they will be until the end. But the young people are not so; besides what they are to-day, there is to be taken into account what they will be to-morrow.

It is not easy to influence the generation of which you are a part by any direct attack, but it is comparatively an easy thing to influence the generation which is just ahead. And this we can do when we work with others and with ourselves who are to be the mature generation of the next few years.

The young people of the Epworth League are called, first of all, to join themselves to Jesus Christ. Now is the one golden opportunity for beginning the life of discipleship. The chances which remain after twenty-five years of age are so small that they may be left out of the account. Of course, there is always opportunity, but once character is fixed there is small likelihood of response to the opportunity. To-day is the time, not merely because there may be no to-morrow, but because to-morrow, if it comes, will in all probability be too late.

The young people are called to the practice of the Christian life. If Christian service and the study of the Bible and interest in all forms of the Kingdom's progress are to mark our mature life, they must be provided for now. You can not force new interests upon old people.

The young people are called to serve and to help. One of the sad things about middle life and old age is that the sympathies are likely to have been blunted. If you are going to possess tenderness and gentleness and pity and helpfulness in the years that are to be, you must care for these things now. That is the educational value which is added to the practical value of the Department of Mercy and Help.

THE EFFICIENT EPWORTHIAN.

The young people are called to be intelligent. There is growing need for wisdom as well as devotion in the service of God. The unintelligent Christian of to-morrow will be at the greatest possible disadvantage. But intelligence concerning the Church, concerning the place of Christianity in the world's life, concerning the relation of all activity to the religious life, must be secured now; to-morrow, when it will be most needed, it will be out of reach.

The young people are called to prepare for their lifework. This is the time of choice. What are you going to be? Why are you going to be that? Have you considered your choice of a life pursuit from the point of view of personal preference or convenience or profit, or have you taken into account the claims of the Kingdom of God?

We must have more preachers or the Church must lose ground; we must have more deaconesses or the multiplied ministry of helpfulness for which they exist will not be provided, to the world's sore loss; we must have more missionaries or the Christian Church must retreat in the very places where it has accomplished its great victories.

How do you know you are not called to be a minister or a deaconess or a missionary? Have you ever asked whether such a call was likely to come to you? Make sure of one thing—that you know what you are going to do, and why you are going to do it, and that it is God's plan for you.

That will make every day Anniversary Day!

FOR THE SUNDAY NEAREST THE FOURTH OF JULY.

Before the meeting write at the top of the blackboard the two words, "Righteousness," "Sin," drawing a line between them down the center of the board. Ask five or six members to be ready to speak, each one giving an example of righteousness in our National life, such as Negro emancipation, the rescue of Cuba, the regeneration of the Philippines, the banishment of lotteries, the Red Cross, universal education, fifteen churches a day, the abolition of the canteen, the quickening of the social conscience, the gains of temperance. Ask five or six to be ready to speak in the like manner on great National sins: the American saloon, our misgoverned cities, the neglected slums, the worship of

THE LEAGUE'S RED-LETTER DAYS.

money, the Mormon disgrace, the divorce evil, the degradation of the day of rest, the widespread passion for gambling, the growing hatred between employer and employed. Confine each speaker to one minute. As they speak, put in the proper column the word or phrase which describes each theme. Then call for additions to the list, on either side of the central line. See where the heaviest total falls.

Ask some one to read or repeat Lincoln's Gettysburg speech.

Drape the speaker's stand with a flag, and place the Bible on the top.

Singing: "Battle-hymn of the Republic."
Prayer, by the leader or pastor.
The Scripture lesson.
One-minute talks on "Things that shame us."
Singing.
General testimony, following the lead of the one-minute talks, and answering the question, "What can Christian citizens do?"
Prayers: of contrition for National sins, of supplication for God's guidance of the Nation, of petition for strength to be Christian citizens.
Singing: "America."
The League benediction.

INDEPENDENCE DAY.

The Epworth League has no mission to celebrate the glorious Fourth in the stereotyped and meaningless fashion which is nowadays so popular. That will be attended to with a vigor worthy of a better method. But it has a call to a better thing—to the work of making Independence Day a day of genuine patriotism and renewed devotion to the highest ideals of American citizenship.

Plan for a celebration. Begin long before the day, and make your preparation as varied and complete as your resources will permit. Enlist everybody in the work. Co-operate with all the other young people's societies, the Sunday schools, the fraternal orders, the Grand Army of the Republic, the World-War Veterans, and everybody else who can be interested in a really patriotic celebration.

THE EFFICIENT EPWORTHIAN.

Provide all the fun-making and noise-making events you choose—the more the better, so long as they do not obscure the real purpose of the day.

The central point of the celebration is the speaking. Get the very best orator you can find. Be sure he is not a mere mouther of braggadocio. On the other hand, do not invite a gloomy-hearted, dyspeptic prophet of National calamity. The Fourth of July oration should be hopeful, yet frank enough to recognize the Nation's dangers; it may leave out some of the old flights of patriotic rhetoric in order to make room for the plain statement of the Christian citizen's plain business in politics and civic life, and it must exalt above all things the Christian ideal of National and individual conduct.

Here is a program which will furnish a hint or two, out of which the particular program you need may be evolved:

6 A. M. Flag raising, with an Independence Day salute. (Let your cannonading, or whatever substitute for it is adopted, be wholly in charge of a competent and careful individual.)

10.30 A. M. Procession to park or grove, with a float or two; organizations in uniform; citizens afoot, mounted, or in carriages; the "thirteen original States," represented by young ladies in costume.

Upon arrival at speaker's stand:

Hymn, "America."

Prayer.

Reading of the Declaration of Independence. (Be careful to choose a good reader.)

Patriotic song by "the thirteen States."

Flag drill.

Recitation, "Liberty Bell."

Adjournment for dinner, picnic fashion.

2. P. M. The orator of the day.

3 P. M. The games and sports.

9 P. M. Co-operative fireworks. (By uniting forces on the fireworks, the smallest community may have a display that will astonish the natives.)

THE LEAGUE'S RED-LETTER DAYS.

The Rally Days.

These days, on which special attention is directed to the definite plans of study and work which the Epworth League presents each year, ought to be observed not merely with enthusiasm, but with an entelligent enthusiasm.

Bible Study Rally Day is fully considered with the other work of the First Department on pages 162 to 164; Mission Study Rally Day has adequate discussion in its place with the work of the Second Department, pages 170 to 172.

After summer's inevitable slackening of effort, many Chapters find it profitable to set a day, usually in September, to mark the resumption of full Epworth League activity. Why should not your Chapter do this? Perhaps it is just the stimulus it needs to start vigorously on the carrying out of the year's program.

The Epworth League year begins now. In a few weeks the Bible study classes will be hard at work. Some mission study and Social Service study courses will be planned for the winter. There are inviting fields waiting to be entered, where half a dozen sorts of courageous labor may be done. What will your Chapter do? What will you do as an individual Christian and Epworthian?

You will not need any new supply of courage to do nothing. That can be done usually by the most cravenhearted weakling. Perhaps you have found out how easy it is to be idle. And how profitless as well. You may have felt in your own soul the woe that comes to those who are at ease in Zion.

Then do something. Remember that every Christian is called to service, and that service is not condescension. God's great service to us did not grow out of the fact that He pities us, but out of the fact that He is God, and Divinity is service. The more we serve, the more godlike we are.

What shall you do? The same old things your Chapter has been doing from the beginning? Yes, if they are profitable. Do not be like the Athenians, carried away by mere novelty. But yet do some new thing also. Consider how many of your Chapter members are active members

THE EFFICIENT EPWORTHIAN.

only in name; how many associate members have very little association with you. Remember that your ideal should be, "To every man his work," and to every woman, too.

Find something worth doing. Do not be satisfied to polish your buttons. Do not fritter away time and talents on things that are not worth while, or that could better be done by some other sort of society. Let your work have definite relation to the aims and ideals of the Epworth League.

As to the specific things to choose there is a wide range. You can suit all Christian tastes and capacities. Here is a mere hint: start a Bible class, or a mission study class, or a class in one of the new study courses. Enroll all you can as Christian Stewards, and as Comrades of the Morning Watch. Adopt the Twenty-four-Hour Day. Get into new avenues of Social Service. Take up some form of literary work. Plan some constructive and helpful recreational activities. Search out some new way of co-operating with the pastor, and ask him to help you in the search. Ask yourselves if there is not some assistance you can render the cause of better citizenship. Get into line in the fight against intoxicants. Tell the pastor he may count on you to help in the revival meetings and in the preliminary home prayer-meetings leading up to the revival.

And, having found something, or several things, that need to be done, do not hesitate because they seem too great for you. Remember whose servant you are, and what He has promised. Read the charge to Joshua in the first chapter of the book of that name. Thank God that He has shown you a task—not only worthy of you, but worthy of Himself—and go about the doing of it as unto the Lord.

A Cabinet meeting should be held a week before this "Fall Opening" meeting, if possible. If the Cabinet decides to take up some new form of work this year, there can be no better time to announce it than now, and to enlist the co-operation of every member.

In case this is done, divide the time of the meeting into three parts: the first, for the discussion of the topic in its larger and more general aspect; the second, for the representation and explanation of the new plans; and the

THE LEAGUE'S RED-LETTER DAYS.

third, for some brief but earnest and definite moments of solemn dedication to and acceptance of the new work.

Some New Departure.

Do you wonder what the "new thing" may be? Look over the list below, and see if you are doing everything it suggests. If not, take up one or more of the enterprises named, and put your Chapter after them in real earnest, of course being careful to neglect no fruitful work already under way.

A class in the study of Christian Experience, and another in the study of Personal Evangelism. These two highly important and closely related subjects are now provided with brief but exceedingly useful courses of study.

The Bible Study Class. There are several courses now available, covering from eight to twenty-five weeks, and with abundant helps from the Central Office.

The Mission Study Class. Write to the Mission Study and Stewardship Department, 740 Rush Street, Chicago, for information concerning the work.

The Social Service Study Class. No Chapter can afford to neglect this phase of its work. The text-books are fascinatingly interesting. Get particulars from the Central Office.

The use of the Morning Watch Enrollment. This is a method of using the early morning hour for Bible reading, meditation, and prayer. Ask the Central Office about it.

The Christian Stewardship Enrollment. This is a plan for those who believe—and who does not?—that the Christian is a steward, a trustee, of all he possesses. The Central Office will explain it fully.

The Parish Abroad Plan. By adopting this plan your Chapter will come into direct communication with some missionary in the foreign field, in whose support you share. Information will be gladly given you by the Board of Foreign Missions, 150 Fifth Avenue, New York.

Co-operation with hospitals and deaconesses. The number of institutions under deaconess control and institutions for the relief of all manner of distress is constantly increasing. They have many needs. Ask your pastor what institutions are so situated that you can easily get into touch with them and help them.

A Chapter survey, surely; and a community survey unless circumstances positively prevent it. See suggestions on page 67.

A reading college. The hints given on page 265 tell how easily this admirable plan can be worked. It has been a notable success in big Chapters and in little, in city and in country. How do you know it would fail with you?

A lecture course. On pages 268 to 270 you will find a well-digested plan for a successful lecture course. Why should not your Chapter have some such provision for winter evening recreation and instruction?

A reading-room. Perhaps you are in a community where there is no public reading-room, and no place where the young men and boys can gather for an evening of pleasant and innocent amusement. Why not establish a reading-room, with a social-room adjoining, furnished with some good periodicals and books, and some harmless games?

Systematic visiting. Do you know the people in your neighborhood? Have you found all the recruits for the League and the Sunday school that the community affords? Has your Social Service Department a working knowledge of the people who should be reached and helped? Look up the suggestions on this subject on pages 230 to 234.

A Suggested Rally Day Program.

Song service, using vigorous songs of dedication and inspiration. For example, instead of singing, "Let us rally, rally, rally," etc., sing, "The Son of God goes forth to war."

Brief prayers, from a number of members who are eager that they and the Chapter shall do large things for God this year. Speak to many people in advance, asking them to be prepared for this part of the service.

Scripture lesson, and the presentation of the general topic by the leader.

"Vision and Task"—a brief but earnest presentation by each Vice-President of the ideals and purposes of the four departments for the year, with sketchy outlines of the

THE LEAGUE'S RED-LETTER DAYS.

various forms of work to be undertaken, and an appeal for new recruits for the department work.

"The Challenge of Our Special Opportunity"—a stirring message from the Chapter President.

"The Gracious Invitation"—an address by the pastor, inviting the Christian young people present to a new dedication of themselves and their powers to Christ, and inviting the unsaved to seek Christ in pardon and new life. This should bring a great company about the altar for the final moments of the service.

After the benediction the officers should get the names of all those who are willing to become members of the League, and of all members who desire to help in the work of the several departments.

ANOTHER PROGRAM: "BETTER WORK OUR CHAPTER SHOULD DO."

Let the Cabinet be consulted before the meeting. There may be some old plans of work which can be strengthened, some new ones begun; and the Cabinet alone has the knowledge of the situation which the leader of this meeting must get. Then build a program something after this fashion:

Song service: Hymns of activity and zeal.

Prayer—many taking part—for God's blessing on what has been done hitherto, with contrition because it was not what it might have been, for the Chapter and its members, for the work to be done in and for the Chapter, for the work to be done in the larger field outside, for the doing of all things from right motives and with holy purposes, for all whom the Chapter may be able to help—the sick, the distressed, the lonely, the discouraged, the unsaved.

The leader speaks: "Things which accompany salvation."

The pastor speaks: "The Christian obligation."

Singing.

A Symposium: "What 'better things' in my department?" by the four Vice-Presidents, the Secretary, and the Treasurer. (Two minutes each.)

Singing.

Seven Questions: What are we here for?

THE EFFICIENT EPWORTHIAN.

What more than I have done can I do?

How can membership in our Chapter be made to mean more than it does now?

How can we—I—get the inactive members of the Chapter to take more interest in its work?

What do I need first—a new method of work, or a new devotion to Jesus Christ?

What is the chief hindrance to better work in our Chapter?

What "better thing" would our Lord ask us to do if He should come in person to our Chapter?

General testimony in answer to one or more of the seven questions printed above (which should be put on a large sheet of paper, or on the blackboard).

A hymn of dedication.

Closing moments of dedication to "better things" for God, the members kneeling and uniting in confession and petition that the work of the Holy Spirit in the meeting may not be lost.

Epworth League Rally Day.

THE RALLY DAY SPIRIT.

Get it. But don't try to "work it up." That way you can have a lively program with plenty of "go" in it, and you may think the meeting has been a success.

And that is the worst thing about all this cheap fuss and folly. It deceives people into thinking they have done something great when, in fact, they have done the one thing that prevents anything great from coming to their Chapter.

No; Rally Day must be a day of large meaning, not only for the moment, but for the whole year. So must you get the spirit of the day.

What is the spirit?

An honest, humble understanding that you and the Chapter have not come up to your best in the service of Jesus Christ.

A deep and sincere purpose to have done with the failures of the past.

A consuming ambition to let the Lord Christ do the

THE LEAGUE'S RED-LETTER DAYS.

work He longs to do in and through every member of the Chapter.

An ardent personal love and devotion to the Christ as the only motive big enough to energize any disciple's life.

An intelligent grasp of the next duty for yourself and your Chapter.

Now, this sort of Rally Day spirit does not depend on the externals of decorations, advertising, special music, attractive speakers. All that is good, but it is incidental. The main business of the day is spiritual, intimate, dealing with the lasting realities.

So there must be some heart searching and much prayer, and a frank sincerity in facing the League's work.

As an aid to the getting of the Rally Day spirit, can not something be done with a Cabinet meeting for prayer and study of the situation? Ask the pastor to be present. Let the keynote of the hour be, for every officer, "Lord, what wilt Thou have *me* to do?" Go over the list of the Chapter's activities. Determine what work needs pushing and what can safely be dropped. Study the whole field of possible new enterprises, and, with the pastor's help, select one or two that with proper effort may be carried on during the year. Unless there are really valid reasons against such work, be sure that Bible study and mission study classes are included in the year's program.

In the Rally Day meeting put the whole responsibility for the League's work where it belongs, on the hearts and consciences of the members. Every one stands in his place in Christ's stead, and Christ's work there depends on him. But he must be Christ's before he can serve Christ.

MULTIPLICATION BY ADDITION, SUBTRACTION, AND DIVISION.

The Rally Day spirit is much more than any mere "hurrah." It is easy to have a lively program, full of a sort of slap-dash enthusiasm, without putting any new interest or definite purpose into the mind and heart of a single member.

Such a program is not only easy, but deceptive. The unthinking say, "Wasn't that a great meeting?" It was; but much ado about nothing. And—the pity of it—so many people were happy over something which actually prevented any real advance in the Chapter's work and life.

Rally by all means. But to what? To a single, fussy, bustling, shallow sort of meeting on Rally Day? There's no gain in that. No; rally to your task! Eight or nine months of splendid opportunity are before you. Discover what that opportunity is, and grip it. The Master whom you serve has work for your Chapter to do. Find it. And then do it.

Rally Day, observed for that purpose, will be worth a dozen ordinary days. Be unwilling that anything shall spoil it or cripple its influence.

Make sure of some things beforehand; among them these:

You have n't done all you could for Jesus Christ in your Chapter, but you mean to change that.

You are not going to measure the prospects of the future by the failures of the past.

You are determined that the Lord Christ shall really be in control of your personal and Chapter life this year.

You are going to discover as many things to do worth doing as your Chapter ought to attempt. Then you will find out how to do those things. And then you will get at them and do them.

If you make sure of these things, you can build a Rally Day program that will be not only vastly more useful and lasting in its influence than the cheap "hurrah" meeting, but that will be in itself more interesting and will rouse more genuine enthusiasm among your members.

Rally—but rally to something worth while!

Rally Day: A Talk With League Leaders.

Rally Day ought not to be a day at all, but a state of mind. It is the beginning of the fall and winter work of the Epworth League. If it is observed as a mass meeting, a mere soda-water substitute for real purpose and power, it will be a cheap performance and barren.

To observe Rally Day rightly there must be a setting up of plans that are worthy of the League's place in the Church and the community.

THE LEAGUE'S RED-LETTER DAYS.

There must be a careful consideration of the things which the Chapter needs to do for its own members. The development of efficiency must come first. True, that efficiency may be secured by what commercial schools call "actual business practice," the learning to do by doing, but the first thing to be sought is not a profit from business, but proficiency in the doing of it.

So give study and training a prominent place.

That means study classes, and conferences with the pastor, and surveys of the Chapter's field, and inquiry as to the forms of local and long-distance ministry which may be best fitted to the Chapter's powers and circumstances.

After study, service. No Epworth League Chapter is so unhappily situated that it must needs spend all its energies on itself. And no Chapter is so poverty-stricken or so incapable that it can not make itself profitable to its own Church and to its own community and to the Kingdom of God.

This is not the place to speak of specific forms of study or of service. The programs published elsewhere in this paper are rich in suggestions which any alert Epworthian can adapt to his own Chapter's work.

But let one thing be said for every Chapter's program. Give it balance! Do not let it be all entertainment or all missionary or all devotional meeting. Our scheme for the departments is ideal; nothing less is sufficient to give the League the training and the chance of service which it needs.

Make the first department a great means of usefulness. Give the devotional meeting most careful thought. Determine to improve it. There's room. The new material offered by *The Herald* will help. Magnify the part of prayer in the meeting. Encourage concerted silent prayer for definite objects. Learn the joy of interceding for people and causes beyond your personal reach. And seek steadily to secure the increase of spiritual power through the work of the devotional meeting.

Keep Bible study to the front. Provide for team work with the Sunday school. Do not use overlapping courses, or permit duplication of effort.

THE EFFICIENT EPWORTHIAN.

Get ready for Win-My-Chum week. Remember that this week is neither a sort of magic, nor yet an empty form. It is the one time of the year when you can unite with Epworthians everywhere in youth's greatest Christian business,—that of winning its own associates to the discipleship of Jesus Christ. Every year the Central Office and *The Epworth Herald* offer special material for this work.

Insist on a real Second Department. This is no time to forget that the Epworth League has had a great place in the missionary revival. The Church needs the League's positive help—not just its sympathy—more to-day than ever. The special opportunities which offer themselves this year to the department of world evangelism are considered on this page. Use them.

Give the Third Department a fair chance to become in very truth a Department of Social Service. Without decreasing its usual ministries, let it undertake something more, so that the Chapter's vision may be broadened and made clearer. For example what better work could it attempt than the making of a community survey? If plans and directions are called for, *The Herald* will be glad to supply them.

And in the Fourth Department follow the bold course! Instead of cataloguing the things your members can not and will not do—let that be taken for granted—set the standard for recreation in your community. Do n't imitate the things that are discredited; displace them! Whatever the recreational form—literary, musical, social, or that most important and beautiful thing called play—give it all the stamp of sincerity and intelligence and thoroughness.

Enough of this. But is it not plain that the field of the Epworth League is a wide and alluring expanse, full of freedoms, of opportunities, of privileges, and of powers to be developed to their utmost?

If you know anybody who has had the narrow view of the League, show him into what room for all the abounding young life of the Church and the community it is the open door.

And invite him in!

THE LEAGUE'S RED-LETTER DAYS.

EPWORTH HERALD DAY.

The Second Sunday in December is *Epworth Herald* Day. The League meeting of that evening is devoted to the presentation of the paper's interests.

If *The Epworth Herald* were an ordinary paper with no special claim on the young people, there would be no reason for making it the subject of a Sunday night service in the Epworth League.

But, to begin with, it is the one official organ of the Epworth League. As such it carries all the messages of the League's officers to our great Epworth League army.

Then, it is of great importance to the Epworth League for helping in the leadership and conduct of the Epworth League's weekly devotional meeting. Every week thousands of leaders turn to this paper for guidance and suggestion in their work of getting ready for the meeting. More thousands of members turn to it that they may be able to take intelligent part in the meeting.

For these two reasons, if for no others, the League authorities feel that they are entirely justified in asking that the Chapters devote this service to the paper which constantly serves them. But many other reasons appear in the paragraphs that follow.

THE EPWORTH HERALD AND ITS USES.

The Epworth Herald is the trade paper of our Methodist young people, teaching them the trade, telling of the trade's progress, describing new trade methods, promoting the acquaintance of workers at the trade, and constantly attracting other young people into the trade.

The trade of Methodist young people is the business of working together in Christian training and service, and it is carried on by an organization of more than three-quarters of a million members.

It is not easy to find out how many Epworthians read *The Epworth Herald*. At the date this book went to press about a hundred thousand were taking the paper, but, of course, two or three times as many read it. One copy may be read by a whole family, and many copies are passed on from reader to reader.

THE EFFICIENT EPWORTHIAN.

Every Epworthian ought to read *The Epworth Herald*, because it is his paper, made to his order, working for his interests, busy with his affairs, speaking in his behalf, providing him with the means of Epworthian efficiency. Every Epworthian who does n't read it puts needless limits to his own League usefulness.

The League could get along without *The Herald*. It did in the beginning. But only for a year. Doubtless the thing could be done again. In the same way, Epworthians could get along without telephones and rural delivery and bathtubs and high schools and vacations. Yet why should they? When a thing does n't exist we get along without it. But nobody wants to end the existence of any good thing on that account.

The Herald does not help all Epworthians equally. Some need it more than others, some read it more than others, some heed it more than others. But no Epworthian, from President to newest member, will say that it has no value for him. It is particularly useful to the officers and the department workers.

The Herald helps the League President to know more about the League than any other member, which is his business. He finds *The Herald* a text-book, a road map, a League barometer, a combination tool, and a tonic for flagging energies. When he can get all these things every week for less than a two-cent stamp, he must be a shortsighted President if he does n't see that in his business it is worth the price.

Its special advantage for the First Department is that it is a constant reminder that personal religion is the central idea of the League. It promotes Bible study; it is as nearly a personal evangelist as paper and ink can become. It gives much space to methods for the First Department.

The Herald can do everything for the devotional meeting if the leader will let it, except what he should do for himself. Its pages of rich material for that meeting will give him so many suggestions that he will not be able to use them all. And he will not use any of them parrot

THE LEAGUE'S RED-LETTER DAYS.

fashion, but intelligently, so that, in spite of all his helps, he will be the real leader of the meeting.

The missionary reason for reading *The Herald* is that without it the Second Department would be almost helpless. Material for the work of World Evangelism appears in *The Epworth Herald* more often than in any other paper within reach of the Epworthian. *The Herald* is a real missionary paper, helping the Second Vice-President in mission study, missionary interest, Christian Stewardship, missionary vision. It has never yet apologized for the missionary enterprise.

The Herald's stand on the Department of Social Service is simply this: with all modesty it can claim some of the credit for the adoption of the new ideas. For a whole year it worked to popularize the name. It printed large portions of what became the first Epworth League text-book on Social Service. It brings to the Third Vice-President all the help afforded by the Methodist Federation for Social Service.

What about Recreation and Culture? Very much. *The Herald* urged strongly the adoption of the recreation idea by the League, and is doing more than any other institution to promote popular and wholesome recreation for the Church's young people. It works ceaselessly for the recognition of play as a great Christian and cultural agency. Nor does it content itself with generalities. It gets down to definite methods, usable everywhere.

Some may ask if there is anything in *The Herald* for the younger folks, the boys and girls. The answer is, never less than two pages a week; often more. The right sort of stories, the right sort of crisp and snappy paragraphs, and a most delightful treatment of the Junior League topics. *The Herald* helps to hold the Juniors through the years when they are sometimes feeling a little too old and sometimes a little too young, the very age when they are hardest to hold and need to be held most steadily.

The Secretary and Treasurer are included in the list of *The Herald's* beneficiaries. The Secretary is the Chapter's information bureau; consequently he himself must always be informed. The Treasurer is a much larger official

THE EFFICIENT EPWORTHIAN.

than would be needed merely to collect dues and pay bills. He's a Professor of Christian Stewardship, and all the Chapter's members are his pupils.

There is plenty inducement held out by *The Herald* to those who are just members. All that has been mentioned so far is also for the "mere members." The League stands for all-round efficiency, and not for mere departmental specializing. Every member needs to keep in touch and sympathy with every part of the League's work. And any member may be called to department leadership at any time. Besides, *The Herald* is the Epworthian's link with the great Church. All the Church's great movements are recorded and interpreted in the paper; because it is for young people it has less to do with the routine and officialism of the Church than the other papers, and can give its attention to things of direct human interest and of universal appeal.

The ideal relation of the Epworthian to *The Herald* is not commercial, at a dollar for fifty-two numbers, nor simply so much reading for leisure hours. The Epworthian and *The Herald* should be as inseparable as the engineer and his engine; each is necessary to the work of the other.

WHY THE CABINET SHOULD TAKE THE HERALD.

The President: Because it is a real leader of young life.

The First Vice-President: Because it makes much of personal religion and personal Christian influences.

The Second Vice-President: Because it shows the reality and reasonableness of world evangelism.

The Third Vice-President: Because it stands for service, love, and mercy as part of every Christian's religion.

The Fourth Vice-President: Because it emphasizes the joy of the Christian life, and insists on recreation, amusement, and intelligence being in the young Christian's program.

The Secretary: Because it records and preserves the best League ideas and describes all noteworthy League events.

THE LEAGUE'S RED-LETTER DAYS.

The Treasurer: Because it reckons all Christians as stewards, and shows them how to operate their stewardship.

The Junior Superintendent: Because it is a large help in training the boys and girls for the League of to-morrow.

IF OUR LEAGUE MEANS BUSINESS.

If our League means business it will demand more intelligence in its leaders, as well as more devotion.

If our League means business it will get better acquainted with itself by finding out what it is doing all over its wide field.

If our League means business it will insist that its Cabinet officers are in possession of the proper tools.

If our League means business it will not wait longer for a more thoughtful and independent devotional meeting.

If our League means business it will get hold of new ideas and new plans that others have worked out and made profitable.

If our League means business it will listen to the General Secretary and follow his guidance in the League's great united enterprises.

If our League means business it will want to keep step with all the other divisions of the Methodist army of Jesus Christ.

If our League means business it will keep its eye on the Junior League, not only in the home Church, but everywhere.

If our League means business it will not be satisfied to be ignorant of the missionary appeal or of missionary facts.

If our League means business it will find out how to do more sincere and direct soul-winning work.

If our League means business it will open its mind to all the newly important truth about Social Service.

If our League means business it will try ever new ways of winning friends and holding them through recreational activities.

If our League means business in all these it will make an *Epworth Herald* Club its first business every year, because ALL LEAGUE BUSINESS IS HERALD BUSINESS.

THE EFFICIENT EPWORTHIAN.

Old People's Day.

It is easy to neglect the aged. But it is neither wise nor kind. "Old People's Day," observed as an annual Church festival, will do much to repair past neglect and prevent future slighting of those whose lifework has been bravely done and who are now a little aside from the main currents of life and affairs.

The Epworth League is the proper organization for the management of this day. The tribute which you pay to age is always grateful to the aged, and graceful in the young.

The proper observance of Old People's Day calls not so much for special talent as for genuine affection and interest. But careful preparation must be made.

First, fix the date. Some prefer an early summer date, about midway in June. But most Chapters have found the fall more convenient, and the season possesses a certain natural appropriateness which will find expression in the decorations, the music, the addresses, and the emotions of the guests.

Make a careful census of the community. If yours is the only Church, put all the old people on the invitation list. If there are other Churches, it may be thought best to confine the list to the families connected with your Church, though even in that case invitations are not to be restricted to the Church membership. There are many old people, not members of the Church, to whom the invitation would bring unmeasured happiness.

Send a written or printed invitation to every person on the list, at least a week in advance. If any age limit is fixed, do not set it below sixty years. Perhaps sixty-five is better. At sixty-five there is usually no sensitiveness about being called elderly, while people under sixty are often in the prime of their powers and do not care to be counted old.

Carriages should be provided for all the guests, if possible. If that can not be done, be sure that there are carriages for those who could not otherwise be present. Of course, there will be careful and interested drivers, so that

THE LEAGUE'S RED-LETTER DAYS.

no timid guest need hesitate about the trip to and from the church.

If the day is observed in the early summer, flowers will be abundant, and they should be freely used in the decorations. If a later date is chosen, the decorations may include autumn leaves, ripe grain, and the fall flowers, especially the old-fashioned sorts. With these, use the League colors and a flag or two. Have a bouquet ready for each guest.

The old-time hymns will be sung, of course, and to the old-time tunes. Do not leave the selection of hymns to the last moment. Ask some of the old people to suggest the favorite hymns of their youth, and be careful to get the music. Some of our modern choirs can not, without the music, sing such hymns as "O Thou in whose presence my soul takes delight," or "How tedious and tasteless the hours," or "Jesus, my All, to heaven is gone."

The pastor will preach an appropriate sermon, or perhaps some aged minister can be selected for that service. Some good themes are: "The pilgrimage of life," "The old paths," "Fruit in old age," "Growing old gracefully," "The pathos of an old age without faith."

At the close of the sermon shall the service end? No, the Lord's Supper may be administered, or a love-feast conducted, or an old-time class meeting held. Whatever is done, let it be arranged so that the guests of the day shall be considered and provided for first.

Many Chapters find it profitable, in connection with Old People's Day, to hold a week-day reception, preferably in the afternoon. The same decorations will serve, in part, and others may be added. The room may be made cozy with rocking-chairs, rugs, and cushions. Two or three short addresses, more or less reminiscent in tone; some good music, and dainty refreshments will make an attractive program. Perhaps letters from former residents may be read.

Old People's Day will fail of its large purpose unless its spirit is projected into the ordinary life of Chapter and Church. Through the year there should be occasional calls on the old people, and frequent reminders that they are loved and reverenced by the younger people of the Church.

THANKSGIVING DAY.

Thanksgiving Day is, first of all, a religious festival. Otherwise it would have no justification. The very name pre-empts the day for the expressing of gratitude to God.

Of course, it is not blameworthy that we have made the day a very human festival also. It is properly a feast day, since the right enjoyment of God's material gifts is one way of being thankful for them. But neither dinner nor play properly shows forth the spirit of the day, unless the distinctively religious side of the occasion is put first.

It has become difficult to arrange for a Thanksgiving service in the church. Many pastors have tried to hold such services, and, after several failures, have fallen back on the expedient of union Thanksgiving services, most of which are no better attended than the denominational attempts which preceded them.

But what one man can not do, a group of interested and resourceful young people can do. The pastor can provide the sermon, and his young people, if they will, can provide the congregation. Let the pastor and his Epworthians get together. They can devise a new dress for the old observance, and it may be made popular once more to go to church on Thanksgiving morning.

Relieve the pastor of all the details of the service. Let him have the opportunity to put into a thirty-minute sermon the best that is in him for this occasion. Tell him if he will provide a message you will see that he gets a hearing.

Prepare special music. Work with and through the leader of the choir, and get the singers to pledge their presence at the service. Usually, you know, singing at a Thanksgiving service is pretty uncertain, but nearly always doleful. If you can promise reform in that direction you will have already interested some people.

Decorate the church. Make it bright with flowers and potted plants, with the National colors, and with the colors of the League. Provide a little buttonhole bouquet for everybody who comes. Post ushers at the doors to welcome the people as they come.

THE LEAGUE'S RED-LETTER DAYS.

Advertise. The media of advertising are numberless—cards, dodgers, newspaper notices, window posters, postal cards, printed invitations, but a living, walking advertisement is the best of them all. Recommend the service. Ask people to recognize it as part of their Thanksgiving program. Invite them to bring their guests. Promise—and keep your word—that the service shall last exactly one hour, and that by twelve o'clock all may be on their way to the turkey.

The offering at this service should be used for charitable purposes. If the Chapter is providing Thanksgiving dinners for those who have special need, the money may properly be used for that. Otherwise, the Mercy and Help Department will know what to do with it.

WHAT HAVE I LEARNED THIS YEAR? A WATCH-NIGHT SERVICE.

It will be small gain to look backward if we can not at the same time face the future. This meeting comes on the last day of the year. What could be more fitting than that it should be a watch-night service?

There will be the usual evening preaching service, of course. But why should not the pastor and the League Chapter join forces? Plan an evening's services that shall begin at nine o'clock, when the pastor will preach such a sermon as the occasion itself will help him to prepare. Of course, it will present Jesus Christ the Savior. Then, at ten o'clock let the congregation break up into little groups, with the distinct understanding that for one hour there shall be conversation on the things of God and on no other theme.

"We never have done such a thing!" And that is precisely the reason it should be done now. Our opportunities for spiritual conversation are not many, and what do come to us are often unused. Make it easy, for once, to talk religion. No argument, of course, but earnest, frank, unconstrained conversation. If there are unsaved people present, what better time could be found for direct appeal to the individual soul? We talk a lot about personal evangelism, and here is a chance to make it gloriously effective.

THE EFFICIENT EPWORTHIAN.

At eleven o'clock begin the League devotional meeting. The combined spiritual influences of the evening will conspire to make everybody unusually tender, receptive, open to the work of the Holy Spirit. Sing nothing for the sake of singing—let every hymn be a necessary part of the hour. Be as little mechanical and formal as possible.

Let the leader's address, the brief talks of those whom he has previously asked to take part, and the testimonies all lead up to the climax of the meeting—the last ten minutes. Of course, that will be a dedication service; a time of prayerful confession, contrition, surrender, hope, and love; and it will be all the holier and more blessed if in those moments you hear the first outpouring of praise from a new-born soul whom you have shown the way into the Kingdom.

At the midnight hour, be still. The passing of the year is not in itself an event, but the coming of every soul into a personal and vital sense of the presence of God is too momentous to suffer any interruption whatever.

After such a meeting there will be such a going home, in the calm of the new year's first moments, as will abide in the memory forever.

CHAPTER XIII.

CEREMONIAL OCCASIONS.

It is entirely Methodistic to make much of occasions. John Wesley advised it, and took his own choice. We are wise when we take it also.

Installation and reception services, when carefully and understandingly conducted, are always profitable. They impress everybody with the seriousness and dignity of the work. They put the stamp of value upon the Epworth League's business. Membership and official responsibility in the League are things of privilege and honor, and ought to be so regarded.

It is not necessary that the same form be always followed. Often a new form may be improvised, or additions may be provided to suit special conditions.

In the installation service the exercises may be enriched by brief addresses from leaders in other departments of the Church work, such as class leaders, stewards, trustees, Sunday school superintendents, workers in various ladies' societies, etc.

At another time the President-elect may speak, followed by the Vice-Presidents in turn, each one emphasizing the scope of the work committed to his department.

Sometimes symbols of the departments may be used effectively: a gavel for the President, a Bible for the First Department, a torch for the Second, a Red Cross flag for the Third, a copy of *The Epworth Herald* and a wreath for the Fourth, a pen for the Secretary, and a purse for the Treasurer.

Reception of New Members.

President.—You have been duly elected to membership in our Chapter of the Epworth League. In welcoming you

THE EFFICIENT EPWORTHIAN.

to its fellowship, we wish to state its object and aims, and to hear your pledge of loyalty to its spirit.

What is the object of the Epworth League?

Response.—The object of the Epworth League is to promote intelligent and vital piety in the younger members and friends of the Church, to aid them in the attainment of purity of heart and in constant growth in grace, and to train them in works of mercy and help.

P.—Will you strive to realize this object?

R.—I will.

P.—Into how large a fellowship do you desire to enter?

R.—I desire a league offensive and defensive with every soldier of Christ.

P.—What is your duty to the Church?

R.—We live to make our Church a power in the land, while we live to love every other Church that exalts our Christ.

P.—Our motto is "Look up, lift up." Will you make this your motto?

R.—I will.

P. (Addressing candidates for active membership)—We understand that you desire to become an active member of our Chapter.

R.—I do.

P.—Will you earnestly seek for yourself, and do what you can to help others attain, the highest New Testament standard of experience and life?

R.—I will.

P.—Will you abstain from all those forms of worldly amusement which can not be taken in the name of the Lord Jesus?

R.—I will.

P.—Will you attend, as far as possible, the religious meetings of the Chapter and Church, and take some active part in the same?

R.—I will.

P. (Addressing candidates for associate membership)—We understand that you desire to become an associate member of our Chapter.

R.—I do.

CEREMONIAL OCCASIONS.

P.—Do you promise to attend the meetings of the League and Church, to serve on committees when appointed, and to more carefully investigate your duty to God?

R.—I do.

P.—In the name of our Chapter and of the Epworth League I extend to you the right hand of fellowship, and welcome you to membership in this great body of Methodist young people. (I take pleasure in assigning you to the Department of ....), and I trust our fellowship may be mutually profitable to ourselves and a blessing to the Church.

Graduation of Juniors.

(They assemble in front and are presented by the Junior League Superintendent.)

Pastor.—You have now reached an age entitling you to membership in the Epworth League. Before transferring your membership thereto, we wish to question you upon the work you have done in the Junior League.

Have you read the four Gospels and Acts and Epistles, and answered the questions thereon?

Response.—We have.

P.—Have you finished the course of study prescribed for the Junior League, and received certificate and seals for the same?

R.—We have.

P.—Will you repeat the Apostles' Creed?

R.—(Juniors repeat the Apostles' Creed.)

P.—Repeat the Ten Doctrines of Grace as held by the Methodist Episcopal Church.

R.—(Juniors repeat Ten Doctrines.)

P.—The President of the Epworth League will now question your knowledge of the purpose and pledge of the Epworth League.

From this point use the form for the reception of new members.

Installation of Chapter Officers.

(Officers present themselves before the pastor in order.)

Pastor.—These persons have been elected or properly appointed as officers, and the President-elect has been approved by the Quarterly Conference.

THE EFFICIENT EPWORTHIAN.

(To the President-elect.) You have been elected to the chief office of the League. It will be your duty to conduct the affairs of the League; to interest yourself in all the details of its organization and work; to counsel with all departments, and to be a pattern for their inspiration; to preside in the Cabinet and business meetings; and to represent the Epworth League in the Quarterly Conference.

(To the First Vice-President.) You have been elected to the office of First Vice-President. You thus become superintendent of the spiritual work. Your duty will require you to arrange for the regular devotional meeting of the Chapter and to look after the spiritual welfare of the members, inviting those who are interested to join the classes of the Church. To you will be committed the work, if possible, of organizing and training a personal workers' class, and a class for the study of Christian experience. It is also your duty, at least once each year, to present the subject of the Morning Watch Enrollment; to interest the young people in systematic daily study of the Bible; to appoint a committee on Bible study; to instruct the membership of the Chapter in the doctrines, polity, history, and present activities of the Methodist Episcopal Church, and the other denominations of the Church universal; to plan special revival meetings, and neighborhood outdoor and cottage services, and other meetings of like purpose; to conduct prayer-meetings for children where there is no Chapter of the Junior League; to supervise all the evangelistic and devotional activities of the Chapter; and, where the work of the League is so divided that the work of the different departments is interwoven, to arrange for the devotional services in sociables, lectures, and all meetings of similar character; to help the Superintendent in building up the Sunday school; and to foster the interests of the Junior League.

(To the Second Vice-President.) Unto you is given the work of the Department of World Evangelism. You are to endeavor to interest our young people in the missionary and other benevolent interests of the Church; to enlist the members in the systematic study of Christian missions; to circulate missionary literature; to arrange for

CEREMONIAL OCCASIONS.

monthly missionary meetings of the Chapter; to circulate a Cycle of Prayer for world evangelism; to present the claims of Christian Stewardship; to interest the members in the systematic study of Christian Stewardship; and to seek to enroll the members in the Christian Stewardship Enrollment. You shall continually keep before our young people the aim of this department as embodied in its motto, "The world for Christ in this generation."

(To the Third Vice-President.) You have been elected to the Department of Social Service. It will be your duty to arrange for the systematic visitation of the members of the Chapter, the sick of the neighborhood, the aged, and the newcomers to the community. You shall interest the Chapter in the charities of the place, and plan to give aid when needed. It will be your duty also to promote a campaign of regard for the law in general and for the laws concerning the illegal liquor traffic in particular, and to assist public officials; to have charge of the social purity work, tract distribution, and kindred activities. All kinds of charitable work, when undertaken by the Chapter—such as visiting hospitals, nursing, distributing flowers, starting industrial schools, conducting employment bureaus, coffee-houses, day nurseries—will be under your care.

(To the Fourth Vice-President.) You are assigned to the Department of Recreation and Culture. It shall be your aim to give stimulus and direction to general Christian culture, and to do what you can to quicken the intellectual and social life of the members of the Chapter and of our community. It shall be part of your duty to open, if practical, libraries, reading-rooms, art-rooms, night schools, and the like; to arrange for lectures and literary gatherings; to extend the circulation of *The Epworth Herald* and the other publications of the Church; to be on the outlook for new members, and be ready to receive them and introduce them at all the meetings of the Chapter; to have charge of all music of the Chapter except that of the devotional meetings; to provide flowers for the pulpit, and ushers when needed. Athletic events, indoors and out-of-doors, and all such recreations as picnics, excursions, and other outings shall be under your care.

THE EFFICIENT EPWORTHIAN.

(To the Secretary.) As Secretary, your duty will be to keep the records of the meetings and of the membership, and of all courses of reading and study pursued by the Chapter. It is desirable that you send reports of its meetings to local papers; also that you keep copies of all programs, newspapers and other notices of Chapter affairs, and all memorabilia relating to its doings. You may carry on correspondence with absent members and other Chapters, and read the replies at the meetings of the Chapter, as the Chapter may order. You are to conduct all correspondence with the Central and District Offices, and be the custodian of all the records of the Chapter. Through you members in good standing shall be recommended to other Chapters. You will keep the District and General League Officers informed as to the status of the work in the local Chapter.

(To the Treasurer.) Into your keeping are committed the financial interests of the Chapter. You are to present to the Chapter plans for meeting the financial needs of the Chapter. You will collect all dues and receive all moneys, disbursing the same as the Chapter may direct; take the special collections; and perform such other financial duties as may be imposed upon you. It is also your duty to forward to the Central Office of the Epworth League in Chicago, Ill., during the month of April, each year, such an amount as the Board of Control shall request to meet the expenses of the general organization.

(To the Junior Superintendent.) It is your task, and a blessed one, to gather the boys and girls into the Junior League, and to secure their conversion to God and their training in the essentials of Christian faith and conduct. You are to teach with carefulness, to guide with watchfulness, to control with love, and to educate in the Spirit of Christ the children committed to your care. You will use the courses of study wisely, and prepare your members for transfer in due time into the senior organization, where they may continue the upright and useful lives begun under your influence.

Fellow-members: You have heard in outline a statement of the work upon which you are now to enter. Will

CEREMONIAL OCCASIONS.

you discharge the duties committed to your care as you have opportunity and to the best of your ability?

Officers.—I will.

Pastor.—"I will lift mine eyes unto the hills, from whence cometh my help."

Officers.—"My help cometh from the Lord, which made heaven and earth."

P.—"Say not ye, There are yet four months, and then cometh the harvest? Behold, I say unto you, lift up your eyes and look on the fields; for they are white already to the harvest."

O.—"We count not our lives dear unto ourselves, so that we may finish our course with joy and the ministry which we have received of the Lord Jesus to testify the Gospel of the grace of God."

P.—"If any man lack wisdom, let him ask of God, that giveth to all men liberally and upbraideth not, and it shall be given him."

O.—"Thou wilt show me the path of life; in Thy presence is fullness of joy; at thy right hand there are pleasures for evermore."

P.—"Delight thyself also in the Lord, and He will give thee the desires of thy heart."

Pastor's address: Having been elected or appointed to fill these responsible positions for the ensuing six months (or "year," as the case may be), much of the success and strength of the work will depend upon you. You will need to plan for it, to work for it. You will need to inspire and assist all the other members, personally to entreat them, and to draw them into closer fellowship.

There are souls among you to be converted; there are erring ones to be uplifted; there are suffering ones to be relieved. You will need discretion, constant watchfulness for opportunities, and the continual presence of the Holy Spirit.

There is no activity in the Church, no movement of reform, in which you may not rightfully engage for the upbuilding of Christlike characters. "Therefore, My brethren, be ye steadfast, unmovable, always abounding in the work of the Lord; forasmuch as ye know that your labor is not in vain in the Lord."

Consecration prayer.

Response by new President.

The Epworth League Benediction: Leader.—The Lord bless thee and keep thee.

Response.—The Lord make His face to shine upon thee and be gracious unto thee.

All.—The Lord lift up His countenance upon thee and give thee peace.

Installation of District Officers.

The District Superintendents' Convention should not adjourn until the new officers are publicly installed. In all but special cases the District Superintendent should be invited to conduct the installation service.

Officers to be installed present themselves at the altar.

Singing.

Responsive service:

Retiring President.—"I will lift up mine eyes unto the hills, from whence cometh my help."

Officers.—"My help cometh from the Lord, which made heaven and earth."

R. P.—"They that sow in tears shall reap in joy."

O.—"He that goeth forth and weepeth, bearing precious seed, shall doubtless come again with rejoicing, bringing his sheaves with him."

R. P.—"The fruit of the righteous is a tree of life; and he that winneth souls is wise."

O.—"And they that be wise shall shine as the brightness of the firmament; and they that turn many to righteousness as the stars for ever and ever."

R. P.—"For we are laborers together with God."

O.—"Till we all come in the unity of the faith, and of the knowledge of the Son of God, unto a perfect man, unto the measure of the stature of the fullness of Christ."

District Superintendent (to the District President.)—We rely upon you to superintend the work of the young people upon this district. Visit the Chapters, organize new Chapters, encourage all by letters, inspire the young people

CEREMONIAL OCCASIONS.

by your example, secure the observance of the Epworth League Anniversary, the promotion of Juniors, increased loyalty to the Church, and co-operation with the pastors on the part of the Epworth League members.

(To the First Vice President.)—Realize fully the spiritual aims of the Epworth League, assist the President in visiting the Chapters, encourage personal evangelism, promote Bible study and the study of Christian experience, form companies of Comrades of the Morning Watch, and set forth by precept and example the highest New Testament standard of experience and life.

(To the Second Vice-President.)—Your task is to energize and direct the work of world evangelism. You will encourage and promote mission study and the study of the Church's manifold benevolent work, recommend and illustrate the blessedness of Christian Stewardship, and in all ways magnify the world-wide mission of every disciple of Jesus Christ.

(To the Third Vice-President.)—To encourage and systematize the varied work of Social Service among the Chapters of the district is the task of your department. The work of every agency that seeks to serve individuals and the community, and to protect them from harm, the ministry of our Methodist hospitals and homes, and of the deaconesses, should receive your heartiest assistance, and you should promote sustained interest in and active support of the law-enforcement crusade by every chapter on the district.

(To the Fourth Vice-President.)—To you is committed the task of directing the cultural interests of the Chapters and their members, and the circulation of *The Epworth Herald*. There are diversions, both intellectual and social, which may be used in the name of the Lord Jesus. Direct the attention of our young people to them. Warn them of the paths of folly, reprove gently, cultivate the widest social intercourse and sympathy, and multiply occasions of genuine recreation.

(To the Secretary.)—Keep the records of the District Cabinet and of the conventions accurately, and see that they are faithfully preserved and promptly turned over to your

THE EFFICIENT EPWORTHIAN.

successor. Co-operate with the President in his correspondence, send out all notices promptly, secure a report from every Chapter Secretary, and carefully transmit the roster of officers to the Central Office of the Epworth League.

(To the Treasurer.)—Look carefully after the expenses of the District Convention, and insist that each Chapter shall contribute, according to the provisions of the Constitution, to the expenses of the general organization.

(To the Junior Superintendent.)—To you is committed a task which angels might envy, to interest every Methodist Church and home in the conversion of the boys and girls, and secure their membership in the Church, that every Junior on this district may be persuaded to read the Bible, complete the work required for promotion to the Epworth League, and become grafted into the Great Vine.

You have heard this brief enumeration of your duties. Will you faithfully perform them?

O.—We will endeavor to do so, in the fear of God.

CHAPTER XIV.

THE EPWORTH LEAGUE PLEDGE.

Those who object to the pledge idea and plead for liberty do not realize that the pledge has positive moral value.

The dependence on the pledged word, on covenants, is well-nigh universal. It is insisted upon when a man changes citizenships, or speaks in a case at law, or borrows money, or sells a farm, or enters upon public office, or gets his life insured, or joins a lodge, or imports dry goods, or is hired to teach school, or gets married. The world is moved by the two words which are implied in the League pledge, "I promise."

It is a recognition of the priceless gift of human freedom. No machine or beast of the field or star of the sky can say, "I will." Man can. He can map out a course and then, by opening his life to the right influences, and by his own powers, he can follow that course to the end. Let metaphysicians worry "the freedom of the will" as Towser worries a bone. We come out of every argument on the subject with the same emphatic conviction, "Nevertheless, I am free."

There is the secret of the pledge's value. It is a free person marking out a course. The purpose to follow that pledge commits the maker. He has cut loose. He is a conqueror who has crossed the Rubicon. He is a discoverer who has burned his ships behind him. He can undo it all—but it is less likely that he will fail than if he relied merely on getting over some kind of a course some time.

That does not fully state the case, either. As a matter of fact, a pledge like that of the Epworth League is always taken after the real promise has been given.

You can not honestly sign a pledge-card unless you have already taken the pledge in heart and mind. And why should a Christian hesitate to commit himself to this form of words? He has already committed himself to everything it stands for, or he is not a Christian.

The Pledge.

I will earnestly seek for myself, and do what I can to help others attain, the highest New Testament standard of experience and life. I will abstain from all those forms of worldly amusement which can not be taken in the name of the Lord Jesus, and I will attend, so far as possible, the religious meetings of the Chapter and the Church, and take some active part in them.

The Pledge Analyzed: Clause One.

The first clause of the pledge is the life of it. It is no mere every-day contract. It is the announcement of a life purpose, a real "quest of the Holy Grail."

In the legend the knight sought the cup of the Last Supper. He who takes this pledge to seek the New Testament standard of experience and life is seeking a holier thing than the cup. He is seeking to drink of the cup of the Lord, it is true, but not in any outward seeming. When our Lord was besought to give great place to two ambitious disciples, He asked of them, "Are ye able to drink of My cup?" They knew not what they asked or promised. To-day's disciple who takes this pledge must know. He is seeking fellowship with Jesus Christ, the inner sacrament, instead of the vessel which held the wine.

The pledge is fully worded, so that there shall be no mistake. But it can be reduced to lower terms. "I will seek the New Testament standard"—there is but one standard in that Book, but we must understand it for what it is, a very high standard.

Let us paraphrase this part of the pledge. It can be re-stated in various forms. "I will seek Jesus Christ." None can live in the New Testament atmosphere without the New Testament life in him. And the life of the new covenant is given by the Christ, who sealed that covenant with His blood. So no one who is unwilling to be a Christian can take this pledge.

THE EPWORTH LEAGUE PLEDGE.

"I will seek the Kingdom of heaven." The pledge does a great service in locating the Kingdom of heaven here on the earth. There is no room for doubt as to the present-day bearing of the pledge. It is of the hour that is passing. But he who is keeping the pledge is really seeking to bring to pass the coming of the Kingdom. The first sentence of the pledge recognizes this, and links salvation and service in an appropriate intimacy.

"I will seek power." There is no going to this warfare of pledge-keeping at one's own charges. The task is too hard, and the way is too long. If you are in search of the New Testament life you will need New Testament power to help you live it. "Ye shall receive power."

What is the New Testament standard? In the terms of the Master's own definition it is twofold. "Ye must be born again," and "A new commandment . . . that ye love one another, as I have loved you." In the terms of the apostle to the Gentiles it is also twofold. "Be not conformed to this world, but be ye transformed," and "Use not liberty for an occasion to the flesh, but by love serve one another."

So it is linked in the pledge. "I will seek for myself, and do what I can to help others attain." Is it not wonderful how these two thoughts find each other and travel together? It is Christianity in a phrase—life and service. The two can not be divorced.

And in the Epworth League there is no effort to separate them. Rather do we put emphasis on personal evangelism as the service which is proof and outflowing of the inner life.

The Christian is by nature an evangelist. By the terms of his own conversion he becomes a preacher of salvation to others. He is pledged to that work in the moment of pardon for sin and the imparting of the new life. So it is no new obligation he is assuming when he promises to help others attain the standard of life which he seeks for himself.

Clause Two.

The rest of the pledge follows as a matter of course. It is merely an expansion of the first clause by going into

THE EFFICIENT EPWORTHIAN.

details. These details are good for information and guidance, but the first part of the pledge has the root in it.

"I will abstain." Surely the new life has its negative side. There are some things a Christian will not do. And what better test than this? He who can not "do all in the name of the Lord Jesus" is not yet Christ's freeman. It is a surer test than any list of doubtful amusements; it includes many things that would not get into such a list, and it can always be applied with the assurance that if honestly used it will always work. It will sometimes exclude one's participation in things which of themselves are innocent enough, for the follower of Jesus Christ often finds it necessary to say of lawful things: "All things are not expedient. What is the best thing to do?" The answer will exclude many a good thing which might otherwise have been included.

CLAUSE THREE.

"I will attend." This is a somewhat narrow clause, relating to only one side of the new life—that side which touches the Chapter and the Church. So far as it goes, it is a great help. It insures a prosperous devotional meeting, and an inspiring preacher. For these things are much more dependent upon interested attendants than is generally supposed. It is not the preacher who makes the Church, nor the leader who makes the meeting. It is the people. The history of many a community has chapters which illustrate this truth. The people have sustained the Chapter in spite of poor leaders, and have made the sermons of a prosy preacher actually inspiring because of the inspiration of their listening and their prayer.

THE HIGHEST STANDARD.

There are those who think that the word "highest" in the Epworth League pledge indicates that "high" and "higher" Scriptural standards exist, which are a little lower than the "highest." But not so. There is in the New Testament only one standard of living. "Highest standard" and "New Testament standard" are equivalent terms. The highest standard is also the lowest. Saint Paul said in one place, "As ye have therefore received Jesus Christ the

THE EPWORTH LEAGUE PLEDGE.

Lord, so walk ye in Him." That is, the Christian life should never get below its beginning. We received Christ Jesus by acceptance of His pardon and by complete surrender to His will. Anything less than that complete surrender is too low a standard for the Christian.

Of course, there will be new knowledge of Christ in the daily doing of His will, and in that sense our standard will rise with experience. But always there must be the "Thy will be done" of the prayer that teaches to pray. There must be the steadfast purpose of loyalty to Christ, and there will be a growing eagerness to serve and obey Him. So the highest New Testament standard, though always the same in requirement, will become through the years a greater and more beautiful ideal, always calling us to fuller and holier life.

What is the Purpose of the Pledge?

We narrow it when we think of it solely as a means to personal advancement in the Christian life. At the very outset, as we declare our purpose to seek the New Testament standard, we find imbedded in the sentence the social purpose of the pledge, the purpose to help others in the attainment of the same standard of experience and life which we seek for ourselves.

There lies the great Christian secret. No man liveth to himself. He that would save his soul shall lose it. No man can be saved while he seeks nothing beyond his own salvation. We are members one of another. "When a hand gathers food it does so for the whole body, itself included, and apart from the general nutrition of the body there could be no nutriment for the hand."

So the purpose of the pledge is to bind us to a plan of life that will bring us closer to God, and closer to our fellows; to make us better children of God at the same time as we become better kinsmen of our brethren in all the world.

Who Should Take the Pledge?

Our pledge is not obligatory. Each Chapter may determine for itself whether it will adopt the pledge. Yet it was not left to discretion because of any doubt as to its wisdom or value, but because its framers believed in local self-government. One can be a Christian without taking the pledge. But it is impossible to be a Christian without, in substance, living the pledge. Its four elements—life, service, abstinence, and duty—are part of the equipment of every follower of Jesus Christ.

Do You Know the Pledge?

We venture to say that there are many active members of the Epworth League who have taken the pledge could not repeat it from memory. Some could not even give an intelligent idea of what it embraces. That is a pity. One of the first things which a Chapter which has adopted the pledge should insist upon is that every active member become thoroughly familiar with the pledge.

There are several ways of aiding new members to memorize the pledge:

1. It should be printed in large type and hung up conspicuously in the room in which the Chapter meets.

2. It should be printed on the topic cards and other literature of the First Department.

3. It should be repeated in concert at least once a month in connection with the regular devotional meeting.

4. It should be taken up by the Chapter, paragraph by paragraph, and fully discussed. A series of "evenings with the pledge" could be arranged. One evening could be devoted to the first clause: "I will earnestly seek for myself, and do what I can to help others attain, the highest New Testament standard of experience and life." Another evening to the second clause, and so on.

When we are left to our better selves it is natural to say "I will" to God, for what He offers is manifestly to our advantage. We should take it as a sign that there is something wrong with us when God's invitations seem to call us to unattractive lives. He who can find nothing winsome in the gospel is most in need of it.

THE EPWORTH LEAGUE PLEDGE.

Some Pledge Questions.

Is the pledge understood?
Is it kept when we are careful to stay just inside the letter of its requirements?
What are some gains of pledge-making?
What are some dangers which grow out of making the pledge?
How does injury come from failure to keep the pledge?
How much importance should be placed on the pledge?
Who should interpret the pledge for me?
Is the pledge a definite vow, or the setting of an ideal, towards which we may work by degrees?
How is it possible to keep the letter of the pledge and violate its spirit?
Why is doing God's will the highest freedom?
What is the great difference between a servant and a friend?
What is the condition of becoming a friend of Jesus Christ?

Reasons for the Pledge.

It is a confession of duty.
It is a help towards faithfulness.
It builds a fence around dangerous places.
It is the expression of our truest convictions.
It provides another bond of fellowship.
It is a practical and constant reminder of our obligations.

Conducting a Pledge Meeting.

Post the pledge in a conspicuous place, and ask the active members to repeat it in concert at some appropriate moment during the meeting.

Use the blackboard for the questions given elsewhere. Keep the blank side of the board in sight until you are ready to call for testimonies. Then swing the questions around.

Ask half a dozen people to explain the "Reasons for the pledge."

Use the questions and other helps towards testimony

THE EFFICIENT EPWORTHIAN.

as a means of getting the more backward members to take part. The others can do without these helps.

Be careful to encourage real testimony that shall be personal and pointed. This is no subject for vague and general essays on abstract themes. Do not be afraid of the first personal pronoun, unless it runs too much to the stating of long-winded views and opinions.

Present the pledge. If you have already adopted it as a Chapter, seek to win the associate members. They ought not to remain associates a moment after they have once seen the beauty and the worth of making full surrender to God's love. If your Chapter has not adopted it, present it for adoption by individual members, and perhaps the Chapter will vote to adopt it as a result of this meeting. What better practical outcome could you desire?

Hymns for a Pledge Meeting.

"Lord, I am Thine, entirely Thine."
"Prince of Peace, control my will."
"King of kings, and wilt Thou deign."
"Walk in the light, so shalt thou know."
"O, for a heart to praise my God."
"Forever here my rest shall be."
"I am Thine, O Lord; I have heard Thy voice."
"My life, my love, I give to Thee."
"Faith of our fathers, living still."
"Take my life and let it be."

CHAPTER XV.

SUPERVISION, INSPIRATION, AND INSTRUCTION.

The District League.

The District League has its necessary place because of the essentially Methodistic character of the Epworth League. The natural grouping of any sort of Methodist societies is the same: first, the pastoral charge; second, the district. This gives the same "sub-bishop" to the Epworth League organization that the Church already possesses. It provides the connecting link between the local Chapter and the general organization. There are Conference Epworth Leagues in some parts of the Church, and a number of State organizations are doing excellent work, while several of the General Conference Districts are organized and active. But the Conference, State, and General Conference District Epworth Leagues are not, strictly speaking, essential to the complete articulation of the League's work. In some places they work well; in others they are not advisable; in still others they are entirely out of the question. But the District Epworth League is essential wherever the Methodist Episcopal Church is in operation.

The District Cabinet is organized with the same list of officers as complete the local Cabinet, and each district officer has supervision over the corresponding officers in the various Chapters throughout the district. Each district department head is the channel through which the information concerning the local Chapter finds its way to the District Cabinet and the District Convention. In many districts the District Cabinet makes more or less formal tours over the district, either as a body or individually, each member going in the interest of his own part of the work.

THE EFFICIENT EPWORTHIAN.

The District Cabinet has large importance as an organizing and reorganizing force. It should see to it that every charge on the district has an Epworth League Chapter, unless conditions plainly indicate that it is impossible. The dead Chapters and the dying must be revived. The members of the Cabinet may profitably visit each charge where such a Chapter is found, in a body, if they can give sufficient time to the work, co-operating with the pastor in looking up members and probable leaders to take charge.

Then, when the reorganizing meeting is held, it will be much easier to secure recruits for a new start than it would be if none but the faithful ones of the almost lifeless local Chapter should make the attempt. The Chapter doubtless failed because it did nothing to justify its existence. It can not be revived unless something is given it to do. Therefore, start something when the Chapter is resuscitated. Start a Bible study class or a mission study class. Organize a class in Christian experience, or a fellow-workers' band. Present the Christian Stewardship enrollment. Enroll the members as Comrades of the Morning Watch. Perhaps some temperance task is ready for vigorous effort. Set people to work. Get something going, and enlist the interest of the local Epworthians in definite work in their own Chapter, and, if possible, in things outside their own little community also. Link them to the great Church of which they are a part.

The work of the district organization continues the year through, but it comes to its highest tide of visible results in the annual District Convention. Here the work of the Cabinet bears fruit that can be seen and tested of all men. Here the officers give an account of the way in which they have discharged the trust committed to them. Here old plans are reported upon and new plans launched. Here the Cabinet feels the pulse of the district and discovers why some things failed last year and what work is most likely to succeed next year. Here the Chapters come together and feel the *esprit de corps* which makes district work easy in the measure that it spreads among the Chapters and the members.

SUPERVISION, INSPIRATION, INSTRUCTION.

The Convention: Master or Servant?

Three cheers for conventions, and three for committees, and three—or, anyway, two—for new organizations!

But in the height of the organizing, delegate-choosing fever, it will do the patient no harm to read a paragraph like this:

> Every idea we have is run into a constitution. We can not think without a chairman. Our whims have secretaries; our fads have by-laws. Literature is a club. Philosophy is a society. Our reforms are mass meetings. Our culture is a summer school. We can not mourn our mighty dead without Carnegie Hall and forty vice-presidents. We remember our poets with trustees, and the immortality of a genius is watched by a standing committee. Charity is an association. Theology is a set of resolutions. Religion is an endeavor to be numerous and communicative. We awe the impenitent with crowds, convert the world with boards, and save the lost with delegates. What Socrates and Solomon would have come to if they had only had the advantage of conventions would be hard to say; but in these days, when the excursion train is applied to wisdom; when, having little enough, we try to make it more by pulling it about; when secretaries urge us, treasurers dun us, programs unfold out of every mail—where is the man who, guileless-eyed, can look in his brother's face; can declare upon his honor that he has never been a delegate, never belonged to anything, never been nominated, elected, imposed on, in his life?

Mr. Gerald Stanley Lee does not mean to be taken altogether literally in this outburst of a pardonable impatience. But he is so far literal that we may as well give heed to him.

The mass meeting is a means of auto-suggestion which makes us reckon the thing discussed as the thing accomplished. All the time we know it is n't; all the time we know that our record will not be tested by what we did in the Committee on Resolutions.

THE EFFICIENT EPWORTHIAN.

If the work of the Epworth League is done with eager desire to make it mean something right on the spot, often we shall be coming together to talk about it, as we ought.

But if coming together to talk about it is beginning and end of our zeal, we need not wonder when the convention and the mass meeting lose their charm for all but the officers and the Executive Committee.

The District Convention.

The Conferences of Methodism are very largely the business meetings of a great and complex institution. They are necessarily cumbered with much serving. The Epworth League, with its minimum of machinery, has had opportunity to provide in its general gatherings for the cultivation of the spirit of fellowship, for the emphasis on the connectional idea, and for the conduct of exceedingly profitable "Conversations on the work of God."

The District President must cultivate the acquaintance of all the pastors and League workers in the district. Every week he will have occasion to draw on his knowledge of these co-laborers. His correspondence will be a heavy item in his work, but it can not be neglected without damage to the activities of the district and of the several Chapters. This is especially true in connection with the district convention. The District President is commander-in-chief of that gathering. If he would marshal his forces effectively he must know them. All the work of the year has been enriching his stores of information and personal knowledge concerning the young people of the district. When the time to arrange for the convention arrives, this equipment of facts and the President's deductions from them will have much to do with the successful building of the program.

Neighboring districts find it profitable to arrange for simultaneous, or, more usually, consecutive conventions. Sometimes all the districts of a Conference adopt this plan. It makes possible the securing of speakers from a distance who could not otherwise come. The expense is small, when shared by four or five districts, and the speakers follow a carefully planned schedule which allows for all minor

SUPERVISION, INSPIRATION, INSTRUCTION.

emergencies and delays in getting from one convention to the next.

Building the Program.—The District Cabinet is usually the Program Committee for the annual convention. A Cabinet meeting should be called not less than four months previous to the date determined on for the convention. The first business is that of blocking out the program's outstanding features and deciding upon the general character of the gathering.

To this meeting a representative of the Chapter which is to entertain the convention should be invited, for many questions will arise which can be settled only by some one who is familiar with the local situation.

The great purposes of a district convention should be kept in mind. It is intended to secure greater effectiveness in the work of the local Chapters, to discover and train League leaders, to push vigorously one or more of the various League enterprises to which the entire organization is committed, to emphasize and intensify the spirit of fellowship and unity among the Epworthians of the district, and to bear immediate fruit in direct evangelism and the spiritual uplift both of the delegates and of the members at home whom they represent.

These things remembered, go over all the available material, in themes and in speakers. Bear in mind that even the longest convention must have a time limit, and see that the program can be fully presented well within the time allotted. In the smaller towns and villages a two-days' convention is usually provided for, while in the larger places the morning, afternoon, and evening of a single day are all that can be given.

Decide on a "dominant note." Let the convention stand for some one specific thing. Of course, a large variety of themes will be provided, but give one of them such importance and prominence that it will stand out above all the others. Next year the emphasis may be changed, so that in a series of conventions a variety of important and timely subjects will have been considered. With some such arrangement as this there will be no opportunity for people to say, when urged to attend the convention, "I went last year, and it was much the same as the year before, and the program seems to be about the same again this year, so I do n't care to go."

Put this "dominant note" into a sentence or a phrase that shall stick out in all the advertising of the convention until everybody knows it by heart and knows what it signifies, and then spread it across the convention room on a banner something after this fashion: "A Bible Study Class in Every Chapter!" "Mission Study and Missionary Zeal!" "A Convention for Soul-Winning!" "Help that Hospital!" "Better Devotional Meetings Next Year!" "Shall We Adopt a Missionary?" "Let Us Double Our Numbers and Quadruple Our Effectiveness!" "Young People's Work for Young People!" "Win One This Year!" "The Union of All Who Love in the Service of All Who Suffer." "Culture, Fellowship, and Evangelism!" Every district can put its aims and purposes into some such attention-compelling mottoes as these.

In stating the themes that are to be discussed, be "different." Avoid sameness of plan and you will not be troubled by its offspring, monotony of result. Put the subjects into question form, or into new and unexpected phrasings. Make the very topics challenge attention and arouse interest.

Keep away from the general themes that were worn out twenty years ago. Do not talk about "The Ideal Epworth League," or "The Relation of the Pastor to the Epworth League," or "The Epworth League and the Church," or "The Work Before Us," or any of those generalities which may have been excusable in the first years of the League's experience, but which long ago served their day and generation. Your themes may be old, but your treatment of them and the very headings under which they are discussed may be suggestive, practical, and fresh.

Make the program too short rather than too long. Remember that delays will happen, even in the best regulated conventions. Do not provide for every five minutes, or arrange the order of exercises like a suburban train schedule. It is much better to print a list of the themes to be discussed without setting down precisely the hour and min-

SUPERVISION, INSPIRATION, INSTRUCTION.

ute when they will be presented. Circumstances almost always compel some transpositions of the original order. If there is no hard-and-fast printed "bill-of-fare," any necessary transposition can be made without the distraction and embarrassment of a public explanation. If a speaker is tardy, another can be substituted, and there is neither waiting nor disappointment. Of course, the speakers who are to deliver the principal addresses do not come within the scope of this suggestion. They must be advertised both as to hour and as to theme.

Make every possible use of the district's indigenous resources. Enlist the workers of the district as far as they are available. That, in most cases, will give a large list of possible participants in the convention program. The Cabinet's acquaintance with leaders in the Chapters will be of great value at this point. It is difficult to build a program in the dark. Each District Vice-President will need to add his knowledge to the common stock. The more work he has done with his local Vice-Presidents, the more valuable his help will be.

On the program, as well as in the convention, the laity should be more in evidence than the preachers. The more preachers take part, as a rule, the less the other delegates will feel like asserting themselves. They have not a preacher's readiness of utterance, or range of observation, or variety of experience. But for precisely these reasons the pastors are willing to give the laymen right of way. Help the ministerial desire to develop lay effectiveness by giving the lay members of the League the large share of the program.

And yet every convention should have a pastors' conference as a part of its program. There are Epworth League problems which concern the pastors directly, and which they ought to discuss among themselves. Give the pastors a conference just as the department leaders are assigned an hour for the consideration of their work.

Of course, every convention program should give large place to distinctly spiritual work. The devotional moments must not be considered as "preliminary exercises." If necessary, avoid this by giving an unusual place to the

THE EFFICIENT EPWORTHIAN.

service of prayer and praise. Put it in the middle of the session, or at the end. Insist that it is an integral part of the program.

Provide for much prayer; prayer by one, prayer by many, silent prayer, prayer in concert, prayer for special ends.

Perhaps it may be possible to plan evangelistic meetings in the open air between sessions of the convention, or at shops and factories at the noon hour. No such opportunity as that should be lost. At these places, and, when occasion serves, in the convention itself, seek to secure immediate decisions for Christ and for salvation. Nothing becomes an Epworth League convention so much as timely and wise work for direct evangelism.

Incorporate the "Institute Idea" into the program. Give the mornings and afternoons largely to the work of considering the real problems and peculiar tasks of the Chapters in the district. The convention that is a normal school for the training of local workers will be of more value than the one which imports speakers to deliver sermons or general addresses. And yet there should be one strong inspirational address at every convention, lest the delegates lose sight of the purpose of the League in the multitude of its plans. Study local problems frankly, but not censoriously. Find the people who are getting things done, and put them on the program to lead conferences in their respective departments.

If reports from the Chapters are provided for, see to it that they are very, very brief. In a district of forty pastoral charges there may be fifty local Chapters. If each one of them makes a one-minute report, an hour is consumed in this one exercise. And a one-minute report is much shorter than the average.

The Question Box is doubly useful. It affords variety, and it awakens interest. But the Question Box may become a dangerous weapon if the one who is handling it "did n't know it was loaded." Few Epworthians are capable of conducting a Question Box hour without having previously seen the questions. That is a risky method unless it is in the hands of an expert. When questions

SUPERVISION, INSPIRATION, INSTRUCTION.

are handed in beforehand, the irrelevant questions and the frivolous ones may be weeded out, which is a necessary process in most cases.

A variation of the Question Box method is used successfully in several district and State organizations. A numbered list of twenty or twenty-five perennially pertinent questions on the work of a single department is made up and distributed just before the open conference on that department. The delegates call for answers by number, and the leader not only gives his own answer to the question, but calls for volunteer answers from the audience. It is a most admirable plan for putting an end to bashfulness and formality, and it is even better as a method of getting at all the available knowledge on the subject under discussion. Program builders will find it profitable to compile their own lists of such questions. As a suggestion of what may be done in this way, a list of questions on the several departments is here given:

GENERAL QUESTIONS.

If one can not be present at both League and Church services on Sunday evening, which of the two should he attend? Give reason.

Tell us some way of bringing the members out to business meeting.

How shall the graduates from the Intermediate League be made to feel at home in the Epworth League and also be encouraged to take in the meetings of the Chapter?

How can we acquaint our members with the workings and victories of the general League? So few see the League clearly and see it whole. Can you suggest any plan outside of reading *The Epworth Herald?* That is the wisest, but all will not subscribe.

Some members of the League have retained their membership through a number of years, simply because there is no plan for graduating them from the young people's society into the other departments of Church life. The "age limit" plan is often unsatisfactory. Is there any better method?

THE EFFICIENT EPWORTHIAN.

After members have been in the League for several years, how should they be treated in order to keep up their interest and enthusiasm?

Is it advisable to lay so much stress on committee work? Does it not detract from the responsibility of the other members?

Is it advisable to drop the names of those members who fail to answer to their names at roll call for a certain length of time?

How can you get young men to take an active interest in the work?

How can a Chapter put to work and keep at work new members, some young, some old in years, but all young in Christian life? Do not give a plan you have not tried.

Is it wise to elect officers without first consulting the persons themselves? Some may serve if elected, who would never consent to their election.

How can the Church membership be brought into closer sympathy with League work?

When members refuse absolutely to take any active part in the work of the League, what is the best method of helping them to see their obligation?

Is there any way to get a good attendance in a country Chapter?

Is it a wise plan, generally considered, to disband a League for the summer months?

In a Chapter of about two hundred members, how can you make every member a worker? Is it a good plan to put every one on one of the departments? If so, how is the plan carried out?

Many young people who have been brought up in good homes, and have been active in Church work, come to our town to attend school, and lose all interest in Church work. How can we reach them?

Is it the aim of the League to fit its members for other departments of Church work and live by giving itself away to these societies?

What is the cure for a society that is more intent on increasing its membership than it is upon doing the work it was organized to do?

SUPERVISION, INSPIRATION, INSTRUCTION.

FIRST DEPARTMENT QUESTIONS.

Should there be a large Devotional Committee, and if so, how can it be used?

In selecting leaders for the year, should the most efficient be chosen or should any one from the membership, and so give all a chance?

What course would you suggest for us to pursue to overcome the "passing-out slips," and "number-calling" habits, when we return to our home Leagues?

Are good results obtained from discarding the regular topics and allowing the leaders to choose their own topics?

Do you think the devotional meeting of the League a good substitute for the class meeting?

What is included in the term "personal evangelism?"

What are the marks of your best meetings?

Should every member be asked to lead sometime? If not, who should not, and why?

Is the meeting helped as a devotional meeting by an orchestra or by special musical features?

What use should be made of helps such as are found in *The Epworth Herald* and elsewhere?

How can the devotional meeting be made a soul-winning agency?

How do you solve the problem of the member who rarely takes part?

How do you interest associate members and non-members in the devotional meeting?

In rural communities, is it advisable to publish in the local newspaper the weekly program—or the program week by week for the devotional meeting?

What simple, workable plan of keeping the Morning Watch can be suggested by one who worked it?

How can we arouse interest in personal work among the members of our Chapter?

Will some Chapter which has successfully helped in revival work please report how it was done?

We have had difficulty in enlisting our members in Bible study. How can the subject be presented so as to be attractive to those who have never yet done systematic study outside of the schoolroom?

THE EFFICIENT EPWORTHIAN.

How can we avoid the danger of making Bible study a mere intellectual exercise?

How can we conduct a Bible study class when we have no person specially qualified to be the leader?

Should we expect every League member to do "personal work?"

What ought the League to expect of the pastor in the devotional meeting?

Shall we call that devotional meeting a failure in which there are long silences and a scarcity of witnesses?

Is it advisable to do much with Bible study classes when the only ones apparently interested are those already busy in the Sunday school?

How shall the League care for the young converts at the close of the revival?

What are the duties of the Spiritual Department toward the absentees in a Chapter where more than half the members are away from home the greater part of the year?

How may a Chapter in a weak country Church, deprived of the Sunday evening preaching, successfully carry on the evening service?

How should open-air meetings be conducted? How often? Where?

In what way would it be best to introduce the Morning Watch to a League which has scarcely heard of it?

What plans can you suggest by which a Chapter could find the young men and women in its community and interest them in the Church?

What is the wisest policy concerning the transaction of business in the devotional meeting?

We have many young, sincere Christians in our Chapter. How can we help to train them for leaders? If any Vice-President has had a class for training members for leadership, will he tell about it, please?

What can we do for our younger members, and the young converts, in training them in the Christian life when they are all busy in school?

SUPERVISION, INSPIRATION, INSTRUCTION.

SECOND DEPARTMENT QUESTIONS.

Should a missionary social be held for the purpose of raising money?

What is the Cycle of Prayer?

Would it be wise to devote the devotional meetings for one month to Christian Stewardship?

Is it wise for a person to lead more than one mission study class during the year?

Is it advisable to hold mission study class meetings during the revival season, providing the meetings are held after Church is dismissed?

How can a district officer interest the Leagues of his district in mission study?

Our Chapter supports a native preacher in India. We send the money to and through a missionary of India who went out from our city. This gives us a more personal interest in the matter. Is there any reason at all why we should not do so, but send the money to the Church Board?

What plan for raising missionary money has proved successful in your Chapter?

Is there a Chapter which can report more than just a few Christian Stewards? If so, how was it accomplished? How often have you found it wise to present the subject?

Is there a practical method of arousing a widespread interest in Christian Stewardship among people who have scarcely heard of it, or who are unprejudiced against it?

How can we teach our members the object, purpose, and importance of the various benevolences other than missions?

What points of missionary truth would you chiefly emphasize in an attempt to arouse interest in foreign missions? To stimulate to action those already somewhat interested?

What can a Second Vice-President do to further the work of his department in a Chapter where it seems impossible to have a separate mission study class? Would it be well for him to bring missionary books sometimes to the devotional meetings and read from them extracts which had definite application to the topic?

THE EFFICIENT EPWORTHIAN.

Is it a good plan to have the Second Vice-President take charge of all missionary meetings?

In a class that has never been especially interested in foreign missions, would you assign much reference work, or would you confine the class more to the text-book?

How can we get our Epworthians interested in reading missionary books?

In an Epworth League whose Sunday evening meetings are distinctly evangelistic, how may the missionary meeting be conducted so that it will not break into this spirit?

Would you recommend a debate when the missionary meeting is held on Sunday evening?

Please give a definition of Christian Stewardship as it is intended to be understood in the work of the Second Department.

Do you think any one could consistently take the office of Second Vice-President who does not believe in the tithing or in the tenth as affecting Christians living under the present condition—that is, under grace rather than law?

THIRD DEPARTMENT QUESTIONS.

What is the greatest reason for Social Service in the Epworth League?

Why should the chairman of this department be a member of the Methodist Federation for Social Service?

How can this department and the Fourth work together in gaining the confidence of the foreign-speaking young people in the community?

What can Epworthians do in the work of encouraging officials to enforce the anti-liquor laws?

With what reform agencies ought the department to become affiliated?

How may we co-operate with other departments of the Church in making a survey of the parish?

How can we avoid duplication with other agencies in doing Social Service work?

What are the good and bad points of Christmas or Thanksgiving dinners for the poor?

What can the rural Chapter do to influence the conditions of farm work?

SUPERVISION, INSPIRATION, INSTRUCTION.

Is there any satisfactory way of exerting a general oversight of the moving picture houses in the neighborhood?

How can the Chapter help in the training of immigrant young people in the rudiments of civics and English?

What can the Chapter do for the away-from-home young people who live in its field?

How much can Epworthians lead in the discussion of proposed legislation in city council or Legislature?

FOURTH DEPARTMENT QUESTIONS.

Is the work of the Fourth Department to have socials to increase League funds? Which, in your opinion, proves to our young people that we want them to have good times, the pay social or the one conducted as a party?

We have a small church without facilities for holding social gatherings. What is the best plan to follow in interesting the older Church members so that they will feel like entertaining the League in their homes?

Is not the department more detrimental than beneficial to the real and proper work of the League as set forth in its "object?"

Many of the attendants at the recreational and social affairs do not come to the devotional meetings. How have you tried to bring them to the latter, and with what success?

Can any one tell of a Fourth Department plan aimed directly at giving an impetus to young people to go to college?

Can anything be done in the Fourth Department to help the boys and girls who have left the public school before graduating, and who now regret it? We have some in our Chapter: young people of promise, but handicapped. No library, no Young Men's Christian Association night school in town. Has the League anything for them?

What can a President do to assist and develop a Fourth Vice-President who is intelligent, eager, and willing, but inexperienced and not really prepared to do such work?

Has any Chapter tried having a central idea running through the literary meetings of the entire year? If so, what was the plan, and with what result?

What is the primary object of the Fourth Department?

THE EFFICIENT EPWORTHIAN.

How can we go about the preparation of a program of recreation for the whole neighborhood?

What plans can be worked that will act as preventives or discouragers of the amusements frowned on by our Church?

Can this department do more towards winning young men to the League?

How can we and they get over the barriers that exist between us and the strangers in our neighborhood?

Can the League do anything through this department to influence the life-work decisions of its members?

Give a list of receptions to various groups of people that an average Chapter can have,—we have them for high school students, railway men, newcomers. What others?

What is the best method of circulating *The Epworth Herald?*

What special days should the Chapter observe?

How fully should we take up athletics?

Is it possible to revive reading circles or clubs?

How can we make the Fourth Department support and serve all the others?

QUESTIONS IN LEAGUE FINANCE.

Do you drop a member from your rolls for non-payment of dues?

What percentage of Chapters pay their dues to district, State, and general funds?

Why do so many Chapters object to paying dues for district and general work?

The object of the League being largely the "attainment of the highest New Testament standard of experience and life," how urgent should the Treasurer be for collection of dues?

What is your method of collecting dues?

Would it not be better in the long run to make an effort to have every member of the League a contributor to the regular benevolences than to try to raise money for extra funds within the League, unless some special reason prompts the special move?

SUPERVISION, INSPIRATION, INSTRUCTION.

How should money be raised for special enterprises undertaken by the Chapter?

How much can the Treasurer help in the teaching and practice of Christian Stewardship?

What is the value of a Chapter Budget, and how do you make one?

Who shall decide the nature and extent of the Chapter's special gifts?

Should delegates at a convention pledge their Chapter's support to district or other larger League enterprises?

SECRETARIAL QUESTIONS.

Discuss methods of League publicity?

How can the Secretary get the support of the local papers?

How many records should the Secretary keep?

What can the Secretary do to keep track of the members who move?

How much reporting of the Chapter's activities should the Secretary do?

Program Committees are constantly searching the four corners of the earth for speakers. The convention programs, as a rule, are taking in a broader sweep, and more and more the subject of missions or world evangelism is being considered as one of the fundamental convention topics. The Mission Study and Stewardship Department of the Central Office is with increasing frequency being asked to give suggestions to Program Committees concerning topics, speakers, and missionary exhibits. It is now prepared to meet the popular demand for information concerning missionary features of convention programs, and invites correspondence. The address, as many times printed in this book, "lest we forget," is 740 Rush Street, Chicago.

The Pageants and Exhibits Division of the Committee on Conservation and Advance has a list of plays, pageants, etc., which will be found most useful by those who are in search of material with a distinct ethical or religious message. Some of the things enumerated are appropriate for the Sunday Vesper Service: as, for in-

THE EFFICIENT EPWORTHIAN.

stance, "The Pilgrim and the Book," and "The Gift of Self." Others are suitable for occasions when a desire for entertainment has brought the audience together, such as "The Birds' Christmas Carol," and "Neighbors."

Costumes and accessories for many of the plays listed may be rented from the office of the Division, 740 Rush Street, Chicago, at reasonable rates.

All the plays, pageants, and books referred to should be ordered of The Abingdon Press (same address as The Methodist Book Concern).

The Division will be glad to correspond with Epworthians who are thinking of taking up more extensively the work of planning and producing pageants and exhibits.

A few of the plays available are as follows:

BISHOP'S CANDLESTICKS, THE. By Norman McKinnel.
One act. Setting simple. Twenty-five minutes. Eight persons, five speaking parts. This is a dramatic version of the scene from "Les Miserables" where the thief steals the Bishop's candlesticks and the Bishop saves him from arrest by declaring that they were a gift. Twenty-five cents.

CROSSROADS MEETIN' HOUSE, THE. By Mary Meek Atkeson.
Three acts. One setting. One hour. Eleven persons. "Presents the problem of the Church in rural communities; pleasingly and sympathetically interpreting the life and characteristics centering about America's historic crossroads, communities, cradles of democracy, and religion." Thirty-five cents.

KOSIKI. By Amy Kellogg.
Two scenes. Fifteen minutes. Twenty to twenty-six persons. Six speaking parts. The transformation of a Korean village through the influence of one Christian convert. Fifteen cents.

SOME HELPFUL BOOKS.

Community Drama and Pageantry—Beegle & Crawford. $4.00. This standard book gives much practical information on the organization and production of community pageants.

SUPERVISION, INSPIRATION, INSTRUCTION.

The Dramatization of Bible Stories—Elizabeth Erwin Miller. $1.00. A concrete description of work done with a group of children in Chicago. Very useful for the teacher in the Junior Department.

Mission Study Through Educational Dramatics—Helen L. Willcox. Twenty-five cents. A brief outline of Educational Dramatic Method as applied with young people and older ones.

The English Religious Drama—Katharine Lee Bates. $2.00. An interesting account of the beginnings of English Drama in the Church.

The success of a convention depends, among other things, upon perfect organization. All the details must be thought out and worked out beforehand. Intelligent instructions must be given to all helpers, and care must be taken to see that they understand their instructions. Hold every helper to direct responsibility for his share in the work. And then, having perfected a smoothly working organization, keep it in the background as much as possible. Do not put the machinery of the convention on exhibition. Have as little business as may be, and make what is essential an integral part of the religious work of the gathering.

Advertising the Convention.—As soon as the program is complete, notify those who have been assigned to work. When it is perfectly clear that all understand what is expected of them, and will do their best to keep their assignments, print the program in an edition sufficient for all advertising purposes. Send a copy to *The Epworth Herald*, so that the convention date may appear in its "Convention Calendar," and circulate the program freely among the Chapters. A copy should be sent to each pastor, together with a request that he make the notice of the convention a part of his regular Church announcements until the date arrives.

Put on the program all possible information about the work in the district, the Conference, the State. Let the printed page tell all that can be told in small compass of what the League is doing. Perhaps a summary of the dis-

THE EFFICIENT EPWORTHIAN.

trict officers' reports can be inserted. It will be a highly profitable use of the space. Other printed matter should be provided; brief notices, posters, letter-heads, postal cards, in as large variety as the district's funds will permit, so that every Epworthian in the district may know that the convention is about to be held, that he is invited, that he needs the convention, that the convention needs him, that "special rates have been arranged for," and all the other facts that should be imparted to him. For what advantage is there in any convention to the Epworthian who hasn't had the desire to go aroused in him until he simply can't stay away?

Appoint a reporter for *The Epworth Herald,* with instructions to send a report at the earliest possible moment after the close of the convention, which report shall not be more than three hundred words long, and which shall state the facts about the convention without attempting to give the number of the hymns which were used, or to indicate the point in the program at which the janitor raised the windows for ventilation.

Convention Hints.—A convention needs order, and the average convention fails to get it because it is supposed that a certain amount of good-natured confusion is inevitable. The wise presiding officer will seek to keep order without himself being disorderly in the effort. Fussiness and scolding make more disturbance than they quell.

The music of the convention demands careful attention. Beware of the tendency to make the singing a mere preliminary or a stop-gap. Therefore, do not sing familiar hymns just because they are familiar. If the occasion calls for a familiar hymn, by all means sing it, for people will appreciate its fitness to the thought of the moment. Sing the best hymns, and depend on their quality to make them familiar. Convention delegates are, as a rule, quite capable of singing any hymn in the book at first sight, and they like to be put to the test. Moreover, if unfamiliar hymns are used, the range of singing appropriate to the work of the convention will be vastly widened.

At frequent intervals give the entire audience something to do. Otherwise people will go to sleep or take to day-

SUPERVISION, INSPIRATION, INSTRUCTION.

dreaming from sheer weariness. Sing not merely for exercise and change, but because the singing has been fitted into the theme of the moment. Pray, not merely to fill the time, or to diversify the program, but because some paper or address has made prayer the most natural thing to turn to. Read a Scripture message, in concert or responsively, as much because the Scripture bears upon the thought of the occasion as because the audience needs variety. All of which means, in a word, this: vary the exercises with all possible ingenuity, but do not permit the variation to be meaningless or perfunctory.

Provide a supply of inexpensive note-books and pencils. The delegates may forget their own, and yet they will be glad of an opportunity to take notes. One dollar will provide one hundred small note-books, and another dollar will provide pencils sufficient for all the delegates.

Furnish the chairman with a bell or buzzer, which is no respecter of persons. Let him be as inexorable as a train dispatcher in his purpose to run things on time.

Serve lunch in the church, or, if the convention meets in a city, at some place near the church, or ask the delegates to pay for their own lunches at near-by restaurants. Do not overburden the people who generously, and at much personal sacrifice, are entertaining the convention.

Seek more efficiency rather than more machinery. To appropriate a famous saying about Christianity in a certain part of London, we might answer the question, "Is our present League machinery a failure?" by saying, "I do n't know; it has never been tried." Do not spend much time over proposed amendments to the Constitution or new arrangements of committees. Put first things first. The people who are getting the most out of the League idea are the ones who have least to say about its imperfection and insufficiency.

Look to the election of officers. The District Cabinet is more important than many seem to think. It decides very largely the complexion and quality of the local work. If you have a good Cabinet, do not change simply because honors should be passed around. The good district officer is worth keeping for a year or two at any cost of doubtful compliments to other people. If changes are made, find the faithful ones, who do not advertise, and promote them. Be careful that you do not aid the ambitious place-seeker, if he should unhappily afflict the convention with his presence. Sooner or later he is sure paralysis to anything he touches.

Convention Themes.—These should not be stated in the bald way here given, but all possible changes should be rung on the method of formulating the topic.

1. General. Inspirational address on "The New Evangelism," "A New View of the Bible," "The Missionary Uprising of the Young People," "The World for Christ in This Generation," "The Modern Good Samaritan," "The Widening Field of Social Service," "The Epworth League's Ideal of Culture," "Social Life and Spiritual Power," "The Moral Value of Play," "Serving God With Pencil and Account Book," "The Christian Ideal of Getting and Using Possessions," "Winning the Next Man," "The League for the Young People and the Young People for the League."

2. Department Conferences. Discussions of the work in the several departments, using such topics as these outlined below.

The First Department. The devotional meeting and its problems of leadership, of participation by all members, of the use of topics, helps, and outlines, of inviting people to Christ. Bible study—its reasons, the courses available, the helps provided, methods of organization and management, essentials to success, reasons for failure, reflex influence on students and Chapter, chief purposes of the study. Studies in Christian Experience—why, how, when, where, by whom, under what circumstances, course to be used, things to avoid, things to seek. Studies in Personal Evangelism—as to motives, subjects, methods, safeguards, helps, related work, actual practice.

The Second Department. Mission study—its justification, its available material, the collateral resources within reach of the class, method of organization and conduct, end to be accomplished. Missionary meetings—their purpose, their supervision, preparation of leader and members, results desired. Missionary literature—its variety, character, value, and necessity; how to secure it and insure its read-

SUPERVISION, INSPIRATION, INSTRUCTION.

ing. Christian Stewardship—as a thing to be studied, as a conviction to be crystallized into practice, methods, literature and study courses available.

The Third Department. Social Service work in the local community, beyond its borders, varieties of service, co-operative mercy and help, the temperance task in public meetings and in private effort, Christian citizenship in elections, general civic affairs, reforms, and efforts at social betterment. The work of visiting—how, when, by whom, for what purpose.

The Fourth Department. The social significance of eating, drinking, and music. Social life and the Scriptures. Friendship as an evangelizing power. Making the Chapter a living unity. What more than socials? The play spirit in action. The League as a recreation center. After the social, what? Reading, with and without others. The League and general culture.

THE INSTITUTES.

The Summer Institutes are not fairly within the scope of this book, as their planning and management calls for expert service of so many sorts.

A few paragraphs are inserted because the subject is of such large interest to so many Epworthians, and it is important to extend the range of that interest.

The goal of the Central Office of the Epworth League is an Institute within reach of every Epworthian every summer. This has not yet been reached, but we are coming nearer to it every year.

The Institutes are all under the direction of the Central Office. Large dependence is placed, however, on local leadership. The Central Office has a Department of Institutes which coöperates fully with the local Institute committees and faculties.

The first thing to do, when any Institute is contemplated or even merely desired, is to write to the General Secretary at Chicago. He will tell what the prospects for a Central Office Institute are, and will outline the method of procedure. He will not only answer such inquiries; he will welcome them, and do all in his power to encourage the desire which prompts them. That is part of his business.

THE LEAGUE EDUCATING ITS EDUCATORS.

The Epworth League will keep on holding Institutes—for one reason, because the Institutes are an education for the League's leaders.

If that were all, it would be pretty expensive business, this bringing together of several hundred young people who, at their own cost in money and time, would be expected to furnish enlightenment and instruction to a more or less interesting Faculty.

That isn't all, nor is it most, of the Institute's profit. But it has a large and distinct value just the same.

At the Institutes the Faculty folk meet young people in free and familiar ways. They get the young people's point of view, and not infrequently are driven to correct a lot of loosely constructed theories as to the intelligent habits and religious processes of the Institute variety of life.

Many a man who has gone to teach a class at the Institute, wondering the while "what's the use of it all," has come away with a new respect for young seriousness and young directness and young insistence on truth.

The Institutes do not represent all the Leagues of to-day—more's the pity—but they represent something better. They stand for what League life is going to be. They define the League's lines of advance, the tendency of its life. What the Institutes were last summer many Chapters will begin to be this winter.

What is the Institute tendency? These, among many things, are part of it:

To be discontented with a devotional meeting
  —that merely "goes" well;
  —that is given to cant, even unconsciously;
  —that does not make easy the freest expression of genuine convictions about personal religion, in unhackneyed and unaffected utterance.

SUPERVISION, INSPIRATION, INSTRUCTION.

To be impatient with a missionary department
  —that supplies knowledge, but produces no consequences;
  —that weeps with Liberian Africa, but ignores the washerwoman's Africa;
  —that studies immigration and is blind to the Italian who sweeps the street or the Slovak who works on the section.

To get away from such notions as
  —that a Thanksgiving basket is the last word in helping the poor;
  —that hot temperance talk scares the saloonkeeper;
  —that flowers for the sick make unnecessary any real fellowship with uninteresting people who are not sick;
  —that everything would be all right with the unfortunate if they would just come to our Church.

To grow away from the idea
  —that a Chapter has done all its duty in recreation when it has given its own members a good time;
  —that athletics are not good form for a religious organization;
  —that young Christians do not need to be intelligent concerning their Church's place in the work of the Kingdom of God;
  —that recreation and culture are ends in themselves, rather than tools of the Chapter's trade of service.

In a word, the Institute tendency, which is to become the whole League's tendency, is to make the League a truly Christian company, seeking intelligence and efficiency because it is more concerned for the Church than for itself, more concerned for the community than for the Church, and more concerned for the Christian world-program than for the community!

Many pastors, and all the men and women who have served on Institute Faculties, see this plainly. When the other pastors and other leaders see it with equal clearness, the League will do better work than it has ever done before, because it will have a larger measure of enlightened leadership.

THE EFFICIENT EPWORTHIAN.

A DISCOVERY AT THE INSTITUTES.

The constant need of the Epworth League is for leadership. We have been present at the telling of that until the hearing of it begins to be a little wearying.

The implication sometimes is that unless we can raise up in the League young people of exceptional powers and unusual gifts, the League can not hope to be anything better than a group of footless, purposeless, and occasionally bewildered youth, a problem to the pastor, an embarrassment to the Church, and a hopeless puzzle to themselves.

The Institutes have always proved that idea to be both false and foolish, and each year's Institutes give new confirmation to the cheerful truth that the League can have all the leadership it needs without waiting for genius.

In every Institute there appears the every-day young man, the commonplace young woman, whose League record is little less than amazing. There is nothing wonderful about these young people but their earnestness. They are just folk.

But they have made their home Chapters very hives of League industry. They have wrought results which the most optimistic pastors had not hoped to see. In a word, they have come to places of leadership, not through extraordinary ability, but by dint of an undiscourageable purpose.

The other young people at the Institutes are beginning to see this thing clearly. It is dawning on them that what one average young person can do under difficult circumstances another can do also. The instructors have been encouraging this attitude with all gladness, for they know what profit for the Church and the Kingdom is in it.

When the Institution and convention time is over the pastor comes to his own again. To him for his comfort the summer gatherings speak this word: You have unsuspected resources among your "average" young people. They need to be won for the service, to be convinced of its value, to be shown a bit of its heroic side. But you have them!

Most League advances of the ten months following any Institute season will not be made by brilliant young people.

SUPERVISION, INSPIRATION, INSTRUCTION.

We haven't enough of them in any case. The work will be done by the ten thousand more-or-less folk. Those who do not seem likely to set the world on fire. If they once get the vision and the purpose, they will not stop at anything to get the equipment they need, and to do the work they have undertaken.

Give them something to do. Put them at a definite piece of service. Leave them a little leeway for inventiveness and initiative and responsibility, and keep your eye on them lest emergencies arise.

Leadership? Yes, indeed we need it. But we have it, though it is undeveloped, is not yet even called out, and certainly does not recognize itself. None the less it is there. It is in our own young people, those we count of only fair capacity.

And, O wise and cunning artificer of the Kingdom and pastor of the flock, yours are the workers and the work! With such workers you can double the doers and double the doing.

"What is that in thy hand?"

HOME FROM DECISION; DOWN TO BUSINESS.

The long procession of suitcases has gone up the hill to the station, or down the hill to the boat, and the Institutes are ended.

They were wonderful times, weren't they? What inspirations, what fellowships, what new outlooks, what new knowledge! And, more than all, what high resolves and holy dedications!

This is the day after the Institute. We are back in the familiar commonplaces of the home Church and Chapter. We are among the unprivileged and uninfluenced majority who did not get to the Institute.

But is it just the same as it was? Is there not new light on the old perplexity? Does not the courage gained at the Institute give difficult work a new allurement? Is there not a strange glow of interest and meaning in the every-day round of the League?

Besides, there is that moment of decision to look back upon and to carry forward into all the plans of the future.

THE EFFICIENT EPWORTHIAN.

It *was* a decision—now comes the steady business of standing by it and transforming it into a deed.

That is the one safeguard against the loss of the Institute's profit. "Methods" may be forgotten, and materials for study may be mislaid, and great messages may grow daily more difficult of recollection.

But the decision stands! That is a contract between the decider and his Lord. It was made with deliberateness; it must be kept with faithfulness.

The sure way to keep it is to begin keeping it at once, by letting people know it was made, and by putting it to work on the nearest task that it was made for.

He who promises his Master a certain service has also promised to discover ways of rendering that service. Therefore, find the beginnings of the deed that will make your decision a thing of life and power.

The Church has heard about your mountain-top exalting and exulting; it waits now to see what, in its actual outworking, your new determination will produce.

The best report of the Institute will be made, not in the "echo meeting," but in the lives that work out the Institute influence and the Institute dedication.

TO THE BUSY AND PATIENT PASTOR.

Were there Epworthians at the Summer Institutes from your Church? Then you have business with them.

They learned some things which make them of more value in the work of the Church than they were before the Institute.

They heard some things which stirred their hearts and quickened their minds and gave them new visions as to the possibilities of Christian living.

They came to great decisions concerning their personal relationship to the work of the Kingdom of Jesus Christ.

These are the Church's young people. But first of all, they are *your* young people. The first fruits of their new ardor and devotion should appear in their home Church and Chapter.

You could not attend the Institute. But now the Institute comes to you.

SUPERVISION, INSPIRATION, INSTRUCTION.

If no more than one of the young people is in your charge, that fact is one of the privileges of your ministry. Besides, you have a new friend, a new sympathizer, a new fellow-laborer.

The League commends these young folk to you; it believes you will be glad to encourage them, to make use of them, to see that their new knowledge is not wasted for want of use, that their new eagerness does not evaporate in an indifferent atmosphere, that their new dedication of life is not overlooked in the press of the Church's routine work.

To be young with the youthful is as great a pastoral privilege as to rejoice with them that do rejoice and to weep with them that weep. But it is more than a privilege. It is an accession of power in a form which makes it available for instant use.

May God make this matter prosper at your hand!

Group Meetings.

The district organization is the next in order after the local Chapter, and the district conventions, of course, are valuable and important gatherings. But they do not provide all the assistance that is needed. In most districts it will be found that a series of subdistrict or group meetings may be held with the utmost profit. They will not interfere with the annual district gathering, but, on the contrary, will tend to make that meeting more popular and increase its attendance and value.

The group meeting provides closer fellowship and better acquaintance between the members of the neighboring Chapters. Moreover, it provides a splendid opportunity for the discussion of local problems, which are important enough, but which may interest only four or five Chapters, and so are not fully discussed in the larger gatherings.

For the organization of group meetings divide the district into four, five, or six groups, with as near as possible the same number of Chapters in each group. Arrange the groups according to convenience of travel between the individual Chapters of the group. Then plan to hold one or two meetings a year in each group.

The program for a subdistrict or group meeting will

be much less formal for a district convention, but it may be much more direct and practical. It will cover usually the morning, afternoon, and evening of a single day. The morning and afternoon sessions should be devoted largely to methods, local problems, and the development of practical effectiveness. The evening session may wisely be given up to one speaker, whose formal address should have large inspirational value. It will be all the better if the evening address can be wholly evangelistic, so that at the close an invitation to begin the Christian life may be extended, with the hope that many people attracted to the exercises of the day may be won over to the Kingdom of God.

The group meeting provides a good opportunity for the adoption by the associated Chapters of some form of united effort, such as the fresh-air work, of concerted evangelistic movements, or flower mission work. If some Chapters of the group are in the country and others in the city, an ideal plan of co-operation in fresh-air and flower mission work may easily be arranged.

Use every Chapter in making up the program. Some Chapters will have good material for one part of the program, other Chapters can help in other things, but no Chapter must be slighted.

Many group organizations find that the awarding of banners for the best attendance is a valuable means of stimulating interest in the group meetings. These banners may be awarded by various methods; for example, for the largest attendance in proportion to membership, or for the largest number of miles traveled, so that the Chapters from the remoter places will not feel that they stand no chance. Or the banner may be awarded on the basis of the largest proportion of dues paid, or the largest number of members in study classes, or the largest proportionate increase in membership since the last group meeting. In fact, there are so many reasons for awarding banners that several banners may profitably be offered for competitive effort.

Group meetings are valuable not only for the reasons already stated, but because:

1. They can be held frequently.

SUPERVISION, INSPIRATION, INSTRUCTION.

2. Many can go a short distance and for a little time who could never attend one of the larger and remoter gatherings.

3. They involve very little expense, which is an important item to many.

4. The social features can be emphasized.

5. You can use material on the program which you could not in a district meeting.

6. Everybody feels a sense of responsibility.

7. It puts the power-house close to the factory and the raw material.

8. So many delegates are present from each Chapter that it is easy to carry enthusiasm home. This can not be said of the great conventions. They generate tremendous power, but lack transmitters.

9. They cultivate good feeling between the Chapters.

Note on the Junior Work.

This book has been purposely limited to the problems of Epworth League work proper. The Junior League is so far-reaching in its scope, and so different in its methods, that it was not deemed wise to attempt its treatment here. That has been better done in another place, by another hand.

But it should always be remembered that these two branches of Epworth League work, though dealing with different material under different conditions, are parts of the same organization, younger and older members of the same family.

The Junior Superintendent is a member of the Epworth League Cabinet, although appointed by the pastor instead of being elected by the Chapter. At all Cabinet meetings the Junior Superintendent should be expected and welcomed. The problems of the Junior work should be considered as carefully as those of any of the departments, and the Chapter should be educated to the point of accepting large responsibility for the Junior branch of the work.

The First Department is especially charged with this work of counsel and supervision. The First Vice-President ought to be a frequent visitor at the Junior meetings, and a sympathetic and intelligent counselor of the Junior workers.

The Junior Superintendent and the other members of the Junior staff have a right to expect support—moral, material, and personal—from the members of the senior Chapter. That the Junior work is done in a different place and at a different time from the other League work affords no reason for ignoring it or for belittling it.

If Epworth League workers are wise, they will see that the preservation of the League itself is largely a question of the success of the Junior work. Given a carefully chosen course of training, conscientiously and enthusiastically followed, and when the Juniors are ready to graduate they will be the finest possible material for the uses of the senior organization. A well-trained Junior has such an advantage over one who has missed the training that it is worth all it costs to provide such education and culture in religious things as the Junior League affords.

INDEX.

A

	PAGE
Abbreviated Social, The	286
Action, As the League Ideal	21
Active Members	35
Advertising	327, 328
Advertising the Convention	411
Age Limit, The	40
Age Question, The	76
Aged, Homes for The	236
Amusements, The Christian and	107
Amusement Question, Tackling the Other Side of The	280
Anniversary Day	341, 344
Anniversary Day, Homily on	351
Anniversary Day, Subjects for Addresses	348
Anniversary Program, The Special	347
Army Camp Fire, The	298
Assembly, A Home	267
Assignment of Members to Departments	32, 34
Associate Members	35
Authors, Hidden	291
Authors' Traits	293

B

Badge, Epworth League	35
Banquet, The Annual	301
Barn Social, A	306
Barter Social, A	288
Baseball Game of Buzz, The	308
Baseball, Indoor	312
Baseball Party, A	311
Better Work Our Chapter Should Do	359
Bible Study	155
Bible Study Class, The Leader of the	160
Bible Study Class, Organization of the	159

	PAGE
Bible Study in the League	158
Bible Study Meetings	160
Bible Study and the Morning Watch	161
Bible Study Rally Day	162
Bible Study Rally Day Programs	163
Bible Study Suggestions	156
Bicycle Tours	304
Bishop Vincent's Summary of Methodist Doctrine	109
Board of Control, The	24, 25, 36
Book and Its Study, The	155
Book Club, The	266
Books, Circulating, Everybody's	264
Budget, The Epworth League	338
Budget Dinner, The	338
Business Meeting, The	45, 54, 57
Business Meeting, The Annual	60
Business Meeting, Order of Business	61
Business Records	323
Businesses, Short Studies of Great	273
Buzz, The Baseball Game of	308
By-Laws, Suggested	33

C

Cabinet and the Epworth League, The	368
Cabinet, The Local	52
Cabinet Meeting, Order of Business	55
Cake, Choosing the	292
Camp Delights	312
Camping Out	307
Candy Making	285
Carnival of the Seasons, The	301

INDEX.

	PAGE
Central Methodist Episcopal Church, Cleveland	10
Ceremonial Occasions	375
Chapter, Organizing a	38
Chapter, The Rural	219
Chapter, Survey, A	67, 358
Chapters, Visiting Between	234
Charades	285
Charter, The Unveiling of the.	41
Charters, Kinds of	41
Charts, Missionary	178, 190
Children's Homes	237
Christ, The Present	106
Christian Citizen, The	259
Christian Citizenship	256
Christian Citizenship Day	341
Christian Education	113
"Christian Stewardship, Our"	203
Christian Stewardship Program, A	205, 206
Christian Stewardship, The Reflex Value of	204
Christmas Gift to the Christ, A	112
Christmas Service, A	341
Church Economy, The Ten Points of	110
Church, The League and the.	18
Church Lyceum, The	7, 8
Church and Youth, The	7
Circulating Library, A Chapter	265
City You Live In, The	294
Citizenship, Women's Relation to Christian	258
Civic Debate, A	274
Cleveland Conference, The	10
Clothespins, A Game With	308
Colored Conferences, Assistant Secretary for	26
Colors, Epworth League	35
Committees, Reducing the Size of	63
Community, What the Chapter Should Know About the	214
Community Field Day, A	307
Community and the League, The	65
Community Study	213

	PAGE
Community Study, How to Begin a	215
Confession, A Service of	114
Congress of Nations, A	272
Congress of Notables, A	272
Constitution, The General	25
Constitution, The Local	27
Contests, Membership	314
Convention, Advertising the.	411
Convention, Questions for Discussion in the	401
Convention, The District, 394,	395
Convention Exhibits	409
Convention Hints	412
Convention Master or Servant, The	395
Convention, Building the Program of the	397
Convention, Speakers of the	399
Convention, Themes of the,	398, 414
Convention, Value of the	15
Corn Social, A	285
Correspondence, The Chapter's	325
Correspondence, Where to Send the Missionary	195
Country Dinner, A	306
Country Epworthians Going to the City	330
Cross, The Epworth	17, 43
Culture	263
Culture and Recreation	262
Culture and Recreation Department	262
Cultural Programs, Suggestions for	270
Cycle of Prayer, The	186

D

Days, Special	341
Deaconess Movement, The	14
Deaconess and the Social Service Department, The.	229
Debate, A Civic	274
Debates, Missionary	178
Debates, Subjects for	275
Decision Meeting, A	114
Denominational Control of League Work	18

INDEX.

Department of Missionary
   Education..........175, 190
Departmental Activities, Evolution of............... 16
Departments, Organizing the. 42
Departure, Some New...355, 357
Descriptive Initials......... 290
Desertions From the League.. 79
Devotional Meeting, The..45, 89
Devotional Meeting, Closing the................... 117
Devotional Meeting, Do n'ts for the................. 98
Devotional Meeting, Hints for the................. 124
Devotional Meeting, How to Magnify the............ 101
Devotional Meeting, How to Take Part in the........ 118
Devotional Meeting, Missionary................... 175
Devotional Meeting, Opening the................... 115
Devotional Meeting, Plans of. 93
Devotional Meeting, Plans for Special.............. 104
Devotional Meeting, Preparation of................ 91
Devotional Meeting, Progress of................... 95
Devotional Meeting, Purpose of................... 97
Devotional Meeting, Scrappiness in the............. 99
Devotional Meeting, Singing in the................. 119
Devotional Meeting, Testimony in the............ 103
Devotional Meeting, Ushers. 121
Devotional Meeting, Variety in the................. 115
Dickens, The Children of.... 272
Dickens Evening, A......... 298
Discipline Evening, A....... 271
District Convention, The.... 394
District League, The........ 393
District Officers, Installation of................... 382
District Superintendents and Pastors................ 33

Dominant Note, The Convention's................. 398
Drawing Party, A.......... 295
Dry Goods Describer, A..... 291
Dues, The Collection of..... 337
Duncan, John W., on Christian Stewardship........ 203

E

Education, Christian........ 113
Efficiency, Hints........... 82
Enterprises, The Inside of Big. 272
Epworth Cross, The......17, 43
Epworth Herald, The....... 276
Epworth Herald in the Devotional Meeting.......... 124
Epworth Herald and League Business................ 369
Epworth Herald, Uses of.... 365
Epworth Herald, Why the Cabinet Should Take the. 368
Epworth Herald Day....341, 365
Epworth League Badge..... 35
Epworth League Colors..... 35
Epworth League Pledge...35, 385
Epworth League Ritual..... 375
Epworth League, Task of the. 350
Epworth League Watchword. 36
Epworth Memorial Church, Cleveland............... 10
Epworth Wheel, The........ 15
Evangelism in the League.... 15
Evangelism of a Person, The. 152
Evolution of League Life, Thoughts on the......... 22
Exclusion of Members, The.. 56
Exhibits for Conventions.... 409
Experts, Evening with...... 273

F

Facts, Finding the Chapter.. 67
Facts, Finding the Community................... 70
Fagot Party, The........... 289
Feather Volley Ball......... 311
Field Day, A Community.... 307
Field Meet, A Parlor........ 310
Finance, Questions on League. 408
Finances of the General Organization............... 26

INDEX.

Financial Man, The Chapter's 335
Financial Plan, The Chapter's 336
First Department and Holy Week, The 149
First Department Questions... 403
First Vice-President, Qualifications of the 49
Flowers, The Message of the. 112
Founders, The Faith and Wisdom of the 12
Fourth Department, Functions of the 262
Fourth Department Questions 407
Fourth of July, The 353
Fourth of July, A New 247
Fourth of July, The Sunday Nearest the 352
Fourth Vice-President, Qualifications of the 146
Freedman's Aid Society Day. 341
Fresh Air Work 244
Full Program and the Empty Life, The 146

G

General Constitution, The... 25
General Conference, The League and the 24
General League Officers... 26, 36
Geography, The Romance of. 273
German Assistant Secretary, The 26
Gifts from the Chapter, Special 239
Gifts to Missionaries 188
Giving, Bible Motives for.... 201
Giving, Four Methods of.... 196
Giving, One Chapter's 194
Giving, One Use of 200
Giving, Questions on 204
Giving, Right and Wrong Motives for 197
Giving, Scripture Questions On 202
Giving, Significance of 198
Giving, Uses of 201
Good Government 223
Graduate Epworthians, Promoting the 27
Group Meetings 421

H

Hall of Fame, A Biblical.... 270
Hallowe'en Games..302, 303, 304
Hallowe'en Happenings..... 302
Health Department and the League, The Local 217
Heavenly Home, Preparing for Our 111
Hidden Authors. 291
Hiking Parties 306
Historic Lovers 300
Holiday Cards 302
Holidays and the Epworth League 249
Holiday Tour, The 308
Holidays, The Redemption of 247
Holy Week, The First Department and 149
Home Assembly, A 267
Homes for the Children 237
Homes for the Aged 236
Hospital Visiting 232
Hospitals and the Social Service Department 235
Hundred Dollar Social, A.... 290
Hymns, Missionary 180

I

Ignorance, The Depths of.... 292
Immigration, Present Day Aspects of 225
Imperfect League Work..... 78
Independence Day 353
Indoor Baseball 312
Industry, Christianizing..... 222
Initiative in the League 81
Institute, After the 419
Institute, A Discovery at the. 418
Institute Idea, The 400
Institute Tendency, The..... 416
Institutes, The 415
Institutes, The Pastor and the 420
Installation of Chapter's Officers 377
Installation of District Officers 382
Interdenominational Evenings 273

428

INDEX.

J

	PAGE
Jumble Social, A	290
Junior Government, A	223
Junior League Superintendent, Duties of the	32
Junior Work, Note on the	423
Juniors, Graduation of	377

L

Labor Day Celebration	301
Language Social, A	287
Leaders of the Devotional Meeting, A School for the	101
Leaders of Social Service Study Classes	224
Leaders, Letters from League	61
Leaders, A Talk with the Devotional Meeting	90
Leader's Twelve Words, The	90
Leadership in the League	418
League Finance, Questions on	408
League Means Business, If Our	369
League Organizations, Forms of	24
League Rally Day	341
League Tested by Time, The	12
League's Value to the Church, The	13
Lecture Course, A	268, 358
Left-Handed Social, A	287
Letters from League Leaders	61
Library, The Envelope	275
Library, The Mission Study	174
Life Work, Evening on Choosing a	272
Lincoln's Birthday	289, 342
Literature, Distribution of Good	246
Literature in Barber Shops	246
Literature in Railway Stations	246
Literary Evenings, Hints for	271
Local Constitution, The	27

M

Maps, Missionary	174
Meetings	45, 46
Meetings of the League	45

	PAGE
Members, Active	35
Members, Assignment to the Departments	32
Members, Associate	35, 315
Members, Developing New	315
Members, Exclusion of,	32, 34, 56
Members, Lists of Prospective	322
Members, Moving Away of	322
Members, Reception of	316, 375
Members, Recognition of New	316
Membership, Conditions of	40
Membership Contests	314, 319
Membership, Discussion of	56
Membership, Recommendations for	55
Membership Record, The Secretary's	321, 322
Membership Roll, Lengthening the	312
Mercy and Help Work, Making It Constructive	216
Methodism, and What It Stands for	109
Methodist Federation for Social Service	215
Methodist Temperance Society	251
Methodist Year Book	192
Methodist Young People's Union	9
Mission Study Class, Work of the	173
Mission Study Libraries	174
Mission Study Rally Day	170
Mission Study Rally Day Programs	172
Mission Study and Stewardship, Dept. of	173, 175, 190
Mission Study, Timeliness of	166
Missions, A Survey of Methodist	177
Missions, Why Study	167
Missionary Boards of the Methodist Episcopal Church	177
Missionary Charts	178, 190
Missionary Devotional Meeting, The	178

429

INDEX.

	PAGE
Missionary Education, Department of	173, 175, 190
Missionary Entertainments, More Formal	192
Missionary Expositions, Scenery for	410
Missionary Field, Women's Work in the	182
Missionary Hymns	180
Missionary Inspiration Meeting, A	182
Missionary Literature	173
Missionary Maps	174
Missionary Material, Other	189
Missionary Meetings, Hints for	179
Missionary Meetings, Special	177
Missionary Pageants	192
Missionary Revival, The	14
Missionary Scrap Book, A	189
Missionaries, Direct Contact with	187
Missionaries, Gifts to	188
Missionaries, The League a Producer of	169
Morning Watch, The	132
Morning Watch and Bible Study	161
Morning Watch Day	341
Morning Watch, Elements of the	132
Morning Watch, How to Keep the	136
Morning Watch Scripture Illustrations	138
Morning Watch Testimony Hints	138
Morning Watch Campaign, The	132
Morning Watch Question, The	138
Musical Evenings	289
My Chum? Who Is	153

N

Nation Social, The	219
Nations, A Congress of	272
Native State Social, A	286
Necessitous Cases	233
Neighbor, My Business with my	108
New Americans, The Third Department and	225
New Members, Canvassing for	314
Nominating Committee	40
North Ohio Conference Methodist Episcopal Alliance	10
Notables, A Congress of	272
Novel, The Composite	293
Numbers, A Menu of	287

O

Officers, Installation of Chapter's	377
Old Members' Social, An	286
Old People's Day	370
Open Air Services	122
Orchestra, A Comic	285
Organic Law, The	24
Organizing a Chapter	38
Outdoors Indoors, Bringing	308
Outdoor Pleasures	304
Oxford League, The	8

P

Pageants and Plays	409
Parlor Field Meet	310
Pastor and the Business Meeting, The	59
Pastor and the Institutes, The	420
Pastor and the District Superintendent, The	33
Pedestrian Sociability	305
Periodicals, The Latest	297
Permanence, The Test of the League's	74
Personal Evangelism Day	341
Personal Evangelism, Imaginary Hindrances	145
Personal Evangelism, Methods of	141, 143
Personal Evangelism, Questions on	143
Personal Evangelism, Real Hindrances to	144
Personal Evangelism, Reasons for	139

INDEX.

	PAGE
Petition, The Right of	249
Picnic Games	306
Picnic, The Indoor	309
Play, Little Paragraphs on	284
Play, The Value of	281
Pledge Analyzed, The	386
Pledge? Do You Know The	391
Pledge, Epworth League..35,	385
Pledge, Purpose of the	389
Pledge, Temperance	250
Pledge, Who Should Take the.	389
Pledge Meeting, A	392
Poems, Identifying the	295
Polar Evening, A	300
Policy, The Chapter	57
Poster Service, The Herald's.	330
Practice of the Presence, The.	132
Prayer, The Cycle of	186
Prayer-meetings	123
"Prayer" Meeting, A	105
Prayer-meetings, Some	123
President, Duties of the	31
President, Qualifications of the	33, 47
Prohibition, The League and.	250
Program Committees, Suggestions for	409
Program, The Convention	397
Public Servants, A Directory of	223, 249
Publicity for League Work	328

Q

Quarterly Conference Recognition	41
Question Box, The Convention	400
Questions for Convention Discussion	401
Questions for First Department	403
Questions for Fourth Department	407
Questions for Second Department	405
Questions, Secretarial	409
Questions for Third Department	406

R

	PAGE
Rally Day, The Annual League	355
Rally Day, A Suggested.358,	359
Rally Day, A Talk with League Leaders	362
Rally Day Spirit	360
Rally to Your Task	361
Rambles	306
Reading Circles, The....266,	275
Reading College, A......265,	358
Reading Rooms	267
Reception of Members	316
Recording Business	323
Recreation for All	219
Recreation, Culture and	262
Recreation, Community	320
Recreation, Literature on	221
Recreation and Culture Department, Duties of the	30
Recreation and Culture Questions	407
Recreation Program, A Simple	282
Recreation and Social Purity.	221
Recreational Work, The	278
Reorganizing Dead Chapters.	394
Reports to the Business Meeting	59
Rural Chapter, The	219
Rural Chapter, Members Leaving the	330

S

School Folk, Winning the	316
Scientific Management in League Work	64
Scrap Book, The Secretary's.	326
Scrappiness in Devotional Meetings	99
Screens, A Game with	309
Scribe, The Epworthian	320
Scribe, Sidelights for the	332
Second Department, Free Helps for the	190
Second Department Questions	405
Second Vice-President, Qualifications of the	50

431

INDEX.

	PAGE
Secretarial Questions	409
Secretary, The	327
Secretary, Duties of the	31
Secretary, The League	320
Secretary, Rules for the	328
Secretary and His Correspondence	325
Secretary and Members Removing, The	322, 326
Secretary and Statistics, The	326
Secretary's Supplies, The	320
Secretary's Committee	321
Secretary's Co-operation with the Treasurer, The	325
Secretary's Membership Record, The	321
Secretary's Record, The	323
Secretary's Scrap Book, The	326
Secretary's Special Records	324
Shakespeare, The Women of	272
Shakespearean Romance, A	296
Sheep, Game of the Stray	309
Sick, Visiting the	231
Social Department, Socializing the	218
Socials in the League, The Test of	279
Socials, Missionary	183
Socials Without Money	278
Social Purity and Recreation	221
Socials of the Senses, The	289
Social Service	14, 208
Social Service, Historical Sketch of	211
Social Service, What Is?	210
Social Service in the Church, Why?	208
Social Service Department Money	230
Social Service Department, Duties of the	29
Social Service Long Distance Work	235
Social Service in Necessitous Cases	233
Social Service Publicity	230
Social Service Questions	406
Social Service Study	212
Social Service Study Class Leaders	224

	PAGE
Social Service Suggestions	238
Social Service Work, Local	229
Socials and Sociability,	279
Social Stunts, Successful	284
Some Prayer-meetings	123
Songs Without Words	286
Soul Winning a Glorious Service	147
Speakers, Convention	399
Special Days	341
Special Records	324
Spiritual Department, Duties of the	28
Spiritual Work Questions	403
St. Patrick's Day Dinner	299
St. Patrick's Day Social	297
Statistics, The Secretary and	326
Stewardship, The Laws of	199
Stewardship Statistics	202
Stranger, Visiting the	232
Stray Sheep, The Game of the	309
Students' Receptions	286
Study Class, The Advantage of the	170
Study Class Day	341
Study Class Meetings	46
Stunts, Successful Social	284
Subjects for Convention Discussion	398
Summer Institutes	415
Sunday Night Service and the League, The	128
Supplies, Chapter	335
Supplies for the Secretary	320
Survey, A Chapter	67
Survey, A Community	70
Surveys, Making Use of	74
Systematic Visitation	230, 358
Systematic Visitation, Books on	216

T

Telegram Social, The	293
Temperance Crusade, The	250
Temperance, Education and Agitation of	251
Temperance Meetings, Themes for	255
Temperance Pledge, The	250
Temperance Programs	254

INDEX.

Temperance Society, The Methodist.............. 251
Tennis Courts? Why Not Two 283
Tennis Tournament, A...... 307
Tennis Tournament Party, A. 311
Tennyson's Religious Poems. 272
Tenth, Finding the......... 203
Testimony in the Devotional Meeting................ 103
Thanksgiving Day...... 248, 372
Third Department and Its Meaning, The........... 209
Third Department Questions. 406
Third Vice-President, Qualifications of the............ 50
Three Deep................ 310
Tithing and the Tithe....... 200
Tongue Twisters........... 288
Topics, Devotional Meeting. 89
Tower of Babel Social, The.. 287
Transfer of Rural Members, The.................... 330
Traveling Social, A......... 290
Treasurer, Duties of the..... 31
Treasurer, The Secretary's Co-operation with the....... 325
Treasurer, Work of the...... 335
Twenty-four-Hour-Day Plan, 338

U

Ushers and the Devotional Meetings............... 121

V

"Vices," The Four.......... 82
"Vision Meeting," A....... 113
Visiting the Sick........217, 358
Visiting Between Chapters... 234
Volley Ball, Feather........ 311

W

Walking Tours............. 304
Washington's Birthday...... 342
Washington's Birthday Party. 299
Washington's Birthday, The Sunday Nearest......... 343
Watch Night Service, The... 373
Watchword, The Epworth League................. 36
Wheel, The Epworth........ 15
Win My Chum Movement, The.................... 150
Win My Chum Reflections.. 151
Winning My Chum, Difficulties of.................. 154
Women and Citizenship..... 258
Word Building............. 290
World Evangelism, Department of................. 165
World Evangelism Departmental Committee....... 165
World Evangelism Department, Duties of the...... 29
World Evangelism Questions. 405

Y

Young Man, The Chapter and the Elusive............. 317
Young People from Abroad.. 218
Young People's Christian League, The............ 9
Young People's Methodist Alliance, The........... 8
Young People, Homeless.... 218
Y-O-I.................... 294
Your Own Initials.......... 294
Younger, Making Way for the.................... 75
Youth and the Church...... 7

www.ingramcontent.com/pod-product-compliance
Lightning Source LLC
Chambersburg PA
CBHW052128010526
44113CB00034B/1024